P9-DDC-586
WITHDRAWN

SCHAUMBURG TOWNSHIP DISTRICT LIBRARY
3 1257 01465 5525

Schaumburg Township District Library
130 South Roselle Road
Schaumburg, Illinois 60193

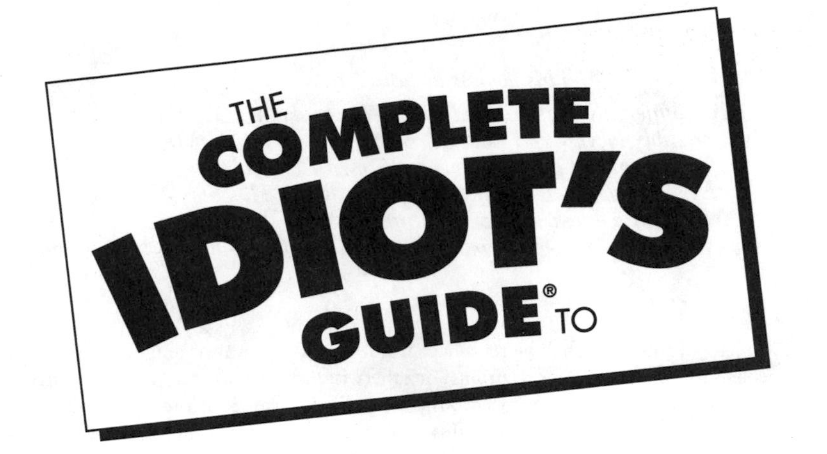

Learning French

Third Edition

by Gail Stein

SCHAUMBURG TOWNSHIP DISTRICT LIBRARY
130 SOUTH ROSELLE ROAD
SCHAUMBURG, ILLINOIS 60193

ALPHA
A member of Penguin Group (USA) Inc.

468
STEIN, G

3 1257 01465 5525

This book is dedicated to:
My wonderfully patient and supportive husband, Douglas
My incredibly loving and understanding sons, Eric and Michael
My proud parents, Jack and Sara Bernstein
My superior consultant and advisor, Roger H. Herz
My mentor from the very beginning, Yetta Rosenblum
The memory of a very special gentleman, Ernest Rothschild—a true professional

Copyright © 2003 by Gail Stein

All rights reserved. No part of this book shall be reproduced, stored in a retrieval system, or transmitted by any means, electronic, mechanical, photocopying, recording, or otherwise, without written permission from the publisher. No patent liability is assumed with respect to the use of the information contained herein. Although every precaution has been taken in the preparation of this book, the publisher and author assume no responsibility for errors or omissions. Neither is any liability assumed for damages resulting from the use of information contained herein. For information, address Alpha Books, 201 West 103rd Street, Indianapolis, IN 46290.

THE COMPLETE IDIOT'S GUIDE TO and Design are registered trademarks of Penguin Group (USA) Inc.

International Standard Book Number: 1-59257-055-0
Library of Congress Catalog Card Number: 2003100695

05 04 03 8 7 6 5 4 3 2 1

Interpretation of the printing code: The rightmost number of the first series of numbers is the year of the book's printing; the rightmost number of the second series of numbers is the number of the book's printing. For example, a printing code of 03-1 shows that the first printing occurred in 2003.

Printed in the United States of America

Note: This publication contains the opinions and ideas of its author. It is intended to provide helpful and informative material on the subject matter covered. It is sold with the understanding that the author and publisher are not engaged in rendering professional services in the book. If the reader requires personal assistance or advice, a competent professional should be consulted.

The author and publisher specifically disclaim any responsibility for any liability, loss, or risk, personal or otherwise, which is incurred as a consequence, directly or indirectly, of the use and application of any of the contents of this book.

Most Alpha books are available at special quantity discounts for bulk purchases for sales promotions, premiums, fund-raising, or educational use. Special books, or book excerpts, can also be created to fit specific needs.

For details, write: Special Markets; Alpha Books, 375 Hudson Street, New York, NY 10014.

Publisher: *Marie Butler-Knight*
Product Manager: *Phil Kitchel*
Senior Managing Editor: *Jennifer Chisholm*
Acquisitions Editor: *Gary Goldstein*
Development Editor: *Michael Koch*
Senior Production Editor: *Katherin Bidwell*
Copy Editor: *Amy Lepore*
Illustrator: *Chris Eliopoulos*
Cover/Book Designer: *Trina Wurst*
Indexer: *Tonya Heard*
Layout/Proofreading: *Megan Douglass, Rebecca Harmon*

Contents at a Glance

Contents

Foreword

In 1066, William the Conqueror of Normandy fought his way to the throne of England and suddenly French became the language to know in Merry Old England. English dictionaries would be far shorter and much less interesting if it weren't for the thousands of French words that have entered and expanded our language. Learning French has intrigued and perplexed many of us ever since. Who hasn't been inspired by the films, art, literature, or music of France to want to rattle off streams of fluent French effortlessly and without hesitation? Imagine stepping into an elegant restaurant after a day on a warm, sunny beach in the Caribbean and ordering *un verre de vin blanc*, or coming off a ski slope in Quebec and asking for *un café au lait*, or stepping into a *pâtisserie* on the Champs-Elysées to buy *une petite tarte aux pommes*, or crossing the Sahara desert and stopping in a village market to ask, "*Avez-vous un peu d'eau?*" Even the most simple and mundane statements sound better in French. When I ask my students why they chose to study French many of them respond, "It always sounds so pretty." All the clichés about it being the language of love, art, philosophy, diplomacy, and literature can be debated endlessly but the simple fact remains that speaking French is fun and knowing the language is a constantly enriching experience.

For years French teachers have used Gail Stein's French language books in their classrooms to aid them in teaching the complexities, nuances, and joys of the French language to their students. Stein consistently offers crisp, concise, and accurate explanations to the thorniest of grammar issues. The vocabulary and examples she chooses to illustrate her topics reinforce the language of everyday communication. In the third edition of *The Complete Idiot's Guide to Learning French*, Gail Stein brings her considerable skills as an educator to the general public and offers the individual learner a practical guide to learning French.

Intimidation is probably the biggest constraint to learning a new language. So, if I ask someone in an unfamiliar city for directions to the subway and I actually use the correct vocabulary and grammar, what if they answer me in French? Then what happens? Fear is the great stumbling block and Gail Stein addresses this concern right away by urging the learner to plunge right in and just do it. I like this book so much because it uses techniques that good teachers have always employed for educating their students. Grammar points are introduced in a logical and sequential manner so the student is moving from the known to the new. Previously learned material is effortlessly reviewed in each chapter. Chapters are focused around topics that are central in the life of a traveler—"Today's Weather," "I Wanna Shop Until I Drop," "Eating Out," and "Money Is the Issue," are some of the chapter headings which, while focusing on the tourist, present vocabulary that is vital to everyone. Exercises and drills are imaginative and taken from actual daily experiences. Throughout the book, Gail Stein offers suggestions to facilitate learning, explanations for cultural differences, and shortcuts for increasing vocabulary.

More and more it appears that English is becoming a universal language and native English speakers can rejoice in their knowledge of this language. Yet while increasing opportunities for travel and the exploding growth of the Internet have shrunk many barriers, speed of communication and access to information have increased the complexity of the world we live in. I don't think we can truly understand another culture or society unless we can speak directly to others in their own language. Certainly France and French-speaking people have contributed greatly to the world. France has been the United States' oldest and perhaps most honest ally. French is spoken on every continent today by more than 300 million people. Knowing another language can have life-altering consequences. I could never have predicted that studying French in Rouen, France, during my junior year of college would have forever changed the course of my life. One year in France led to four years as a Peace Corps teacher in Niger, West Africa, which has led to almost 25 years as a high school French teacher. If you have ever considered learning French, I would urge you to get a copy of this book and plunge in.

—John Garnet Lord
French teacher
Packer Collegiate Institute, Brooklyn, New York

Introduction

You have at your fingertips a completely updated, user-friendly book that will help you enjoy your language-learning experience to the fullest. This book's light, simple, clear-cut approach will give you all the confidence you need to start communicating almost instantly with a reasonable amount of success and an encouraging sense of achievement.

Learning French enables you to broaden your horizons and will open a path to endless opportunities, intriguing experiences, exotic adventures, and exciting challenges. Just open your eyes, ears, heart, and soul to the new cultures, creative ideas, varying perspectives, and unique situations that await you all over the world. Knowledge of French is a handy and useful tool that will serve you well when you least expect it.

This book has been designed for people from all walks of life and with wide and varied interests: from travel to business to a pure and simple love for learning. Seize the chance to put the French-speaking world at your doorstep. Do it now!

How This Book Is Organized

This book takes you from the most basic material to a broader understanding of the structural patterns of the French language and finally to a higher level of expertise and proficiency. This book is not a phrase book, a dictionary, a grammar text, or a tour guide. It is unique in that it is a combination of these four all wrapped up in one. Its goal is to teach you to communicate effectively in common, everyday situations. You'll be able to socialize, ask for information, express your opinions, and be persuasive. Plain and simply, you'll be able to get what you want and need. Whether you are a student, tourist, businessperson, or lover of languages, the simple, easy-to-use format of this book will provide you with the knowledge and skills you need. Each thematically constructed chapter ties together vocabulary, useful phrases, and grammar and furnishes authentic materials and activities that will give you a thorough understanding of French-speaking people and their culture. Here's what you can expect to find in this book:

Part 1, "The Bare Basics," begins with a discussion of the importance of French in today's world. This is followed by an easy-to-use, phonetic pronunciation guide designed for the shy and easily intimidated speaker. Next there's a demonstration of your pre-existing knowledge of many French words, phrases, and expressions. Don't agonize over grammar; basic elementary terms and rules are presented painlessly along with idioms, slang, and typical gestures. From the outset, you'll be able to ask and answer simple questions and engage in basic conversations.

Part 2, "Travel Time," provides useful information and tips for how to plan a trip to a French-speaking country and get the most out of it. You'll learn how to meet and greet others and how to introduce and speak about yourself and your traveling companions. For the curious type, asking questions will be quite easy. There are chapters to help you navigate the airport, find ground transportation, and even rent a car. You'll also become proficient at giving and receiving directions. Finally, this section helps you acquire a room with the creature comforts you prefer.

Part 3, "Fun Time," helps you have a fantastic, fun-filled time. Everything that makes your dream vacation a reality is featured in this section: food, shopping, sports, tourist attractions, musical events, and leisure activities. You'll learn to plan your activities around the weather, to offer suggestions, and to express your opinions and preferences. The chapters about food ensure that your appetite will be satisfied and your diet maintained. If you love to shop, there's a chapter that enables you to buy anything from *haute couture* fashions to souvenirs for the crowd back home.

Part 4, "Time Out: Problems," helps you deal with simple, minor inconveniences as well as those of a more serious nature. Turn to this section when you need your hair cut, a spot removed, your camera repaired, a replacement contact lens, new heels on your shoes, a prescription filled, or your mail sent. You'll even be able to explain what happened in the past.

Part 5, "It's Time for Business," was written to meet the needs of people who want to conduct business transactions at the bank. You'll learn how to make deposits and withdrawals, open a checking account, and take out a loan. You'll also learn tasks such as sending faxes, making photocopies, and using the computer. This section includes mini-dictionaries for banking-, computer-, business-, and stock market–related terms. When you're through, you'll be able to buy or rent property abroad and express your present and future needs.

If you are truly committed to learning French, by the time you've completed this book, you will have studied and practiced skills that enable you to feel confident in both social and business situations. With time, patience, and the willingness to make a sincere effort, you will be able to communicate successfully in a beautiful language in a relatively short period of time.

Extras

In addition to all the vocabulary lists, useful phrases and expressions, and grammatical explanations, this book provides many interesting and informative facts set apart from the text in boxes.

Un, Deux, Trois

These boxes feature tips for learning and perfecting your French in a fast, fun way.

Attention!

These warnings help you avoid unnecessary or embarrassing mistakes.

Memory Enhancer

Consult these boxes for a speedy refresher course of grammar or a quick understanding of new rules.

Culture Capsule

Refer to these boxes for useful facts and an increased cultural understanding of the customs of the French-speaking world. These useful tidbits will certainly make your travel experience more fulfilling.

How to Use This Book

This book is tailor-made for you whether you are a beginner or a more seasoned French student, whether you are learning for business or for pleasure, and whether you are trying to perfect oral, reading, or writing skills. You can use this book in any way that will help you achieve the goals you've set for yourself.

- The conversational introductory paragraphs help you understand, by means of personal, funny, anecdotal examples, why you may need the information about to be provided.
- The extensive vocabulary lists offer a wide choice of words you may need in a particular situation. These lists are ideal for reference: They are *not* meant to be memorized in their entirety. Choose only the words you think you'll need and concentrate on learning them. The others will be at your fingertips just in case you have to rely on them. You never know when they may come in handy.
- The grammar is presented with concise, clear-cut explanations and examples. Your goal should be to develop an understanding of the rules that make French work so that you can apply them automatically without agonizing over awkward, often incomprehensible literal translations that don't make the grade. You only need a basic knowledge of grammar before you can communicate on a level at

which you can be understood and before you can understand what is said to you. The more you listen to and speak French, the quicker the grammar rules will fall into place and become an internalized part of the communicative process, in much the same way as they did when you were a child learning your native tongue.

- Authentic reading materials are presented to give you an idea of what you might expect to encounter in a variety of situations in a French-speaking country: from general information contained in a tourist brochure, to directions to a monument, to instructions on how to get things to work properly, to newspaper ads, to weather reports. Use these selections to perfect your comprehension skills. While reading, remember that it is unreasonable to expect to recognize and understand each and every word. A more reasonable goal is to simply get the gist of what you've read and be able to use it to your advantage.

- Writing exercises, many based on authentic materials, are provided to reinforce grammar rules and to allow you to use what've internalized to the fullest. As your listening, speaking, and reading skills improve, so will your ability to write. Bear in mind that, as in any language, the more you read, the better you will write.

Tips for the Beginner

For beginners, learning a foreign language must seem like an intimidating task. There is so much to learn: proper pronunciation, vocabulary, grammar, and so on. How and where does one begin? Here are a few do's and don'ts to get you started:

Do's

- Start by concentrating on the pronunciation guide. Practicing and mastering the sounds of the language first will make the chapters that follow easier to master.

- Examine your immediate language goals and focus on them. If you plan on traveling, learn the vocabulary and expressions you'll use on your trip. If you're a student, pay more attention to grammatical structures and verb conjugations. If you're a businessperson, familiarize yourself with the words and phrases that will lead to a successful deal.

- Learn the basics first, especially the idiosyncrasies of the language that make it different from English: the fact that nouns have a masculine or feminine gender, the fact that adjectives must agree in number and gender with the nouns and pronouns they modify and that they generally are placed after these words, and the differing irregular verbs.

- Enjoy your learning experience. Take your time. Study one small segment at a time until you've mastered it.

Don'ts

- Don't be intimidated by the amount of material in a chapter. You certainly aren't expected to learn or retain it all, even after you've made significant progress. Use this book as a resource and a reference guide and read and reread the most personally challenging and useful material repeatedly until you feel comfortable with it. Over time you'll find that the chapters become easier and easier as you build on what you've already mastered.
- Don't feel compelled to be in a rush. This is a book that needs to be studied and restudied. Keep it handy for easy reference.
- Don't be afraid to skip the parts that you won't use or that you find too difficult at the beginning. You can always pick up the book again at a later date.
- Don't be too hasty to lend this book to a friend, to give it away, or to put it up for auction on your favorite website. Even if you feel you've mastered French, you never know when you'll have a simple question whose answer lies within these pages.

Tips for Those Who Know Some French

If you've already had the opportunity to study French, you may feel familiar and confident enough with your speaking and linguistic skills to quickly pass over the beginning chapters that cover the bare basics. For you, parts of this book will be a refresher course that will enable you to fine-tune your skills. Here are a few do's and don'ts for those with more intermediate abilities:

Do's

- Briefly review what you already know and then spend time perfecting the language skills you'll need the most.
- Understand that there is more than one way to express most ideas and that this book provides choices. Select the phrases and expression that are easiest for you to remember. Concentrate on learning them while keeping in mind that other alternatives exist, should you need them.
- Strive to develop your oral and written communication skills as much as possible because these are most important if you travel or are part of the business world. To speak well, listen carefully. To write well, concentrate on reading everything you can get your hands on.
- Focus on your long-range goals. Ask yourself what you feel you'd like to have accomplished after having read and studied the various chapters in this book.

Don'ts

- Don't expect perfection. Native speakers of any language make mistakes without even realizing it.
- Don't worry about your accent and then shy away from communicating. Any attempts at speaking or writing a foreign language will be respected and appreciated by native speakers who will, in most instances, go out of their way to help you.
- Don't expect to translate word for word from language to language. In most cases, it doesn't work. In a best-case scenario, translating will make your French sound very stilted and awkward. Use idioms and colloquial expressions to speak the way a native would.
- Don't expect to learn every vocabulary word and grammar rule in the book. That's unrealistic and therefore frustrating and self-defeating. Whatever you don't learn or can't remember, you can always look up. So just like the beginners, don't give away your copy of *The Complete Idiot's Guide to Learning French*. Let it serve as a constant resource guide.

Acknowledgments

I would like to acknowledge the contributions, input, support, and interest of the following people:

Natercia Alves, Marie-Claire Antoine, Monika Bergenthal, Vivian Bergenthal, Richard Calcasola (of Maximus Hair Salon), Nancy Chu, Raymond Elias, Barbara Gilson, Robert Grandt, François Haas (of the Office of the French Treasury), Martin Hyman, Roger Herz (of Roger Herz, Inc.), Martin Leder, Christina Levy, Nancy Lasker (of L'Oréal), Max Rechtman, Marie-Madeleine Saphire, and Barbara Shevrin.

Special Thanks to the Technical Reviewer

To help us ensure that this book gives you everything you need to know about French, *The Complete Idiot's Guide to Learning French, Third Edition*, was reviewed by an expert who double-checked the accuracy of what you'll learn here. Special thanks are extended to Stephanie Rosenfeld.

Trademarks

All terms mentioned in this book that are known to be or are suspected of being trademarks or service marks have been appropriately capitalized. Alpha Books and Penguin Group (USA) Inc. cannot attest to the accuracy of this information. Use of a term in this book should not be regarded as affecting the validity of any trademark or service mark.

Part 1

The Bare Basics

Learning simple, basic grammar is the fastest, easiest, most efficient way to pick up French effortlessly. All it takes is a quick study of a few simple rules. Be honest: Does the thought of grammar turn you off? Surprise! As you'll learn in Part 1, the rules are easy and don't test your memorization skills in the slightest. You'll also learn to speak idiomatically so that you'll be mistaken for a native! Just dive right in and, before you know it, you'll be communicating in French with ease and confidence.

Chapter 1

The Top Ten Reasons You Should Study French

In This Chapter

- Where and when you can use French
- Developing a workable learning strategy
- Where in the world French is spoken
- Twenty phrases you should know

You've picked up this book, and as you're leafing through it you're probably wondering, "Should I or shouldn't I?" Undoubtedly, you're asking yourself if it will be difficult, if you'll have the time, if it's going to be worth the effort, and if you'll stick with it. My name may not be Dave, but here are my top 10 reasons why you need to study French:

10. You can't put down Colette's romance novels.
9. You'd like to root for the Montréal Canadiens in French.
8. You loved the musical *Les Misérables* so much that you decided to read the original version in its entirety—all 600 plus pages.
7. You want to avoid ordering francs with mustard and sauerkraut.

6. You never know when you're going to run into Catherine Deneuve.
5. You want to impress your date at a French restaurant.
4. You love French movies but find the subtitles too distracting.
3. They won't let you onto the topless beach in Martinique without it.
2. Two words: French fries.

And finally, the best reason of all:

1. You want to meet St. Exupéry's *Little Prince.*

Are you now totally convinced that French is the language for you? If you're still a little doubtful, let's look at some more down-to-earth, realistic reasons why you should study French.

Reality Check

The following are some serious and credible reasons why this book is for you:

10. **You're a musician, and France is a country where culture is taken seriously.** You long to go to L'Opéra and admire its sculptured façade, its magnificent marble staircase, and its elegant foyer. You really like classical music (although you'd never admit it to your friends) and would like to enjoy the operas you love in their native language: Bizet's *Carmen*, Gounod's *Faust*, Massenet's *Manon*, Saint-Saëns's *Samson et Dalila*. Yes, you want to take your studies further.
9. **You're an *artiste*.** Your dream is to sit in the Place du Tertre in Montmartre and paint watercolor scenes of Paris or do charcoal portraits of the tourists who stop by your easel to admire your work.

Culture Capsule

Paris has many museums: the Musée du Louvre with its *Mona Lisa* and *Vénus de Milo,* the Musée d'Orsay with its impressionist collection, the Centre Georges-Pompidou with its fabulous modern art museum, the well-hidden Musée Picasso, and many more. You can have a picnic lunch at the Musée Rodin while you sit and admire *Le Penseur* (*The Thinker*) or *Le Baiser* (*The Kiss*). In Paris, art is respected and loved.

8. **You love French movies and long to understand the actors without the distraction of poorly translated subtitles.** You know that those subtitles don't tell it all, and you want to know what's really happening. You are also aware that this is a good way to pick up some up-to-date slang expressions.

7. **You're not greedy, but you do want to make more money.** France, a leading nation in the European Union, has the fourth largest economy in the world, and you'd like to take advantage of that. *Haute couture* (high fashion), perfume, leather goods, precision instruments, automobiles, chemical and pharmaceutical products, and jewelry are all thriving French industries.

6. **You want to prove you're smart.** The French language has the reputation of being difficult to learn. This myth dates back to a time when only the smartest junior high school students were offered French. Of course, anyone who's ever studied French knows that it really isn't any more difficult than any other foreign language.

5. **You want to live in a French-speaking country.** You love the language, you love the people, or maybe your company has relocated you. Whatever the reason, if you're going to be staying in a French-speaking country for an extended period of time, you've got to learn the language.

4. **You love to cook and have a special passion for fabulous dishes and desserts.** You want to go to the original sources to understand all the food terms and culinary techniques. If you decide to take a cooking course in France, you want to know what's going on.

3. **You love to eat.** Are you a gourmet? Even if you love food but don't study it, a basic knowledge of French, especially the culinary terms, is a must. Whether you prefer *nouvelle*, *haute*, or traditional cuisine, Cajun specialties, or regional or native dishes, French cooking is the world's greatest. Whether you eat in Paris or New Orleans, Algeria or Port-au-Prince, the city or the country, you can be sure that the food you are served is fresh and appetizing and that it has been expertly and lovingly prepared by a chef who takes great pride in his or her work—and a good French wine can improve even the best meal.

Culture Capsule

Remember that champagne is made only from the grapes grown in the Champagne valley in France. So if you crave the real bubbly, make sure it's from France.

2. **You want to be totally irresistible, and you believe that speaking French will attract that special someone.** You're probably right. French, more than any other language, has the reputation of being "the language of love." It doesn't even matter what you say. Just whisper any of the beautiful, flowing, song-like phrases in someone's ear to "Wow!" that person and make his or her heart beat faster. It's practically foolproof.

1. **You love to travel.** In addition to France, there are more than 40 French-speaking countries around the world where more than 100 million people speak French on a daily basis. Whether you travel for business or pleasure, romance or adventure, excitement or relaxation, your choices include sensuous tropical islands with white, sandy beaches; lush rain forests with luxuriant, native vegetation; tempting, snow-covered mountains perfect for winter sports; sweaty, sultry jungles where special thrills lurk everywhere; fortified ancient villages where history comes to life; or bustling, modern cities where the future rapidly unfolds.

Un, Deux, Trois

You don't have to go far to speak French. For example, you could go to parts of Louisiana, Maine, New Hampshire, Vermont, Massachusetts, or Canada. Or you could go across the globe to distant, exotic lands in Africa or Asia. More than 60 million tourists visit France each year. The possibilities and opportunities are endless.

Fast Forward

The best, most foolproof way to become proficient in something is to plunge right in. Immerse yourself in anything and everything that is French. Have a love affair with the language and the culture. Follow these suggestions to ensure an enduring and fulfilling relationship:

- **Examine your goals, honestly evaluate your linguistic abilities, and pace yourself accordingly.** Take your time, don't rush, and set aside special time each day that you devote only to French.
- **Invest in or borrow a good bilingual dictionary.** Pocket varieties (usually running between $6 and $15) may suit the needs of some learners but prove somewhat deficient for others. Carefully peruse what is available in your local bookstore or library before making a decision as to what is best for you. Current popular dictionaries that are easy to use and that provide a comprehensive listing of modern, colloquial vocabulary words are published by a number of companies. The best include those by Simon & Schuster, Collins/Robert, and

Larousse. They can be found in any bookstore to fit any size pocketbook. Ultralingual is a highly regarded, up-to-the minute software dictionary that can be downloaded for computer use for a nominal fee. Unlike its printed counterparts, this dictionary contains a huge vocabulary that can be updated on a regular basis and is available for Mac, Windows, and Palm devices.

- **Take advantage of all available opportunities to listen to the language.** Rent French movies and try not to read the English subtitles. If broadcast in your area, listen to public service radio or television stations that provide French programs. Search bookstores and public or college libraries for language tapes that will help you hear and master the French sound system. Create your own tapes and use them to perfect your accent. Ask to use language laboratories and computer programs that are available in many high schools and universities.
- **Read everything you can get your hands on.** Read fairy tales, children's books, comic books (*Astérix* is my personal favorite, but you may want to sample *Iznogud*, *Lucky Luke*, and *Tintin*), newspapers (*Le Monde*, *France-Soir*, *Le Figaro*, *Libération*, *Le Dauphiné Libéré*), and magazines (*Paris Match*, *Elle*, *L'Express*, *Marie-Claire*). If you're not too bashful, read aloud to practice your pronunciation and comprehension at the same time.
- **Surf the Internet.** There are so many places you can go and things you can see at home on your computer. Take advantage of everything the Web has to offer.

Un, Deux, Trois

If you're planning a trip to France, visit the official website of the French Government Tourist Office at www.Frenchtourism.com.

Create *un coin français* (a French corner) in a convenient spot in your home. Decorate it with posters or articles. Label items whose names you want to learn and display them for easy viewing. Keep all your materials together and organized in this special French spot.

Forget Your Fear

Some people are truly afraid to study a foreign language. They think that it'll be too much work, too hard, too time-consuming. In reality, if you take it slow and don't allow yourself to become overly concerned with grammar and pronunciation, you will manage very well. To help you feel more at ease, try to remember the following:

- **Don't be intimidated by the grammar.** Everyone makes mistakes—even native speakers. Besides, you usually need only one or two correct words (especially verbs) to be understood.
- **Don't be intimidated by the pronunciation.** Put on your best French accent. Don't be shy and speak, speak, speak. In any country, there are many different regional accents. Certainly yours will fit in somewhere!
- **Don't be intimidated by the French.** They are perfectly lovely people and accept anyone who makes a sincere attempt to communicate.
- **Don't be intimidated when people tell you that French is difficult.** As you will see almost immediately, French is easy and fun.

How to Study

As a more than 32-year veteran New York City public junior-high and high school French and Spanish teacher, I have seen and dealt with every type of student imaginable: from those who've gone on to graduate with honors from the finest Ivy League schools to those who have dropped out. Except for the extraordinarily rare individual who defies all odds and excels at a second language without opening a book, the rest of us have to study. Over the years, I compiled a list of suggestions to help students acquire better study habits and to make the task of learning a foreign language more enjoyable. I'll share them with you because I want you to succeed.

How to Succeed in a Foreign Language Without Trying Too Hard

Let's face it: The overwhelming majority of us don't and can't intuitively learn a foreign language. Understand that you have to study to succeed. There's no getting around it. With that said, the more effort you exert, the more rewards you will reap.

- You should commit certain key phrases to memory because they will be useful in a tremendous amount of situations. For example, *Je voudrais* (I would like) can be used to say the following: *Je voudrais manger.* (I'd like to eat.) *Je voudrais aller en France.* (I'd like to go to France.) *Je voudrais acheter ceci.* (I'd like to buy this.) *Je voudrais une chambre.* (I'd like a room.) Learn the expressions and then plug in the vocabulary word or phrase that fits the circumstances. You'll only need a few key phrases before you'll be able to comfortably communicate in French.
- Psychological studies have proven that, for the maximum retention of facts, the optimal times to study are first thing in the morning or right before you go to bed. So keep your *Complete Idiot's Guide* on your night table.

- While studying, use as many of your senses as you can. This will help reinforce the new material you've learned in as many ways as possible. Remember that language is acquired in four steps: listening, speaking, reading, and then writing.
- Think in French as often as possible. Don't stop to translate. See if you can make yourself formulate your ideas in your second language.
- Practice a little every day. Short practice and study periods are much more effective than one long, drawn-out cramming session.
- Use what you already know in English to help you communicate and understand French. Many French and English words have the same Latin roots, so if you hear or see words that seem familiar, there's a good chance you will be able to correctly guess their meaning. Learn and use as many cognates (words that are the same or almost the same in both languages) as you can.
- Be organized. Keep all your language materials together in one place.
- If you can, find a partner who wants to learn the language with you. You'll see rapid results if you work together closely. Practice and test each other regularly.
- The absolute best way to learn and master a foreign language is to teach it to another person. You cannot teach something you don't understand or don't know well, so if you can teach it, you know it.

Learning Specifics

Pronunciation: If one of your goals is to sound like a native, here are some tips you should follow:

- Listen to everything that's available to you in French: television and radio shows, films, music CDs. The more you listen, the sooner you'll be able to speak.
- Speak as much as you can with whomever you can. Don't be shy. If you're alone, record yourself on tape and then play it back. Keep your very first tape. Study and practice some more and then rerecord yourself. Compare the two tapes to see how much progress you've made.

Vocabulary: Knowing the proper vocabulary words to use in various situations is the key to perfecting good communication skills. Here are some ideas for acquiring the words and phrases you'll use the most:

- Make flash cards for various groups of words (vegetables, hotel words, business terms, and so on) by writing the English word on one side and the French on the other. Start with the easier of the two tasks: Look at the French word and see if you can give its English meaning. Now for the hard part: Look at the English word and see if you can give its French equivalent. Set aside a specific amount of time every day for vocabulary practice.

- Label things in your house (furniture, rooms, food) or your car. This way, you will immerse yourself as much as possible in the language and will learn as you go through the motions of doing your daily chores.
- Take a sheet of loose-leaf paper. Fold it into four long columns. Write in English all the words you want to learn down the first column. Put your book away. Try saying and also writing the French words in the second column. Once you've completed the second column, fold back the first column to see if you can write the English words again in column 3. Now check your work. All the correct words can be considered words you've mastered. All the words you got wrong or didn't know have to be studied more carefully before you fold back the first two columns to try to complete the fourth column with the correct French word again. Continue in this manner using both sides of the paper until you've mastered all the words you deem important. Remember that writing down what you've studied helps reinforce what you've learned.

Column 1	Column 2	Column 3	Column 4
pear	poire	pear	(mastered word)
apple	pome	apple (incorrect; needs more work)	pomme (correct)

Verb Conjugations: You'll want to make sure that your verbs agree with the subjects you use so that your French sounds impeccable. Two good study guidelines are:

- Use flash cards to practice learning how to give the proper oral conjugation of verbs.
- Practice saying the verbs as you write them on a piece of paper. Write the verb several times until you have it memorized.

Where in the World Is French Spoken?

French is a language that can be used throughout the world as well as in the United States. There are more than 100 million native French speakers, and more than 125 million people speak French on a daily basis. As a second language, French is the second most frequently taught language after English. French is the official language of 28 countries and is the official working language of the United Nations, UNESCO, NATO, and the International Red Cross. Let's take a closer look at the French-speaking world.

- **France and her neighbors.** We are all well aware that French is spoken in France, but it is also the major language of Belgium, Luxembourg, and Switzerland, as well as in the principality of Monaco and on the mountainous Mediterranean island of Corsica. French is also spoken in Andorra, a small country that borders Spain and France.
- **Caribbean and South America.** Haiti, in the Greater Antilles, shares the island of Hispañola with the Spanish-speaking Dominican Republic. Although it's a totally independent country, French influence continues to play an important role in Haiti. French is its official language, but most people speak Creole, a French dialect influenced by African elements.

  Martinique and Guadeloupe are overseas subdivisions of France know as Départements d'Outre-Mer (D.O.M.). Their residents are French citizens and have the same rights, privileges, laws, president, government, system of education, and responsibilities as French citizens in France. Several small islands near Guadeloupe (Les Saintes, Marie Galante, La Désirade, St. Barthélemy, and St. Martin) are part of the same administrative subdivision.

  French Guiana, an overseas French subdivision, is the only country in South America where French is the official language and the residents are French citizens.
- **Africa.** Réunion and Mayotte are two African colonies that remain overseas departments of France. Many former African colonies that are now independent from France still continue to have close cultural and economic ties to France and have retained French as their official language. French is spoken in 24 African countries, and the French government provides them with financial and technical assistance. Algeria, Morocco, and Tunisia belong to a region referred to as the Mahgreb (the setting sun). Although Arabic is the official language of these countries, they continue to use French and have institutions and school systems that are based on those originally established by the French. Two other African countries that use French as a common language are Senegal and the Ivory Coast.
- **Far and Middle East.** In Indochina, vestiges of French culture and heritage remain in Vietnam, Laos, and Cambodia, although these countries maintain their independence. In the Middle East, French is spoken in Lebanon.

  Overseas islands of France in the Pacific Ocean include Tahiti and New Caledonia. Although they maintain close ties with France, their inhabitants have no voice in French politics.

- **North America.** Believe it or not, according to U.S. census figures from the year 2000, French is spoken by almost 2 million Americans in their home. The history of Louisiana dates back to the seventeenth century when French settlers colonized various lands. The Cajuns, descendants of the French-speaking Acadian settlers, maintain many of the traditions and customs of their ancestors.

  North of the United States, in Canada, about one third of the population, descendants of French colonists, speak French. Most reside in Quebec, Canada's largest province and one of its oldest, where about 83 percent of the 7 million inhabitants speak French. French has been the official language of Quebec since 1977. These people take pride in maintaining and promoting their language, traditions, and cultural identity. French influence is apparent everywhere. After Paris, Montréal is the second-largest French-speaking city in the world.

Is French the Same Throughout the French-Speaking World?

As we all know, the English spoken in the northern part of the United States sounds a lot different from the English spoken in the South. People from New England have an accent that is quite distinct from those from the Midwest. Let's not forget about our overseas friends, the British. Not only does their pronunciation differ greatly from ours, sometimes they even have different words for things. We refer to an "elevator," but they call it a "lift." Despite differences in words and accents, somehow we manage to understand, albeit with a certain degree of difficulty, those who are speaking the same language as we are but who hail from different regions.

The same holds true for French, which is not spoken in exactly the same way throughout the French-speaking world. Since French is the native language of so many different countries, there are many regional differences in pronunciation and vocabulary, and there is no standard dialect. Just as we can understand and communicate with others who speak English, speakers of French can do the same with their language. As far as writing goes, there are fewer differences than in speaking, and this shouldn't pose a problem.

Parisian French sets the standard for the world. If other French-speaking countries had had strong, forceful governments that rose to power and rivaled France—for example, had Quebec remained a separate country or had Haiti been a larger country with a more stable government—other dialects might have possibly become more accepted. The French used in your *Complete Idiot's Guide to Learning French*, therefore, is standard Parisian French. Should you expect to hear differences in French used around the world? The answer is yes. Should you be able to understand that French with relative ease? The answer is again yes. The vast majority of words and structures used in the French-speaking world can be recognized and understood. Here are the differences you can expect to hear:

- Within France itself, certain regional dialects are still spoken: *provençal* in the south of France, *celtic* in Brittany, *basque* in the Pyrenées, and *bas-allemand* in Alsace. If you're in these regions, the dialects will prove quite a bit of a challenge to understand.
- Cajun French differs from the standard in several ways. In some cases, Cajun French has kept words, structures, and pronunciations from old French that were long ago abandoned by modernists. In other instances, Cajun words have evolved: They've become shortened versions of the original French, they've become Americanized, or they've borrowed from other languages.
- Canadian French is typified by the use of archaic and/or dialectical words, expressions, and pronunciations, Anglicisms, and words that the Canadians have made up along the way. The Canadians have also internalized many English words that they pronounce with a French-Canadian accent.
- Most words in Haitian Creole would not be understood by a native French speaker. Haitian French, however, is virtually the same as the French spoken in France. The more educated the speaker, the less likely the chance that Creole words will be mixed or interchanged with French words.
- The more educated the Moroccan speaker, the more likely it is that his or her French will be flawless and free of any Arabic influence. Less educated Moroccans speak a heavily accented dialect.

Twenty Phrases You Should Know

No matter what your reason for studying French, these 20 phrases are an absolute must. (See the section "You're Supposed to Sound Nasal" in Chapter 2 for an explanation of the uppercase "N" in the pronunciations.)

Phrase	French	Pronunciation
Please	S'il vous plaît	*seel voo pleh*
Thank you very much.	Merci beaucoup.	*mehr-see boh-koo*
You're welcome.	De rien; Pas de quoi.	*duh ryaN; pahd kwah*
Excuse me.	Pardon; Excusez-moi.	*pahr-dohN; ehk-skew-zay mwah*

continues

continued

Phrase	French	Pronunciation
My name is …	Je m'appelle …	*zhuh mah-pehl*
I would like …	Je voudrais …	*zhuh voo-dreh*
I need …	Il me faut …; J'ai besoin de …	*eel muh foh; zhay buh-zwaN duh*
Do you have …?	Avez-vous …?	*ah-vay voo*
Please give me …	Donnez-moi s'il vous plaît …	*doh-nay mwah seel voo pleh*
Could you help me please?	Pourriez-vous m'aider?	*poo-ryay voo meh-day*
Do you speak English?	Parlez-vous anglais?	*pahr-lay voo ahn-gleh*
I speak a little French.	Je parle un peu le français.	*zhuh pahrl uhN puh luh frahN-seh*
I don't understand.	Je ne comprends pas.	*zhuh nuh kohN-prahN pah*
Please repeat.	Répétez, s'il vous plaît.	*ray-pay-tay seel voo pleh*
What did you say?	Qu'est-ce que vous avez dit?	*kehs-kuh voo zah-vay dee*
I'm lost.	Je me suis égaré(e).	*zhuh muh swee zay-gah-ray*
I'm looking for …	Je cherche …	*zhuh shehrsh*
Where is the bathroom?	Où sont les toilettes?	*oo sohN lay twah-leht*
Where is the police station?	Où est le commissariat de police.	*oo eh luh koh-mee-sah-ryah duh poh-lees*
Where is the American embassy?	Où est l'ambassade américaine?	*oo eh lahN-bah-sahd ah-may-ree-kehn*

Bonne chance! (*bohn shahNs;* Good luck!)

The Least You Need to Know

- Anyone and everyone, from all walks of life, can benefit from studying French.
- French is very useful to know because it is an international language spoken daily throughout the world.
- You'll always get by despite imperfections in your grammar and pronunciation.
- Fear not! Learning French is really easier than you might think.
- To become a francophone (French speaker), you must first be a francophile (lover of French).

Chapter 2

Pronounce It Properly

In This Chapter

- When there's stress involved
- Go with the flow
- Perfecting your accent
- Phonetically fine

When you speak French, you want to sound like they do in the movies: irresistible, romantic, sexy, sophisticated, chic. It's only natural. So lose your inhibitions, put on your best French accent, and repeat and practice the sounds of the language. Although different from English, these sounds are not too difficult to master. Just follow the rules, learn the proper pronunciation of the phonetic symbols, be patient, and you're on your way!

This is a *work* chapter. It's not terribly exciting; it's not particularly fun; and it's not especially amusing—but don't be reluctant to see it through. Just like anything you might have to learn (a sport, a hobby, a trade, or a profession), there's work involved, and you must be committed to putting in a certain amount of effort and energy. Think of learning a language as a mental fitness routine. Start slowly and carefully work up to a pace that suits you. Remember, you don't want to burn yourself out at the first workout. So give it your best shot and practice, practice, practice. *Oh là là*, you'll be sounding like a native in no time!

The Stress of It All

In French, each syllable of a word has just about equal stress. When speaking, try to pronounce each syllable of a word with equal emphasis. When you remember, place a slightly stronger emphasis on the last syllable of a group of words. Speak smoothly, speak musically, and speak evenly. My best advice: For maximum results, stay on an even keel.

Not Dangerous Liaisons—Elisions

Liaison (linking) and *elision* (sliding) are two elements of the French language that give it its fluidity and melodious beauty by smoothing out rough spots.

Liaison

Liaison refers to the linking of the final consonant of one word with the beginning vowel of the next word. There are many rules in French explaining when a liaison is mandatory, optional, and forbidden. I could go on for pages boring you with rules you'll probably never remember. Instead, simply follow the pronunciation guide provided in this chapter and the phonetic keys for words and phrases throughout the book.

Memory Enhancer

Liaison links a final consonant with a beginning vowel. **Elision** eliminates a final pronounced *a*, *e*, or *i* and replaces it with an apostrophe before a beginning pronounced vowel.

Make a liaison when you see that the pronunciation of the last consonant sound of one word precedes the beginning vowel of the next word. Take for example the expression *vous arrivez*. The final *s* (pronounced *z*) of the first word *vous* (pronounced *voo*) is linked to the beginning of the next word, *arrivez*. The pronunciation of this word is now *zah-ree-vay*, and the necessary liaison has been painlessly achieved.

Words	Liaison
Vous arrivez	*voo zah-ree-vay*
Mon ami	*mohN nah-mee*

Elision

Elision occurs when there are two pronounced vowel sounds: one at the end of a word, and the other at the beginning of the next word. The first vowel is dropped and replaced by an apostrophe. To pronounce the words, simply slide them together. If you try to say them separately, the vowel sounds will clash, and you will probably feel like you have a word stuck in your throat. Elision is a very natural device and gives the language fluidity. The following is an example of elision.

Words	Elision	Pronunciation
Je arrive	J'arrive	*zah-reev*
Le hôtel	L'hôtel	*lo-tehl*

Add a Little Accent Here

If this is your first experience with a foreign language, you'll probably be mystified by accent marks. Just think of them as pronunciation guideposts that help you speak like an old pro.

Working on Your Own Personal Accent

For some, French pronunciation is a breeze. If you are lucky enough to have been born with a "good ear," chances are you can carry a tune or play a musical instrument. You'll imitate the lilt, intonation, and stress without a problem.

For most of us, however, pronunciation is not without problems. If this is you, you're in good company. Consider my former college French literature teacher, a Rhodes scholar from Oxford University, who later went on to become chairman of the Romance Language Department. He was charming, interesting, sweet, very, very intellectual, well-read, and knowledgeable. He also had the worst French accent I have ever heard. He pronounced every word, every syllable, every letter so harshly and with such stress and emphasis that the students would sit in class squinting in pain. He butchered the pronunciation so much that it was memorable.

In my more naïve days, I often wondered why he would teach a language he obviously had so much trouble speaking. When I think back, I realize that it really didn't matter at all. Why? Because we all understood him despite his terrible pronunciation. And that, *débutant(e)s*, is a very valuable lesson for us all. No matter what you sound like (and you couldn't sound any worse than this teacher), if you use the correct vocabulary, you will be able to make yourself understood. That should be your goal. Nobody is going to laugh at you; they might just say "*Pardon*" more than usual. In the end, your level of competence in pronunciation is no big deal. So relax, try your best, and, above all, don't be discouraged.

Accent Marks

There are five different accent marks in French that may be used to change the sounds of letters (*é* versus *è*, *à* versus *â*, and so on), to differentiate between the meanings of two words whose spellings are otherwise the same—*a* (has) and *à* (to, at); *ou* (or) and *où* (where), and so on—or to replace an *s* that was part of the word many centuries ago in old French.

- An *accent aigu* (´) is seen only on an *e* (*é*). *É* produces the sound (*ay*), as in *day*.
- An *accent grave* (`) is used with *a* (*à*), *e* (*è*), and *u* (*ù*). On an *e*, an *accent grave* produces the sound of (*eh*), as in the *e* in the English word *met*. It doesn't change the sound of the *a* (*à*) or *u* (*ù*).
- An *accent circonflexe* can be used on all vowels: *â*, *ê*, *î*, *ô*, *û*. The vowel sounds are longer for *â* and *ô*, are slightly longer for *ê*, and are practically imperceptible on *î* and *û*.
- A *cédille* (¸) is used only on a *c* (*ç*). When the *c* comes before *a*, *o*, or *u*, it means that you pronounce the letter as a soft *c* (the sound of *s*).
- A *tréma* (¨) occurs on a second vowel in a series. This accent indicates that the two vowels are pronounced separately, each having its own distinct sound: Haïti (*ay-ee-tee*), Noël (*noh-ehl*).

Memory Enhancer

Keep the following in mind: *H* and *Y* are usually considered vowels in French.

Vowel Sounds Simplified

French vowels are a bit complicated. Why? In general, each vowel has a number of different sounds, and there are specific rules and accent marks that help you determine how a vowel is to be pronounced. I've included some practice words to help you.

French Letter	Symbol	Pronunciation Guide
a, *à*, *â*	ah	Say ***a*** as in ***spa***

Open wide (but not too wide) and say *ahhh* …

ça	la	ma	sa	ta	va	papa	Canada
sah	*lah*	*mah*	*sah*	*tah*	*vah*	*pah-pah*	*kah-nah-dah*

French Letter	Symbol	Pronunciation Guide
é, final *-er* and *-ez*; *es* in some one-syllable words; a few *ai*, *et* combinations	ay	Say ***ay*** as in ***day***

é, final *-er*, and *-ez* are always pronounced *ay*. Instead of driving yourself crazy trying to remember the rules (which are vague), just look at the following guide:

bébé *bay-bay*	télé *tay-lay*	météo *may-tay-o*	été *ay-tay*	René *ruh-nay*
danser *dahN-say*	arriver *ah-ree-vay*	désirer *day-zee-ray*	parler *pahr-lay*	tourner *toor-nay*
chez *shay*	nez *nay*	allez *ah-lay*	passez *pah-say*	assez *ah-say*
des *day*	les *lay*	mes *may*	tes *tay*	ces *say*
ai *ay*	gai *gay*	et *ay*		

French Letter	Symbol	Pronunciation Guide
e in one-syllable words or in the middle of a word followed by a single consonant	uh	Say ***e*** as in ***the***

Again, this is another rule that requires too much thought for simple conversational French. Consult the pronunciation guide until the rule becomes second nature.

ce *suh*	je *zhuh*	le *luh*	ne *nuh*	de *duh*
regarder *ruh-gahr-day*	venir *vuh-neer*	repasser *ruh-pah-say*	demander *duh-mahN-day*	prenons *pruh-nohN*

French Letter	Symbol	Pronunciation Guide
è, *ê*, and *e* (plus two consonants or a final pronounced consonant), *et*, *ei*, *ai*	eh	Say ***e*** as in *met*

At this point, don't overwhelm yourself with rules. When in doubt, let the guide do the work for you. With practice, you'll get the hang of it.

très *treh*	mère *mehr*	père *pehr*	achète *ah-sheht*	bibliothèque *bee-blee-oh-tehk*
fête *feht*	tête *teht*	être *ehtr*	même *mehm*	prêter *preh-tay*
est *eh*	sept *seht*	rester *reh-stay*	concert *kohN-sehr*	Suzette *sew-zeht*
quel *kehl*	sel *sehl*	chef *shehf*	cher *shehr*	cette *seht*
ballet *bah-leh*	bonnet *bohN-neh*	jouet *zhoo-eh*	complet *kohN-pleh*	cabinet *kah-bee-neh*
seize *sehz*	treize *trehz*	Seine *sehn*	peine *pehn*	pleine *plehn*
aider *eh-day*	jamais *zhah-meh*	chaise *shehz*	mais *meh*	américaine *ah-may-ree-kehn*

French Letter	Symbol	Pronunciation Guide
i, *î*, *y*, *ui*	ee	Say ***i*** as in *magazine*

Smile and show your teeth when you say *ee*.

il *eel*	ici *ee-see*	midi *mee-dee*	timide *tee-meed*	visiter *vee-zee-tay*
Sylvie *seel-vee*	lycée *lee-say*	mystère *mee-stehr*	dîne *deen*	île *eel*
huit *weet*	nuit *nwee*	qui *kee*	guide *geed*	bruit *brwee*

French Letter	Symbol	Pronunciation Guide
i + *ll*, *il* when preceded by a vowel	y	Say ***y*** as in ***your***

For the *ill*, *ail*, or *eil* combinations, remember to keep the *l* silent.

fille	famille	gentille	billet	travail
fee-y	*fah-mee-y*	*zhahN-tee-y*	*bee-yeh*	*trah-vahy*
soleil	oeil	détail		
soh-lehy	*uhy*	*day-tahy*		

French Letter	Symbol	Pronunciation Guide
i + *ll* in these words only	eel	Say the word ***eel***

Every rule has an exception; or in this case, because there aren't too many, the words might be worth memorizing—especially because they're used frequently.

ville	village	mille	million	tranquille
veel	*vee-lahzh*	*meel*	*mee-lyohN*	*trahN-keel*

French Letter	Symbol	Pronunciation Guide
o (before *se*), *o* (last pronounced sound of word), *ô*, *au*, *eau*	o	Say ***o*** as in ***no***

Keep your lips rounded to pronounce this very open *o* sound. Once again, for o, there are many letter combinations you will have to eventually learn. For the time being, follow the pronunciation guide.

radio	trop	mot	stylo	vélo
rah-dyo	*tro*	*mo*	*stee-lo*	*vay-lo*
hôtel	allô	tôt	bientôt	hôpital
o-tehl	*ah-lo*	*to*	*byaN-to*	*o-pee-tahl*
au	aussi	jaune	autre	auteur
o	*o-see*	*zhon*	*otr*	*o-tuhr*
eau	beau	cadeau	gâteau	manteau
o	*bo*	*kah-do*	*gah-to*	*mahN-to*

French Letter	Symbol	Pronunciation Guide
o when followed by a pronounced consonant other than *s*	oh	Say ***o*** as in ***love***

This *o* sound is not nearly as rounded and open as the one before. It may take some practice to distinguish between the two. If you can't, don't worry—chances are no one is listening that closely anyway. As you practice, try to hear the difference.

notre	pomme	donner	téléphone	octobre
nohtr	*pohm*	*doh-nay*	*tay-lay-fohn*	*ohk-tohbr*

French Letter	Symbol	Pronunciation Guide
ou, où, oû	oo	Say ***oo*** as in ***tooth***

Round your lips to say *oo*.

toujours	écouter	douze	doux	beaucoup
too-zhoor	*ay-koo-tay*	*dooz*	*doo*	*bo-koo*
où	goût			
oo	*goo*			

French Letter	Symbol	Pronunciation Guide
oy, oi	wah	Say ***w*** as in ***watch***

moi	trois	soir	froid	voiture
mwah	*trwah*	*swahr*	*frwah*	*vwah-tewr*
pourquoi	voyage	voyez		
poor-kwah	*vwah-yahzh*	*vwah-yay*		

French Letter	Symbol	Pronunciation Guide
u, û	ew	No equivalent

There really is no English sound that is equivalent to the French *u* sound. Try the following for best results: Say the sound *oo* as in *Sue* while trying to say *ee* as in *see*. As you try to make the sound, concentrate on puckering your lips as if you just ate a very sour pickle. That's about as close as you can get. If you say *oo*, don't worry, you'll be understood. This is a foreign sound that requires concentration and practice.

super	sur	tu	du	une	salut
sew-pehr	*sewr*	*tew*	*dew*	*ewn*	*sah-lew*

You're Supposed to Sound Nasal!

You must use your nose and your mouth to produce a French nasal sound. Here's how it's done: Hold your nose, then use your mouth to say the vowel sound. It's that simple. Of course you're not going to walk around with your hand on your nose. That's just a technique to get you started and to make you aware of what a nasal sound should sound like. We are so accustomed to English pronunciation that we never stop to consider how we produce sounds. When learning a foreign language, it's necessary to pause and think about the sounds we want to make.

Attention!

Be careful! There is no nasal sound in the following combinations: vowel + MM, vowel + M + vowel, vowel + NN, vowel + N + vowel. For example: *homme* is pronounced *ohm; bonne* is pronounced *bohn.*

Nasal sounds occur when a vowel is followed by a single *N* or *M* in the same syllable. In the pronunciation guide, you will see a vowel sound followed by *N*. This indicates that you must make a nasal sound.

French Nasal	Symbol	Pronunciation Guide
an (am), en (em)	ahN	Similar to ***on*** with little emphasis on ***n***

Now hold your nose, say *on*, and you'll quickly get the hang of it. Watch for the *N* indicating the vowel sound.

Français *frahN-seh*	dans *dahN*	anglais *ahN-gleh*	grand *grahN*	lampe *lahNp*
maman *mah-mahN*	ambiance *ahN-byahNs*	ambition *ahN-bee-syohN*	en *ahN*	encore *ahN-kohr*
souvent *soo-vahN*	attendre *ah-tahNdr*	décembre *day-sahNbr*	temps *tahN*	sembler *sahN-blay*
employé *ahN-plwah-yay*				

French Nasal	Symbol	Pronunciation Guide
in (im), ain (aim)	aN	Similar to ***an*** with little emphasis on ***n***

continues

continued

French Nasal	Symbol	Pronunciation Guide		
Hold your nose again and practice the sounds:				
cinq *saNk*	Martin *mahr-taN*	cousin *koo-zaN*	demain *duh-maN*	américain *ah-may-ree-kaN*
simple *saNpl*	important *aN-pohr-tahN*	impossible *aN-poh-seebl*	impatient *aN-pah-syahN*	faim *faN*

French Nasal	Symbol	Pronunciation Guide		
oin	waN	Similar to ***wa*** of ***wa**g*		
You should be getting the hang of nasals by now. Try these:				
loin *lwaN*	coin *kwaN*	moins *mwaN*	point *pwaN*	soin *swaN*

French Nasal	Symbol	Pronunciation Guide		
ien	yaN	Similar to ***yan*** of ***Yan**kee*		
Try these sounds:				
bien *byaN*	rien *ryaN*	vient *vyaN*	italien *ee-tahl-yaN*	Lucien *lew-syaN*

French Nasal	Symbol	Pronunciation Guide		
on (om)	ohN	Similar to ***on*** as in ***lon**g*		
Here are some more to try:				
on *ohN*	bon *bohN*	sont *sohN*	non *nohN*	onze *ohNz*
pardon *pahr-dohN*	tomber *tohN-bay*	bombe *bohNb*	comprendre *kohN-prahNdr*	compter *kohN-tay*
combien *kohN-byaN*				

French Nasal	Symbol	Pronunciation Guide		
un (um)	uhN	Similar to ***un*** as in ***un**der*		
Be patient for the last of the nasal sounds:				
un *uhN*	brun *bruhN*	lundi *luhN-dee*	parfum *pahr-fuhN*	emprunter *ahN-pruhN-tay*

Consonants Are Easy!

Most final consonants are not pronounced except for final *c*, *r*, *f*, and *l* (think of careful). A final *s* is not pronounced in French, so avoid the temptation. Doing so will quickly unveil your amateur status.

Éric *ay-reek*	Luc *lewk*	avec *ah-vehk*	parc *pahrk*
amour *ah-moor*	bonjour *bohN-zhoor*	tour *toor*	cour *koor*
neuf *nuhf*	sauf *sof*	chef *shehf*	actif *ahk-teef*
il *eel*	Michel *mee-shehl*	journal *zhoor-nahl*	cheval *shuh-vahl*

But

salut *sah-lew*	dessert *duh-sehr*	beaucoup *bo-koo*	minutes *mee-newt*

French Letter	Symbol	Pronunciation Guide
b, *d*, *f*, *k*, *l*, *m*, *n*, *p*, *s*, *t*,*v*, *z*	The same	Same as English

These letters are all so easy because they are pronounced exactly the same in French and in English. You will, however, have to follow the rules for the pronunciation of other consonants.

French Letter	Symbol	Pronunciation Guide
c (hard sound before *a*, *o*, *u*, or consonant) *qu*, final *q*	k	Say ***c*** as in ***card***

carte *kahrt*	court *koor*	document *doh-kew-mahN*	classe *klahs*	qui *kee*
quoi *kwah*	quatre *kahtr*	pourquoi *poor-kwah*	cinq *saNk*	

French Letter	Symbol	Pronunciation Guide
c (soft sound before *e*, *i*, *y*), *ç*, *s* at beginning of word, *s* next to a consonant, *-tion* (*t*), *x* (only in the words given)	s	*cent*

As you can see, there are lots of ways to get the *s* sound. Practice them all:

ce *suh*	cinéma *see-nay-mah*	Nancy *nahN-see*	ça *sah*	nation *nah-syohN*
attention *ah-tahN-syohN*	invitation *aN-vee-tah-syohN*	action *ahk-syohN*	six *sees*	dix *dees*
soixante *swah-sahNt*				

French Letter	Symbol	Pronunciation Guide
ch	sh	Say the ***ch*** in *machine*

We've all had practice with this sound—especially those of us with children. *Shhh.*

chanter *shahN-tay*	chocolat *shoh-koh-lah*	sandwich *sahNd-weesh*	toucher *too-shay*

French Letter	Symbol	Pronunciation Guide
g (hard sound before *a*, *o*, *u*, or consonant), *gu* (before *i*, *e*, *y*)	g	Say the **g** in *good*

These words should present no problem:

garçon *gahr-sohN*	goûter *goo-tay*	glace *glahs*	légume *lay-gewm*
Guy *gee*	bague *bahg*	fatigué *fah-tee-gay*	guide *geed*

French Letter	Symbol	Pronunciation Guide
g (soft sound before *e, i, y*), *ge* (soft before *a, o*), *j*	zh	Say the ***s*** as in *pleasure*

This might take a little practice before you get used to it:

garage *gah-razh*	girafe *zhee-rahf*	Gisèle *zhee-zehl*	Égypte *ay-zheept*
âge *ahzh*	orange *oh-rahNzh*	manger *mahN-zhay*	voyageons *vwah-yah-zhohN*
je *zhuh*	jour *zhoor*	jaune *zhon*	jupe *zhewp*

French Letter	Symbol	Pronunciation Guide
gn	ny	Say the ***n*** as in ***union***

This sound will take some practice, too. Be careful not to overemphasize it:

montagne *mohN-tah-nyuh*	Espagne *ehs-pah-nyuh*	gagner *gah-nyay*	accompagner *ah-kohN-pah-nyay*

French Letter	Symbol	Pronunciation Guide
h	—	Always silent

We've come to the easiest letter of all. *H* is always silent. Most of the time, it is used as a vowel and, therefore, requires elision with a vowel that might precede it: *l'homme* (*the man*). In other instances, *h* is used as a consonant and does not require elision with the preceding vowel: *le héros*. To tell how *h* is being used, you must look in a dictionary, where the consonant *h* is usually indicated with an *.

huit *weet*	hôtel *o-tehl*	heure *uhr*	homme *ohm*

French Letter	Symbol	Pronunciation Guide
r	r	No equivalent

The French *r* requires the participation of your throat. First, drop your tongue to the bottom of your mouth and rest it against your teeth. Keep it pressed there, out of your way. Now clear your throat or gargle and say "r" at the back of your throat at the same time. That's it; you've got the French *r*. A few words of advice: Do not roll your *r*; that's what they do in Spanish. Do not roll your tongue; that's what we do in English. This will require a fair amount of practice on your part until you get it down pat.

merci	au revoir	parler	rentrer
mehr-see	*o ruh-vwahr*	*pahr-lay*	*rahN-tray*

French Letter	Symbol	Pronunciation Guide
s (between vowels), *-sion*	z	Say ***z*** as in ***zero***

This sound is easy:

musée	musique	cousin	télévision
mew-zay	*mew-zeek*	*koo-zaN*	*tay-lay-vee-zyohN*

French Letter	Symbol	Pronunciation Guide
th	t	Say ***t*** as in ***to***

There is no *th* sound in French. Native French speakers have a tremendous amount of difficulty with our words *the*, *this*, and *there* because they pronounce *th* as *t*. You, of course, will want to say *th*. Don't. Your nationality will be showing again.

Catherine	thé	théâtre	sympathique
kah-treen	*tay*	*tay-ahtr*	*saN-pah-teek*

French Letter	Symbol	Pronunciation Guide
x	ks	Say ***xc*** as in ***excel***

This last sound (that's right, we've finally reached the end) is a little tricky. Practice it well:

extra	mixte	excellent	exprimer
ehks-trah	*meekst*	*ehk-seh-lahN*	*ehks-pree-may*

Wow Them with Your Accent

Now that you are an expert, put on your best accent and practice pronouncing these names that were taken from a Parisian phone book:

1. Éric Le Parc
2. Colette Lapierre
3. Michel Lechien
4. Alain Lechat
5. Agnès Leloup
6. Roland Lamouche
7. Patrick Leboeuf
8. Solange Laforêt

Culture Capsule

Many French family names begin with *Le* and *La* and are taken from elements in nature. It really does lend an extra beauty to the language when the people are named for beautiful things. However, I am sure that Jean Lavache (*John the Cow*) would probably have been happier had his ancestors been associated with something different.

The Least You Need to Know

- Reading aloud from French newspapers, magazines, and literature will help you lose your inhibitions and perfect your accent.
- While speaking the language, allow yourself to slide the sounds together by using liaison and elision.
- Even if your accent isn't up to snuff, you'll still be understood and your attempts will be appreciated.
- Practice and good listening skills will improve your accent.
- Use your nose correctly to pronounce French nasal sounds.

The French You Know

In This Chapter

- Cognates help with comprehension
- Tricks that work
- French words used in English
- Avoiding mistakes

Café, *restaurant*, *amateur*, *boutique*, *bureau*—you already know many French words. You see, you really do know a lot of French. You don't realize it yet, but your vocabulary is filled with French words and phrases. And there are plenty of French words and expressions that you will find very easy to use and understand with a minimal amount of effort. By the end of this chapter, you will be well on your way to producing simple but intelligent sentences that allow you to express feelings, thoughts, and opinions.

I Know This Already!

There is absolutely nothing on television. After watching the French news on a local cable station, my husband (who has no French blood coursing through his veins) takes off for the local video rental store to choose some entertainment for the evening. An hour later he returns with a wide grin on his face and cheerfully exclaims: "*Oiseau* ([*wah-zo*] that's French for bird, his term of endearment for me), I've got a surprise for you." I wait in eager anticipation to hear that he rented a hot, new release fresh from the theater. Instead, he informs me that he picked out the latest French film.

As a francophile, I should be jumping for joy. But he can read the disappointment on my face. Truth be told, I find French movies lacking in adventure, and I don't love character studies. The subtitles are extremely distracting. He, on the other hand, can't wait to get the film into the VCR, and I can't understand why. It's true that he had two years of college French, but that was over 30 years ago. And I did all his homework. The Cs he passed with were certainly not an indication of a love affair with the language. So why French films? He likes exotic movies, he loves to hear the language, and, believe it or not, he can understand what the actors and actresses are saying. How can that be? He never listened as a student. How does the man do it?

The answer is *cognates*. What are they? Quite simply, a cognate is a word that is spelled exactly the same, or almost the same, as a word in English and that has the same meaning. Sometimes we've actually borrowed the word from the French, letter for letter, and have incorporated it into our own vocabulary. Sure, the cognates are pronounced differently in each language, but the meaning of the French word is quite obvious to anyone who speaks English.

A Perfect Match

The following table contains a list of cognates, words that have exactly the same meaning in both French and English. Take your time pronouncing the French words and compare them to their English equivalents. Your goal is to sound French.

Un, Deux, Trois

There is no way to easily determine the gender of a French noun, so it is best to learn the noun with its corresponding article. See Chapter 6 for a more detailed explanation. For now, just remember:

le is for masculine singular nouns.

la is for feminine singular nouns.

l' is for any singular noun that begins with a vowel.

All French nouns (people, places, things, *and* ideas) have an assigned gender. This might seem strange to you at first, because we do not have anything similar in English. For now, just remember that if you want to say that French is easy, you must use the definite article: "Le français est facile."

When you look at the following list, notice that most French nouns are listed under a specific definite article: *le* or *la*. These articles both mean "the" and indicate the gender of the noun (masculine or feminine, respectively). If you are very observant, you will see that *l'* is used with nouns beginning with a vowel.

Perfect Cognates

Adjectives	Nouns		
	Le	***La***	***L'***
blond *blohN*	ballet *bah-leh*	blouse *blooz*	accident *ahk-see-dahN*
certain *sehr-taN*	chef *shehf*	date *daht*	ambulance *ahN-bew-lahNs*
content *kohN-tahN*	client *klee-yahN*	dispute *dees-pewt*	animal *ah-nee-mahl*
horrible *oh-reebl*	hamburger *ahm-bewr-gehr*	note *noht*	olive *oh-leev*
immense *ee-mahNs*	journal *zhoor-nahl*	photo *foh-to*	orange *oh-rahnzh*

You Understand So Much Already!

I'd venture to guess that, by now, you're in the same league as my husband. The following sentences should be a snap to understand, and the pronunciation should be no problem if you patiently follow the key. Don't be shy! Give it your best effort.

Read the following sentences in French. What are you saying? (*Est* means *is* in French.)

1. La blouse est orange.
   lah blooz eh toh-rahNzh
2. Le service est horrible.
   luh sehr-vees eh toh-reebl
3. Le sandwich est immense.
   luh sahN-weesh eh tee-mahNs
4. Le chef est excellent.
   luh shehf eh tehk-seh-lahN

Now try a few with some new words:

1. Le pull-over est rose.
   luh pewl-oh-vehr eh roz
2. Le film est important.
   luh feelm eh taN-pohr-tahN
3. La question est unique.
   lah kehs-tyohN eh tew-neek
4. Le voyage est urgent.
   luh vwah-yahzh eh tewr-zhahN

An Almost Perfect Match

The following table lists the cognates that are nearly the same in both French and English. Take your time pronouncing the French words and compare them to their English equivalents. Remember: Your goal is to sound French. (Note all adjectives in French must agree in number and gender with the nouns they modify. I discuss the rules governing the agreement of adjectives in detail in Chapter 9.)

Near Cognates

Adjectives	**Nouns**		
	Le	***La***	***L'***
confortable *kohN-fohr-tahbl*	docteur *dohk-tuhr*	cathédrale *kah-tay-drahl*	agence *ah-zhahNs*
difficile *dee-fee-seel*	jardin *zhahr-daN*	chambre *shahNbr*	anniversaire *ah-nee-vehr-sehr*
élégant *ay-lay-gahN*	professeur *proh-feh-suhr*	couleur *koo-luhr*	appartement *ah-pahr-tuh-mahN*
intéressant *aN-tay-reh-sahN*	programme *proh-grahm*	famille *fah-mee-y*	artiste *ahr-teest*
populaire *poh-pew-lehr*	supermarché *sew-pehr-mahr-shay*	fontaine *fohN-tehn*	employé *ahN-plwah-yay*
sérieux *say-ryuh*	téléphone *tay-lay-fohn*	musique *mew-zeek*	hôtel *o-tehl*
sincère *saN-sehr*	théâtre *tay-ahtr*	personne *pehr-sohn*	oncle *ohNkl*
splendide *splahN-deed*	touriste *too-reest*	salade *sah-lahd*	opticien *ohp-tee-syaN*
superbe *sew-pehrb*	vendeur *vahN-duhr*	soupe *soop*	orchestre *ohr-kehstr*

Versatile Verbs

Many French verbs (words that show action or a state of being) are so similar to their English counterparts that you'll recognize their meaning almost immediately. The majority of French verbs fall into one of three families: the *-er* family, the *-ir* family, and the *-re* family. This concept is foreign to us, since English has borrowed so much from so many different languages that no "verb families" exist. For now, you'll see that the largest French family, by far, is the *-er* family. Any verbs belonging to a family are considered *regular*, while those that do not belong to a family are designated as *irregular*. Each family has its own set of rules, which are explained in Chapter 7. All irregular verbs must be memorized.

Attention!

Verbs in French are conjugated to agree with their subjects. The rules governing verb conjugation are explained in Chapter 7.

Look at the three major verb families and see if you can determine the meanings of the verbs presented in the following table.

Verb Families

The *-er* Family			
accompagner *ah-kohN-pah-nyay*	demander *duh-mahN-day*	observer *ohb-sehr-vay*	recommander *ruh-koh-mahN-day*
adorer *ah-doh-ray*	désirer *day-zee-ray*	pardonner *pahr-doh-nay*	refuser *ruh-few-zay*
aider *eh-day*	dîner *dee-nay*	passer *pah-say*	regarder *ruh-gahr-day*
blâmer *blah-may*	échanger *ay-shahN-zhay*	payer *peh-yay*	regretter *ruh-greh-tay*
changer *shahN-zhay*	embrasser *ahN-brah-say*	persuader *pehr-swah-day*	remarquer *ruh-mahr-kay*
chanter *shahN-tay*	entrer *ahN-tray*	porter *pohr-tay*	réparer *ray-pah-ray*
commander *koh-mahN-day*	hésiter *ay-zee-tay*	préférer *pray-fay-ray*	réserver *ray-zehr-vay*
commencer *koh-mahN-say*	ignorer *ee-nyoh-ray*	préparer *pray-pah-ray*	signer *see-nyay*
danser *dahN-say*	inviter *aN-vee-tay*	présenter *pray-zahN-tay*	tourner *toor-nay*
décider *day-see-day*	marcher *mahr-shay*	prouver *proo-vay*	vérifier *vay-ree-fyay*
déclarer *day-klah-ray*	modifier *moh-dee-fyay*		

continues

Verb Families (continued)

The *-ir* and *-re* Families	
accomplir *ah-kohN-pleer*	défendre *day-fahNdr*
applaudir *ah-plo-deer*	répondre *ray-pohNdr*
finir *fee-neer*	vendre *vahNdr*

You've Got It!

As a matter of fact, this is so easy that you can easily read and understand these sentences without any problem at all.

1. Le docteur aide le bébé.

   ____

2. Maman prépare de la soupe et de la salade.

   ____

3. La famille regarde la télévision.

   ____

4. Le touriste réserve la chambre.

   ____

5. L'enfant adore la musique moderne.

   ____

What Do You Think?

Imagine that you are a tourist in a French-speaking country. Use what you've learned to express the following opinions to a fellow tourist.

1. The garden is splendid.
2. The fountain is superb.
3. The artist is popular.
4. The music is splendid.
5. The restaurant is elegant.
6. The hotel is elegant.

Special Pronunciation Tricks

Some special tricks on pronunciation help you determine the meaning of words. When you look at the following table, you will see how adding an *s* after an accent circonflexe (ˆ) and how substituting an *s* for an *é* or adding one after it will help you figure out the meanings of many words. Then see if you can complete the list.

Special Tricks

Accent (ˆ)	English	Accent (é)	English
arrêter *ah-ruh-tay*	to arrest	écarlate *ay-kahr-laht*	scarlet
bête *beht*	beast	échapper *ay-shah-pay*	to escape
conquête *kohN-keht*	conquest	école *ay-kohl*	school
coûter *koo-tay*	to cost	épars *ay-pahr*	sparse
croûte *kroot*	crust	épellation *ay-puh-lah-syohN*	spelling
fête *feht*	feast	épice *ay-pees*	spice
forêt *foh-reh*	forest	épier *ay-pyay*	to spy
hôpital *o-pee-tahl*	hospital	éponge *ay-pohNzh*	sponge
hôte *ot*	host	épouser *ay-poo-zay*	to espouse
hôtesse *o-tehs*	________	état *ay-tah*	________
île *eel*	________	étrange *ay-trahNzh*	________
pâte *paht*	________	étude *ay-tewd*	________
intérêt *aN-teh-reh*	________	répondre *ray-pohNdr*	________

What We've Borrowed

Are you a *gourmet* cook or a *chef*? Do you live near a large *avenue* or *boulevard*? Do you enjoy *ballet*? In America, a truly multicultural society, we readily borrow and accept things from other backgrounds that suit our wants and needs and that make our life more meaningful, fulfilling, and interesting. And so we've borrowed a great many words from the French that we use on a daily basis. We've adopted these words and have made them a part of our everyday vocabulary. We even assume, incorrectly, that these words are English when they are not.

Culture Capsule

The French are very resistant to the infiltration of American words, politely called *franglais*, into their language. Many of our words have, indeed, slowly crept into French: *le jean*, *le fax*, *le walkman*, *le C.D.*, *le club*, *le jazz*, *le steak*, and *le week-end*, for example. The French government, through the Académie Française, tries to limit their use as much as possible by prohibiting foreign words in official texts, advertisements, and announcements for employment opportunities.

French Awareness

The following French words and expressions are widely used by most of us. Define as many of them as you can.

1. à la carte ____________
2. c'est la vie ____________
3. carte blanche ____________
4. chic ____________
5. coup d'état ____________
6. crème de la crème ____________
7. déjà vu ____________
8. esprit de corps ____________
9. fait accompli ____________
10. faux pas ____________
11. joie de vivre ____________
12. objet d'art ____________
13. pièce de résistance ____________
14. R.S.V.P. ____________
15. rendez-vous ____________

False Friends (*Faux Amis*)

Just when you think you know it all, exceptions pop up to prevent you from becoming overly confident. *Faux amis* (false friends) are words spelled exactly the same or almost the same in both French and English, but which have very different meanings in each language and might even be different parts of speech. Don't fall into the trap of thinking that every French word that looks like an English one is automatically a cognate. It's not quite that simple. Beware of the *faux amis* listed in the following table.

False Friends

French	Part of Speech	Meaning	English	Part of Speech
attendre *ah-tahNdr*	verb	to wait	attend	verb
blesser *bleh-say*	verb	to wound	bless	verb
comment *koh-mahN*	adverb	how	comment	noun
la figure *lah fee-gewr*	noun	face	figure	noun
la librairie *lah lee-breh-ree*	noun	bookstore	library	noun
le livre *luh leevr*	noun	book	liver	noun
l'occasion *loh-kah-zyohN*	noun	opportunity	occasion	noun
la prune *lah prewn*	noun	plum	prune	noun
le raisin *luh reh-zaN*	noun	grape	raisin	noun
rester *rehs-tay*	verb	to remain	rest	verb
sale *sahl*	adjective	dirty	sale	noun
le sang *luh sahN*	noun	blood	sang	verb
sensible *sahN-seebl*	adjective	sensitive	sensible	adjective

continues

False Friends (continued)

French	Part of Speech	Meaning	English	Part of Speech
le stage *luh stahzh*	noun	internship	stage	noun
le store *luh stohr*	noun	shade	store	noun
travailler *trah-vah-yay*	verb	to work	travel	verb

You Are Well Read

The famous French literary titles listed here all contain cognates. Give their English equivalents.

1. Balzac—*La Comédie humaine* ________________
2. Camus—*L'Étranger* ________________
3. Cocteau—*La Machine infernale* ________________
4. Cocteau—*Les Enfants terribles* ________________
5. Flaubert—*L'Éducation sentimentale* ________________
6. Hugo—*Les Misérables* ________________
7. Laclos—*Les Liaisons dangereuses* ________________
8. Malraux—*La Condition humaine* ________________
9. Molière—*Le Malade imaginaire* ________________
10. Sartre—*La Nausée* ________________

The Least You Need to Know

- Cognates are words that look exactly or almost the same in English and French and that have the same meaning in both languages. They allow you to express yourself in French with a minimal amount of effort.
- We use many French words and expressions in English every day.
- Beware of false friends—words spelled the same or almost the same in both languages—that have different meanings in each language. Don't let them trap you into mistakes.

Idiomatically Speaking

In This Chapter

- What are idioms and how do we use them?
- What is slang and should we use it?
- Using body language to express yourself

Idioms are very important to a complete and correct understanding of the language. Imagine a beautiful young woman walking along the Champs-Élysées, an elegant, tree-lined avenue in Paris. Two men approach from the opposite direction and look her up and down. She hears one man casually say to the other *"Oh là là. Elle a du chien."* The young lady, having taken a year or two of French in school hears *elle* (she) and *chien* (dog). She immediately puts two and two together and thinks these men have called her a "dog." If she is extraordinarily brazen, perhaps she even smacks one across the face. She has just made a terrible mistake. What she doesn't understand is the idiomatic expression *avoir du chien*, which in English means *to be alluring, sexy.* The English equivalent of what the men said was really: "Boy, is she attractive."

Idioms Aren't for Idiots!

So what exactly is an idiom? In any language, an *idiom* is a particular word or expression whose meaning cannot be readily understood by either its grammar or the words used. Examples of some common English idioms are:

To look on the bright side.	To fall head over heels.
On the other hand.	To be down and out.

Idioms Versus Slang

What's the difference between an idiom and slang? *Slang* refers to colorful, popular words or phrases that are not part of the standard vocabulary of a language. Slang is considered unconventional. Many of these words evolved as needed to describe particular things or situations. Here are some examples of English slang:

Give me a break!	Get real!
Tough luck!	Get a life!

Idioms are acceptable in oral and written phrases, whereas slang, although freely used in informal conversations, generally is considered substandard in formal writing or speaking. Much slang is, at best, x-rated.

Take Your Pick

Take a look at some of these popular expressions used in sentences. I'm sure you will immediately realize that it would be impossible to translate them into French. Certainly they couldn't be translated word for word. Which are they, idioms or slang?

You drive me crazy!	Keep your shirt on!
Don't jump the gun!	I'm always on the go.
It's raining cats and dogs!	We'll just have to kill some time.
I'm going to call your bluff.	Did you fall for it?

Did you recognize that these are idiomatic expressions we use in English all the time? Good for you. Now compare those sentences with the following:

That's tacky!	What a cop out!
She just flipped out!	Don't dis my friend.

Do you notice how these slang sentences differ from the idiomatic ones? Excellent! You probably won't be using much French slang, but the idioms sure will come in handy.

There are many idioms in French. In this chapter, we will look at six categories of idioms that you might find helpful: travel and transportation, time, location and direction, expressing opinions, physical conditions, and weather conditions. Other idiomatic expressions will appear in their appropriate chapters.

Getting Off to a Fast Start

Let's say you are taking a trip. We might ask: "Are you going on a plane or on a boat?" The French word for *on* is *sur* (*sewr*). If you said: "*Je vais sur l'avion*," however, that would imply you were flying on the exterior of the plane, which is truly impossible. It is well worth your time to learn the idiomatic expressions covered in the following table.

Memory Enhancer

The preposition *en* is usually used when you are traveling inside of something, such as a subway. Use *à* when you expect to feel your hair blowing in the breeze.

Idioms for Travel and Transportation

L'idiome	Pronunciation	Meaning
à bicyclette	*ah bee-see-kleht*	by bicycle
à cheval	*ah shuh-vahl*	on horseback
à moto	*ah moh-to*	by scooter
à pied	*ah pyeh*	on foot
en automobile	*ahN no-toh-moh-beel*	by car
en avion	*ahN nah-vyohN*	by plane
en bateau	*ahN bah-to*	by boat
en bus	*ahN bews*	by bus
en métro	*ahN may-tro*	by subway
en taxi	*ahN tahk-see*	by taxi
en train	*ahN traN*	by train
en voiture	*ahN vwah-tewr*	by car

Memory Enhancer

Use the preposition *à* to express *until* before a time period when you expect to see someone at a later time. For example: *à lundi* (until Monday).

It's That Time

For some travelers, time is of the essence. They make sure they get that wake-up call bright and early in the morning. They want to be on the go as soon as possible. For others, it's not important at all. They don't even wear a watch. They're on vacation, and time is simply unimportant. Whether you're time-conscious or not, the idioms in the following table will serve you well.

Time Expressions

L'idiome	Pronunciation	Meaning
à bientôt	*ah byaN-to*	see you soon
à ce soir	*ah suh swahr*	until this evening
à demain	*ah duh-maN*	until tomorrow
à l'heure	*ah luhr*	on time
à la fois	*ah lah fois*	at the same time
à samedi	*ah sahm-dee*	until Saturday
à temps	*ah tahN*	on time
à tout à l'heure	*ah too tah luhr*	see you later
au bout de	*o boo duh*	at the end of
au revoir	*o ruh-vwahr*	goodbye
de bonne heure	*duh boh nuhr*	early
de jour en jour	*duh zhoor ahN zhoor*	from day to day
de temps à autre	*duh tahN zah o-truh*	from time to time
de temps en temps	*duh tahN zahN tahN*	from time to time
du matin au soir	*dew mah-taN o swahr*	from morning until evening
en même temps	*ahN mehm tahN*	at the same time
en retard	*ahN ruh-tahr*	late
il y a (+ time)	*eel yah*	ago (+ time)
par jour (semaine, mois)	*pahr zhoor (suh-mehn, mwah)*	by day, week, month
tout à l'heure	*too tah luhr*	in a while
tout de suite	*toot sweet*	immediately

Using Your Idioms I (or What Time Is It?)

What French idioms of time would you use in the following situations?

1. When you leave a friend for the day you would say:

 ____

2. If your boss wants something done right away, he wants it done:

 ____

3. If you have an interview at 9 A.M. and you arrive at 10 A.M., you arrive:

 ____

4. If you have an interview at 9 A.M. and you arrive at 8 A.M., you arrive:

 ____

5. If you are going to see a friend later today, you will see him/her:

 ____

6. If you go to the movies every once in a while, you go:

 ____

7. If you work all day long, you work:

 ____

8. If you are leaving a friend for today but know that you will see him/her tomorrow, you would say:

 ____

Where To?

Probably among the most useful idioms are those telling you how to get where you want to go. Most men, of course, would never dream of asking for directions. They have to prove that they can find it themselves. So when my husband and I find ourselves off the beaten path, I'm the one who goes into the nearest gas station. I like to know exactly where I'm going and, if I get lost, I want precise directions. The idioms of location and direction in the following table are quite important for any traveler, don't you think? (This list is for men, too.)

Idioms Showing Location and Direction

L'idiome	Pronunciation	Meaning
à côté (de)	*ah ko-tay (duh)*	next to, beside
à droite (de)	*ah drawht (duh)*	to the right (of)
à gauche (de)	*ah gosh (duh)*	to the left (of)
à l'étranger	*ah lay-trahN-zhay*	abroad
à la campagne	*ah lah kahN-pah-nyuh*	in the country
à la maison	*ah lah meh-zohN*	at home
à part	*ah pahr*	aside
à travers	*ah trah-vehr*	across, through
au loin	*o lwaN*	in the distance
au milieu (de)	*o mee-lyuh (duh)*	in the middle (of)
au-dessous de	*o duh-soo duh*	beneath, below
au-dessus de	*o duh-sew duh*	above, over
de l'autre côté (de)	*duh lohtr ko-tay (duh)*	on the other side (of)
du côté de	*dew ko-tay duh*	in the direction of, toward
en bas (de)	*ahN bah (duh)*	at the bottom (of)
en face (de)	*ahN fahs (duh)*	opposite, facing
en haut (de)	*ahN o (duh)*	at the top (of)
en plein air	*ahN pleh nehr*	in the open air, outdoors
en ville	*ahN veel*	downtown
le long de	*luh lohN duh*	along
par ici (là)	*pahr ee-see (lah)*	this way (that way)
tout droit	*too drwah*	straight ahead
tout près	*too preh*	nearby

Culture Capsule

No one in France is going to tell you how many blocks away a certain tourist attraction is located. The concept of "blocks" is strictly American. When giving directions in France, the average man or woman in the street will tell you the number of streets (rues—*rew*) or traffic lights (feux—*fuh*) you will encounter.

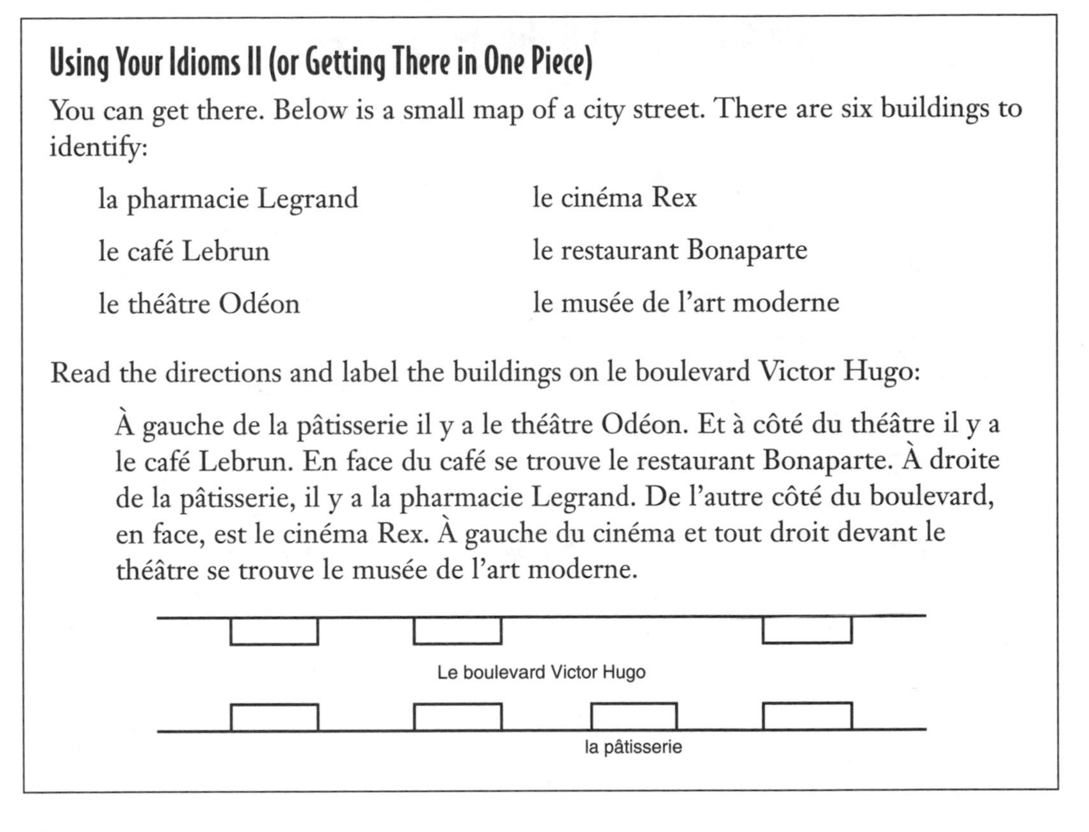

Using Your Idioms II (or Getting There in One Piece)

You can get there. Below is a small map of a city street. There are six buildings to identify:

la pharmacie Legrand	le cinéma Rex
le café Lebrun	le restaurant Bonaparte
le théâtre Odéon	le musée de l'art moderne

Read the directions and label the buildings on le boulevard Victor Hugo:

À gauche de la pâtisserie il y a le théâtre Odéon. Et à côté du théâtre il y a le café Lebrun. En face du café se trouve le restaurant Bonaparte. À droite de la pâtisserie, il y a la pharmacie Legrand. De l'autre côté du boulevard, en face, est le cinéma Rex. À gauche du cinéma et tout droit devant le théâtre se trouve le musée de l'art moderne.

So, What's Your Opinion?

Everyone, at one time or another, has an opinion about something. Some people are certainly more expressive than others. Whether you're talking about your flight, the food you ate, the movie you watched, the people you met, or life in general, you will need to know how to properly express your feelings. The following table should help.

Expressing Your Opinions with Idioms

L'idiome	Pronunciation	Meaning
à mon avis	*ah mohN nah-vee*	in my opinion
à vrai dire	*ah vreh deer*	to tell the truth
au contraire	*o kohN-trehr*	on the contrary
bien entendu	*byaN nahN-tahN-dew*	of course

continues

Expressing Your Opinions with Idioms (continued)

L'idiome	Pronunciation	Meaning
bien sûr	*byaN sewr*	of course
bon marché	*bohN mahr-shay*	cheap
c'est-à-dire	*seh-tah-deer*	that is to say
ça m'est égal	*sah meh tay-gahl*	that's all the same to me (I don't care.)
ça ne fait rien	*sah nuh feh ryaN*	that doesn't matter
d'accord	*dah-kohr*	agreed, okay
de mon côté	*duh mohN ko-tay*	as for me, for my part
jamais de la vie	*zhah-meh duh lah vee*	never, out of the question
n'importe	*nahN-pohrt*	it doesn't matter
ressembler à	*ruh-sahN-blay ah*	to resemble
sans doute	*sahN doot*	without a doubt
tant mieux	*tahN myuh*	so much the better
tant pis	*tahN pee*	too bad
tout à fait	*too tah feh*	entirely
tout de même	*too dmehm*	all the same

Are You All Right?

Let's say you are freezing cold. So you say to your French host: "*Je suis froid,*" and he cracks up laughing. Why? In English we use adjectives to describe how we are feeling, thus you've chosen (so you think): "I am cold." The French say: "I have cold" (which doesn't mean that they are sick and have a cold). Your French host would literally interpret what you said as that you are cold to the touch of a hand. Of course this sounds very strange and silly to us. Just remember, our idioms sound very off-beat to others.

Memory Enhancer

Always use the verb *avoir* (to have) to express your physical condition (even though the English uses the verb "to be").

You will notice that all the following idioms begin with the verb *avoir,* which means *to have.* Of course, it will be necessary to conjugate *avoir* as the subject of the sentence changes, but that will be discussed further in Chapter 9. For now, concentrate on how you feel—*J'ai* (*zhay,* I have)—using the expressions for physical conditions in the following table.

Idiomatic Physical Conditions

L'idiome	Pronunciation	Meaning
avoir besoin (de)	*ah-vwahr buh-zwaN (duh)*	to need
avoir chaud	*ah-vwahr sho*	to be hot (person)
avoir envie (de)	*ah-vwahr ahN-vee (duh)*	to need
avoir faim	*ah-vwahr faN*	to be hungry
avoir froid	*ah-vwahr frwah*	to be cold (person)
avoir honte (de)	*ah-vwahr ohNt (duh)*	to be ashamed (of)
avoir l'air (+ adj.)	*ah-vwahr lehr*	to seem, look
avoir l'air de (+ inf.)	*ah-vwahr lehr duh*	to seem to, look as if
avoir mal à	*ah-vwahr mahl ah*	to have an ache in
avoir peur (de)	*ah-vwahr puhr (duh)*	to be afraid (of)
avoir quelque chose	*ah-vwahr kehl-kuh shohz*	to have something wrong
avoir raison	*ah-vwahr reh-zohN*	to be right
avoir soif	*ah-vwahr swahf*	to be thirsty
avoir sommeil	*ah-vwahr soh-mehy*	to be sleepy
avoir tort	*ah-vwahr tohr*	to be wrong
avoir ___ ans	*ah-vwahr ___ ahN*	to be ___ years old

Using Your Idioms III (or What's Happening?)

Express how you feel, using idioms.

1. sleepy

   ____

2. hot

   ____

3. hungry

   ____

4. thirsty

   ____

5. being wrong

   ____

6. on your 30th birthday

   ____

7. being correct

   ____

8. cold

   ____

Baby, It's Cold Outside

Travelers tend to be obsessed with weather, which makes sense given that many plans are contingent on it. The French way of discussing weather differs from ours. If you said to your French host: "*Il est chaud*," he or she would assume that you were speaking about something that was warm to the touch. The French use the verb *faire* (to make, to do) to describe most weather conditions. We wouldn't use the verbs *make* and *do* to express ourselves in English; we'd be laughed at. But in France, do as the French do as you study the following table.

Attention!

Never use *faire* when speaking about snow or rain: *Il neige* (*eel nehzh;* it's snowing). *Il pleut* (*eel pluh;* it's raining).

Weather conditions are always expressed impersonally with the expression *il fait* … (it's …) even though English uses the verb "to be." *Faire* can be used with other subject nouns and pronouns but not when discussing the weather.

Idiomatic Weather Expressions

L'idiome	Pronunciation	Meaning
faire beau	*fehr bo*	to be nice weather
faire chaud	*fehr cho*	to be hot weather
faire des éclairs	*fehr day zay-klehr*	to be lightning
faire doux	*fehr doo*	to be mild
faire du soleil	*fehr dew soh-lehy*	to be sunny
faire du tonnerre	*fehr dew toh-nehr*	to be thundering
faire du vent	*fehr dew vahN*	to be windy
faire frais	*fehr freh*	to be cool
faire froid	*fehr frwah*	to be cold
faire jour	*fehr zhoor*	to be daytime, light
faire mauvais	*fehr mo-veh*	to be bad weather
faire nuit	*fehr nwee*	to be night, dark
Quel temps fait-il?	*kehl tahN feh-teel*	What is the weather?

Using Your Idioms IV (or How's the Weather?)

Look at a weather map of France for the day. Tell what the weather will be in each of the following cities:

1. À Paris il fait ______________.
2. À Nice il fait ______________.
3. À Bordeaux il fait ___________.
4. À Strasbourg il fait __________.
5. À Toulouse il fait ___________.

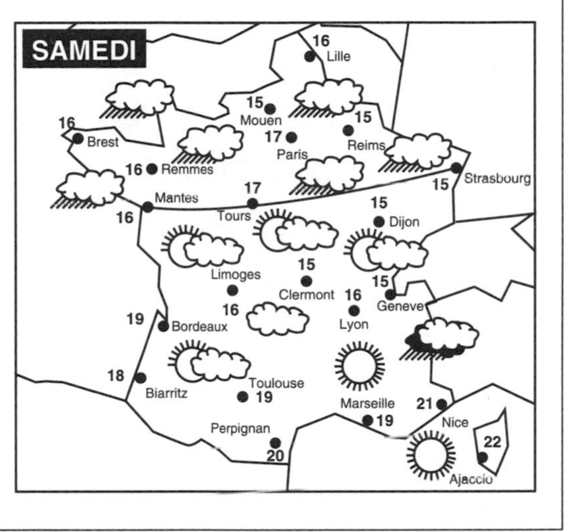

It's in Your Hands

The French are very expressive people and tend to speak a lot with their hands. Facial expressions and body language are also an important part of communicating feelings and emotions. Many gestures perfectly convey certain French slang expressions without the use of words. These gestures play an important role in the French language.

1. Mon oeil *(mohN nuhy)* My eye. You can't fool me.

2. J'en ai par-dessus la tête. *(zhahN nay pahr-duh-sew lah teht)* I've had it up to here.

3. Au poil! *(o pwahl)* Perfect!

4. Extra! *(ehks-trah)* Super!

5. C'est la barbe!
   (seh lah bahrb)
   It's boring!

6. Qu'est-ce que tu veux que j'y fasse?
   (kehs-kuh tew vuh kuh zhee fahs)
   What do you want me to do about it?

In many instances, it is unwise to attempt to translate word for word from English to French. This can backfire and cause embarrassment, especially in situations where specific idiomatic expressions are necessary.

When you can't think of the words you need, do not hesitate to use body language and gestures to convey your thoughts and feelings.

The Least You Need to Know

- Idioms are expressions that can't be translated word for word from one language to another.
- Idioms, not slang, will help you speak the language the way it should be spoken.
- Proper body language can help you communicate without even uttering a word.

Chapter 5

Grasp That Grammar!

In This Chapter

- A crash course in very basic grammar
- Using a bilingual dictionary

Today's approach to learning a foreign language is certainly much different than it was in the past. There's been a de-emphasis on grammatical rules and an emphasis on communication. So if you really want to speak like a Frenchman/woman, you will be happy to know that speaking a foreign language doesn't mean you'll mentally have to translate word for word from one language to the other or concentrate on memorizing endless pages of rules. Sure, that's how they tried to teach you in school way back when (and it was pure drudgery). But the powers that be have finally come to realize that communicating doesn't mean walking around with a dictionary under your arm. On the contrary, it means learning to use the language and its patterns the way a native speaker does. To do this, you need to know basic grammar as well as the idioms and colloquialisms used by native speakers.

If grammar is a weak spot for you, don't despair. Today's focus is strictly on your communicative skills. So if you're lacking in one area, make up for it in another: Use body language, facial gestures, common sense, and a dictionary to get your point across.

Grappling with Grammar

When you hear the word *grammar*, do you get a sinking feeling in the pit of your stomach like when someone mentions *math?* Did you ever have the pleasure of diagramming a sentence? I still have very vivid memories of many seemingly useless grammatical terms. You don't have to be an expert grammarian to learn a foreign language. All you really need is a basic understanding of four simple parts of speech: nouns, verbs, adjectives, and adverbs. Now don't get all nervous. You'll see how simple it really is.

Nouns

Nouns refer to people, places, things, or ideas. Just like in English, nouns can be replaced by pronouns (he, she, it, they). Unlike English, however, all nouns in French have a gender. That means that all nouns have a *sex*. That ought to grab your attention. Sorry to disappoint you, but in this case sex refers to the masculine or feminine designation of the noun. In French, all nouns also have a number (singular or plural). Little articles (words that stand for "the" or "a") serve as noun markers and usually help to indicate gender and number. But even if you can't figure out the gender of a noun, you will still be understood, as long as you use the correct word. You will learn more about gender in Chapter 6.

Verbs

Verbs are words that show action or a state of being. In both English and French, we conjugate verbs. That word "conjugate" sounds a lot scarier than it really is. In English, conjugating is so automatic (because we've been doing it practically since birth) that we don't even realize that we are doing it. I had a friend who took four years of high school French and never understood the concept of verb conjugation. (She was absent that day.) I explained it to her, and she realized that it's really quite simple. *Conjugating* means giving the correct form of the verb so that it agrees with the subject. For example: In English, we say *I am* but *you are*, *he is*, and so on; *I look* but *she looks*. It just doesn't work to mix and match the subjects and verb forms whether you are speaking English or French. Imagine how silly it would sound to you if a French person said, "I are." You will have to strive to give the form of the verb that matches the subject. But don't despair. Even if you use the wrong verb form, you will be understood. Surely you would understand a foreigner who said, "You is very nice."

That's enough for now. Verb conjugation will be explained in greater depth in Chapter 7.

Adjectives

Adjectives help to describe nouns. Unlike English, in French all adjectives agree in number and gender (sex) with the nouns they modify. In other words, in a French sentence, all the words have to match. If the noun is singular, then its adjective must also be singular. If the noun is feminine, then you must be sure to give the correct feminine form of the adjective you are using.

In English, adjectives are generally placed before the nouns they modify: for example, *the blue house*. In French, most adjectives come after the nouns they describe: for example, *la maison bleue*. Don't get nervous. If you make a mistake, you will still be understood. You will find out more about adjectives in Chapter 9.

Adverbs

Adverbs are words that describe verbs, adjectives, or other adverbs. In English, most adverbs end in *-ly*: for example, *He dances slowly*. In French, they end in *-ment*: *Il danse lentement*. Adverbs will probably pose few problems as you learn the language. Adverbs are discussed in greater detail in Chapter 18.

I'm No Idiot—Using a Bilingual Dictionary Is Easy

Sure you know how to use an *English* dictionary. Even if you don't know how to spell the word you're looking up, you usually stumble across it eventually. But using a bilingual dictionary requires a certain, albeit minimal, amount of grammatical expertise. Believe it or not, an open-book dictionary test is probably harder than any test you would have to study for.

Your Bilingual Dictionary—a Crash Course

The very first thing you should do is open to the front of your dictionary and find the list of abbreviations. Generally, there is a rather long, comprehensive list. There are only a few abbreviations that are truly essential and that need attention. They are:

- ***adj.*** adjective.
- ***adv.*** adverb.
- ***f.*** indicates a *feminine* noun. The gender of nouns will be explained in Chapter 6.
- ***n.*** noun (sometimes an *s* is used). The *n.* designation is generally used only if the noun can be either masculine or feminine.

- ***m.*** indicates a *masculine* noun.
- ***pl.*** indicates a *plural* noun. More on plural nouns in Chapter 6.
- ***p.p.*** indicates the *past participle* of a verb. A past participle is necessary when a verb is used in the past tense. An explanation follows in Chapter 21.
- ***v.i.*** indicates an *intransitive* verb, which can stand alone: *I eat.*
- ***v.t.*** indicates a *transitive* verb that may be followed by a direct object: *He removes his hat* (*removes* may not stand alone) or may be used in the passive, where the subject is acted upon: *I was seen.*
- ***v.r.*** indicates a *reflexive* verb, where the subject acts upon itself: *I brush my teeth.* Reflexive verbs will be treated in Chapter 20.

Now, let's see how well you can do with your bilingual French-English, English-French dictionary. We'll start with the English word *mean*. Consider the following sentences and how the meaning of the word *mean* changes:

That man is **mean.** (adjective)

What can that **mean?** (verb)

What is the **mean** (average)? (noun)

Attention!

Some verbs can be used transitively and intransitively according to their meaning. Be careful to use a direct object when a transitive verb is indicated.

If you change ***mean*** to the plural, its meaning changes:

What is the **means** of transportation? (noun)

Look up the word ***mean*****,** and you see:

mean [min] *v.t.* signifier; *adj.* (miserly) radin, (nasty) méchant, (vicious) sauvage;
n. (math) moyenne *f.*; (method) moyen; *m.*
means ressources *f.pl.*

Now try completing the following sentences with the correct form of the word mean:

1. *That man is* ***mean.*** Determine the part of speech. Did you choose an adjective? Good! Now complete the French sentence: *Cet homme est* __________.
   The correct choice is *méchant.*
2. *What can that* ***mean?*** In this sentence, did you select ***mean*** as a verb? You got it! The French sentence would read: *Qu'est-ce que ça peut* __________. I hope you chose *signifier*.

3. *What is the **mean?*** This term refers to the *average* of two numbers. Because the correct word is feminine, you will have to use the article *la* before the noun you choose. Articles will be discussed in Chapter 6. The French is: *Quelle est la* __________. The answer is *moyenne*.
4. *What is the **means** of transportation? **Means*** is plural in English but masculine, singular in French. Use *le* before the noun you choose. The French is: *Quel est* __________ *de transport*. The answer is *le moyen*.

As you can see, to successfully look up the meanings of the word you want to use, you must do three things:

- Check to make sure that you are using the correct part of speech: noun, verb, adjective, or adverb.
- Check your work by looking up the French word you have chosen and by verifying that the English meaning given is the one you want.
- Check that you are using the correct form of the word: the right number (singular or plural) and the right gender (masculine or feminine).

Just Look It Up

Use a bilingual dictionary to see if you can find the correct word to complete each of the following French sentences. For now, I've supplied the proper articles. *Write all verbs in the infinitive form.* We'll move on to conjugation later, in Chapter 7.

1. Look at the fire!	Regarde le ______________.
2. The boss is going to fire the employee.	Le patron va ______________ l'employé.
3. I see the light.	Je vois la ______________.
4. I am going to light the barbecue.	Je vais ______________ le barbecue.
5. The land is fertile.	La ______________ est fertile.
6. The plane is going to land.	L'avion va ______________.
7. He dances better than you.	Il danse ______________ que toi.
8. The chocolate cake is better.	Le gâteau au chocolat est ________.

The Least You Need to Know

- The parts of speech are the same in both French and English.
- To use a bilingual dictionary effectively, you must know the different parts of speech.
- You must use both sides of a bilingual dictionary to obtain the proper definition of a word.

Chapter 6

French—the Sexy Language

In This Chapter

- Determining gender
- Switching gender
- Going from singular to plural

Unlike in English, where girls are girls, and boys are boys, and everything else is neuter, every single noun (person, place, thing, or idea) in French is designated as *masculine* or *feminine*, *singular* or *plural*. How is this determination made? Sometimes it's obvious, sometimes there are clues, and sometimes it's just downright tricky. This chapter teaches you to make the right connections.

The Battle of the Sexes

If you're speaking about a man or a woman, gender is obvious. But what if you want to talk about a lovely boutique you passed the other day? There is no obvious clue to you as yet, telling you the gender of the word *boutique*. Do you assume that it's feminine because women like to go to boutiques? In this day and age, that's a dangerous thing to do. There are, however, tricks for determining gender that you will learn as you read and study this chapter. For instance, the word *boutique* ends in *que*; most French words with this ending are feminine.

Attention!

Beware of trying to use common sense to guess gender: make-up, stockings, and pocketbook are masculine, while car, shirt, and fishing are feminine.

Memory Enhancer

For words beginning with a vowel or vowel sound (*h*, *y*), the definite articles *le* and *la* become *l'*. Therefore, learn the indefinite article *un* or *une* for any word that begins with a vowel.

Suppose that you want to purchase a tie that you saw in the boutique. It would be normal to assume that *cravate* is masculine because men wear ties more often than women do. But you would be wrong in your assumption. In fact, *cravate* is a feminine word. "Why?" you're probably asking yourself. "That really doesn't make any sense." You're right. It doesn't. And unfortunately, there are no clues and no tricks to help you with this word and many others like it. So what do you do? You learn which endings are usually masculine and which are feminine; for the others, you try to learn the word with its *noun marker* (le [un] or la [une]). If you forget the noun marker, you can always resort to a good French dictionary. Just remember: Even if you make a gender mistake, as long as you have the correct vocabulary word, you'll be understood.

Noun Markers

Noun markers are articles or adjectives that tell you whether a noun is *masculine* (m.) or *feminine* (f.), *singular* (sing.) or *plural* (pl.). The most common markers, shown in the table below, are *definite articles* expressing "the" and *indefinite articles* expressing "a," "an," "one," or "some."

Singular Noun Markers

	Masculine	**Feminine**
the	le (l') (*luh*)	la (l') (*lah*)
a, an, one	un (*uhN*)	une (*ewn*)

Singular Nouns

The nouns in the following table are very easy to mark because they obviously refer to males or females.

Gender-Obvious Nouns

Noun	Pronunciation	English
Masculine		
le père	*luh pehr*	father
le grand-père	*luh grahN-pehr*	grandfather
le garçon	*luh gahr-sohN*	boy
l'ami	*lah-mee*	friend
un homme	*uhN nohm*	man
un oncle	*uhN nohN-kluh*	uncle
un cousin	*uhN koo-zaN*	cousin
un ami	*uhN nah-mee*	friend
Feminine		
la mère	*lah mehr*	mother
la grand-mère	*lah grahN-mehr*	grandmother
la fille	*la fee-y*	girl
l'amie	*lah-mee*	friend
une femme	*ewn fahm*	woman
une tante	*ewn tahNt*	aunt
une cousine	*ewn koo-zeen*	cousin
une amie	*ewn nah-mee*	friend

All nouns must be identified as either masculine or feminine. Use *le* to express the definite article (the) and *un* to express the indefinite article (a, an, or one) before a masculine singular noun. Use *la* to express the definite article (the) and *une* to express the indefinite article (a, an, or one) before a feminine singular noun. Use *l'* before any singular noun that begins with a vowel, regardless of gender.

Memory Enhancer

The *e* is never dropped from the indefinite article *une*. The final *e* does, however, change the sound of the word *un* (*uhN*) to *une* (*ewn*).

Mark Your Nouns

Choose the correct definite article noun marker (le, la) when referring to these people.

Example:
reine (*rehn;* queen): C'est la reine. (*It's the queen.*)

1. fils (*fees;* son) ______
2. vendeur (*vahN-duhr;* salesman) ______
3. mari (*mah-ree;* husband) ______
4. soeur (*suhr;* sister) ______
5. neveu (*neh-vuh;* nephew) ______
6. nièce (*nyehs;* niece) ______
7. frère (*frehr;* brother) ______
8. femme (*fahm;* woman, wife) ______

Nouns for Both Sexes

Some nouns can be either masculine or feminine. To indicate whether you are speaking about a male or female, simply change the marker to suit the identity of the person, as shown in the following example:

Le touriste (male) prend (is taking) des photos.

La touriste (female) aussi prend des photos.

When you come across these words in a dictionary, you will not see a simple *m.* or *f.* Some dictionaries will designate them with an *n.* for noun or *s.* for substantive (which stands for noun) or will simply show *m/f.* The following table lists nouns that can be either masculine or feminine. To distinguish between the two you must choose the correct marker according to the person you are speaking about.

Nouns for Both Sexes, Part 1

Word	Pronunciation	Meaning
artiste	*ahr-teest*	artist
camarade	*kah-mah-rahd*	friend

Word	Pronunciation	Meaning
concierge	*kohN-syehrzh*	concierge
élève	*ay-lehv*	student
enfant	*ahN-fahN*	child
malade	*mah-lahd*	sick person
secrétaire	*seh-kray-tehr*	secretary
touriste	*too-reest*	tourist

Let's take a look at an interesting sentence:

Jacques Cousteau est une personne importante.

Did you notice the use of the feminine indefinite article *une?* Are you perplexed? After all, Jacques Cousteau is a man. Shouldn't the indefinite article reflect this? Not really. The answer is simple, although somcwhat unsatisfactory for men and women alike.

Whether we agree or not, some nouns are always masculine or feminine no matter what the sex of the person to whom you are referring. These nouns always use the masculine or feminine marker no matter what the gender of the person. Notice that the "Always Masculine" list, which generally refers to professions, is much longer than the "Always Feminine" list.

Nouns for Both Sexes, Part 2

Always Masculine	Always Feminine
agent de police (*ah-zhahN duh poh-lees;* police officer)	connaissance (*koh-neh-sahNs;* acquaintance)
bébé (*bay-bay;* baby)	personne (*pehr-sohn;* person)
chef (*shehf;* chef, head)	star (*stahr;* star)
dentiste (*dahN-teest* dentist)	vedette (*vuh-deht;* star)
écrivain (*ay-kree-vaN;* writer)	victime (*veek-teem;* victim)
ingénieur (*aN-zhay-nyuhr;* engineer)	
mannequin (*mahn-kaN;* model)	
médecin (*mayd-saN;* doctor)	
pompier (*pohN-pyeh;* firefighter)	
peintre (*paNtr;* painter)	
professeur (*proh-feh-suhr;* teacher)	

The endings in the following table can be helpful in determining the gender of the noun and can make marking easier. This will require some memorization and practice on your part. When in doubt, always consult your dictionary for the gender of a word. An *m.* or an *f.* will always appear. Make sure to look carefully in case the gender is in doubt.

Masculine and Feminine Endings

Masculine Endings	Example	Feminine Endings	Example
-acle	spectacle (*spehk-tahkl*)	-ade	limonade (*lee-moh-nahd*)
-age*	garage (*gah-rahzh*)	-ale	cathédrale (*kah-tay-drahl*)
-al	animal (*ah-nee-mahl*)	-ance	chance (*shahNs*)
-eau**	château (*shah-to*)	-ence	essence (*eh-sahNs*)
-et	ticket (*tee-keh*)	-ette	chaînette (*sheh-neht*)
-ier	papier (*pah-pyay*)	-ie	magie (*mah-zhee*)
-isme	cyclisme (*see-kleez-muh*)	-ique	boutique (*boo-teek*)
-ment	changement (*shahNzh-mahN*)	-oire	histoire (*ees-twahr*)
		-sion	expression (*ehks-preh-syohN*)
		-tion	addition (*ah-dee-syohN*)
		-ure	coiffure (*kwah-fewr*)

* *except page (pahzh) (f.); plage (plahzh) (f.) beach*

** *except eau (o) (f.) water; peau (po) (f.) skin*

Mark More Nouns

You are looking around a gift shop. In order to tell the salesperson what you would like, use the indefinite article noun marker *un* or *une*. After #2, you're on your own.

Example:
chaînette *f.* (*sheh-neht;* chain)
Je voudrais une chaînette, s'il vous plaît.
I would like a chain, please.

1. ______________________ écharpe *f.* (*ay-shahrp;* scarf)
2. ______________________ tee-shirt *m.* (*tee-shehrt;* T-shirt)

3. ______________________ tableau (*tah-blo;* picture)
4. ______________________ collier (*koh-lyeh;* necklace)
5. ______________________ ceinture (*saN-tewr;* belt)
6. ______________________ bougie (*boo-zhee;* candle)
7. ______________________ bracelet (*brahs-leh;* bracelet)
8. ______________________ journal (*zhoor-nahl;* newspaper)

Gender Benders

Marking some nouns is as easy as adding an *e* to the masculine form to get the corresponding feminine form. When you do this, there will be a change in the pronunciation of any feminine noun whose masculine form ended in a *consonant.* For the masculine noun, the final consonant is not pronounced. When the *e* is added to form the feminine, the consonant must then be pronounced. Another change is that the final nasal sound of a masculine *in* (*aN*) ending loses its nasality when the feminine ending becomes *ine* (*een*). Observe these changes in the following table.

Gender Benders

Le (L'), Un	La (L'), Une
ami (*ah-mee;* friend)	amie (*ah-mee;* friend)
avocat (*ah-vo-kah;* lawyer)	avocate (*ah-vo-kaht;* lawyer)
client (*klee-yahN;* client)	cliente (*klee-yahNt;* client)
cousin (*koo-zaN;* cousin)	cousine (*koo-zeen;* cousin)
employé (*ahN-plwah-yay;* employee)	employée (*ahN-plwah-yay;* employee)
étudiant (*ay-tew-dyahN;* student)	étudiante (*ay-tew-dyahNt;* student)
voisin (*vwah-zaN;* neighbor)	voisine (*vwah-zeen;* neighbor)

Some masculine noun endings (usually referring to professions) very conveniently have a corresponding feminine ending. Most of the feminine endings sound different, as you will notice in the table below.

More Gender Benders

Masculine Ending	Feminine Ending
-an	paysan (*peh-ee-zahN;* peasant)
-anne	paysanne (*peh-ee-zahn;* peasant)
-el	contractuel (*kohN-trahk-tew-ehl;* traffic enforcer)
-elle	contractuelle (*koh-trahk-tew-ehl;* traffic enforcer)
-er	pâstissier (*pah-tee-syay;* pastry chef)
-ère	pâtissière (*pah-tee-syehr;* pastry chef)
-eur	vendeur (*vahN-duhr;* salesman)
-euse	vendeuse (*vahN-duhz;* saleswoman)
-ien	mécanicien (*may-kah-nee-syaN;* mechanic)
-ienne	mécanicienne (*may-kah-nee-syehn;* mechanic)
-on	patron (*pah-trohN;* boss)
-onne	patronne (*pah-trohn;* boss)
-teur	spectateur (*spehk-tah-tuhr;* spectator)
-trice	spectatrice (*spehk-tah-trees;* spectator)

What's Their Line?

Review what you've learned so far and then complete the list with the missing professions. Be very careful before you choose an ending. Remember, some nouns do not change.

Il est	Elle est	Il est	Elle est
avocat	__________	infirmier	__________
__________	dentiste	pompier	__________
coiffeur	__________	__________	patronne
__________	factrice	mannequin	__________
boucher	__________	__________	pâtissière
__________	étudiante	médecin	__________
__________	chef	__________	ouvrière

If you did well in this exercise, then it's time to continue. The good news is: There are no more rules. However, because most nouns in French do not follow any specific set of rules, you should learn them with their markers. You'll see that you'll get the hang of it in no time. And if you make a gender mistake, it's really not that serious—as long as you've chosen the correct noun, you'll be understood.

When There's More Than One

When a French noun refers to more than one person, place, thing, or idea, just like in English, it must be made plural. But it is not enough to simply change the noun; the marker must be made plural, as well. As you study the following table, you will see that in the plural, the masculine and feminine noun markers for *the* and *some* are exactly the same.

Plural Noun Markers

	Masculine	Feminine
the	les	les
some	des	des

What does this mean? Because *le*, *la*, and *l'* all become *les* in the plural, and *un* and *une* become *des*, using a plural noun marker does not enable you to determine the gender of any noun. Plural noun markers indicate only that the speaker is referring to more than one noun. This means that you must learn each noun with its singular noun marker.

Un, Deux, Trois

In a mixed group of males and females, the masculine plural form always prevails. *Les amis*, for example, can refer to male friends or a group of male and female friends. If there are only females present, use *les amies*.

Plural Nouns

Forming the plural of most nouns in French is really quite easy. All you have to do is add an *unpronounced s* to the singular form:

le garçon (*luh gahr-sohN*), un garçon (*uhN gahr-sohN*)	les garçons (*lay gahr-sohN*), des garçons (*day gahr-sohN*)
la fille (*lah fee-y*), une fille (*ewn fee-y*)	les filles (*lay fee-y*), des filles (*day fee-y*)
l'enfant* (*lahN-fahN*), un enfant** (*uhN nahN-fahN*)	les enfants** (*lay zahN-fahN*), des enfants** (*day zahN-fahN*)

**elision*

***liaison*

Remember elision and liaison? Use the pronunciation guide and slide the sounds joined by the apostrophe: *l'homme* (*lohm*) and *j'écoute* (*zhay-koot*), and link the sound of the final consonant with the beginning vowel: *les hôtels* (*lay zo-tehl*) and *nous arrivons* (*noo zah-ree-vohN*). Don't pronounce the final *s* if you want your French to sound authentic.

The letters *s*, *x*, and *z* are all letters that are used to make plurals in French. So what happens if you have a French noun that ends in one of these letters? Absolutely nothing!

le prix (*luh pree;* the price, prize)	les prix (*lay pree*)
le fils (*luh fees;* the son)	les fils (*lay fees*)
le nez (*luh nay;* the nose)	les nez (*lay nay*)

Common words that end in *-s:*

l'ananas (*lah-nah-nah;* pineapple)	le héros (*luh ay-ro**; hero)
l'autobus (*lo-toh-bews;* bus)	le mois (*luh mwah;* month)
le bas (*luh bah;* stocking)	le jus (*luh zhew;* juice)
le bras (*luh brah;* arm)	le palais (*luh pah-leh;* palace)
le colis (*luh koh-lee;* package)	le pardessus (*luh pahr-duh-sew;* overcoat)
le corps (*luh kohr;* body)	le pays (*luh pay-ee;* country)
le dos (*luh do;* back)	le repas (*luh ruh-pah;* meal)
la fois (*lah fwah;* time)	le tapis (*luh tah-pee;* rug)

Common words that end in *-x:*

la croix (*lah krwah;* cross)	la voix (*lah vwah;* voice)

More Than One

Chances are that when you travel, you're going to see more than one château, museum, church, and so forth. If you choose to discuss or describe these things, you'll want to make sure that you've got your plurals down pat. Practice makes perfect, so try to express that you see more than one of the things in the following list.

Example:
héros: Je vois des héros

1. boutique ____________________
2. automobile ____________________
3. croix ____________________
4. tapis ____________________
5. restaurant ____________________
6. magazine ____________________
7. palais ____________________
8. autobus ____________________

Other Plurals

The letter *x* is used in French to make plurals.

- For nouns ending in *eau:*

le bateau (*luh bah-to;* boat)	les bateaux
le bureau (*luh bew-ro;* office, desk)	les bureaux
le cadeau (*luh kah-do;* gift)	les cadeaux
le chapeau (*luh shah-po;* hat)	les chapeaux
le château (*luh shah-to;* castle)	les châteaux
le couteau (*luh koo-to;* knife)	les couteaux
l'eau *f.* (*lo;* water)	les eaux
le gâteau (*luh gah-to;* cake)	les gâteaux
le manteau (*luh mahN-to;* coat)	les manteaux
le morceau (*luh mohr-so;* piece)	les morceaux
l'oiseau (*lwah-zo;* bird)	les oiseaux
le rideau (*luh ree-do;* curtain)	les rideaux
le tableau (*luh tah-blo;* picture, chalkboard)	les tableaux

Attention!

Although you can refer to one hair in French as *un cheveu*, (for example, if there were a hair in your food), *hair*, in general, is always plural and is referred to as *les cheveux*.

- For nouns ending in *eu*, except *le pneu* (*luh pnuh;* tire)/*les pneus:*

le cheveu (*luh shuh vuh;* hair)	les cheveux
le jeu (*luh zhuh;* game)	les jeux
le lieu (*luh lyuh;* place)	les lieux
le neveu (*luh nuh-vuh;* nephew)	les neveux

- For nouns ending in *al*, change *al* to *aux* except for *le bal* (*luh bahl;* ball)/*bals*; *le festival* (*luh fehs-tee-vahl;* festival)/*festivals:*

l'animal (*lah nee mahl;* animal)	les animaux
le cheval (*luh shuh-vahl;* horse)	les chevaux
l'hôpital (*lo-pee-tahl;* hospital)	les hôpitaux
le journal (*luh zhoor-nahl;* newspaper)	les journaux

- For some nouns ending in *ou*, add *x* to form the plural:

le bijou (*luh bee-zhoo;* jewel)	les bijoux
le caillou (*luh kah-yoo;* pebble)	les cailloux
le genou (*luh zhuh-noo;* knee)	les genoux
le joujou (*luh zhoo-zhoo;* toy)	les joujoux

- Just as we have some words in English that are always plural (*pants*, *sunglasses*, *shorts*, *news*), so do the French. Here are some nouns that might prove useful to you:

les ciseaux *m.* (*lay see-zo;* scissors)	les lunettes *f.* (*lay lew-neht;* eyeglasses)
les gens *m.* (*lay zhahN;* people)	les vacances *f.* (*lay vah-kahNs;* vacation)

Learning a foreign language wouldn't be a challenge if there weren't some irregularities. Here are some irregular plurals you might find useful:

l'oeil *m.* (*luhy;* eye)	les yeux (*lay zyuh*)
le travail (*luh trah-vahy;* work)	les travaux (*lay trah-vo*)
madame (*mah-dahm;* Mrs.)	mesdames (*may-dahm*)
mademoiselle (*mahd-mwah-zehl;* Miss)	mesdemoiselles (*mayd-mwah-zehl*)
monsieur (*muh-syuh;* Mr.)	messieurs (*meh-syuh*)

Some compound nouns (nouns made up of two nouns usually joined by a hyphen) do not change in the plural—only their markers do:

le gratte-ciel (*luh graht-syehl;* skyscrapers)	les gratte-ciel
le hors d'oeuvre* (*luh ohr-duhvr;* appetizers)	les hors d'oeuvre
le rendez-vous (*luh rahN-day-voo;* appointments)	les rendez-vous

Practice with Plurals

If you're anything like me, you're always looking for something because you're either (a) very absent-minded or (b) totally lacking a sense of direction. Try your luck at telling someone what you are looking for.

Example:
boats: Je cherche les bateaux.

1. castles

 ____

2. eyeglasses

 ____

3. people

 ____

4. newspapers

 ____

5. packages

 ____

6. palaces

 ____

7. scissors

 ____

8. toys

 ____

The Least You Need to Know

- You can change some nouns from masculine to feminine by adding an *e* or by changing the ending of the word.
- You must memorize the gender of most nouns.
- Certain endings are almost always masculine (*-acle*, *-age*, *-al*, *-eau*, *-et*, *-ier*, *-isme*, *-ment*); others are almost aways feminine (*-ade*, *-ale*, *-ance*, *-ence*, *-ette*, *-ie*, *-ique*, *-oire*, *-sion*, *-tion*, *-ure*).
- Most nouns can be made plural by adding *s*.

- Some nouns ending in *-eau*, *-eu*, and *-ou* can be made plural by adding *x*.
- Nouns ending in *-al* change to *-aux* in the plural.
- Singular and plural nouns sound the same—only the markers change in spelling and pronunciation.

On the Move!

In This Chapter

- Subject pronouns
- Conjugation of regular verbs
- How to ask a question
- Common regular verbs

In the preceding chapter, you learned about nouns: how to determine their gender and how to make them plural. Nouns, and the pronouns used to replace them, are very important because you can use them as the subject of a sentence. In this chapter, you will see how you can communicate your thoughts in French by using nouns or pronouns and the verbs that convey the actions being performed.

Planning and taking an imaginary trip to a French-speaking country will teach you how to get along in most everyday situations where you would need French. Picture the places you could go: the bustling cities, the sandy beaches, the medieval towns. Imagine the sites you could see: the museums, the cathedrals, the parks, the gardens. Consider the people you could meet: French, Canadians, Haitians, Africans. The possibilities are endless. Let's start with the basics.

Who's the Subject?

You're on a group tour, and everyone involved seems to have his or her own agenda. *You* would like to take pictures of the beautiful stained-glass windows of Notre Dame. The woman next to you, *she* insists on the Eiffel Tower. The couple to your right, *they* would prefer to spend the day shopping. And the tour guide, well, *he*'s just disgusted at this point. To express the things people do, you need to learn about verbs. Verbs require a subject, whether it is stated as in:

> *I* would like to go to the Louvre.
> *The guide* is waiting for us.

Or understood, as in a command:

> *Go* to the Pompidou Center. (The subject is understood to be *you*.)

A subject can be either a noun or a pronoun that replaces the noun:

> *The artist* is painting a landscape.
> *He (she)* is painting a landscape.

Un, Deux, Trois

On (which can mean one, you, we, or they) comes in very handy if you want to speak about people in general. For example: One shouldn't hitchhike. Even though *on* may refer to more than one person, the third person singular verb form follows it.

Subject Pronouns

Just as in English, the French subject pronouns in the following table are given a person and a number (singular or plural).

Subject Pronouns

Person	Singular		Plural	
first	je* (*zhuh*)	I	nous (*noo*)	we
second	tu** (*tew*)	you	vous*** (*voo*)	you
third	il (*eel*)	he	ils****(*eel*)	they
	elle (*ehl*)	she	elles (*ehl*)	they
	on (*ohN*)	one, you, we, they		

* *The subject pronoun* je *requires elision and becomes* j' *before a vowel or vowel sound (h, y).*
In English, the subject pronoun "I" is always capitalized, regardless of its position in the sentence.
In French, je *is capitalized only at the beginning of a sentence, just like any other word.*

** *The subject pronoun* tu *is used when speaking to a single (one) friend, relative, child, or pet.* Tu *is called the familiar form. The* u *from* tu *is never dropped for elision:* tu arrives.

*** *The subject pronoun* vous *is used in the singular to show respect to an older person or when speaking to someone you don't know very well.* Vous *is always used when speaking to more than one person, regardless of familiarity.* Vous *is referred to as the polite form.*

**** *The subject pronoun* ils *is used to refer to more than one male or a combined group of males and females.*

Culture Capsule

Tu is used by the French when speaking to their pets, which are considered to be family members and are held in very high regard. It is not unusual to see a family accompanied by its dog in a French restaurant. No, the dog doesn't sit at the table. It eats on the floor as usual, out of its own bowl. And, believe it or not, there are special takeout restaurants catering strictly to the family canine.

Tu or *Vous*?

Would you use *tu* or *vous* when speaking to the following people: A doctor? Your cousin? Your friend? A salesman? A woman waiting in line for a bus? Two friends? A policeman from whom you are asking directions? A group of friends?

Pronouns are very useful because they enable you to speak fluidly without having to constantly repeat the noun. Imagine how tedious it would be to hear: Luc is French; Luc is from Paris; Luc would make a wonderful guide. A better version would be: Luc is French; he's from Paris, and he'd make a wonderful guide. Use pronouns to replace proper nouns (the name of a person or persons), as follows.

Noun	Pronoun	Noun	Pronoun
Lucien	il	le restaurant	il
Marie-Claire	elle	la boutique	elle
Luc et Jean	ils	le restaurant et le café	ils
Marie et Anne	elles	la boutique et la poste	elles
Luc et Anne	ils	le restaurant et la boutique	ils

Who's Who?

Are you like me, an incurable gossip? Imagine you've just attended a fabulous party and now you're driving your best friend home. Of course, the two of you can't wait to talk about all the *invites* (guests). Which pronoun would you use when speaking about the following people: *Charles? Lucie et Sylvie? Berthe? Pierre? Luc et Henri? Robert et Suzette? Janine, Charolotte, Michèle, et Roger? Paul, Roland, et Annick?*

Which pronoun would you substitute for the following nouns, subjects that came up in your conversation about the festivities: *La fête? Le bal costumé? La musique et le décor? Les vêtements? Le travail et le coût? La cuisine et la nourriture? L'ambiance? L'hôte et l'hôtesse?*

Moving Along with Verbs

Do you like to bungee jump? Participate in ballroom dancing competitions? Skydive? Or are you a couch potato attracted to activities like reading a book or watching television? No matter what your preferences, you'll have to learn to use verbs to express any action, motion, or state of being. Verbs are referred to as "regular" if they follow a set pattern of rules and "irregular" if they don't. This chapter will look at regular verbs only.

Regular Verbs

Verbs are generally shown in the infinitive, the basic "to" form of the verb: to live, to laugh, to love. An infinitive, whether in French or English, is the form of the verb before it has been conjugated. We conjugate verbs all the time in English without even paying attention to the fact that we're doing it. Conjugation refers to changing the ending of a regular verb so that it agrees with the subject. For example, think of the verb "dance." The infinitive is "to dance," and it is conjugated as follows:

I dance	We dance
You dance	You dance
He/she dances	They dance

With irregular verbs, such as the verb "to be," the entire verb form changes:

I am	We are
You are	You are
He/she is	They are

Regular verbs in French belong to one of three large families: verbs whose infinitives end in *-er*, *-ir*, or *-re*. The verbs within each family are all conjugated in exactly the same manner, so after you've learned the pattern for one family, you know them all.

When they stand alone, verbs are generally written in their infinitive form. If you want to express what someone is doing, you must choose a subject pronoun and then learn the conjugations.

The *-er* Verb Family

Let's start with the biggest and easiest family. This will give you an introduction to conjugation that will put you at ease right from the start. To conjugate *-er* verbs, drop *er* from the infinitive and then add the following endings.

Singular Forms	Plural Forms
Je parl**e** (I speak)	Nous parl**ons** (We speak)
Tu parl**es** (You speak)	Vous parl**ez** (You speak)
Il parl**e** (He speaks)	Ils parl**ent** (They speak)
Elle parl**e** (She speaks)	Elles parl**ent** (They speak)
On parl**e** (One, we, they speak[s])	

Now you can conjugate any *-er* verb that belongs to the family. So, if you want to brag about your accomplishments to impress a member of the opposite sex, the sky's the limit.

Je gagne beaucoup d'argent.	I earn a lot of money.
Je joue très bien aux sports.	I play sports very well.
Je dîne dans les restaurants les plus élégants.	I dine in the finest restaurants.

See how easy it is?

Common *-er* Verbs

Le Verbe	Pronunciation	Meaning
aider	*eh-day*	to help
annoncer	*ah-nohN-say*	to announce
bavarder	*bah-vahr-day*	to chat
changer	*shahN-zhay*	to change

continues

Common *-er* Verbs (continued)

Le Verbe	Pronunciation	Meaning
chercher	*shehr-shay*	to look for
commencer	*koh-mahN-say*	to begin
danser	*dahN-say*	to dance
demander	*duh-mahN-day*	to ask
dépenser	*day-pahN-say*	to spend (money)
donner	*doh-nay*	to give
écouter	*ay-koo-tay*	to listen (to)
étudier	*ay-tew-dyay*	to study
expliquer	*ehks-plee-kay*	to explain
exprimer	*ehks-pree-may*	to express
fermer	*fehr-may*	to close
fonctionner	*fohNk-syohN-nay*	to function
garder	*gahr-day*	to keep, watch
habiter	*ah-bee-tay*	to live (in)
indiquer	*aN-dee-kay*	to indicate
jouer	*zhoo-ay*	to play
laver	*lah-vay*	to wash
manger	*mahN-zhay*	to eat
marcher	*mahr-shay*	to walk
nager	*nah-zhay*	to swim
oublier	*oo-blee-yay*	to forget
parler	*pahr-lay*	to speak
penser	*pahN-say*	to think
préparer	*pray-pah-ray*	to prepare
présenter	*pray-zahN-tay*	to present, introduce
quitter	*kee-tay*	to leave, remove
regarder	*ruh-gahr-day*	to look at, watch
regretter	*ruh-gruh-tay*	to regret
rencontrer	*rahN-kohN-tray*	to meet
retourner	*ruh-toor-nay*	to return
sembler	*sahN-blay*	to seem
signer	*see-nyay*	to sign

Le Verbe	Pronunciation	Meaning
téléphoner	*tay-lay-foh-nay*	to telephone
travailler	*trah-vah-yay*	to work
voyager	*vwah-yah-zhay*	to travel

Note: A subject can be followed by two consecutive verbs. When this occurs, conjugate only the first verb. The second verb remains in the infinitive: *Je désire danser.* (I want to dance.) *Il aime jouer au tennis.* (He loves to play tennis.)

Conjugation 101

Use the correct form of the verb to express what each individual is doing on vacation.

Example:
(regarder) Je *regarde* le spectacle.

1. (traverser) Il ____________________ la rue.
2. (demander) Elles ____________________ l'adresse.
3. (chercher) Nous ____________________ le musée.
4. (accompagner) J'____________________ ma famille.
5. (louer) Vous ____________________ un appartement.
6. (présenter) Sylvie et Luc ____________________ leurs amis à leurs parents.
7. (réserver) Robert ____________________ une chambre d'hôtel.
8. (monter) Tu ____________________ à la tour.
9. (parler) Marie ____________________ avec ses amis.
10. (poser) Jean et Robert ____________________ des questions.

The *-ir* Verb Family

To conjugate *-ir* verbs, drop *ir* from the infinitive and then add the endings. Let's take a look at the conjugated forms of *choisir* (to choose).

Singular Forms	Plural Forms
Je chois**is** (I choose)	Nous chois**issons** (We choose)
Tu chois**is** (You choose)	Vous chois**issez** (You choose)
Il chois**it** (He chooses)	Ils chois**issent** (They choose)
Elle chois**it** (She chooses)	Elles chois**issent** (They choose)
On chois**it** (One, we, they choose[s])	

Common *-ir* Verbs

Le Verbe	Pronunciation	Meaning
agir	*ah-zheer*	to act
avertir	*ah-vehr-teer*	to warn
blanchir	*blahN-sheer*	to bleach, whiten
choisir	*shwah-zeer*	to choose
finir	*fee-neer*	to finish
guérir	*gay-reer*	to cure
jouir	*zhoo-eer*	to enjoy
maigrir	*meh-greer*	to become thin
obéir	*oh-bay-eer*	to obey
punir	*pew-neer*	to punish
réfléchir	*ray-flay-sheer*	to reflect, think
réussir	*ray-ew-seer*	to succeed

Conjugation 102

It's time to see if you're up to the challenge. Be careful with infinitives, such as *choisir* and *réussir*, that already have i's and s's in them. By the time you're finished conjugating them, they may look a little strange (*Nous réussissons, Tu choisis*), but they are correct. Be confident and give the correct form of the verb to express what each tourist does.

1. (finir) Nous ____________________ à huit heures.
2. (réfléchir) On ____________________.

3. (jouir) Ils __________________ de tout.
4. (applaudir) Tu __________________ au théâtre.
5. (réussir) Elle__________________ à parler français.
6. (choisir) Je __________________ un bon tour.
7. (agir) Vous __________________ bien.
8. (remplir) Alice et Berthe __________________ les formulaires.

The *-re* Verb Family

The *-re* verb family is by far the smallest. The verbs *attendre* (to wait for), *entendre* (to hear), and *vendre* (to sell) are high-frequency verbs that you'll be using and hearing on a regular basis, so it will be necessary to commit this conjugation to memory. To conjugate *-re* verbs, drop *re* from the infinitive and then add the endings.

Singular Forms	Plural Forms
J'attend**s** (I wait)	Nous attend**ons** (We wait)
Tu attend**s** (You wait; fam. sing.)	Vous attend**ez** (You wait; polite sing. and pl.)
Il attend (He waits)	Ils attend**ent** (They wait)
Elle attend (She waits)	Elles attend**ent** (They wait)
On attend (One, we, they wait[s])	

Common *-re* Verbs

Le Verbe	Pronunciation	Meaning
attendre	*ah-tahNdr*	to wait for
descendre	*deh-sahNdr*	to go (come) down
entendre	*ahN-tahNdr*	to hear
perdre	*pehrdr*	to lose
répondre	*ray-pohNdr*	to answer
vendre	*vahNdr*	to sell

The third person singular forms of *rompre* (to break) and *interrompre* (to interrupt) are slightly irregular:

il/elle rompt il/elle interrompt

Conjugation 103

People on vacation do all sorts of different things. Use your knowledge of *-re* verbs to describe their actions. In this exercise, choose the verb that best completes the sentence. Then, provide the correct verb form to explain what each tourist is doing.

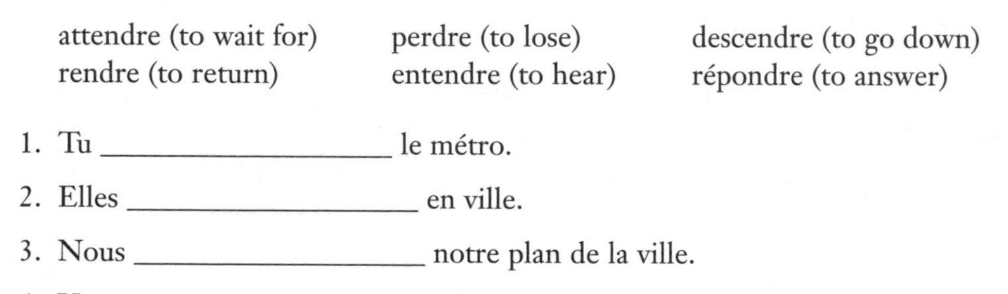

attendre (to wait for) perdre (to lose) descendre (to go down)
rendre (to return) entendre (to hear) répondre (to answer)

1. Tu ____________________ le métro.
2. Elles ____________________ en ville.
3. Nous ____________________ notre plan de la ville.
4. Vous ____________________ à des questions.
5. Il ____________________ les nouvelles (the news).
6. Je ____________________ les documents.

Verb Family Review

To review, all regular verbs follow a pattern of conjugation consistent with their infinitive endings. Simply drop the final *-er*, *-ir*, or *-re* and add the ending that corresponds to the subject, as shown in the following table.

Review of Regular Verbs

	-er **Verbs**	***-ir*** **Verbs**	***-re*** **Verbs**
je	-e	-is	-s
tu	-es	-is	-s
il, elle, on	-e	-it	(no ending)
nous	-ons	-issons	-ons
vous	-ez	-issez	-ez
ils, elles	-ent	-issent	-ent

Go Ahead! Ask Me a Question!

When planning a trip, you'll find a lot of questions that you'll want to ask. Let's concentrate on the easy ones—those that require a simple yes or no answer.

There are four ways to show that you're asking a question:

- Intonation
- The tag *n'est-ce pas* (isn't that so?)
- *Est-ce que* at the beginning of your phrase
- Inversion

It's Okay to Raise Your Voice

The easiest way to show that you're asking a question is to simply change your intonation and raise your voice at the end of the sentence. To do this, place an imaginary question mark at the end of your statement and speak with a rising inflection.

Tu penses au voyage?	Are you thinking about the trip?

Notice how your voice starts out lower and gradually keeps rising until the end of the sentence.

When using the same sentence as a statement of fact, notice how your voice rises and then lowers by the end of the sentence.

Tu penses au voyage.	You are thinking about the trip.

The *n'est-ce pas* Tag

Another simple way to ask a question is to add the tag *n'est-ce pas* (*nehs pah;* isn't that so?) at the end of the sentence.

Tu penses au voyage, n'est-ce pas?

Est-ce que

Yet another way to ask the same question is to put *est-ce que* (*ehs-kuh*) at the beginning of the sentence. *Est-ce que* is not translated but does indicate that a question follows.

Est-ce que tu penses au voyage?

Est-ce que becomes *est-ce qu'* before a vowel or vowel sound (h, y):

Est-ce qu'il pense au voyage?

Doing an About Face

The last way to form a question is by inversion, which is used far more frequently in writing than in conversation. Inversion means reversing the word order of the subject pronoun and the conjugated verb form. Several rules govern inversion, which can get tricky. Don't despair, however. If you feel more comfortable using one of the other three methods mentioned, by all means use them. You will still be speaking perfectly correct French, you will be understood, and your question will be answered. For those who are up to the challenge, the rules are as follows:

Attention!

You can only invert a verb with a subject pronoun. If you try to do this with a noun, you will sound like an amateur. If you find this rule hard to remember, use one of the other three easier ways to ask a question.

- **Avoid inverting with *je*.** It's awkward and is very rarely used.
- **You can only invert subject pronouns with conjugated verbs. Do *not* invert with nouns!** Look at some examples to see how inversion works with the subject pronouns:

Tu penses au voyage.	Penses-tu au voyage?
Nous expliquons bien.	Expliquons-nous bien?
Vous parlez français.	Parlez-vous français?
Ils commandent du vin.	Commandent-ils du vin?
Elles habitent à Paris.	Habitent-elles à Paris?

- **A *-t-* must be added with *il* and *elle* to avoid having two vowels together.** This usually happens only with verbs in the *-er* family. For the *-ir* and *-re* families, the *il* and *elle* verb forms end in a consonant:

Il travaille aujourd'hui.	Travaille-**t-**il aujourd'hui?
Elle contacte l'agent.	Contacte-**t-**elle l'agent?
Il finit son dessert.	Finit-il son dessert?
Elle attend le bus.	Attend-elle le bus?

- **When you have a noun subject and you want to use inversion, you *must* replace the noun with the appropriate pronoun.** You may retain the noun at the beginning of the question, but then you must invert the corresponding pronoun with the conjugated verb form. For example:

Le chanteur **est-il** français?
The pronoun *il* was chosen because *le chanteur* (the singer) is a singular, masculine noun. No *-t-* was necessary because the verb ends in a consonant.

La robe **est-elle** trop petite?
The pronoun *elle* was chosen because *la robe* (the dress) is a feminine, singular noun. Again, no *-t-* was necessary because the verb ends in a consonant.

Le docteur et le dentiste **travaillent-ils** aujourd'hui?
The pronoun *ils* was chosen because we are referring to more than one male noun.

Les brochures **sont-elles** à notre disposition?
The pronoun *elles* was chosen because we are referring to a feminine, plural noun.

Le gâteau et la mousse **sont-ils** excellents?
The pronoun *ils* was chosen because, when referring to two nouns of different genders, the male noun is always given precedence.

Remember that whether you are using intonation, *est-ce que*, *n'est-ce pas*, or inversion, you are asking for exactly the same information: a yes/*oui* (*wee*) or no/*non* (*nohN*) answer.

Tu poses des questions intelligentes?
Est-ce que tu poses des questions intelligentes?
Tu poses des questions intelligentes, n'est-ce pas?
Poses-tu des questions intelligentes?

Ask Me—I Dare You

Imagine you're sitting on a bus with your tour group stuck in traffic on the *autoroute*. To keep yourselves occupied, you decide to ask questions about everyone on board, including yourselves. Using the subjects and actions listed, write questions in as many ways as you can.

1. nous/parler trop
____
2. il/descendre souvent en ville
____
3. vous/accomplir beaucoup
____
4. Marie/téléphoner toujours à sa famille
____
5. tu/attendre toujours les autres
____
6. les garçons/jouer au tennis
____
7. elles/écouter le guide
____
8. Luc et Anne/sembler heureux
____

And the Answer Is ...

If you're an upbeat person who enjoys doing a lot of things, you'll surely want to know how to answer "yes." To answer "yes" to an affirmative question, use *oui* (*wee*) and then give your statement.

Vous dansez?	Oui, je danse.

To answer "yes" to a negative question, use *si*.

Tu ne danses pas bien?	Si, je danse bien.

Perhaps you're in a foul mood, and everyone and everything is getting on your nerves. Or maybe "no" is just an honest answer. To answer negatively (no), use *non* (*nohN*) and then add *ne* and *pas* (not), respectively, before and after the conjugated verb form. Remember, if there are two verbs, only the first is conjugated.

Vous fumez?	Non, je ne fume pas. Non, je ne désire pas fumer.

You can easily vary your negative answers by putting the following negative phrases before and after the conjugated verb.

ne … jamais (*nuh … zhah-meh*)	never
Je ne fume jamais.	I never smoke.
Ne … plus (*nuh … plew*)	no longer
Je ne fume plus.	I no longer smoke. (I don't smoke anymore.)
ne … rien (*nuh … ryaN*)	nothing, anything
Je ne fume rien.	I'm not smoking anything.

It's All About You

What are your good or bad habits? Do you have hobbies? Are there activities you really enjoy doing to relax? Read the following list and answer with a yes or no sentence. (Sample responses are located in Appendix A.)

Fumer? ______________________________

Crier? ______________________________

Jouer au tennis? ______________________________

Danser bien? ______________________________

Parler français? ______________________________

Bavarder avec des amis? ______________________________

Dîner tôt? ______________________________

Aimer réussir? ______________________________

Your Trip Awaits

You're finally going to take that dream trip. Read the following ads for travel agencies and match them with the services you think they provide.

a)

MAISON DE VOYAGES

VOYAGES EN GROUPES
FORFAIT INDIVIDUEL
BILLETS ET LOCATIONS
LIVRAISON À DOMICILE
(PARIS)

b)

VOYAGES de la JEUNESSE
Jeunes 18/35
voyagez à des
prix exceptionnels
séjours, circuits
expéditions ... club 18/35

c)

LOISIRS ET VACANCES

DES VACANCES PARTOUT DANS LE MONDE AVEC UNE SEULE CLEF

AVEC LE DROIT DE SÉJOUR

ÉCHANGEABLE

Consultez l'Annuaire électronique
11 Nom: LOISIRS ET VACANCES
Loc: BOULOGNE
Dept: 92

d)

SPORTS ET LOISIRS
TOUS LES VOYAGES
POUR TOUS LES SPORTS

Jeux olympiques
Football
Rugby "5 Nations"
Marathons, Formule 1
Basketball, Volleyball
Tennis, Voile
Sports loisirs
Stages tous sports

continues

1. This agency caters to a younger crowd. _____
2. This agency provides for an exchange of residences. _____
3. This agency will take you home if you live in Paris. _____
4. This agency caters to an athletic crowd. _____

The Least You Need to Know

- Subject pronouns can be used to replace any subject noun.
- Any verb that follows a subject noun or pronoun must be properly conjugated.
- There are different rules for conjugating verbs belonging to the *-er*, *-ir*, and *-re* families.
- There are four ways to ask a question in French: intonation, using the *n'est-ce pas* tag, using *est-ce que*, and inversion.
- Use *ne* + verb + *pas* (not), *jamais* (never), *plus* (no longer), or *rien* (never) to answer a question negatively.

Part 2 Travel Time

You never know where life will take you and whom you'll meet along the way. In an ever-growing, multicultural society—where foreign travel not only is a luxury but has become a business necessity—you might easily find yourself in a French-speaking country one day soon. Undoubtedly, your French will serve you well around the globe.

Being able to introduce yourself and your traveling companions will help you meet new people from different cultures and will allow you to pick up useful travel tips before the plane has landed. Upon arrival, you'll be able to get around the airport so that there's no delay in reaching your destination. Your comfort, of course, will also be very important to you.

The highlights of Part 2 include how to get where you're going in a timely fashion and how to procure some necessary creature comforts once you've arrived.

Chapter 8

Greetings and Salutations

In This Chapter

- Hellos and good-byes
- The irregular verb *être* (to be)
- Jobs and professions
- When you need information

The time has come to put what you've learned to good use. Now that you can create simple French sentences (using subject nouns, pronouns, and regular verbs) and ask yes-or-no questions, you're ready to engage in a short conversation.

While you're sitting on the plane on your way to a glorious vacation in a French-speaking country, you might want to strike up a conversation with the person sitting next to you. If that person speaks French, you're in luck. This is an excellent opportunity for you to introduce yourself and perhaps to get a few helpful hints and recommendations about places to visit, restaurants to go to, and things to do in the country you're visiting.

Becoming Friends

Even though you've read every travel book in your local bookstore, you may still be a little nervous about your trip. What you really need to do is speak to someone from the country you're visiting—someone who lives there and can fill you in on everything to do and see and everywhere to go. Where can you find this person? Probably sitting right next to you on the plane! There's plenty of time before you arrive at your destination, so why not strike up a conversation?

Culture Capsule

Out of respect, older women in France are generally addressed as *Madame* (Mrs.) whether they are married or not. At what age is one considered "older"? It's hard to say. When in doubt, use *Madame*. *Mademoiselle* (Miss, Ms.) is used for younger women.

It's considered quite a *faux pas* (a mistake) to address someone informally if a strong friendship or relationship has not been established. One would not *tutoyer* (use *tu* with) a new business acquaintance or a stranger. Never use the familiar form *tu* when speaking to someone you don't know well. It's considered very rude and insulting. Since you don't know the person at all, a formal approach is *de rigueur* (mandatory). A typical opening conversation might start with many of these phrases.

Phrase	Pronunciation	Meaning
Bonjour.	*bohN-zhoor*	Hello.
Bonsoir.	*bohN swahr*	Good evening.
Monsieur	*muh-syuh*	Sir
Madame	*mah-dahm*	Miss, Mrs.
Mademoiselle	*mahd-mwah-zehl*	Miss
Je m'appelle …	*zhuh mah-pehl*	My name is … (I call myself …)
Comment vous appelez-vous?	*kohN-mahN voo zah-play voo*	What is your name?
Comment allez-vous?	*kohN-mahN tah-lay voo*	How are you?
Très bien.	*treh byaN*	Very well.
Pas mal.	*pah mahl*	Not bad.
Comme ci comme ça.	*kohm see kohm sah*	So-so.

When you're ready to leave, remember to say *au revoir* (*o ruh-vwahr;* good-bye). If you plan on seeing the person sometime soon, use à + the period of time, as in *à demain* (see you tomorrow), *à tout à l'heure* (see you soon), or *à lundi* (see you Monday). During an informal opening conversation (between young people or friends), you might use the following phrases.

Phrase	Pronunciation	Meaning
Salut!	*sah-lew*	Hi!
Je m'appelle …	*zhuh mah-pehl*	My name is … (I call myself …)
Comment t'appelles-tu?	*kohN-mahN tah-pehl tew*	What's your name?
Ça va?	*sah vah*	How's it going?
Ça marche?	*sah mahrsh*	How's it going?
Ça boume?	*sah boom*	How's it going?
Ça va.	*sah vah*	Okay.
Ça marche.	*sah mahrsh*	Okay.
Ça boume.	*sah boom*	Okay.

To Be or Not to Be

If you'd really like to get to know the person you are talking to, ask him or her a few questions about himself or herself such as where he or she is from. You'll also want to respond correctly when others ask where you are from. To do this, you will need the verb *être* (to be). Just as it is in English, the verb "to be" (*être*) is irregular, and all of its forms must be memorized. Because you will be using this verb so frequently, make it a top priority to memorize its forms. Compare the conjugations in the following table. As you will see, there are more irregular forms in French than there are in English.

The Verb *Être* (to Be)

Conjugation	Pronunciation	Meaning
je suis	*zhuh swee*	I am
tu es	*tew eh*	you are
il, elle, on est	*eel, ehl, ohN eh*	he, she, one is

continues

The Verb *Être* (to Be) (continued)

Conjugation	Pronunciation	Meaning
nous sommes	*noo sohm*	we are
vous êtes	*voo zeht*	you are
ils, elles sont	*eel, ehl sohN*	they are

Do you detect an unfamiliar accent when speaking to an acquaintance? Get ready to satisfy your curiosity by using the verb *être* to ask about a person's origins. You're ready to proceed:

Formal use

Vous êtes d'où? *voo zeht doo* Where are you from?

Informal use

Tu es d'où? *tew eh doo* Where are you from?

To express the city or state you come from, keep the following in mind:

- Use *de* (from) for all cities and feminine states, meaning any state ending in *-e* and any state whose name has an adjective:

  Je suis de Maine.
  Je suis de New York.

- Use *du* (from) for all masculine states, meaning states ending in any letter other than *-e:*

  Je suis du Vermont.

- Use *des* (from) to say that you come from the United States:

  Je suis des États-Unis.

Idioms with *Être*

Imagine you are on the phone with your French relative, Uncle Gaston. You think you hear him say to you, "*Je suis en train de préparer le dîner.*" Hearing the cognates *train, préparer,* and *dîner,* you immediately assume that Uncle Gaston is a chef on one of France's trains, perhaps on the *T.G.V.* (*Train à Grande Vitesse,* a very modern and fast train). But how could this be? The last you heard, he was a nephrologist at a leading teaching hospital in Paris. Did he have a change of heart? If you think you hear something that sounds wildly implausible, chances are you're right. Just when you think you have a handle on the language, idioms, those linguistic bugaboos, are ready to trip you up. In this case, your uncle was using an idiomatic expression that means he's busy preparing dinner (bouillabaisse perhaps?). The following table shows you some new idioms with *être*.

Idioms with *Être*

L'idiome	Pronunciation	Meaning
être à	*ehtr ah*	to belong to
être d'accord (avec)	*ehtr dah-kohr ah-vehk*	to agree (with)
être de retour	*ehtr duh ruh-toor*	to be back
être en train de + infinitive	*ehtr ahN traN duh*	to be in the act of, to be busy
être sur le point de + infinitive	*ehtr sewr luh pwaN duh*	to be on the verge of

Make sure to conjugate the verb when you use it in context:

Je suis d'accord.	I agree.
Nous sommes en train de manger.	We are busy eating.
Es-tu sur le point de finir?	Are you on the verge of finishing?

Using Être

Complete the sentence with the correct form of *être* and the idiom that fits:

être à	être de retour
être d'accord	être en train de
être sur le point de	

1. Je travaille. Je ______________ préparer le dîner.
2. Je dis "oui." Tu dis "oui." Nous __________________.
3. Les filles arrivent dans six minutes. Elles ______________ arriver.
4. Le sac bleu __________________ M. Dupont.
5. Vous ______________ depuis quand (since when)?

What's Your Line?

You can also use *être* to ask about a person's job or to talk about your own job. The feminine forms are given in parentheses in the following table. Some occupations have only masculine or feminine forms despite the gender of the person employed.

Formal use

Quel est votre métier?
kehl eh vohtr may-tyay
What is your profession?

Attention!

The indefinite article *un* (*une*) is not used with someone's profession (for example, *Elle est artiste*) unless the profession is qualified by an adjective (as in *Elle est une artiste célèbre*).

Informal use

Quel est ton métier?
kehl eh tohN may-tyay
What is your profession?

Je suis …
zhuh swee
I am …

Professions

Profession	La Profession	Pronunciation
accountant	comptable	*kohn-tahbl*
actor (actress)	acteur (actrice)	*ahk-tuhr (ahk-trees)*
artist	artiste *m.* or *f.*	*ahr-teest*
business man (woman)	homme (femme) d'affaires	*ohm (fahm) dah-fehr*
cashier	caissier (caissière)	*kehs-yay (kehs-yehr)*
dentist	dentiste *m.*	*dahN-teest*
doctor	docteur *m.*, médecin *m.*	*dohk-tuhr; mayd-saN*
electrician	électricien(ne)	*ay-lehk-tree-syaN (ay-lehk-tree-syehn)*
engineer	ingénieur *m.*	*ahN-zhay-nyuhr*
firefighter	pompier *m.*	*pohN-pyay*
government employee	fonctionnaire *m.*	*fohNk-syoh-nehr*
hairdresser	coiffeur (coiffeuse)	*kwah-fuhr (kwah-fuhz)*
jeweler	bijoutier (bijoutière)	*bee-zhoo-tyay (bee-zhoo-tyehr)*

Profession	La Profession	Pronunciation
landlord	propriétaire *m.* or *f.*	*proh-pree-ay-tehr*
lawyer	avocat(e)	*ah-voh-kah(t)*
manager	gérant(e)	*zhay-rahN(t)*
mechanic	mécanicien(ne)	*may-kah-nee-syaN (may-kah-nee-syehn)*
musician	musicien(ne)	*mew-zee-syaN (mew-zee-syehn)*
nurse	infirmier (infirmière)	*ahN-feer-myay (ahN-feer-myehr)*
optician	opticien(ne)	*ohp-tee-syaN (ohp-tee-syehn)*
photographer	photographe *m.* or *f.*	*foh-to-grahf*
pilot	pilote *m.*	*pee-loht*
police officer	agent de police *m.*	*ah-zhahN duh poh-lees*
postal worker	facteur (factrice)	*fahk-tuhr (fahk-trees)*
programmer	programmeur (programmeuse)	*proh-grah-muhr (proh-grah-muhz)*
salesperson	vendeur (vendeuse)	*vahN-duhr (vahN-duhz)*
secretary	secrétaire *m.* or *f.*	*seh-kray-tehr*
student	étudiant(e)	*ay-tewd-yahN(t)*
teacher	professeur *m.*	*proh-feh-suhr*
waiter	garçon *m.*, serveur *m.*	*gahr-sohN, sehr-vuhr*
waitress	serveuse *f.*	*sehr-vuhz*

To refer to a woman in a profession that always uses the masculine word form, simply add the word *femme* (*fahm;* woman) before the job title: *Elle est femme pilote.* (She's a woman pilot.)

An Introductory Conversation

You're sitting on the plane reading your traveler's guide to France when your seat-mate decides to get talkative. How would you respond when she says the following? (Sample responses can be found in Appendix A.)

1. Bonjour. ______________________________
2. Comment vous appelez-vous? ______________________________

continues

continued

3. Comment allez-vous? ______________________________
4. Vous êtes-d'où? ______________________________
5. Quel est votre métier? ______________________________

Curiosity Killed a Cat ... but Not You

Picture this: That sublime hunk/babe in seat 6B—you think he's/she's cute. What phrases do you need to probe more deeply and develop the relationship of your dreams? You have a million questions, and you want thorough answers. You're going to have to ask information questions to find out all the relevant facts you seek. Whatever the situation or problem, you'll be able to see it through with the words and expressions in the following table.

Questions

Word/Phrase	Pronunciation	Meaning
à quelle heure	*ah kehl uhr*	at what time
à qui	*ah kee*	to whom
à quoi	*ah kwah*	to what
avec qui	*ah-vehk kee*	with whom
avec quoi	*ah-vehk kwah*	with what
de qui	*duh kee*	of, about, from whom
de quoi	*duh kwah*	of, about, from what
combien (de + noun)	*kohN-byaN (duh)*	how much, many
comment	*kohN-mahN*	how
où	*oo*	where
d'où	*doo*	from where
pourquoi	*poor-kwah*	why
quand	*kahN*	when
qui	*kee*	who, whom
que	*kuh*	what
qu'est-ce que	*kehs-kuh*	what
quoi	*kwah*	what

Getting Information 1-2-3

You're ready to make your move. What's your opening line? Something corny like "Excuse me, where are you from?" or "Where are you going?" Or perhaps you have a more interesting question to break the ice. No matter how you choose to pursue your line of questioning, you'll find that the easiest way to ask for information is to put the question word immediately after the verbal phrase or thought. Here are some questions you might want to ask a traveling companion:

Vous voyagez (Tu voyages) **avec qui?**

Vous voyagez (Tu voyages) **pourquoi?**

Vous voyagez (Tu voyages) **comment?**

Vous parlez (Tu parles) **de qui? de quoi?**

Vous regardez (Tu regardes) **quoi?**

Vous êtes (Tu es) **d'où?**

Vous habitez (Tu habites) **où** en France?

Le vol (The flight) arrive **quand? à quelle heure?**

Un soda coûte **combien?**

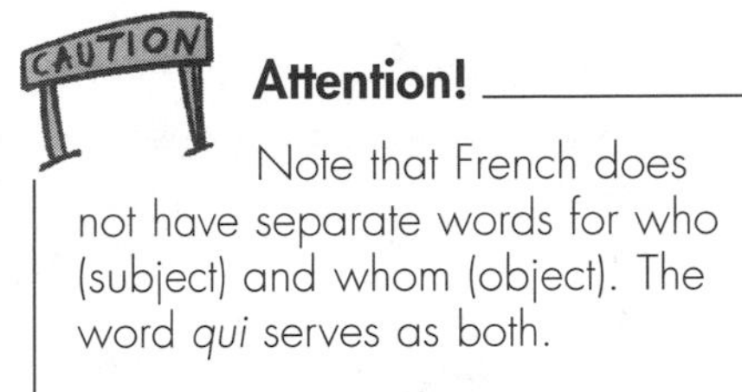

Attention!

Note that French does not have separate words for who (subject) and whom (object). The word *qui* serves as both.

Getting Information Using *Est-ce Que*

Information questions can also be asked by using *est-ce que*. This is done by putting the question word at the very beginning of the sentence and then adding *est-ce que* before the verbal phrase or thought:

Avec qui est-ce que vous voyagez (tu voyages)?

Pourquoi est-ce que vous voyagez (tu voyages)?

Comment est-ce que vous voyagez (tu voyages)?

De qui/De quoi est-ce que vous parlez (tu parles)?

Qu'est-ce que vous regardez (tu regardes)?

Attention!

Quoi, when it stands alone, becomes *que* (*qu'*) before *est-ce que*, as follows:

Tu veux faire quoi?

Qu'est-ce que tu veux faire? (What do you want to do?)

D'où est-ce que vous êtes (tu es)?

Où est-ce que vous habitez (tu habites) en France?

Quand/À quelle heure est-ce que le vol (the flight) arrive?

Combien est-ce qu'un soda coûte?

Getting Information Using Inversion

Finally, you can use inversion to ask information questions. Put the question word(s) (as listed in the previous table) before the inverted subject pronoun and conjugated verb form:

Avec qui voyagez-vous (voyages-tu)?

Pourquoi voyagez-vous (voyages-tu)?

Comment voyagez-vous (voyages-tu)?

De qui/De quoi parlez-vous (parles-tu)?

Que regardez-vous (regardes-tu)?

D'où êtes-vous (es-tu)?

Où habitez-vous (habites-tu) en France?

Quand/À quelle heure le vol (the flight) arrive-t-il?

Combien coûte-t-il un soda?

You will probably ask for information in a variety of different ways. No doubt you'll choose the way that feels more comfortable and seems to flow. Most of the time, however, you will probably tack the question word or phrase onto the end of your statement (as in *Vous êtes d'où?*). Why not? It's easy and it works. Using *est-ce que* may be your choice on occasion, especially if you have a noun subject (as in *À quelle heure est-ce que l'avion arrive?*). At other times, you might find it preferable to invert (as in *Que cherches-tu?*). Whichever way you choose, you will be perfectly understood and will get the information you need.

CAUTION

Attention!

Quoi, when it stands alone, becomes *que* (*qu'*) when inversion is used:

Tu veux faire ***quoi?***

Que veux-tu ***faire?***

Getting the Scoop

Read each of the following paragraphs. Ask as many questions as you can based on the information given to you in each selection. In paragraph A, you are asking about Robert. In paragraph B, you must ask Georgette questions about herself. Sample responses can be found in Appendix A.

A. Robert est des États-Unis. Il voyage avec sa famille en France en voiture. Ils passent deux mois en France. Ils désirent visiter tous les villages typiques. Ils retournent à Pittsburgh en septembre.

____

____

____

____

B. Je m'appelle Georgette. Je suis de Nice. Je cherche une correspondante américaine parce que je désire pratiquer l'anglais. Je parle anglais seulement quand je suis en classe. J'adore aussi la musique. Je suis sérieuse.

____

____

____

____

The Least You Need to Know

- Choose your words carefully! The greeting words you use depend on your familiarity with that person.
- The verb *être* is one of the most useful verbs in French. It is essential to memorize it because it is irregular.
- You can ask yes-or-no questions by using intonation, the tag *n'est-ce pas*, the phrase *est-ce que* at the beginning of a sentence, and inversion.
- You can get information easily by learning a few key words and phrases and then placing them at the end of the thought, before *est-ce que* at the beginning of the sentence, or before an inverted question form.

Chapter 9

I'd Like to Get to Know You

In This Chapter

- Family members
- Showing possession
- Introducing family and friends
- The irregular verb *avoir* (to have)
- Describing people and things

If you've successfully used the linguistic tools provided in the preceding chapter, you should be well on your way to introducing yourself and making new friends. You certainly don't want to appear rude, so how about introducing your family members to your new acquaintances? Perhaps you, too, will meet a new friend and be introduced to members of his or her family. Whatever the circumstances, it helps to be prepared.

Let's say there is someone in particular you would like to meet. Before you make your introduction, however, you'd like to find out a few things about this person. This chapter gives you the tools to find out what your potential pal is really like.

Here's the Clan

How many times have you opened your mouth during the course of a conversation only to find that you've done a magnificent job of sticking your foot in it? If you're anything like me, it's probably happened more often than you care to remember. Have you ever (as I have done) mistaken someone's father for his grandfather? Or, worse yet, someone's wife for his mother? I've learned not to make any assumptions when I meet someone. The following table helps you avoid a potentially embarrassing situation.

Family Members

French	Pronunciation	Meaning
Male		
le père	*luh pehr*	father
le grand-père	*luh grahN-pehr*	grandfather
le beau-père	*luh bo-pehr*	father-in-law
l'enfant	*lahN-fahN*	child
le frère	*luh frehr*	brother
le demi-frère	*luh duh-mee frehr*	stepbrother
le beau-fils	*luh bo-fees*	stepson
le fils	*luh fees*	son
l'oncle	*lohNkl*	uncle
le cousin	*luh koo-zahN*	cousin
le neveu	*luh nuh-vuh*	nephew
le mari	*luh mah-ree*	husband
le gendre	*luh zhahNdr*	son-in-law
le petit ami	*luh puh-tee tah-mee*	boyfriend
Female		
la mère	*lah mehr*	mother
la grand-mère	*lah grahN-mehr*	grandmother
la belle-mère	*lah behl-mehr*	mother-in-law
l'enfant	*lahN-fahN*	child
la soeur	*lah suhr*	sister
la demi-soeur	*lah duh-mee suhr*	stepsister
la belle-fille	*lah behl-fee-y*	stepdaughter
la fille	*lah fee-y*	daughter

French	Pronunciation	Meaning
la tante	*lah tahNt*	aunt
la cousine	*lah koo-zeen*	cousin
la nièce	*lah nyehs*	niece
la femme	*lah fahm*	wife
la belle-fille	*lah behl-fee-y*	daughter-in-law
la petite amie	*lah puh-tee tah-mee*	girlfriend

So you've got a large family. Sometimes it can be easier to group our kids, parents, and grandparents together when we speak about them. Here are some useful plurals and their spellings.

les enfants	*lay zahN-fahN*	the children
les parents	*lay pah-rahN*	the parents
les grands-parents	*lay grahN-pah-rahN*	the grandparents
les beaux-parents	*lay bo pah-rahN*	the in-laws

You Belong to Me

Don't be upset, but you're probably possessed. That is, you're somebody's somebody: your mother's child, your friend's friend, your brother's sister, or your sister's brother. There are two ways to show possession in French: by using the preposition *de* and by using possessive adjectives.

Possession with *de*

To show possession in English, we put apostrophe + s ('s) or s + apostrophe (s') after a noun, but there is no 's in French to show possession. To translate "Roger's mother" into French, a speaker would have to say "the mother of Roger," as in *la mère de Roger*. The preposition *de* means "of" and is used to express possession or relationship. *De* is repeated before each noun and becomes *d'* before a vowel.

C'est le père de Jean et d'Anne.
He's John and Anne's father.

If the possessor is referred to not by name but by a common noun, such as "the boy" or "the parents" ("He is the boy's father"—the father of the boy; or "That's the parents' car"—the car of the parents), then *de* contracts with the definite articles *le* and *les* to express "of the," as shown here.

Contractions with *de*

de + le	du	Ce sont les parents *du* garçon.
de + les	des	Ce sont les parents *des* jeunes filles.

No changes are necessary for *de + la* or *de + l'*.

Ce sont les parents *de la* fille.
Ce sont les parents *de l'*homme.

A Sense of Belonging

Now that you understand how to use *de* to express possession, how would you say the following?

1. Michael's mother
   ____
2. André and Marie's father
   ____
3. The girls' grandparents
   ____
4. The boy's uncle
   ____
5. The family's grandfather
   ____
6. The child's brother
   ____

Possessive Adjectives

The possessive adjectives "my," "your," "his," "her," and so on show that something belongs to someone. In French, possessive adjectives agree with the nouns they describe (the person or thing possessed) and not with the subject (the person possessing them). See how this compares with English.

English	French
He loves *his* mother.	Il aime *sa mère.*
She loves *her* mother.	Elle aime *sa mère.*
He loves *his* father.	Il aime *son père.*
She loves *her* father.	Elle aime *son père.*

Son and *sa* both mean "his" or "her" because the possessive adjective agrees with the noun it modifies, not with the subject. Therefore, "her father" translates into *son père* because *son* agrees with the word *père*, which is masculine, and "his mother" translates into *sa mère* because *sa* agrees with the word *mère*, which is feminine. This difference makes French very tricky to English speakers. Just remember that it is important to know the gender (masculine or feminine) of the noun possessed. When in doubt, look it up! The following list summarizes the use of possessive adjectives.

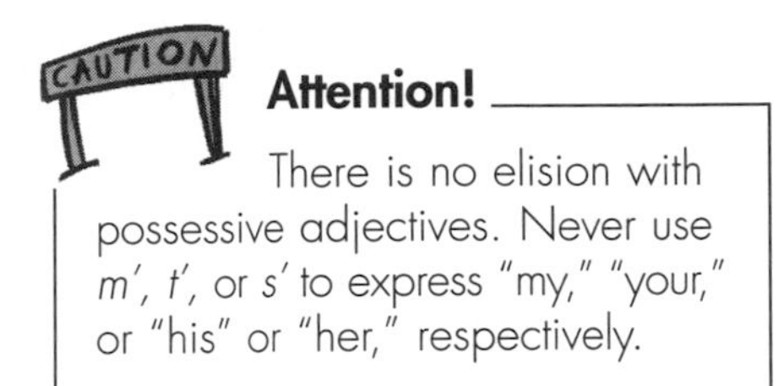

Attention!

There is no elision with possessive adjectives. Never use *m'*, *t'*, or *s'* to express "my," "your," or "his" or "her," respectively.

- Possessive adjectives used before masculine singular nouns or feminine singular nouns beginning with a vowel:

mon (*mohN*) my	notre (*nohtr*) our
ton (*tohN*) your (fam.)	votre (*vohtr*) your (pol.)
son (*sohN*) his, her	leur (*luhr*) their

Note: The French use *mon*, *ton*, and *son* before feminine nouns beginning with a vowel to prevent a clash between two pronounced vowel sounds:

mon ami (my male friend)	mon amie (my female friend)

- Possessive adjectives used before feminine singular nouns beginning with a consonant only:

ma (*mah*) my	notre (*nohtr*) our
ta (*tah*) your (fam.)	votre (*vohtr*) your (pol.)
sa (*sah*) his, her	leur (*luhr*) their

- Possessive adjectives used before all plural nouns:

mes (*may*) my	nos (*no*) our
tes (*tay*) your (fam.)	vos (*vo*) your (pol.)
ses (*say*) his, her	leurs (*luhr*) their

It's a Matter of Preference

Do you have a favorite song, color, restaurant, or vacation spot? We all have our own individual preferences. What are yours? Express them by using the correct possessive adjective (*mon*, *ma*, *mes*).

continues

continued

Examples:
acteur favori: Mon acteur favori est Danny DeVito.
acteurs favoris: Mes acteurs favoris sont Mel Gibson et Patrick Swayze.

1. actrices favorites: ______________________________
2. restaurants favoris: ______________________________
3. couleur favorite: ______________________________
4. chanson (song) favorite: ______________________________
5. sport favori: ______________________________
6. film favori: ______________________________

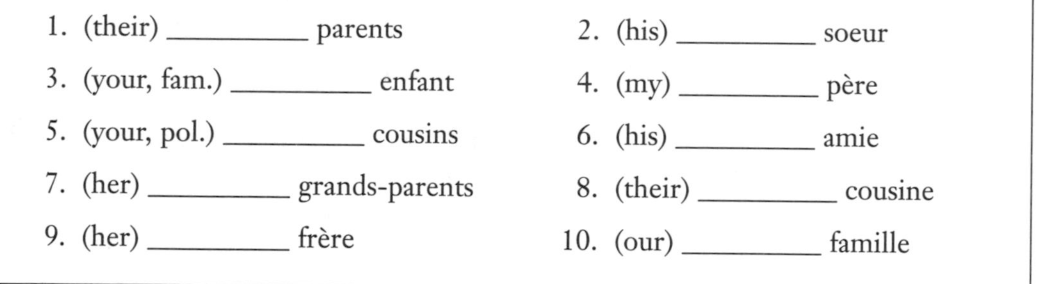

Totally Possessed

Give the possessive adjective you would use to talk about these people:

1. (their) __________ parents
2. (his) __________ soeur
3. (your, fam.) __________ enfant
4. (my) __________ père
5. (your, pol.) __________ cousins
6. (his) __________ amie
7. (her) __________ grands-parents
8. (their) __________ cousine
9. (her) __________ frère
10. (our) __________ famille

Introductions

Let me introduce myself. My name is Gail. And I'd love for you to meet my husband, Doug, who's helped me tremendously with this book. Do you know my sons, Eric and Michael? Eric is a computer wiz. This manuscript couldn't have been typed without him. Michael, a U.S. naval officer, is my source of moral support and is a terrific salesman. Now let's make some introductions in French:

> Permettez-moi de me présenter. Je m'appelle __________.
> *pehr-meh-tay mwah duh muh pray-zahN-tay. zhuh mah-pehl*
> Let me introduce myself. My name is __________.

You might ask about a companion:

Vous connaissez (Tu connais) mon cousin, Roger?
voo koh-neh-say (tew koh-neh) mohN koo-zahN, roh-zhay
Do you know my cousin, Roger?

If the answer is *no* (*non*), you would say:

Je vous présente (Je te présente) mon cousin, Roger.
zhuh voo pray-zahNt (zhuh tuh pray-zahNt) mohN koo-zahN, roh-zhay
Let me introduce my cousin, Roger.

or

C'est mon cousin, Roger.
seh mohN koo-zahN, roh-zhay
This is my cousin, Roger.

To express pleasure at having met someone, you might say:

Formally

Je suis content(e) [heureux (heureuse), enchanté(e)] de vous connaître.
zhuh swee kohN-tahN [zuh-ruh(z), zahN-shahN-tay] duh voo koh-nehtr
I am glad (happy, delighted) to know you.

Informally

Enchanté(e). C'est un plaisir.
ahN-shahN-tay. seh tuhN pleh-zeer
Delighted. It's a pleasure.

The correct reply to an introduction is:

Moi de même.
mwah dmehm
The pleasure is mine.

CAUTION

Attention!

If you want to know a person's address and phone number, simply ask *Quelles sont tes (vos) coordonnées?* (*kehl sohN tay [voh] koh-ohr-doh-nay;* What's your address and phone number?)

Taking the Conversation a Little Further

Perhaps you would like to discuss how many children you have or your age, or you might want to describe family members or friends who aren't present. A verb that you will find most helpful is *avoir* (to have). Like the verb *être* (to be), *avoir* is an irregular verb, and all of its forms (as seen in the following table) must be memorized.

The Verb *Avoir* (to Have)

Conjugation	Pronunciation	Meaning
j'ai	*zhay*	I have
tu as	*tew ah*	you have
il, elle, on a	*eel, ehl, ohN ah*	he, she, one has
nous avons	*noo zah-vohN*	we have
vous avez	*voo zah-vay*	you have
ils, elles ont	*eel, ehlz ohN*	they have

Idioms with *Avoir*

In Chapter 4, I presented many idioms with *avoir* that express physical conditions. To refresh your memory, refer to that chapter.

Now you are ready for some new *avoir* idioms. Perhaps you would like to thank a family for giving you the opportunity to stay in their home. You might be tempted to give a French twist to our word "opportunity." After all, *opportunité* does have a French ring to it. When you look up your creation (*opportunité*) in a bilingual dictionary, you will find that the word does exist, but it doesn't mean what you had hoped. (In fact, it means "expediency, advisability, fitness.") To avoid other mistakes, study the *avoir* idioms in the following table.

Idioms with *Avoir*

L'idiome	Pronunciation	Meaning
avoir l'occasion de	*ah-vwahr loh-kah-zyohN duh*	to have the opportunity to
avoir de la chance	*ah-vwahr duh lah shahNs*	to be lucky
avoir l'habitude de	*ah-vwahr lah-bee-tewd duh*	to be accustomed to
avoir l'intention de	*ah-vwahr laN-tahN-syohn duh*	to intend to
avoir le temps de	*ah-vwahr luh tahN duh*	to have the time to
avoir lieu	*ah-vwahr lyuh*	to take place

Make sure to conjugate the verb when you use it in context.

J'ai l'occasion de voyager.
I have the opportunity to travel.

Avez-vous l'intention de partir?
Do you intend to leave?

Ils n'ont pas le temps d'attendre.
They don't have the time to wait.

Using Avoir

Avoir is a verb that you'll be constantly using. Now that you've taken the time to learn all of its forms and useful idiomatic expressions, see if you can properly complete the following thoughts:

avoir de la chance	avoir l'occasion de
avoir l'habitude de	avoir le temps de
avoir l'intention de	avoir lieu

1. Tu ne travailles pas. Alors tu ________________ aider tes parents.
2. Il regarde la télévision tous les jours. Il ________________ regarder la télévision.
3. Vous avez gagné (*won*) la loterie. Vous ________________.
4. Elles sont riches. Elles ________________ visiter la France chaque année (*every year*).
5. J'étudie le français. Un jour j'________________ d'aller (*to go*) à Paris.
6. La cérémonie ________________ aujourd'hui (*today*).

What's He/She Like?

I've been blabbing about myself for several chapters now. Are you curious to know what I'm like? Do you have a mental picture of what a French author looks like? Did you guess brunette (thank you, L'Oréal), brown eyes, 5'4", thin, and young at heart? (I'd tell you my real age, but my students might be curious enough to read this book and discover the answer to a very well-kept secret.) That's me.

If you want to describe a person, place, thing, or idea in detail, you must use adjectives. French adjectives always agree in gender (masculine or feminine) and number (singular or plural) with the nouns or pronouns they modify. In other words, all the words in a French sentence must match:

Son père est *content.*	Sa mère est *contente.*
Her father is happy.	Her mother is happy.

Memory Enhancer

Fortunately, many adjectives follow the same, or almost the same, rules for gender and plural formation as the nouns you studied in Chapter 6.

Adjectives Show Gender

With most adjectives, you form the feminine by simply adding an *e* to the masculine form, as shown in the following table. A pronunciation change occurs when an *e* is added after a consonant. That consonant, which is silent in the masculine, is pronounced in the feminine form. When the *e* is added after a vowel, there is no change in pronunciation.

Forming Feminine Adjectives

Masculine	Pronunciation	Feminine	Pronunciation	Meaning
âgé	*ah-zhay*	âgée	*ah-zhay*	old, aged
américain	*ah-may-ree-kahN*	américaine	*ah-may-ree-kehn*	American
amusant	*ah-mew-zahN*	amusante	*ah-mew-zahNt*	amusing, fun
bleu	*bluh*	bleue	*bluh*	blue
blond	*blohN*	blonde	*blohNd*	blond
charmant	*shahr-mahN*	charmante	*shahr-mahNt*	charming
content	*kohN-tahN*	contente	*kohN-tahNt*	glad
court	*koor*	courte	*koort*	short
dévoué	*day-voo-ay*	dévouée	*day-voo-ay*	devoted
élégant	*ay-lay-gahN*	élégante	*ay-lay-gahNt*	elegant
fatigué	*fah-tee-gay*	fatiguée	*fah-tee-gay*	tired
fort	*fohr*	forte	*fohrt*	strong
français	*frahN-seh*	française	*frahN-sehz*	French
grand	*grahN*	grande	*grahNd*	big
haut	*o*	haute	*ot*	tall, big
intelligent	*aN-teh-lee-zhahN*	intelligente	*aN-teh-lee-zhahNt*	intelligent
intéressant	*aN-tay-reh-sahN*	intéressante	*aN-tay-reh-sahNt*	interesting
joli	*zhoh-lee*	jolie	*zhoh-lee*	pretty
lourd	*loor*	lourde	*loord*	heavy
occupé	*oh-kew-pay*	occupée	*oh-kew-pay*	busy
ouvert	*oo-vehr*	ouverte	*oo-vehrt*	open
parfait	*pahr-feh*	parfaite	*pahr-feht*	perfect
petit	*puh-tee*	petite	*puh-teet*	small

Masculine	Pronunciation	Feminine	Pronunciation	Meaning
poli	*poh-lee*	polie	*poh-lee*	polite
prochain	*proh-shaN*	prochaine	*proh-shehn*	next
situé	*see-tew-ay*	située	*see-tew-ay*	situated

If an adjective already ends in *-e*, it is not necessary to make any changes at all. Both the masculine and feminine forms are spelled and pronounced exactly the same. (See also the adjectives in Chapter 3.)

- aimable (*eh-mahbl;* nice)
- célèbre (*say-lehbr;* famous)
- célibataire (*say-lee-bah-tehr;* single)
- chauve (*shov;* bald)
- comique (*koh-meek;* comical)
- drôle (*drohl;* funny)
- facile (*fah-seel;* easy)
- faible (*fehbl;* weak)
- formidable (*fohr-mee-dahbl;* great)
- honnête (*oh-neht;* honest)
- maigre (*mehgr;* thin)
- magnifique (*mah-nyee-feek;* magnificent)
- malade (*mah-lahd;* sick)
- mince (*maNs;* thin)
- moderne (*moh-dehrn;* modern)
- pauvre (*pohvr;* poor)
- populaire (*poh-pew-lehr;* popular)
- propre (*prohpr;* clean)
- riche (*reesh;* rich)
- sale (*sahl;* dirty)
- splendide (*splahN-deed;* great)
- sympathique (*saN-pah-teek;* nice)
- triste (*treest;* sad)
- vide (*veed;* empty)

If a masculine adjective ends in *-x*, the feminine is formed by changing *-x* to *-se*, which gives the feminine ending a *z* sound, as shown in the following table.

Adjectives Ending in *-eux* and *-euse*

Masculine	Pronunciation	Feminine	Pronunciation
affectueux	*ah-fehk-tew-uh*	affectueuse	*ah-fehk-tew-uhz*
ambitieux	*ahN-bee-syuh*	ambitieuse	*ahN-bee-syuhz*
courageux	*koo-rah-zhuh*	courageuse	*koo-rah-zhuhz*
curieux	*kew-ryuh*	curieuse	*kew-ryuhz*
dangereux	*dahNzh-ruh*	dangereuse	*dahNzh-ruhz*
délicieux	*day-lee-syuh*	délicieuse	*day-lee-syuhz*
furieux	*few-ryuh*	furieuse	*few-ryuhz*
généreux	*zhay-nay-ruh*	généreuse	*zhay-nay-ruhz*
heureux (happy)	*uh-ruh*	heureuse	*uh-ruhz*

continues

Adjectives Ending in *-eux* and *-euse* (continued)

Masculine	Pronunciation	Feminine	Pronunciation
malheureux (unhappy)	*mahl-uh-ruh*	malheureuse	*mahl-uh-ruhz*
paresseux (lazy)	*pah-reh-suh*	paresseuse	*pah-reh-suhz*
sérieux	*say-ryuh*	sérieuse	*say-ryuhz*

If a masculine adjective ends in *-f*, the feminine is formed by changing *-f* to *-ve*. See the following table for pronunciation changes.

Adjectives Ending in *-f* and *-ve*

Masculine	Pronunciation	Feminine	Pronunciation
actif	*ahk-teef*	active	*ahk-teev*
attentif	*ah-tahN-teef*	attentive	*ah-tahN-teev*
imaginatif	*ee-mah-zhee-nah-teef*	imaginative	*ee-mah-zhee-nah-teev*
impulsif	*aN-pewl-seef*	impulsive	*aN-pewl-seev*
intuitif	*aN-tew-ee-teef*	intuitive	*aN-tew-ee-teev*
naïf	*nah-eef*	naïve	*nah-eev*
neuf (new)	*nuhf*	neuve	*nuhv*
sportif	*spohr-teef*	sportive	*spohr-teev*
vif (lively)	*veef*	vive	*veev*

If a masculine adjective ends in *-er*, the feminine is formed by changing *-er* to *-ère*, as shown in the following table.

Adjectives Ending in *-er* and *-ère*

Masculine	Pronunciation	Feminine	Pronunciation	Meaning
cher	*shehr*	chère	*shehr*	dear, expensive
dernier	*dehr-nyay*	dernière	*dehr-nyehr*	last
entier	*ahN-tyay*	entière	*ahN-tyehr*	entire
étranger	*ay-trahN-zhay*	étrangère	*ay-trahN-zhehr*	foreign
fier	*fyehr*	fière	*fyehr*	proud
léger	*lay-zhay*	légère	*lay-zhehr*	light
premier	*pruh-myay*	première	*pruh-myehr*	first

Culture Capsule

Although French men become *âgé* or *vieux* as they mature, French women are considered forever young. Until her teens, a girl is *tout jeune* (very young). During adolescence and her 20s, she becomes *une jeune fille* (a young girl). In her 30s, she is *encore jeune* (still young). A middle-aged woman remains *jeune toujours* (as young as ever). And an older woman, in her 70s or 80s, is considered *éternellement jeune* (forever young).

Some masculine adjectives double the final consonant and then add *e* to form the feminine, as shown in the following table.

Adjectives That Double Their Consonants

Masculine	Pronunciation	Feminine	Pronunciation	Meaning
ancien	*ahN-syaN*	ancienne	*ahN-syehn*	ancient, old
bas	*bah*	basse	*bahs*	low
bon	*bohN*	bonne	*bohn*	good
européen	*ew-roh-pay-aN*	européenne	*ew-roh-pay-ehn*	European
gentil	*zhahN-tee-y*	gentille	*zhahN-tee-y*	nice, kind
gros	*gro*	grosse	*gros*	fat, big
mignon	*mee-nyohN*	mignonne	*mee-noyhn*	cute

Finally, the adjectives in the following table have irregular feminine forms that must be memorized.

Irregular Adjectives

Masculine	Pronunciation	Feminine	Pronunciation	Meaning
beau*	*bo*	belle	*behl*	beautiful
blanc	*blahN*	blanche	*blahNsh*	white
complet	*kohN-pleh*	complète	*kohN-pleht*	complete
doux	*doo*	douce	*doos*	sweet, gentle
faux	*fo*	fausse	*fos*	false
favori	*fah-voh-ree*	favorite	*fah-voh-reet*	favorite
frais	*freh*	fraîche	*frehsh*	fresh
long	*lohN*	longue	*lohNg*	long

continues

Irregular Adjectives (continued)

Masculine	Pronunciation	Feminine	Pronunciation	Meaning
nouveau*	*noo-vo*	nouvelle	*noo-vehl*	new
vieux*	*vyuh*	vieille	*vyay*	old

**The French use special forms*—bel, nouvel, *and* vieil—*before masculine nouns beginning with a vowel or vowel sound to prevent a clash between two pronounced vowel sounds. This allows the language to flow.*

un bel appartement *un nouvel appartement* *un vieil appartement*

If the adjective comes *after* the noun, the regular masculine form is used:

L'appartement est beau.
L'appartement est vieux.
L'appartement est nouveau.

When There's a Crowd

Perhaps you'd like to describe a physical or personality trait that is common to more than one of your family members. This is relatively simple because adjectives are often made plural in the same way as the nouns you've already studied.

The plural of most adjectives is formed by adding an unpronounced *s* to the singular form.

Singular	Plural
timide	timides
charmant(e)	charmant(e)s
joli(e)	joli(e)s
fatigué(e)	fatigué(e)s

If an adjective ends in *-s* or *-x*, it is unnecessary to add the *s*.

Singular	Plural
exquis	exquis
heureux	heureux

Most masculine singular adjectives that end in *-al* change *-al* to *-aux* in the plural.

Singular	Plural
spécial	spéciaux

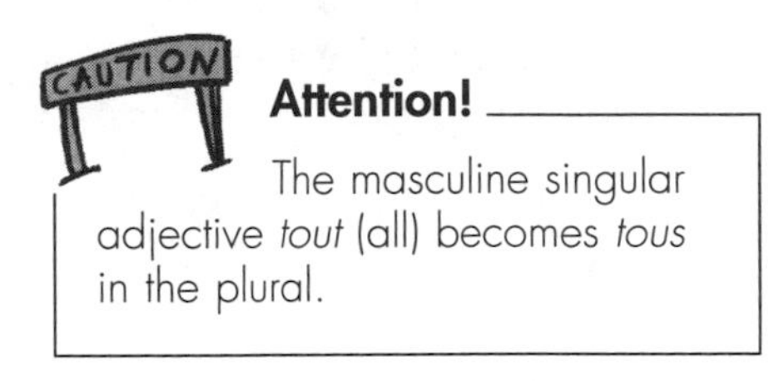

Attention!

The masculine singular adjective *tout* (all) becomes *tous* in the plural.

Attention!

Des becomes *de* before an adjective.

For the irregular, masculine, singular adjectives *beau*, *nouveau*, and *vieux*, the problem of having two conflicting vowel sounds (one at the end of the adjective and the other at the beginning of the noun that follows) is eliminated by adding an *s* or an *x* when the plural is formed. This eliminates the need for a plural form for the special masculine singular adjectives *bel*, *nouvel*, and *vieil* that are used only before nouns beginning with a vowel or a vowel sound. Note the plural formation for these masculine adjectives.

Singular	Plural	Example
beau	beaux	de beaux films
bel	beaux	de beaux appartements
nouveau	nouveaux	de nouveaux films
nouvel	nouveaux	de nouveaux appartements
vieux	vieux	de vieux films
vieil	vieux	de vieux appartements

Get in Position

In French, most adjectives are placed after the nouns they modify. Compare this with English, in which we do the opposite:

un homme intéressant
an interesting man

Adjectives showing …

Beauty: beau, joli
Age: jeune, nouveau, vieux
Goodness (or lack of it): bon, gentil, mauvais, vilain
Size: grand, petit, court, long, gros, large

… generally precede the nouns they modify. Remember **BAGS,** and you'll have no trouble with these adjectives:

un beau garçon	une large avenue
a handsome boy	a wide avenue

If more than one adjective is being used in a description, put each adjective in its proper position:

une bonne histoire intéresante
a good, interesting story

Creative Descriptions

How would you describe the Eiffel Tower, the car of your dreams, the mayor of your city? Here's an opportunity to give your opinions about certain things by using appropriate adjectives. Complete your descriptions carefully using the rules you've learned. Sample responses can be found in Appendix A.

1. La Tour Eiffel est une ________ tour ________.
2. Les film français sont de ________ films ________.
3. Le président des États-Unis est un ________ homme ________.
4. Les boutiques parisiennes sont de ________ boutiques ________.
5. Le musée du Louvre est un ________ musée ________.

The Least You Need to Know

- There are no apostrophes in the French language to show possession. To show possession, you can use the following formula: thing possessed + *de* + possessor.
- To show possession using an adjective, the adjective must agree with the person or thing possessed, not with the possessor.
- *Avoir* is an important irregular verb that expresses not only physical conditions but also luck, intention, and opportunity.
- Adjectives agree in number and gender with the nouns they describe.
- Many adjectives follow the same rules for gender and plural formation as nouns.
- There are irregular adjectives and verbs. They follow no rules, so you'll have to memorize them.
- Adjectives generally are placed after the nouns they modify.

Chapter 10

Navigating the Airport

In This Chapter

- The ins and outs of airplanes and airports
- The irregular verb *aller* (to go)
- How to give and receive directions
- Getting help when you just don't understand

Congratulations! You've planned a trip, you've gotten on the plane, and you've had a very pleasant conversation with the person sitting next to you. You've gotten the names of some good restaurants, places you want to be sure to visit, and perhaps the phone number of someone to call who will show you around town.

Your plane hasn't even landed yet, but you are mentally preparing for all the things you'll have to do before you start off for your hotel—you must get your bags, go through customs, change some money, and find a means of transportation to get to your hotel. By the end of this chapter, you'll have accomplished these things and more.

On the Plane

A plane ride is often long and tedious. Sometimes you might experience some minor inconveniences or delays. During your trip, you might want to see about changing your seat, or perhaps you have some questions for the flight crew. Maybe they've stuck you in the smoking section and you're a militant nonsmoker, or maybe your traveling companion is seated a few rows in front of you, and you'd like to join him or her. Perhaps you'd simply like to ask the crew about takeoff and landing. The words and phrases in the following table will help you get information and solve simple problems you may encounter on board.

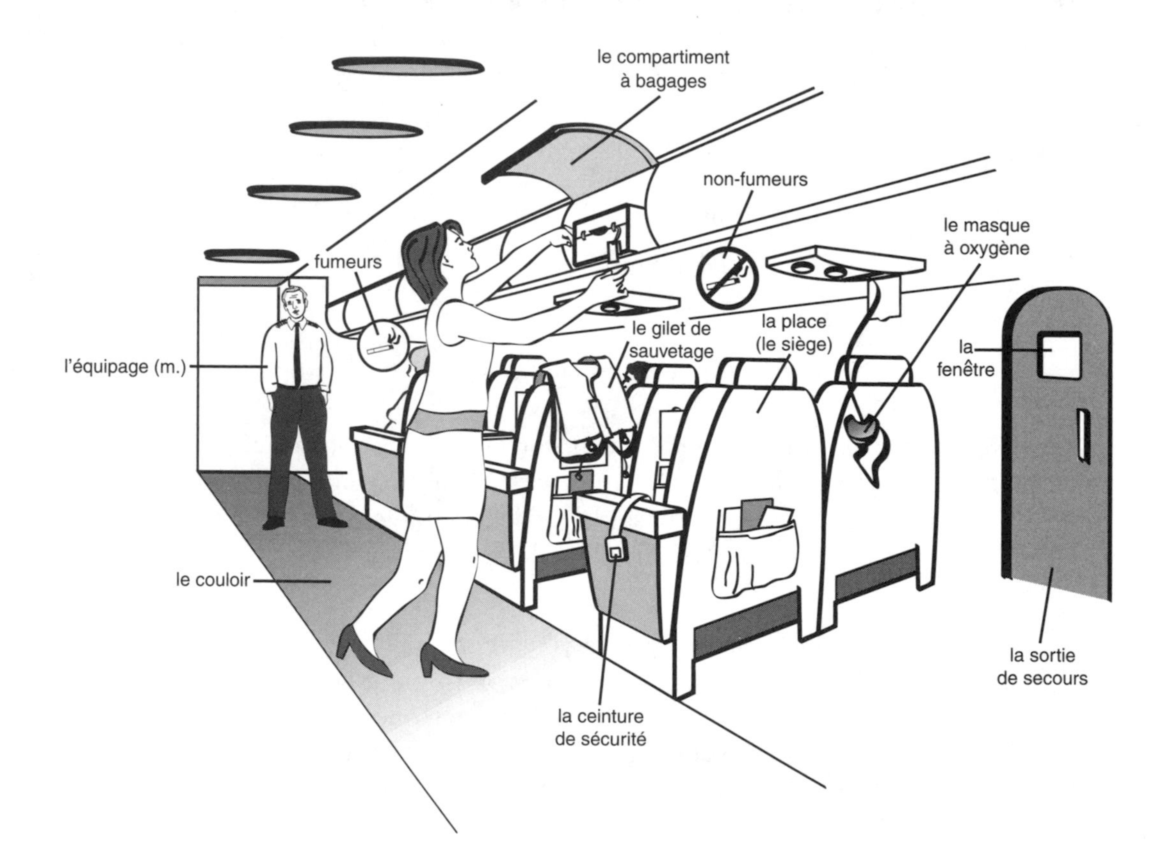

Inside the Plane

Airplane Term	French	Pronunciation
airplane	l'avion *m.*	*lah-vyohN*
aisle	le couloir	*luh kool-wahr*
(on the) aisle	côté couloir	*koh-tay kool-wahr*
crew	l'équipage *m.*	*lay-kee-pahzh*
emergency exit	la sortie (l'issue) de secours	*lah sohr-tee (lee-sew) duh suh-koor*
life vest	le gilet de sauvetage	*luh zhee-leh duh sohv-tahzh*
(non)smokers	(non)fumeurs	*(nohN) few-muhr*
row	le rang	*luh rahN*
seat	la place, le siège	*lah plahs, luh syehzh*
seatbelt	la ceinture de sécurité	*lah saN-tewr duh say-kew-ree-tay*
(by the) window	côté fenêtre	*koh-tay fuh-nehtr*

Airline Advice

If you've flown before, you know that airlines always have instructions about boarding, safety, and emergency procedures. Once on board, you will find an emergency card in your seat pocket, and your flight attendant will demonstrate any number of devices, from seat belts to oxygen masks. Read the following information to see if you can decipher the information the airline is trying to convey. A translation is shown in Appendix A.

En cabine (In the plane)

Pour votre confort et votre sécurité, n'emportez avec vous qu'un seul bagage de cabine.

N'y placez pas d'objets considerés comme dangereux (armes, couteaux, ciseaux, etc.). Ils seront retirés lors des contrôles de sécurité.

____

____

____

continues

continued

What advice are they giving about your bags?

En soute (In the hold)

Choisissez des bagages solides, fermant à clé. Fixez à l'intérieur et à l'extérieur une étiquette d'identification. Évitez les articles suivants: médicaments, devises (securities), chèques, papiers d'affaires ou importants, bijoux et autres objets de valeur. Conservez-les avec vous en cabine.

____

____

____

____

____

____

Customs

Upon entering a country all travelers must pass through passport control, where certain paperwork is filled out and a computer verifies identity.

Customs is next. Since every nation has different rules, it is best to find out beforehand what you may and may not bring into a country. Weapons and arms of any kind are strictly prohibited, as are illegal drugs and items made from endangered animals. So, if you're taking medication, don't forget to bring along a copy of your prescription. Most countries do not allow fruits, vegetables, or plants to pass through their borders for fear of insect infestation, and any pet purchased abroad will be thoroughly examined and then quarantined before allowed entry. Generally, there is a limit on tobacco items, perfumes, wines and spirits, and jewelry, and some items may be taxed if purchased in excess. Despite all the rules, most tourists have an easy time passing through customs. In many instances, your bags aren't even opened, and your dirty laundry will remain your little secret.

The following is an example of the information required of you upon entering a foreign country. The only words that might be unfamiliar to you are *imprimerie* (printing), *lieu* (place), and *naissance* (birth). You are now ready to fill out this card exactly as if you were a newly arrived tourist. Note that this card is not necessary for French nationals or for subjects of the European Union.

At the Airport

There is a lot to do after you are inside the airport, but don't worry—there will be plenty of signs to point you in the right direction. Sometimes it's hard to judge where to go first. My first stop is usually the bathroom. After that, I slowly progress from one area to the next, taking care of all my business at a slow and steady pace. The following table gives you all the words you need to know in the airport as well as outside on the way to your first destination.

Inside the Airport

Term	Le Terme	Pronunciation
airline	la ligne aérienne	*lah lee-nyuh ahy-ryehn*
airline terminal	l'aérogare *f.*, le terminal	*lahy-roh-gahr, luh tehr-mee-nahl*
airport	l'aéroport	*lahy-roh-pohr*
arrival	l'arrivée	*lah-ree-vay*
baggage claim area	la bande, les bagages *m.*	*lah bahnde, lay bah-gahzh*
bathrooms	les toilettes *f.*	*lay twah-leht*
to board, embark	embarquer	*ahN-bahr-kay*
bus stop	l'arrêt de bus *m.*	*lah-reh duh bews*
car rental	la location de voitures	*lah loh-kah-syohN duh vwah-tewr*
carry-on luggage	les bagages à main *m.*	*lay bah-gahzh ah maN*
cart	le chariot	*luh shah-ryoh*
counter	le comptoir	*luh kohN-twahr*
customs	la douane	*lah doo-ahn*
departure	le départ	*luh day-pahr*
to deplane, disembark, exit	débarquer	*day-bahr-kay*
destination	la destination	*lah dehs-tee-nah-syohN*
elevators	les ascenseurs *m.*	*lay zah-sahN-suhr*
entrance	l'entrée *f.*	*lahN-tray*
exit	la sortie	*lah sohr-tee*
flight	le vol	*luh vohl*
gate	la porte	*lah pohrt*
information	les renseignements *m.*	*lay rahN-seh-nyuh-mahN*
landing	l'atterrissage *m.*	*lah-teh-ree-sahzh*

continues

Inside the Airport (continued)

Term	Le Terme	Pronunciation
lost and found	les objets trouvés *m.*	*lay zohb-zheh troo-vay*
to miss the flight	manquer (rater) le vol	*mahN-kay (rah-tay) luh vohl*
money exchange	le bureau de change	*luh bew-ro duh shahNzh*
passport control	le contrôle des passeports	*luh kohN-trohl day pahs-pohr*
porter	le porteur	*luh pohr-tuhr*
security check	le contrôle de sécurité	*luh kohN-trohl duh say-kew-ree-tay*
stop-over	l'escale *f.*	*lehs-kahl*
suitcase	la valise	*lah vah-leez*
take-off	le décollage	*luh day-koh-lahzh*
taxis	les taxis	*lay tahk-see*
ticket	le billet, le ticket	*luh bee-yeh, luh tee-keh*
trip	le voyage	*luh vwah-yahzh*

Signs Tell It All

With airport security at a maximum due to terrorist threats and bomb scares, you can be sure that you will see many signs indicating the rules that must be followed. It is very important that you understand what you may and may not do. Even if you break a rule unintentionally, it can be scary to be approached by an armed *gendarme* speaking a language in which you have limited fluency. The following are the signs you can expect to see in Charles de Gaulle airport. Read them carefully and then match each sign with the information it gives you. Students traveling abroad would be well advised to inquire about the International Student Identity Card issued by the Council on International Educational Exchange and the Youth International Educational Exchange Card issued by the Federation of International Youth Travel. For a very reasonable rate, these agencies offer enticing discounts to students.

Airport Signs

Which of the following signs is telling you each of the following?

1. If you leave something behind, it might be destroyed. ___
2. All of your baggage will be checked, even carry-on luggage. ___

3. You can be searched for hidden weapons. ___
4. You may carry a weapon if you declare it. ___
5. You can only use the baggage cart within the airport. ___
6. You shouldn't carry a suitcase for someone else. ___

a.

AVIS AUX PASSAGERS

Il est formellement interdit par la loi de transporter une arme dissimulée à bord d'un avion.

Les règlements en vigueur imposent l'inspection des passagers et des bagages à main lors de contrôle de sécurité.

Cette inspection peut être refusée. Les passagers refusant cette inspection ne seront pas autorisés à passer le contrôle de sécurité.

b.

Chariot reservé aux passagers; utilisation interdite au-delà du trottoir de l'aérogare.

c.

ATTENTION

Pour des raisons de sécurité, tout objet abandonné peut être détruit par les services de police.

Les passagers sont donc instamment priés de conserver leurs bagages avec eux.

d.

ATTENTION

Ne mettez pas votre sécurité en péril: n'acceptez aucun bagage d'une autre personne.

e.

Veuillez présenter tous vos bagages à l'enregistrement, y compris vos bagages à main.

f.

TRANSPORT DES ARMES À FEU

Les armes à feu transportées dans les bagages enregistrés doivent être déchargés et faire l'objet d'une déclaration auprès de nos services.

Les passagers transportant des armes sans les déclarer ou chargées sont passibles d'une amende de 1,000 dollars ou équivalent.

Going Places

It's easy to get lost in sprawling international airports. To get yourself back on track, you'll need to know how to ask the right questions. One of the verbs you'll use a lot is *aller* (to go), an irregular verb that you must memorize.

The Verb *Aller* (to Go)

Conjugation	Pronunciation	Meaning
je vais	*zhuh veh*	I go
tu vas	*tew vah*	you go
il, elle, on va	*eel, ehl, ohN vah*	he, she, one goes
nous allons	*noo zah-lohN*	we go
vous allez	*voo zah-lay*	you go
ils, elles vont	*eel, ehl vohN*	they go

Aller is generally followed by the preposition *à* (to). If the location to which the subject is going is masculine, *à* contracts with *le* (the) to become *au* (to the) and with *les* (the) to become *aux* (to the), as in the following examples:

Je vais au contrôle des passeports.
I'm going to the passport control.

No changes are necessary with *l'* or *la:*

Il va à l'aéroport.
He's going to the airport.

Use *aller* + *en* to express the many different ways to go someplace:

Je vais à Paris en voiture.
I'm going to Paris by car.

One exception is when you decide to walk:

Nous allons au restaurant à pied.
We're walking to the restaurant.

Aller is most commonly used idiomatically to express health:

Comment allez-vous?	Je vais bien (mal).
Comment vas-tu?	
How are you?	I'm fine (doing poorly).

Where To?

Tell where each person is going by giving the correct form of *aller.*

1. Nous __________ à Paris.
2. Marie __________ à Nice.
3. Tu __________ à Marseille.
4. Ils __________ à Grenoble.
5. Je __________ à Cannes.
6. Vous __________ à Bordeaux.

Where's the ...?

If the airport is unfamiliar to you, you may need to ask for directions. This is relatively easy to do. There are two different ways of asking:

Où est le comptoir? *Oo eh luh kohN-twahr?* Where is the counter?	Le comptoir, s'il vous plaît. *Luh kohN-twahr, seel voo pleh.* The counter, please.
Où sont les bagages? *Oo sohN lay bah-gahzh?* Where is the baggage claim?	Les bagages, s'il vous plaît. *Lay bah-gahzh, seel voo pleh.* The baggage claim, please.

Remember that you must use the verb *être* in its singular form *est* (is) if the place you are asking for is singular. If it is plural, use the plural *sont* (are).

Ask for It

Imagine you are lost at the airport. Ask for the following places in two ways.

1. bathrooms ____

   ____
2. passport control ____

   ____
3. customs ____

   ____
4. elevators ____

   ____

continues

continued

5. exit ______________________________

____

6. money exchange ______________________________

____

There It Is

Sometimes the place you are trying to find is right in front of you. For instance, suppose you're trying to locate the ticket counter. With all the noise and confusion, you lose your bearings and don't realize that you are standing near the very place you are trying to find. When you ask the gentlemen next to you for directions, he may reply:

Voici le comptoir.	Voilà le comptoir.
vwah-see luh kohN-twahr	*vwah-lah luh kohN-twahr*
Here is the counter.	There is the counter.

Memory Enhancer

To be very polite, use *veuillez* + infinitive to say please: *Veuillez entrer* (*vuh-yay ahN-tray;* Please enter).

More Complicated Directions

If the place you want to get to is not within pointing distance, you'll need other directions. The verbs in the following table are very helpful in getting you where you want to go or perhaps in helping someone else who is lost.

Verbs Giving Directions

Le Verbe	Pronunciation	Meaning
aller	*ah-lay*	to go
continuer	*kohN-tee-new-ay*	to continue
descendre	*day-sahNdr*	to go down
marcher	*mahr-shay*	to walk
monter	*mohN-tay*	to go up
passer	*pah-say*	to pass
prendre	*prahNdr*	to take
tourner	*toor-nay*	to turn
traverser	*trah-vehr-say*	to cross

When someone directs you to a location, that person is giving you a command. The subject of a command is understood to be you since you are being told where to go or what to do. Because there are two ways to say *you* in French (the familiar *tu* and the polite and always plural *vous*), there are two different command forms. Choose the form that best suits the situation. To form commands, simply drop the *tu* or *vous* subject pronoun:

Va tout droit.	Allez à gauche.
vah too drwah	*ah-lay ah gohsh*
Go straight ahead.	Go to the left.

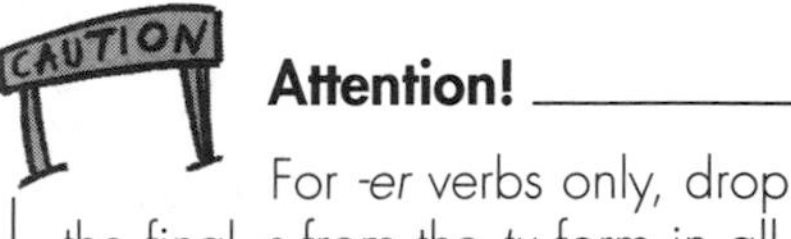

Attention!

For -*er* verbs only, drop the final -*s* from the *tu* form in all commands. Example: *Regarde!*

Giving Commands

You must use the command form to give directions. Use the *tu* or *vous* form (depending on your relationship to the person or the number of people to whom you are speaking) of the present tense of the verb.

Do not use the subject *tu* or *vous* when giving a command. Imagine for a moment that in Orly Airport a Hungarian tourist approaches you and asks for directions. He doesn't speak English, and you don't know a word of Hungarian. Fortunately, you both bought *The Complete Idiot's Guide to Learning French* and know a little French. Help the poor lost Hungarian man by practicing your commands. Complete the following table by filling in the missing command forms and their meanings.

Command Forms

Verb	Tu	Vous	Meaning
aller	Va!	Allez!	Go!
continuer	_____	_____	_____
descendre	_____	_____	_____
marcher	_____	_____	_____
monter	_____	_____	_____
passer	_____	_____	_____
prendre (Chapter 11)	Prends!	Prenez!	Take!
tourner	_____	_____	_____
traverser	_____	_____	_____

Two verbs that have very irregular command forms are *être* and *avoir*. Although they are used infrequently, you should memorize them.

	Être	Avoir
Tu form	Sois! *swah* Be!	Aie! *ay* Have!
Vous form	Soyez! *swah-yay* Be!	Ayez! *ay-yay* Have!

Prepositions

Prepositions are used to show the relation of a noun to another word in a sentence. Refresh your memory with the idiomatic expressions for direction and location from Chapter 4 that are, in fact, prepositional phrases. Then add the simple prepositions in the following table. They are useful for giving and receiving directions.

Simple Prepositions

La Préposition	Pronunciation	Meaning
à	*ah*	to, at
après	*ah-preh*	after
avant	*ah-vahN*	before
chez	*shay*	at the house (business) of
contre	*kohNtr*	against
dans	*dahN*	in
de	*duh*	from
derrière	*deh-ryehr*	behind
devant	*duh-vahN*	in front of
en	*ahN*	in
entre	*ahNtr*	between
loin (de)	*lwaN (duh)*	far (from)
par	*pahr*	by, through
pour	*poor*	for, in order to
près (de)	*preh (duh)*	near
sans	*sahN*	without

La Préposition	Pronunciation	Meaning
sous	*soo*	under
sur	*sewr*	on
vers	*vehr*	toward

Contractions

In certain cases, contractions form with the prepositions *à* and *de*, whether they are used alone or as part of a longer expression.

	le	les
à	au	aux
de	du	des

Allez à la douane.	La porte est à côté de la douane.
Allez à l'entrée.	La porte est à côté de l'entrée.

but

Allez *au* bureau de change.	La porte est à côté *du* bureau de change.
Allez *aux* bagages.	La porte est à côté *des* bagages.

Are You Dazed and Confused?

What if someone gives you directions that you don't understand? Perhaps the person to whom you are speaking is mumbling, is speaking too fast, has a strong accent, or uses words you don't know. Don't be embarrassed. Ask for help in a kind, polite manner. You'll find the phrases in the following table to be an invaluable aid if you need to have something repeated or if you need more information.

Expressing Confusion

Expression	L'expression	Pronunciation
Excuse me.	Excusez- (Excuse-) moi.	*ehk-skew-zay (ehk-skewz) mwah*
Excuse me.	Je m'excuse.	*zhuh mehk-skewz*

continues

Pardon me.	Pardon.	*pahr-dohN*

Expressing Confusion (continued)

Expression	L'Expression	Pronunciation
Pardon me.	Pardonnez- (Pardonne-) moi.	*pahr-doh-nay (pahr-dohn) mwah*
I don't understand.	Je ne comprends pas.	*zhuh nuh kohN-prahN pah*
I didn't understand.	Je n'ai pas compris.	*zhuh nay pah kohN-pree*
I didn't hear you.	Je ne vous (t') ai pas entendu(e).	*zhuh nuh voo zay (tay) pah zahN-tahN-dew*
Please repeat it.	Répétez (Répète), s'il vous (te) plaît.	*ray-pay-tay (ray-peht) seel voo (tuh) pleh*
One more time. (Again.)	Encore une fois.	*ahN-kohr ewn fwah*
Speak more slowly.	Parlez (Parle) plus lentement.	*pahr-lay (pahrl) plew lahNt-mahN*
What did you say?	Qu'est-ce que vous avez (tu as) dit?	*kehs-kuh voo zah-vay (tew ah) dee*
Did you say _____ or _____?	Vous avez (tu as) dit _____ ou _____?	*voo zah-vay (tew ah) dee _____ oo _____*

The Least You Need to Know

- The irregular verb *aller* is used to give directions and to speak about health and well-being.
- A few verbs are tremendously useful in giving and taking directions: *aller* (to go), *continuer, descendre, marcher, monter, passer, prendre* (to take), *tourner,* and *traverser* (to cross).
- Leave out the subject (*tu* or *vous*) when you give a command.
- Use prepositions to show the relationship of a noun to another word in the sentence.
- *À* + *le* contracts to *au. À* + *les* contracts to *aux.*
- *De* + *le* contracts to *du. De* + *les* contracts to *des.*
- If you don't understand what someone is saying to you, don't be afraid to say, "*Je*

Chapter 11

Getting There Without Delay

In This Chapter

- Planes, trains, and automobiles—getting around
- The irregular verb *prendre* (to take)
- Renting a car
- Cardinal numbers
- How to tell time

You'll probably find that it's far less painful and far more time-consuming than you thought to get through customs, find your bags, and change some money into francs. If you're lucky, you will have transfers (transportation provided as part of your travel package) to your hotel and someone waiting to whisk you away. If not, you must figure out on your own how you are going to get to the hotel. This chapter discusses your options.

For example, if you're visiting Paris, the Parisian R.A.T.P. (*Régie Autonome des Transports Parisiens*) is in charge of the user-friendly bus and subway system. Green Parisian buses post their route and destination on the outside front of the bus and their major stops on the bus's sides. The route of each line is indicated on a sign at every stop it makes. Free bus maps (*autobus Paris—Plan du Réseau*) are readily available at tourist offices and some *métro* booths. Buy tickets ahead of time at a *métro* station or *bureau de tabac* (tobacconist) because they cannot be purchased aboard the bus.

Planes, Trains, and Automobiles

Several means of transportation can get you from the airport to your hotel: bus, subway, train, taxi, or car. To make the decision that is right for you, keep the following considerations in mind: Do you really want to carry your bags on a bus or the subway? (Remember what you packed!) Although taxis are fast and efficient, they are costly. Do you feel up to renting a car in a foreign country where you are unfamiliar with the traffic laws and street signs? Think carefully before you make a choice.

A *Paris Visite* card, available through travel agencies, tourist offices, or subway and train stations, allows you to choose unlimited bus, subway, and train travel for three or five consecutive days. The *Formule 1* card is a one-day pass.

Means of Transportation	French	Pronunciation
bus	le bus (l'autobus)	*le bews (loh-toh-bews)*
car	l'auto *f.*	*lo-to*
car	la voiture	*lah vwah-tewr*
subway	le métro	*luh may-tro*
taxi	le taxi	*le tahk-see*
train	le train	*luh traN*

Culture Capsule

The 13 numbered Parisian subway lines are indicated by different colors on maps distributed everywhere: at *métro* stops, hotels, department stores, tourist offices, and so on. Each station displays a *plan du quartier,* a detailed map of the surrounding area. Transfers from one subway line to another are free, and connections are indicated by orange *correspondance* signs. You can transfer as often as you like on one ticket provided you do not exit to the street. Exits are clearly marked by blue *sortie* signs.

The Best Way to Go

Regardless of how you decide to get where you are going, you will need to use the irregular verb *prendre* (*prahNdr;* to take) to express which mode of transportation you have chosen. *Prendre* is a tricky verb: All singular forms end in a nasal sound, but the third person plural, *ils/elles*, is pronounced quite differently. The double *n*'s eliminate the need for an initial nasal sound and give the first *e* a more open sound. Pay close attention to the following table.

The Verb *Prendre* (to Take)

Conjugation	Pronunciation	Meaning
je prends	*zhuh prahN*	I take
tu prends	*tew prahN*	you take
il, elle, on prend	*eel, ehl, ohN prahN*	he, she, one takes
nous prenons	*noo pruh-nohN*	we take
vous prenez	*voo pruh-nay*	you take
ils, elles prennent	*eel, ehl prehn*	they take

Something Different

Travelers interested in visiting France from England and Belgium may now make use of the Chunnel. Although you can't drive through these new tunnels, *Le Shuttle* carries freight and cars with passengers (up to 180 vehicles) between England and France. Just drive a car onto a train at one end and drive off at the other—in just 35 minutes. Service is available 24 hours a day, and at peak times, trains depart every 15 minutes. No reservations are accepted, so drivers are accommodated on a first-come, first-served basis. Drivers pay a charge per car regardless of the number of occupants.

The other Chunnel service, *Eurostar*, carries only passengers (each train carries 800 people) and provides through service from London to Paris and London to Brussels.

It's Up to You

When asking questions about the mode of transportation you've chosen, you'll use the interrogative adjective *quel* (which, what). Just like all adjectives, "which" agrees with the noun it modifies. The following table shows how easy it is to make a match between the correct form of *quel* (keeping gender and number in mind) and the noun that follows it.

The Possessive Adjective *Quel*

	Masculine	Feminine
Singular	quel	quelle
Plural	quels	quelles

Be prepared for questions such as the following:

> Quel bus est-ce que vous prenez (tu prends)?
> *kehl bews ehs-kuh voo pruh-nay (tew prahN)*
> Which bus are you taking?
>
> Quelle marque de voiture est-ce que vous louez (tu loues)?
> *kehl mahrk duh vwah-tewr ehs-kuh voo loo-ay (tew loo)*
> What make of car are you renting?

The only verb that may separate *quel* from its noun is the verb *être:*

> Quel est votre (ton) nom?
> *kehl eh vohtr (tohN) nohN*
> What's your name?

Using *Quel*

Have you ever had a conversation with a friend who rambles on and on about a fabulous film she's just seen but never mentions the title? You're ready to explode from frustration when she finally decides to come up for air. You grab your chance and quickly interject: Which film? Here are some typical answers that don't give enough information. Pursue your line of questioning by using *quel.*

> Example:
> J'aime le film. *Quel film?*

1. Je prends le train. ______________________
2. J'aime la couleur. ______________________
3. J'achète (buy) les jolies blouses. ______________________
4. Je lis (read) de bons journaux. ______________________
5. Je loue une voiture. ______________________
6. Je cherche de bonnes cassettes. ______________________
7. Je regarde le match. ______________________
8. Je prépare des plats délicieux. ______________________

Fill 'er Up

If you are adventurous, you might want to rent a car at *une location de voitures.* Check out rates of a few car rentals before you make a decision because rates vary from agency to agency. Keep in mind that gasoline is very expensive in most foreign countries, usually more than double the price Americans pay. Familiarize yourself with all driving and traffic laws. The following phrases are very useful when renting a car:

Je voudrais louer une …
zhuh voo-dreh loo-ay ewn …
I would like to rent a (give make of car).

Je préfère la transmission automatique.
zhuh pray-fehr lah tranhz-mee-syohN o-toh-mah-teek
I prefer automatic transmission.

Quel est le tarif à la journée (à la semaine, au kilomètre)?
kehl eh luh tah-reef ah lah zhoor-nay (ah lah suh-mehn, o kee-lo-mehtr)
How much does it cost per day (per week, per kilometer)?

Quel est le montant de l'assurance?
kehl eh luh mohn-tahN duh lah-sew-rahNs
How much is the insurance?

Le carburant est compris?
luh kahr-bew-rahN eh kohN-pree
Is the gas included?

Acceptez-vous des cartes de crédit? Lesquelles?
ahk-sehp-tay voo day kahrt duh kray-dee? lay-kehl
Do you accept credit cards? Which ones?

If you've decided to rent a car, take a tip from me: Carefully inspect the car—inside and out—because you never know what might go wrong after you're on the road. Make sure there is *un cric* (*uhN kreek;* a jack) and *un pneu de secours* (*uhN pnuh duh suh-koor;* a spare tire) in the trunk.

Make sure to carefully inspect the outside of your rental car before driving away. You wouldn't want to be charged for damage you didn't do. The following table gives you the words you need to talk about the car's exterior.

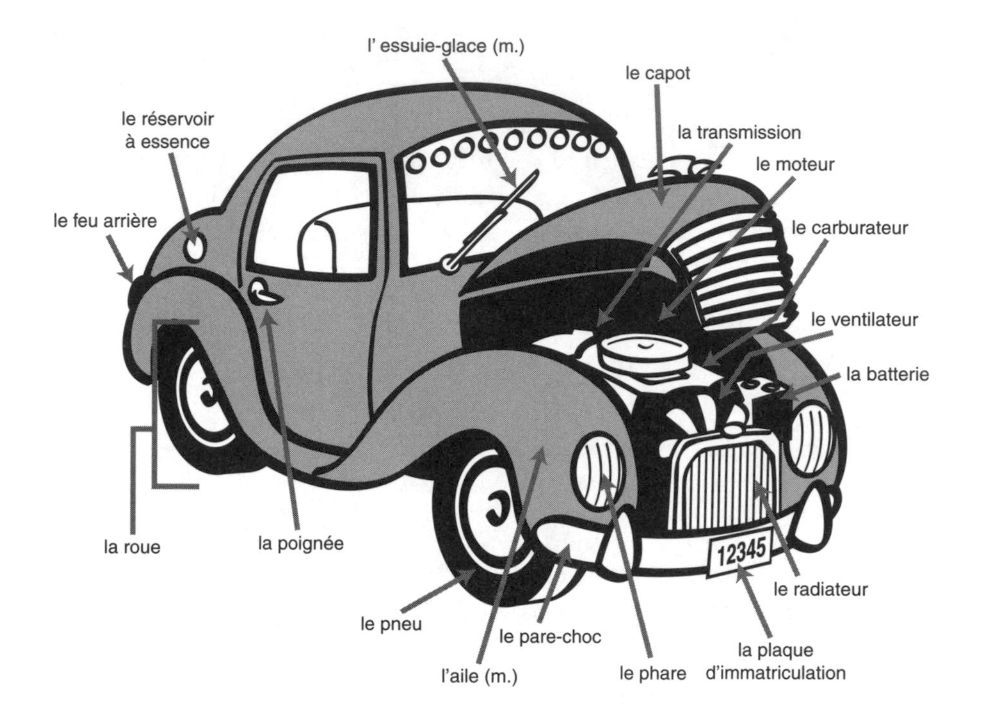

Outside the Car

Car Part	French	Pronunciation
battery	la batterie	*lah bah-tree*
bumper	le pare-choc	*luh pahr-shohk*
carburetor	le carburateur	*luh kahr-bew-rah-tuhr*
door handle	la poignée	*lah pwah-nyay*
fan	le ventilateur	*luh vahN-tee-lah-tuhr*
fender	l'aile *f.*	*lehl*
gas tank	le réservoir à essence	*lah ray-sehr-vwahr ah eh-sahNs*
headlight	le phare	*luh fahr*
hood	le capot	*luh kah-po*
license plate	la plaque d'immatriculation	*lah plahk dee-mah-tree-kew-lah-syohN*
motor	le moteur	*luh moh-tuhr*
radiator	le radiateur	*luh rahd-yah-tuhr*
tail light	le feu arrière	*luh fuh ah-ryehr*
tire	le pneu	*luh pnuh*

Car Part	French	Pronunciation
transmission	la transmission	*lah trahNz-mee-syohN*
trunk	le coffre	*luh kohfr*
wheel	la roue	*lah roo*
windshield wiper	l'essuie-glace *m.*	*leh-swee glahs*

You'll also want to verify that everything on the inside is functioning properly. The following table gives you the words you need to know to talk about the car's interior parts.

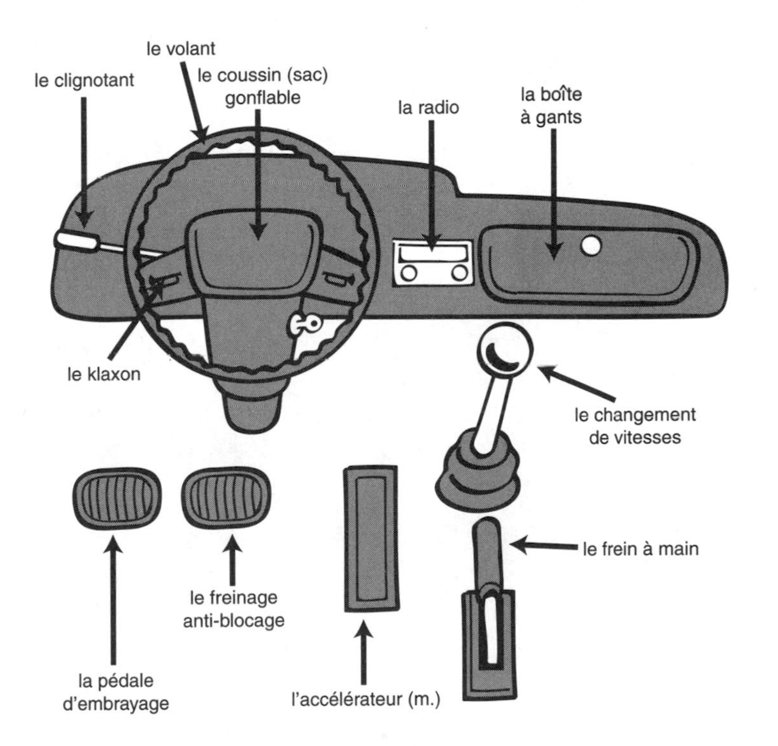

Inside the Car

Car Part	French	Pronunciation
accelerator	l'accélérateur *m.*	*lahk-say-lay-rah-tuhr*
air bag	le coussin (sac) gonflable	*luh koo-saN (sahk) gohn-flahbl*
antilock brake system	le freinage anti-blocage	*luh freh-nahzh ahn-tee bloh-kahzh*
brakes	les freins *m.*	*lay fraN*
clutch pedal	la pédale d'embrayage	*lah pay-dahl dahN-brah-yahzh*

continues

Inside the Car (continued)

Car Part	French	Pronunciation
directional signal	le clignotant	*luh klee-nyoh-tahN*
gear shift	le changement de vitesses	*luh shahNzh-mahN duh vee-tehs*
glove compartment	la boîte à gants	*lah bwaht ah gahN*
hand brake	le frein à main	*luh fraN ah maN*
horn	le klaxon	*luh klahk-sohN*
ignition	l'allumage *m.*	*lah-lew-mahzh*
radio	la radio	*lah rahd-yo*
steering wheel	le volant	*luh voh-lahN*

Feu (fire) refers to a traffic light. You are required to stop *au feu rouge* (at the red light), of course, and you may go *au feu vert* (at the green light).

Off You Go

If you decide to rent a car, you are required to fill out a rental agreement. Before renting a car, familiarize yourself with the terms and conditions of your rental contract. Read the fine print so that there is no misunderstanding when you return the car. You'll want everything to go smoothly. What does the following notice say?

MODALITÉS D'APPLICATION

RÉSERVATION

La réservation est recommandée au minimum vingt-quatre heures à l'avance.

CONDITIONS

Le forfait PARISCAR est applicable dans toutes les agences PARISCAR en France continentale. La durée de location facturée (minimum un jour) se calcule par tranche de vingt-quatre heures non fractionnable. Une tolérance de cinquante-neuf minutes est accordée. Au-delà de celle-ci, une journée supplémentaire sera facturée.

KILOMÉTRAGE

Le kilométrage inclus dans le forfait PARISCAR est illimité.

LOUEZ ICI, LAISSEZ AILLEURS

Ce service, permettant de restituer le véhicule dans une agence différente de l'agence de départ, est compris dans ce forfait.

ASSURANCES

En cas de dommages, seul un montant forfaitaire de 300 euros reste à la charge du locataire.

En cas de vol, seul un montant forfaitaire reste à la charge du locataire.

Il y a une garantie d'assistance technique et médicale vingt-quatre heures sur vingt-quatre.

CARBURANT

Le carburant n'est pas compris dans nos tarifs et reste à la charge du locataire.

VALIDITÉ

Les prix indiqués sont exprimés en euros. Ils sont modifiables sans préavis.

See Appendix A for translations. Remember that it is always a good idea to purchase extra insurance.

You're Going in the Right Direction

By all means, learn those road signs—some of them are not as obvious as they should be. It took a one-week vacation and a near accident in Saint-Martin for me to figure out that the sign with a horizontal line through it means NO ENTRY. Here are some road signs you need to be familiar with before you venture out on your own in a car.

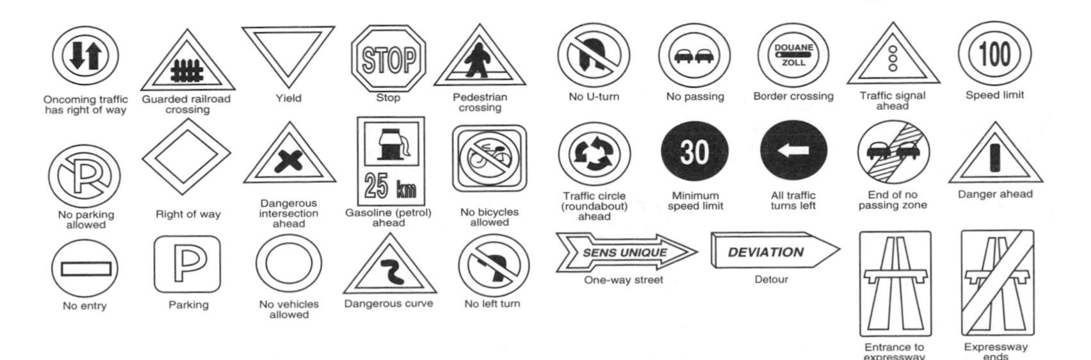

If you plan on driving, make sure you know your compass directions. They're all masculine.

au nord	à l'est	au sud	à l'ouest
o nohr	*ah lehst*	*o sewd*	*ah lwehst*
to the north	to the east	to the south	to the west

Having Trouble?

Here are some expressions you will need if you have trouble with a rental car:

Pourriez-vous m'aider, s'il vous plaît.
poo-ryay voo meh-day sel voo pleh
Could you help me please?

La voiture est en panne.
lah vwah-tewr eh tahN pahn
The car has broken down.

Pouvez-vous la réparer?
poo-vay voo lah ray-pah-ray
Can you fix it?

Quand sera-t-elle prête?
kahN suh-rah tehl preht
When will it be ready?

______ ne fonctionne(nt) [marche(nt)] pas.
______ *nuh fonNk-syohn [mahrsh] pah*
______ doesn't (don't) work.

How Much Does It Cost?

To tell someone what flight or bus you are taking or to figure out how much a rental car is going to set you back, you'll need to learn the French numbers listed below. Believe it or not, these very same numbers will come in handy when you want to tell time, count to 10, or reveal your age.

Cardinal Numbers

Le Numéro	Pronunciation	Digit
zéro	*zay-ro*	0
un	*uhN*	1
deux	*duh*	2
trois	*trwah*	3
quatre	*kahtr*	4
cinq	*saNk*	5
six	*sees*	6
sept	*seht*	7

Le Numéro	Pronunciation	Digit
huit	*weet*	8
neuf	*nuhf*	9
dix	*dees*	10
onze	*ohNz*	11
douze	*dooz*	12
treize	*trehz*	13
quatorze	*kah-tohrz*	14
quinze	*kaNz*	15
seize	*sehz*	16
dix-sept	*dee-seht*	17
dix-huit	*dee-zweet*	18
dix-neuf	*dee-znuhf*	19
vingt	*vaN*	20
vingt et un	*vaN tay uhN*	21
vingt-deux	*vaN-duh*	22
trente	*trahNt*	30
quarante	*kah-rahNt*	40
cinquante	*saN-kahNt*	50
soixante	*swah-sahNt*	60
soixante-dix	*swah-sahNt-dees*	70
soixante et onze	*swah-sahNt ay ohNz*	71
soixante-douze	*swah-sahNt-dooz*	72
soixante-treize	*swah-sahNt-trehz*	73
soixante-quatorze	*swah-sahNt-kah-tohrz*	74
soixante-quinze	*swah-sahNt-kaNz*	75
soixante-seize	*swah-sahNt-sehz*	76
soixante-dix-sept	*swah-sahNt-dee-seht*	77
soixante-dix-huit	*swah-sahNt-dee-zweet*	78
soixante-dix-neuf	*swah-sahNt-dee-znuhf*	79
quatre-vingts	*kahtr-vaN*	80
quatre-vingt-un	*kahtr-vaN-uhN*	81
quatre-vingt-deux	*kahtr-vaN-duh*	82
quatre-vingt-dix	*kahtr-vaN-dees*	90
quatre-vingt-onze	*kahtr-vaN-onze*	91

continues

Cardinal Numbers (continued)

Le Numéro	Pronunciation	Digit
quatre-vingt-douze	*kahtr-vaN-dooz*	92
cent	*sahN*	100
cent un	*sahN uhN*	101
deux cents	*duh sahN*	200
deux cent un	*duh sahN uhN*	201
mille	*meel*	1,000
deux mille	*duh meel*	2,000
un million	*uhN meel-yohN*	1,000,000
deux millions	*duh meel-yohN*	2,000,000
un milliard	*uhN meel-yahr*	1,000,000,000
deux milliards	*duh meel-yahr*	2,000,000,000

When you begin, you may find that the numbers from 70 to 100 take a little mathematical finesse. But you'll get the hang of it.

When numbers are used before plural nouns beginning with a vowel, the pronunciation of the numbers changes to allow for elision:

Before a Consonant	Before a Vowel Sound
deux jours (*duh zhoor*)	deux oncles (*duh zohNkl*)
trois cartes (*trwah kahrt*)	trois opinions (*trwah zoh-pee-nyohN*)
quatre valises (*kahtr vah-leez*)	quatre hôtels (*kaht ro-tehl*)
cinq dollars (*saN doh-lahr*)	cinq années (*saN kah-nay*)
six femmes (*see fahm*)	six hommes (*see zohm*)
sept francs (*seht frahN*)	sept heures (*seh tuhr*)
huit mois (*wee mwah*)	huit enfants (*wee tahN-fahN*)
neuf billets (*nuhf bee-yeh*)	neuf artistes (*nuh fahr-teest*)
dix personnes (*dee pehr-sohn*)	dix ans (*dee zahN*)

French numbers are a little tricky until you get used to them. Look carefully at the preceding table and pay special attention to the following:

- The conjunction *et* (and) is used only for the numbers 21, 31, 41, 51, 61, and 71. Use a hyphen in all other compound numbers through 99.
- *Un* becomes *une* before a feminine noun:

  vingt et un hommes et vingt et une femmes

  twenty-one men and twenty-one women

- To form 71 to 79, use 60 + 11, 12, 13, and so on.
- To form 91 to 99, use 80 (four 20s) + 11, 12, 13, and so on.
- 80 (*quatre-vingts*) and the plural of *cent* for any number over 199 drop the *s* before another number but not before a noun:

quatre-vingts dollars	80 dollars
quatre-vingt-trois dollars	83 dollars
deux cents dollars	200 dollars
deux cent cinquante dollars	250 dollars

- Do not use *un* (one) before *cent* and *mille.*
- *Mille* doesn't change in the plural.

The *f* sound in *neuf* becomes a *v* sound when liaison is made with *heures* (hours, o'clock) and *ans* (years):

Il est neuf heures.	Il a neuf ans.
eel eh nuh vuhr	*eel ah nuh vahN*
It is nine o'clock.	He is nine years old.

Un, Deux, Trois

You can learn the numbers more quickly if you practice counting by 2s, 3s, 4s, 5s, and 10s. Try it. You'll see how quickly you remember all you need to know.

Culture Capsule

The French write the number 1 with a little hook on top. To distinguish a 1 from the number 7, they put a line through the 7 when they write it: 7̶. In numerals and decimals, where we use commas, the French use periods and vice versa. For example (English/French): 1,000/1.000; .25/0,25; $9.95/$9,95.

Your Number's Up

Parisian phone numbers consist of eight numbers grouped in pairs of two. The regional code for Paris is 1. You must dial this number before the phone number when calling from outside the city. How would you ask the operator for these numbers?

45 67 89 77 ____________________

48 21 15 51 ____________________

46 16 98 13 ____________________

43 11 72 94 ____________________

Memory Enhancer

Instead of saying the hour minus the number of minutes, you can say the number of minutes after the hour. For example, here's how you'd say "It's 4:35": *Il est cinq heures moins vingt-cinq,* or *il est quatre heures trente-cinq.*

What Time Is It?

Now that you are familiar with French numbers, it is relatively easy to learn how to tell time. The following is a question that you will probably ask or hear asked very often:

Quelle heure est-il?
kehl uhr eh-teel
What time is it?

Telling Time

L'heure	Pronunciation	Translation
Il est une heure.	*eel eh tewn nuhr*	It is 1:00.
Il est deux heures cinq.	*eel eh duh zuhr saNk*	It is 2:05.
Il est quatre heures et quart.	*eel eh kahtr uhr ay kahr*	It is 4:15.
Il est cinq heures vingt.	*eel eh saN kuhr vaN*	It is 5:20.
Il est six heures vingt-cinq.	*eel eh see zuhr vaN-saNk*	It is 6:25.
Il est sept heures et demie.	*eel eh seh tuhr ay duh-mee*	It is 7:30.
Il est neuf heures moins vingt.	*eel eh nuh vuhr mwaN vaN*	It is 8:40 (20 minutes to 9).

L'heure	Pronunciation	Translation
Il est dix heures moins le quart.	*eel eh dee zuhr mwaN luh kahr*	It is 9:45 (a quarter to 10).
Il est onze heures moins dix.	*eel eh ohN zuhr mwaN dees*	It is 10:50 (10 minutes to 11).
Il est midi moins cinq.	*eel eh mee-dee mwaN saNk*	It is 11:55 (5 minutes to noon).
Il est minuit.	*eel eh mee-nwee*	It is midnight.

Keep the following in mind when you tell time:

- To express the time after the hour, the number of minutes is simply added. Use *et* only with *quart* and *demi(e).*
- To express time before the hour, use *moins* (before, less, minus), and use *moins le* before quart.
- To express half past noon or midnight, use the following:

  Il est midi et demi.
  Il est minuit et demi.

- With all other hours, *demie* is used to express half past.

Culture Capsule

In public announcements, such as time schedules and timetables, the official 24-hour system is commonly used. Midnight is the 0 hour: 0 h 15 = 12:15 A.M.; 15 *heures* = 3:00 P.M.

Fractions of Time

It's not enough to know how to say what time it is—you might want to know at what time an activity is planned or whether it is taking place in the morning, afternoon, or evening. Imagine you asked someone at what time a play was being presented, and he responded, "*Il y a deux heures.*" You might mistake this as meaning "At two o'clock" or "There are two hours," which, to you, might mean you have two hours before the play begins. In fact, you've missed the play because it started two hours ago. The expressions in the following table will help you deal with time.

Time Expressions

L'expression	Pronunciation	Meaning
une seconde	*ewn suh-gohNd*	a second
une minute	*ewn mee-newt*	a minute

continues

Time Expressions (continued)

L'expression	Pronunciation	Meaning
une heure	*ewn nuhr*	an hour
du matin	*dew mah-taN*	in the morning (A.M.)
de l'après-midi	*duh lah-preh mee-dee*	in the afternoon (P.M.)
du soir	*dew swahr*	in the evening (P.M.)
à quelle heure	*ah keh luhr*	at what time
à minuit précis	*ah mee-nwee pray-see*	at exactly midnight
à une heure précise	*ah ewn uhr pray-seez*	at exactly 1:00
à deux heures précises	*ah duh zuhr pray-seez*	at exactly 2:00
vers deux heures	*vehr duh zuhr*	at about 2:00
un quart d'heure	*uhN kahr duhr*	a quarter of an hour
une demi-heure	*ewn duh-mee uhr*	a half hour
dans une heure	*dahN zew nuhr*	in an hour
jusqu'à deux heures	*zhew-skah duh zuhr*	until 2:00
avant trois heures	*ah-vahN trwah zuhr*	before 3:00
après trois heures	*ah-preh trwah zuhr*	after 3:00
depuis quelle heure	*duh-pwee kehl uhr*	since what time
depuis six heures	*duh-pwee see zuhr*	since 6:00
il y a une heure	*eel yah ewn nuhr*	an hour ago
par heure	*pahr uhr*	per hour
tôt (de bonne heure)	*to (duh boh nuhr)*	early
tard	*tahr*	late
en retard	*ahN ruh-tahr*	late (in arriving)

The Least You Need to Know

- The irregular verb *prendre* means "to take."
- *Quel* is an adjective expressing "which." It must agree in gender and number with the noun it modifies.
- If you plan on renting a car, you'll need to know French numbers and the metric system.
- You can tell time easily by giving the hour and the number of minutes past the hour.

Chapter 12

In This Chapter

- Hotel amenities
- Ordinal numbers
- "Shoe verbs"

You've successfully chosen a suitable means of transportation to get you where you want to go. Now, as you ride along, you try to get a feel for your new environment. You can hardly wait to get to the hotel so that you can unpack and start your glorious vacation. Just as your patience is wearing thin, you catch a glimpse of the hotel in the distance. Your first impression reassures you that you've chosen wisely.

Are you a traveler who is happy with the bare minimum in accommodations? Do you feel that because you won't be spending much time in your room, you'd be wasting money on something you wouldn't truly enjoy? Perhaps you'd rather spend more money on consumables: food, drink, side trips, and souvenirs. On the other hand, you might be someone who prefers the creature comforts of home at the very least and, at most, outright luxury. Do you want it all and expect to be treated royally? In this chapter, you learn how to get the room and services you expect from your hotel.

It's a Great Hotel! But Does It Have ...?

Before leaving home, you will probably want to check with your travel agent or the hotel management to be sure the hotel you've chosen has the amenities you desire. Depending on your requirements, you will need to know the words for everything from "bathroom" to "swimming pool." In the 1970s, my husband and I backpacked around Europe with a copy of Arthur Frommer's *Europe on $5 a Day* under our arms. We hadn't made any reservations, so most nights we had to take whatever room we could get. In Paris, we wound up in a small room in the red-light district. The room didn't have its own bathroom, and we were not thrilled with having to share the *W.C.* down the hall; sometimes the wait was unbearable. Even with reservations, however, you may end up with some surprises; it never hurts to ask questions when you are making your arrangements. See the following table for a basic list of hotel amenities.

Hotel Services

Service	Le Service	Pronunciation
bar	le bar	*luh bahr*
business center	le centre d'affaires	*luh sahNtr dah-fehr*
cashier	la caisse	*lah kehs*
concierge (caretaker)	le (la) concierge	*luh (lah) kohN-syehrzh*
doorman	le portier	*luh pohr-tyay*
elevator	l'ascenseur *m.*	*lah-sahN-suhr*
fitness center	le club santé	*luh klewb sahN-tay*
gift shop	la boutique	*lah boo-teek*
laundry and dry-cleaning service	la blanchisserie	*lah blahN-shees-ree*
maid service	la gouvernante	*lah goo-vehr-nahNt*
restaurant	le restaurant	*luh rehs-toh-rahN*
swimming pool	la piscine	*lah pee-seen*
valet parking	l'attendance (*f.*) du garage	*lah-tahN-dahNs dew gah-rahzh*

When I was planning a trip to Martinique, my travel agent told me about a terrific hotel where the best rooms had balconies facing the ocean. She described the views as breathtaking. Unfortunately, we were not able to confirm a room with a balcony at the time of the reservation, but I figured I'd give it a shot after we arrived. As fate would have it, a travel agent and her large family arrived just as we did. She, too, was eager to trade up to a room with a view. Unfortunately, she was not able to make herself understood to the French-speaking staff. My husband and I, however, were rewarded for our fluency; we got a spectacular room overlooking the ocean! Study the following table to get a jump on the others, just as we did.

Culture Capsule

In French buildings, the ground floor is called *le rez-de-chaussée*, and the basement is called *le sous-sol* (literally, the "under ground"). The "first floor" is really on the second story of any building.

Getting What You Want Nicely Furnished

Amenities	Les Agréments	Pronunciation
a single (double) room	une chambre à un (deux) lits	*ewn shahNbr ah uhN (duh) lee*
air conditioning	la climatisation	*lah klee-mah-tee-zah-syohN*
alarm clock	le réveil	*luh ray-vehy*
balcony	le balcon	*luh bahl-kohN*
bathroom (private)	la salle de bains (privée)	*lah sahl duh baN (pree-vay)*
key	la clé (clef)	*lah klay (klay)*
on the courtyard	côté cour	*koh-tay koor*
on the garden	côté jardin	*koh-tay zhahr-daN*
on the sea	côté mer	*koh-tay mehr*
safe (deposit box)	le coffre	*luh kohfr*
shower	la douche	*lah doosh*
telephone (dial-direct)	le téléphone (direct)	*luh tay-lay-fohn (dee-rehkt)*
television (color)	la télévision (en couleurs)	*lah tay-lay-vee-zyohN (ahN koo-luhr)*
toilet facilities	les toilettes	*lay twah-leht*

Do You Need Something?

Don't you just hate it when your hotel skimps on towels? They often provide four small bath towels and expect them to be enough for a couple with two kids. I could use three just for myself: hair, top half, and bottom half. Imagine how the rest of my family feels when they're left with my soggy remains! If you need something for your room to make your stay more enjoyable, the following phrases may help you:

Je voudrais …
zhuh voo-dreh …
I would like …

J'ai besoin d'un (d'une) …
zhay buh-zwaN duhN (dewn) …
I need a (for plural use *de* + noun) …

Il me faut un (une)(des) …
eel muh foh tuhN (tewn) (day) …
I need a (some) …

Okay. You're all checked in, you've unpacked, and now you're ready for a nice hot bath. But wait! The housekeeper has forgotten to provide you with any towels at all! Rather than making your sheets do double duty, call the front desk and ask for towels. The management, after all, is there to make sure your stay is enjoyable. The following table lists a few things you might need.

Necessities

Necessity	La Nécessité	Pronunciation
an ashtray	un cendrier	*uhN sahN-dree-yay*
a bar of soap	une savonnette	*ewn sah-voh-neht*
a beach towel	un drap de bain	*uhN drah dbaN*
a blanket	une couverture	*ewn koo-vehr-tewr*
hangers	des cintres *m.*	*day saNtr*
ice cubes	des glaçons *m.*	*day glah-sohN*
mineral water	de l'eau minérale	*duh lo mee-nay-rahl*
a pillow	un oreiller	*uhN noh-reh-yay*
tissues	des mouchoirs en papier	*day moo-shwahr ahN pah-pyay*
a roll of toilet paper	un rouleau de papier hygiénique	*uhN roo-lo duh pah-pyay ee-zhyay-neek*
a towel	une serviette	*ewn sehr-vyeht*
a transformer (an electric adaptor)	un transformateur	*uhN trahnz-fohr-mah-tuhr*

Hotel Amenities

Imagine that your travel agent has sent you a brochure for a hotel where French is spoken. Read what is available and list the services offered. Answers can be found in Appendix A.

A LIBREVILLE
LE GRAND HOTEL VOUS ATTEND

Au coeur des activités de Libreville, le Grand Hôtel allie la qualité de ses services à l'élegance d'un hôtel moderne de luxe, 5 étoiles. Situé directement sur la plage, le Grand Hôtel dispose de 300 chambres dont 10 suites de très grand confort, 3 salons de conférences et réceptions, 1 restaurant ouvert 24 hr., 1 snack bar, 1 restaurant gastronomique, et d'un piano bar.

Pour vos loisirs, le Grand Hôtel met à votre disposition, piscine, plage, sauna, tennis, massages, galeria marchande, ainsi qu'un élégant casino. Un service de navette gratuite (hôtel–aéroport) est mis à votre disposition.

____

____

____

____

____

Going Up

We've all had an elevator experience in which we've felt like a large sardine in a small can. When you're pushed to the back or squished to the side, you have to hope that a kind and gentle soul will wiggle a hand free and ask, "*Quel étage, s'il vous plaît* (*kehl ay-tahzh seel voo pleh*)?" You will need the ordinal numbers in the following table to give a correct answer, such as "*Le deuxième étage, s'il vous plaît* (*luh duh-zyehm ay-tahzh seel voo pleh*)."

Ordinal Numbers

Le Numéro	Pronunciation	English
premier (première)	*pruh-myay (pruh-myehr)*	1st
deuxième (second[e])	*duh-zyehm (suh-gohN[d])*	2nd
troisième	*trwah-zyehm*	3rd
quatrième	*kah-tree-yehm*	4th
cinquième	*saN-kyehm*	5th
sixième	*see-zyehm*	6th
septième	*seh-tyehm*	7th
huitième	*wee-tyehm*	8th
neuvième	*nuh-vyehm*	9th
dixième	*dee-zyehm*	10th
onzième	*ohN-zyehm*	11th
douzième	*doo-zyehm*	12th
vingtième	*vaN-tyehm*	20th
vingt et un(e)ième	*vaN-tay-uhN (ewn)-nyehm*	21st
soixante-douzième	*swah-sahNt doo-zyehm*	72nd
centième	*sahN-tyehm*	100th

Keep the following in mind when using ordinal numbers:

- *Premier* and *second* (and *un* when used with another number) are the only ordinal numbers that must agree in gender (masculine or feminine) with the noun they describe. All other ordinal numbers must agree in number with the noun:

  son premier fils — sa première fille
  his (her) first son — his (her) first daughter

- Except for *premier* and *second*, *ième* is added to all cardinal numbers to form the ordinal number. Drop the silent *e* before *ième*.
- Note that *u* is added in *cinquième*, and *v* replaces *f* in *neuvième*.
- *Second(e)* is generally used in a series that does not go beyond two.
- There is no elision with *huitième* and *onzième*. The definite article *le* or *la* does not drop its vowel:

  le huitième jour — la onzième personne
  the eighth day — the eleventh person

- In French, cardinal numbers precede ordinal numbers:

  les deux premières fois
  the first two times

Making a Change

Imagine you want to sample a famous French delicacy, eat in a special restaurant, pay with your credit card, or buy a special gift. Naturally, you'll want some recommendations and will probably get opinions from everyone from the concierge to the chambermaid. In the course of your conversations, you'll have to use many verbs to get the information you seek. There are a few categories of regular *-er* verbs whose endings require spelling changes in certain forms. In some instances, this is necessary to maintain the proper sound of the verb. In other instances, it's just one of the idiosyncrasies of the language. You should familiarize yourself with some of these verbs in each group because they are high-frequency words that you will use and see quite often.

These verbs are referred to as "shoe verbs" because the rules of conjugation work as if you put the subject pronouns that follow one set of rules within the shoe and the others outside the shoe. To make this clearer, look at the pronouns that go in and out of the shoe.

Attention!

The letter *c* has a hard sound before *a*, *o*, and *u*. The letter *c* has a soft sound before *e* and *i*. A hard *c* can be made soft by attaching a cedilla under the *c*, as in *ç*.

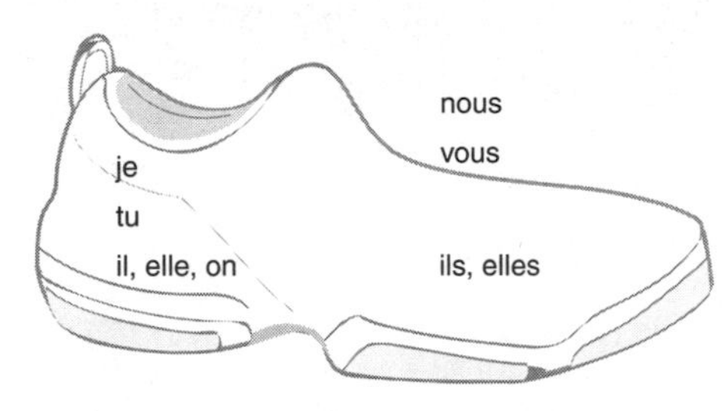

In other words, all verbs in these categories, *je*, *tu*, *il*, *elle*, *on*, *ils*, and *elles*, follow one set of rules, whereas *nous* and (generally but not always) *vous* follow a different set of rules. Now let's look at the different categories.

-cer Verbs

For *-cer* verbs, the *nous* form needs *ç* to maintain the soft sound of the *c* (s). This cedilla is added before the vowels *a*, *o*, and *u*.

***placer* (to place, set)**

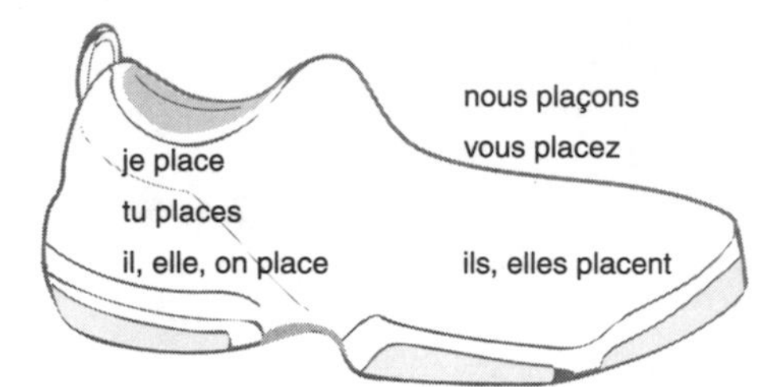

Other verbs conjugated like *placer* include:

annoncer	*ah-nohN-say*	to announce
avancer	*ah-vahN-say*	to advance (be fast—clocks and watches)
commencer (à)	*koh-mahN-say (ah)*	to begin
menacer	*muh-nah-say*	to threaten
remplacer	*rahN-plah-say*	to replace
renoncer à	*ruh-nohN-say ah*	to give up, renounce

Using *-cer* Verbs

You should find *-cer* verbs quite easy since there is really only one small change involved. Practice vocabulary and conversation by completing the sentence with the correct form of the verb provided.

1. Le spectacle (commencer) _______________ à neuf heures.
2. Nous (renoncer) _______________ à faire des projets.
3. Tu (remplacer) _______________ ta valise?
4. Ma montre (avancer) _______________.
5. Ils (annoncer) _______________ le départ du train.

-ger Verbs

For *-ger* verbs, the *nous* form needs an extra *e* to maintain the soft sound of the *g* (zh). This extra *e* is always added after the *g* before the vowels *a*, *o*, and *u*.

manger (to eat)

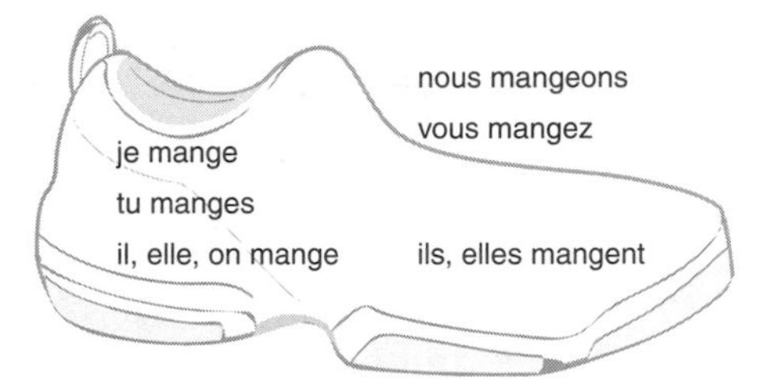

Other verbs that are conjugated like *manger* include:

arranger	*ah-rahn-zhay*	to arrange
changer	*shahN-zhay*	to change
corriger	*koh-ree-zhay*	to correct
déranger	*day-rahN-zhay*	to disturb
diriger	*dee-ree-zhay*	to direct
nager	*nah-zhay*	to swim
obliger	*oh-blee-zhay*	to oblige
partager	*pahr-tah-zhay*	to share, divide
ranger	*rahN-zhay*	to tidy

Memory Enhancer

The letter *g* has a hard sound before *a, o,* and *u*. The letter *g* has a soft sound before *e* and *i*. The letter *g* can be made soft by adding an *e* after it.

Using *-ger* Verbs

Like *-cer* verbs, *-ger* verbs have only one change to memorize. Giving the correct form of the verb in each sentence should prove to be a snap.

1. La fille de chambre (ranger) _______________ la chambre.
2. Tu (déranger) _______________ les autres clients.
3. Nous (partager) _______________ notre sandwich parce qu'il est très grand.
4. Vous (nager) _______________ bien.
5. Ils (arranger) _______________ tout.

-*yer* Verbs

In *-yer* verbs, the *y* is retained in the *nous* and *vous* forms. Within the shoe, an *i* is used instead of the *y*.

employer **(to use)**

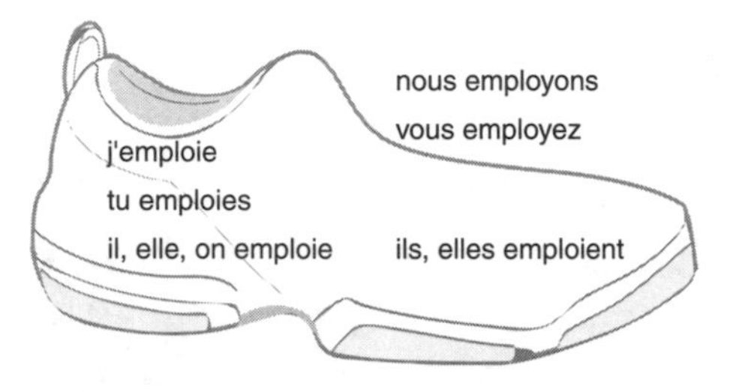

Other verbs that are conjugated like *employer* include:

ennuyer	*ahN-nwee-yay*	to bother, bore
envoyer	*ahN-vwah-yay*	to send
nettoyer	*neh-twah-yay*	to clean

Verbs ending in *–ayer* may or may not change *y* to *i* in the forms inside the shoe:

payer **(to pay)**

je paie (paye)	nous payons
tu paies (payes)	vous payez
il, elle, on paie (paye)	ils, elles paient (payent)

essayer **(to try)**

j'essaie (essaye)	nous essayons
tu essaies (essayes)	vous essayez
il, elle, on essaie (essaye)	ils, elles essaient (essayent)

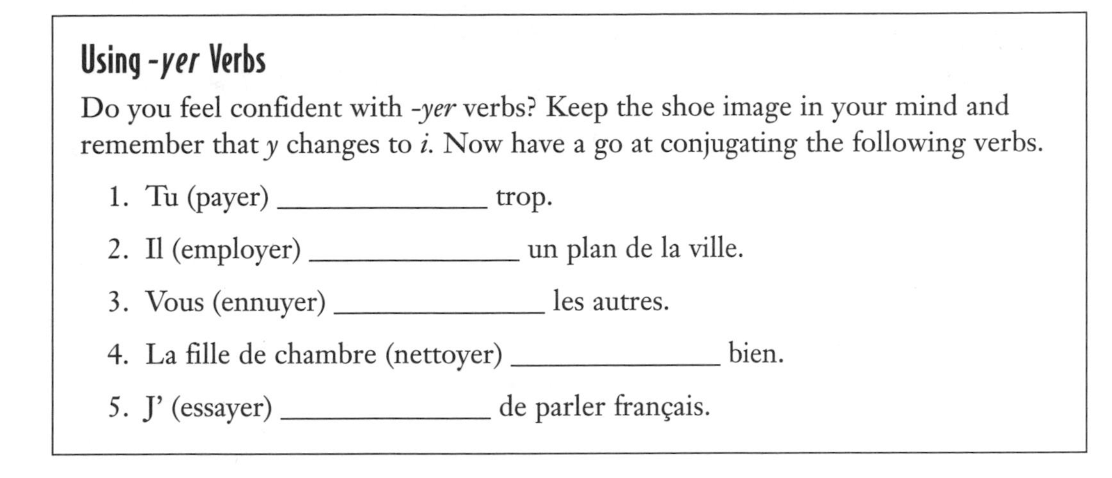

Using *-yer* Verbs

Do you feel confident with *-yer* verbs? Keep the shoe image in your mind and remember that *y* changes to *i*. Now have a go at conjugating the following verbs.

1. Tu (payer) ______________ trop.
2. Il (employer) ______________ un plan de la ville.
3. Vous (ennuyer) ______________ les autres.
4. La fille de chambre (nettoyer) ______________ bien.
5. J' (essayer) ______________ de parler français.

e + Consonant + *-er* Verbs

Verbs with a silent *e* in the syllable before the *-er* infinitive ending (*acheter*: to buy; *peser*: to weigh) change the silent *e* to *è* for all forms in the shoe. Within the shoe, all the endings of the verbs are silent.

***acheter* (to buy)**

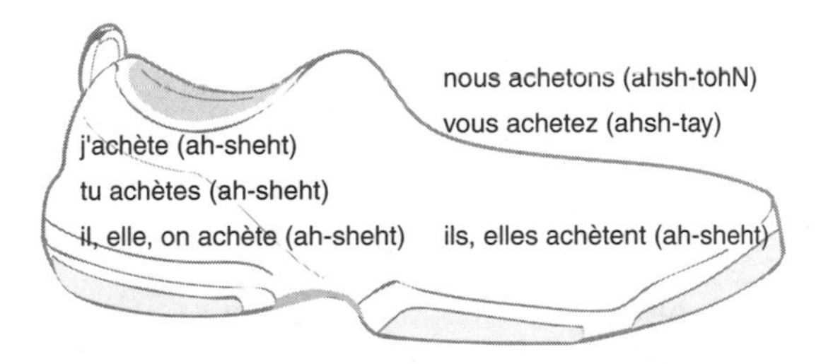

Notice the difference in pronunciation of the verb inside and outside the shoe. Within the shoe, the first *e* has an *accent grave* and *è* is pronounced. Outside the shoe, the first *e* is unpronounced.

Other verbs that are conjugated like *acheter* include:

achever	*ahsh-vay*	to finish, complete
amener	*ahm-nay*	to bring, lead to

Memory Enhancer

Because all the endings within the shoe are silent, adding an *accent grave* (è) to the silent *e* before the ending gives sound to that silent *e*. Two silent *e*'s would make the word virtually impossible to pronounce.

emmener	*ahNm-nay*	to take, lead away
enlever	*ahN-lvay*	to take off, remove
peser	*puh-zay*	to weigh
promener	*prohm-nay*	to walk

Appeler (to call) and *jeter* (to throw) are two verbs with a silent *e* that double the consonant before the *-er* infinitive ending instead of adding the *accent grave*.

***appeler* (to call)**

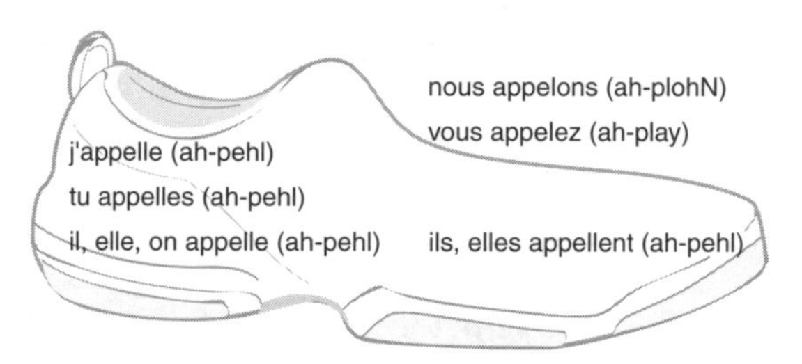

***jeter* (to throw)**

je jette (*zheht*)	nous jetons (*zhuh-tohN*)
tu jettes (*zheht*)	vous jetez (*zhuh-tay*)
il, elle, on jette (*zheht*)	ils, elles jettent (*zheht*)

Using *e* + Consonant + *-er* Verbs

It's very important to practice the correct spelling of *e* + consonant + *-er* verbs—and not because spelling is so important. Let's face it; you're probably not going to be writing many letters in French. Why spend time on this? Because if you understand that accents give sounds to silent letters, you'll be much more successful at perfecting your pronunciation. Take this opportunity to read and write at the same time.

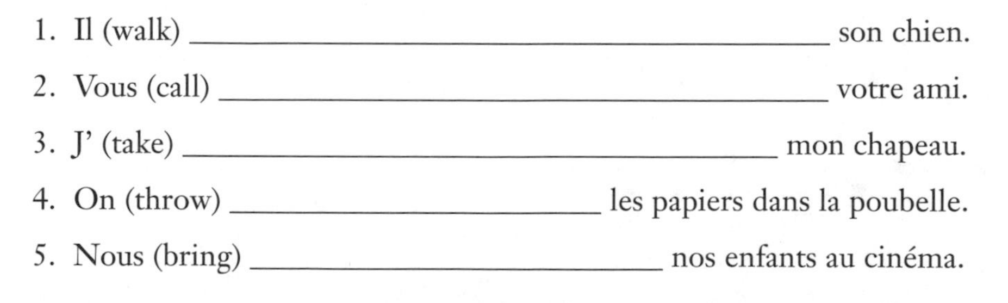

1. Il (walk) ____________________ son chien.
2. Vous (call) ____________________ votre ami.
3. J' (take) ____________________ mon chapeau.
4. On (throw) ____________________ les papiers dans la poubelle.
5. Nous (bring) ____________________ nos enfants au cinéma.

é + Consonant + *-er* Verbs

Verbs with *é* in the syllable before the infinitive ending change *é* to *è* in the shoe, where the endings to the conjugated verb forms are all silent.

***préférer* (to prefer)**

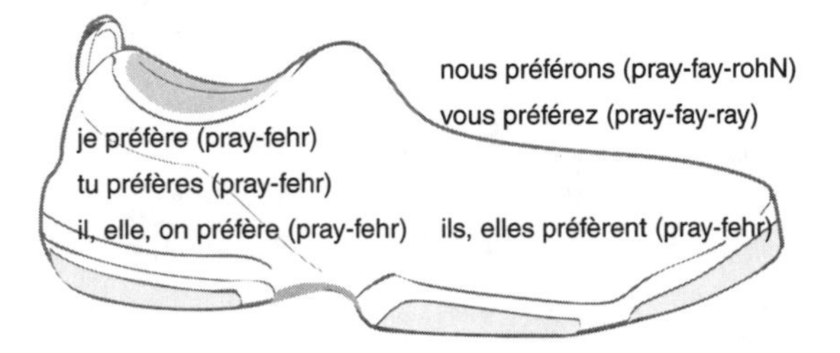

Other verbs that are conjugated like *préférer* include:

célébrer	*say-lay-bray*	to celebrate
espérer	*ehs-pay-ray*	to hope
posséder	*poh-say-day*	to own, possess
protéger	*proh-tay-zhay*	to protect
répéter	*ray-pay-tay*	to repeat

Using *é* + Consonant + *-er* Verbs

Once again, using accents correctly will ensure that you're speaking properly. You can practice vocabulary, spelling, and pronunciation all in one fell swoop by completing the following sentences.

1. Je (celebrate) ______________________ mon anniversaire demain.
2. (Repeat) ______________________ la phrase, s'il vous plaît.
3. Nous (protect) ______________________ nos amis.
4. Ils (hope) ______________________ voyager.
5. Elle (owns) ______________________ une jolie voiture.

Memory Enhancer

"Shoe verbs" may have changes within or outside the shoe. The following changes occur.

Verb	Change	Subject Affected
-cer	c > ç	nous
-ger	g > ge	nous
-yer	y > i	nous, vous
e + consonant + er	e > è	je, tu, il, elle, ils, elles
é + consonant + er	é > è	je, tu, il, elle, ils, elles

Verbs ending in *-ayer* may or may not change *y* to *i*.

The verbs *appeler* and *jeter* double the consonant before the *-er* ending instead of adding an accent.

The Least You Need to Know

- To be happy in your hotel, learn the vocabulary for facilities and furnishings to facilitate asking for what you want and need.
- Ordinal numbers (except for *premier* and *second[e]*, which is used only for the second in a series of two) are formed by adding *ième* to the cardinal number.
- "Shoe verbs" follow a pattern of conjugation that resembles the outline of a shoe. If you remember the shoe, you'll remember how to conjugate the verbs.

Part 3 Fun Time

You want to have fun no matter where you go or what the reason, so your trip will surely include games, amusements, and diversions. This is the place to be when you're seeking a good time.

No matter what weather conditions prevail, there's always something to do. Naturally, you'll want to sightsee. Then there are other exciting activities for the most athletic and adventuresome among us: a wide gamut of sports, including parasailing, scuba diving, windsurfing, and much more. Don't forget all the cultural opportunities: museums, concerts, ballets, and operas. Perhaps traveling is a shopping experience for you. Maybe it's a gastronomic feast.

The six chapters in Part 3 deal with how to get the most fun out of your vacation. You'll learn how to express what you want to do, when you want to do it, and how much you're enjoying yourself.

Chapter

Today's Weather Is ...

In This Chapter

- Weather conditions
- Days of the week
- Months of the year
- The four seasons
- Expressing the date
- The irregular verb *faire* (to make, do)

Your hotel is fabulous. Your room suits you to a T and has all the creature comforts and then some. But it is time to get up and out. Before you head to the lobby, you glance out the window and notice that the sky is overcast, and you want to be prepared in case it rains. By the way, what are you going to do if that happens?

If you were at home, you'd probably tune into the weather channel to get the latest forecast. You could give this approach a shot, but remember that in a French-speaking country, all the announcers speak in French—and when it comes to weather, your knowledge of cognates won't take you too far. In this chapter, you'll tackle the weather report, and you'll also learn how to find out the hours at museums, movie theaters, and other places that may beckon on a rainy day.

It's 30 Degrees, but They're Wearing String Bikinis!

Let's say you turn on the television and manage to understand the weatherman when he reports that it is 30 degrees. But it's summer—how can this be? Is it possible that *la météo* (the forecast) is wrong? Perhaps it's time to consult the friendly *concierge* (caretaker/manager) at the front desk. The phrases in the following table will help you talk about the weather.

Weather Expressions

Expression	L'expression	Pronunciation
What's the weather?	Quel temps fait-il?	*kehl tahN feh-teel*
It's beautiful.	Il fait beau.	*eel feh bo*
It's hot.	Il fait chaud.	*eel feh sho*
It's sunny.	Il fait du soleil.	*eel feh dew soh-lehy*
It's nasty (bad).	Il fait mauvais.	*eel feh moh-veh*
It's cold.	Il fait froid.	*eel feh frwah*
It's cool.	Il fait frais.	*eel feh freh*
It's windy.	Il fait du vent.	*eel feh dew vahN*
It's lightning.	Il fait des éclairs. *m.*	*eel feh day zay-klehr*
It's thundering.	Il fait du tonnerre.	*eel feh dew toh-nehr*
It's foggy.	Il fait du brouillard. Il y a du brouillard.	*eel feh dew broo-yahr* *eel yah dew broo-yahr*
It's humid.	Il fait humide. Il y a de l'humidité.	*eel feh tew-meed* *eel yah duh lew-mee-dee-tay*
It's cloudy.	Il y a des nuages. Le ciel est nuageux.	*eel yah day new-ahzh* *luh syehl eh new-ah-zhuh*
It's overcast.	Le ciel est couvert.	*luh syehl eh koo-vehr*
It's raining.	Il pleut.	*eel pluh*
It's pouring.	Il pleut à verse.	*eel pluh ah vehrs*
It's snowing.	Il neige.	*eel nehzh*
There are gusts of wind.	Il y a des rafales. *f.*	*eel yah day rah-fahl*
There's hail.	Il y a de la grêle.	*eel yah duh lah grehl*
There are sudden showers.	Il y a des giboulées. *f.*	*eel yah day zhee-boo-lay*

So why is everyone wearing tank tops and bikinis when it's 30 degrees outside? The answer is really quite simple. The French-speaking world uses Celsius (centigrade) rather than Fahrenheit to tell the temperature. This means that when it is 30 degrees Celsius, it's 86 degrees Fahrenheit.

And the Temperature Is ...

You never were that great in math, but you're determined to have a pretty good idea of what the temperature is. You arm yourself with a mini solar calculator and ask the concierge:

Il fait quelle temperature?
eel feh kehl tahN-pay-rah-tewr
What's the temperature?

If someone asks you what the temperature is (and you happen to know), respond with the phrase *il fait* followed by the number of degrees. If it is below zero, throw a *moins* (minus) before the number.

Il fait moins dix.
eel feh mwaN dees
It's 10 below.

Il fait zéro.
eel feh zay-ro
It's zero.

Il fait soixante.
eel feh swah-sahNt
It's 60 degrees.

In the Paper It Says ...

French newspapers, like American newspapers, contain weather information complete with maps and symbols. Take a look at the following map to see if you can decipher the symbols. If you have trouble, consult the guide for help.

Meteorological Expressions

L'expression	Pronunciation	Expression
brouillards	*broo-yahr*	fog
fraîcheur	*freh-shuhr*	chilly
soleil	*soh-lehy*	sun
ciel clair	*syehl klehr*	clear sky
couvert	*koo-vehr*	cloudy
neige	*nehzh*	snow
peu nuageux	*puh new-ah-zhuh*	slightly cloudy

continues

Meteorological Expressions (continued)

L'expression	Pronunciation	Expression
pluies	*plwee*	rain
verglas	*vehr-glah*	sleet
variable	*vah-ree-yahbl*	changeable
bruines	*brween*	drizzle
orages	*oh-rahzh*	storms
très nuageux	*treh new-ah-zhuh*	very cloudy
averses	*ah-vehrs*	showers (heavy rain)
brumeux	*brew-muh*	hazy, foggy
vent	*vaN*	winds
faibles	*fehbl*	weak
modérés	*moh-day-ray*	moderate
fort	*fohr*	strong
tempête	*tahN-peht*	storm

MÉTÉO

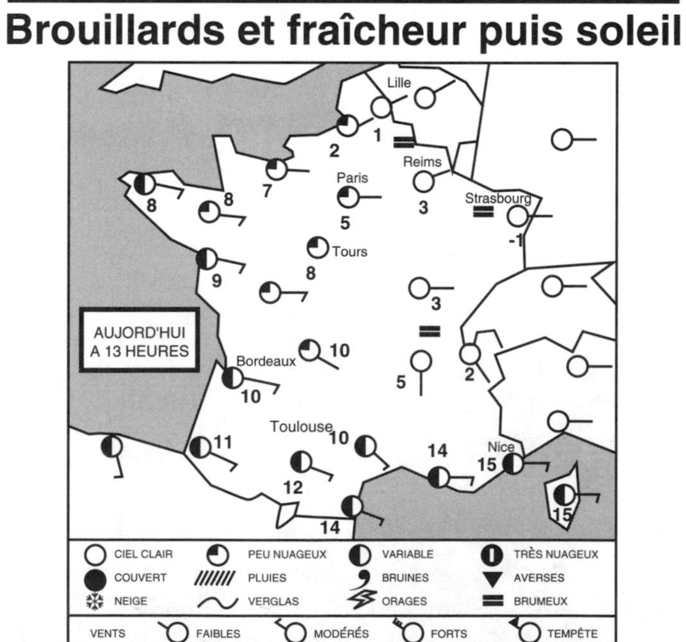

What Day Is It?

If you're anything like me, the day your vacation starts is the day your watch comes off. You get so involved in having a good time that you lose all track of time. Every day seems like Saturday or Sunday, and you frequently have to ask, "What day is it, anyway?" If you're on a sightseeing vacation, you really have to keep track of the days of the week so that you don't wind up at the attraction you're dying to see on the day that it's closed. That can happen very easily in Paris, where schedules differ from museum to museum. When you study the days of the week in the following table, you'll notice that they all end in *-di* except for Sunday, which begins with *di-*.

Note: The days of the week in French (which are all masculine) are not capitalized (unless they are at the beginning of a sentence).

Attention!

Unlike our calendars, French calendars start with Monday.

Days of the Week

Day	Le Jour	Pronunciation
Monday	lundi	*luhN-dee*
Tuesday	mardi	*mahr-dee*
Wednesday	mercredi	*mehr-kruh-dee*
Thursday	jeudi	*zhuh-dee*
Friday	vendredi	*vahN-druh-dee*
Saturday	samedi	*sahm-dee*
Sunday	dimanche	*dee-mahNsh*

To say that something is happening "on" a certain day, the French use the definite article *le:*

> Le lundi je vais en ville.
> *luh luhN-dee zhuh veh zahN veel*
> On Monday(s) I go downtown.

The Best Month for a Trip

It's August and you want to go to Nice. Disappointment sets in when your travel agent says, "Sorry, there's nothing available." So you book your own trip to Paris during this same time period. When you get there, the city is empty. Where *is* everyone?

In France, many stores and businesses are closed during the month of August, when everyone seems to head south to La Côte d'Azur (the Riviera) for a vacation. The following table gives you the months of the year. Thus, when you glance through all those glossy vacation brochures, you can figure out the best time to take your trip.

Note: Like the days of the week, all months in French are masculine and are not capitalized (unless they are used at the beginning of a sentence or are special days such as Good Friday—le *Vendredi saint*).

Months of the Year

Month	Le Mois	Pronunciation
January	janvier	*zhahN-vyay*
February	février	*fay-vree-yay*
March	mars	*mahrs*
April	avril	*ah-vreel*
May	mai	*meh*
June	juin	*zhwaN*
July	juillet	*zhwee-eh*
August	août	*oo(t)*
September	septembre	*sehp-tahNbr*
October	octobre	*ohk-tohbr*
November	novembre	*noh-vahNbr*
December	décembre	*day-sahNbr*

To make clear that something is expected to happen in a certain month, use the preposition *en.* For example:

Je vais en France en avril.
zhuh veh zahN frahNs ahN nah-vreel
I am going to France in April.

The Four Seasons

Some seasons are better for traveling in certain countries than in others. Make sure to plan your trip when the weather will be great so that you don't have to worry about hurricanes, storms, or other adverse conditions. Maybe you're not a traveler but enjoy doing crossword puzzles where clues often call for "season (Fr.)." Perhaps you'd like to know which sports and activities are performed in each season. Whatever your reason, the following table gives you the names of the seasons.

The Seasons

Season	La Saison	Pronunciation
winter	l'hiver	*lee-vehr*
spring	le printemps	*luh praN-tahN*
summer	l'été	*lay-tay*
autumn, fall	l'automne	*lo-tohn*

To express "in" with the seasons, the French use the preposition *en* for all the seasons except spring, which uses *au* instead:

> Je vais en France en hiver (en été, en automne, **au** printemps).
> *zhuh veh zahN frahNs ahN nee-vehr (ahN nay-tay, ahN no-tohn, o praN-tahN)*
> I'm going to France in the winter (summer, fall, spring).

You Have a Date

Do you also lose track of the date when you're away from home or work? The date is something people tend to forget on a fairly regular basis, especially when they're on vacation. (I finally broke down and bought a minicomputer so that I can always have a calendar on hand.) See the following table for a few words you will need to know when making plans.

Dates

Date	Le Date	Pronunciation
a day	un jour	*uhN zhoor*
a week	une semaine	*ewn suh-mehn*
a month	un mois	*uhN mwah*
a year	un an, une année	*uhN nahN,* *ewn ah-nay*

The word for "year," *an*, is used with cardinal numbers (one, two, three, and so on) unless an adjective is used to describe the word "year." In that case, the word *année* is used. Sometimes either word is acceptable.

un an	une année	deux bonnes années
one year	a year	two good years

quelques années	l'an dernier	l'année dernière
some years	last year	last year

You've decided to take the plunge and get a new French coif. Perhaps you're on a business trip and have to arrange for an important meeting, or maybe you've decided to make unexpected travel plans. Whatever the reason, you'll have to know how to express the date for your appointment.

- Dates in French are expressed as follows:

  (*le*) day of week + (*le*) (cardinal) number + month + year

  lundi onze juillet 2003
  lundi le onze juillet 2003
  le lundi onze juillet 2003

- The first day of each month is expressed by *premier*. Cardinal numbers are used for all other days:

le premier janvier	le deux janvier
January 1st	January 2nd

- Just as in English, years are usually expressed in hundreds. When the word for "thousand" is written in dates only, *mil* is often used instead of *mille:*

1999	dix-neuf cent quatre-vingt dix-neuf
	mil neuf cent quatre-vingt dix-neuf
2003	deux mil(le) trois

- To get information about the date, you need to ask the following questions:

Quel jour est-ce aujourd'hui?	Quelle est la date d'aujourd'hui?
kehl zhoor ehs oh-zhoor-dwee	*kehl eh lah daht doh-zhoor-dwee*
What day is today?	What is today's date?

  or

  Quel jour sommes-nous aujourd'hui?
  kehl zhoor sohm noo oh-zhoor-dwee
  What day is today?

  The answer to your questions would be one of the following:

C'est aujourd'hui + (day) date.	Aujourd'hui nous sommes + (day) date.
seh toh-zhoor-dwee …	*oh-zhoor-dwee noo sohm …*
Today is …	Today is …

Heaven help those of us who forget important dates. It's not intentional, but it often creates problems. Practice what you've learned by giving the day and dates for these important events of the year:

> Your birthday, the birthday of a friend, Thanksgiving, New Year's, Mother's Day, Valentine's Day, Father's Day, Memorial Day

Culture Capsule

When the French write the date in numbers, the sequence is day + month + year. In the United States, we tend to lead with the month, followed by the day, and then the year.

When you have to make plans and schedule your time wisely, you'll need certain time-related words and expressions. Keep the expressions in the following table in mind when time is of the essence.

Time Expressions

Expression	L'expression	Pronunciation
in	dans	*dahN*
ago	il y a	*eel yah*
per	par	*pahr*
during	pendant	*pahN-dahN*
next	prochain(e)	*proh-shaN (proh-shehn)*
last	dernier (dernière)	*dehr-nyah (dehr-nyehr)*
last	passé(e)	*pah-say*
eve	la veille	*la vehy*
day before yesterday	avant-hier	*ah-vahN yehr*
yesterday	hier	*yehr*
today	aujourd'hui	*oh-zhoor-dwee*
tomorrow	demain	*duh-maN*
day after tomorrow	après-demain	*ah-preh duh-maN*
next day	le lendemain	*luh lahN-duh-maN*
from	dès	*deh*
a week from today	d'aujourd'hui en huit	*doh-zhoor-dwee ahN weet*
two weeks from tomorrow	de demain en quinze	*duh duh-maN ahN kaNz*

What's the Date?

Yesterday? Tomorrow? Two weeks from today? What if you don't have a calendar with you and you need the exact date? Practice your understanding of the phrases in the preceding table. If today were *le sept août*, give the date for the following. Answers can be found in Appendix A.

1. avant-hier ____________________
2. d'aujourd'hui en huit ____________
3. de demain en quinze ____________
4. demain ____________________
5. la veille ____________________
6. il y a sept jours ______________

What Do You Make of This?

A French friend phones and says to you, *"Il fait si beau aujourd'hui. On fait du golf?"* You have already seen that, in speaking about the weather, you can use the irregular verb *faire* in an impersonal way: *il fait* + the weather condition. The verb *faire*, shown in the following table, means "to make" or "to do" and is often used to speak about household chores. *Faire* can also be used to speak about playing a sport, even though it translates poorly into English. So, will you be playing golf with your friend today?

The Verb *Faire* (to Make, to Do)

Conjugation	Pronunciation	Meaning
je fais	*zhuh feh*	I make, do
tu fais	*tew feh*	you make, do
il, elle, on fait	*eel, ehl, ohN feh*	he, she, one makes, does
nous faisons	*noo fuh-zohN*	we make, do
vous faites	*voo feht*	you make, do
ils, elles font	*eel, ehl fohN*	they make, do

Expressions with *Faire*

Let's say you don't want to talk about sports or the weather. How else can you use the verb *faire* to your best advantage? There are many useful idioms with the verb *faire*. If your host asked you, "*Voudriez-vous faire une partie de tennis?*" would you think he was inviting you to a tennis party? Common sense and a knowledge of cognates would trick you into thinking so. In reality, he'd only be inviting you to play in a match. Similarly, if he told you "*Je l'ai fait exprès*," would you think he did something in a rush? Again, your knowledge of English would make you think so. Actually, whatever he did, he did it on purpose. You can see why it is very important to study the idiomatic expressions with *faire* in the following table.

More Idioms with *Faire*

L'expression	Pronunciation	English
faire à sa tête	*fehr ah sah teht*	to do as one pleases
faire attention à	*fehr ah-tahN-syohN ah*	to pay attention to
faire de son mieux	*fehr duh sohN myuh*	to do one's best
faire des achats (emplettes)	*fehr day zah-shah (ahN-pleht)*	to go shopping
faire des courses	*fehr day koors*	to do errands (shop)
faire exprès	*fehr ehks-preh*	to do on purpose
faire la connaissance de	*fehn lah koh-neh-sahNs duh*	to meet, to become acquainted with
faire la queue	*fehr lah kuh*	to stand in line
faire mal à	*fehr mahl ah*	to hurt
faire peur à	*fehr puhr ah*	to frighten
faire plaisir à	*fehr pleh-zeer ah*	to please
faire semblant de	*fehr sahN-blahN duh*	to pretend
faire ses adieux	*fehr say zah-dyuh*	to say good-bye
faire une partie de	*fehr ewn pahr-tee duh*	to play a game of
faire une promenade	*fehr ewn prohm-nahd*	to take a walk
faire un voyage	*fehr uhN vwah-yahzh*	to take a trip
faire venir	*fehr vuh-neer*	to send for

Make sure to conjugate the verb when you use it in context:

Je fais les courses le lundi.
I go on errands on Mondays.

Faites venir le médecin.
Send for the doctor.

Ils font un voyage en France.
They are taking a trip to France.

In the preceding expressions, wherever the possessive adjective *son*, *sa*, or *ses* appears, any of the equivalent possessive adjectives may be used, depending on the subject:

Je fais à ma tête.	Nous faisons nos adieux.
zhuh feh ah mah teht	*noo fuh-zohN no zah-dyuh*
I do as I please.	We say our good-byes.

Using Faire

Because the verb *faire* has so many different uses, it's quite important to practice it thoroughly. After you feel confident with the conjugation of *faire* and have learned its various idioms, complete the following sentences. Answers can be found in Appendix A.

1. (to take a trip) Ils ____________________.
2. (to wait in line) Vous ____________________.
3. (to send for) Tu ____________________ le docteur.
4. (to take a walk) Nous ____________________.
5. (to meet) Elle ____________________ M. Renaud.
6. (to go shopping) Je ____________________.
7. (to pay attention) On ____________________ au directeur.
8. (to play a game of) Elles ____________________ golf.

The Least You Need to Know

- Use *il fait* to express weather conditions and the temperature.
- To express the date, use the day of the week + the number of the day + the month + the year.
- The irregular verb *faire* is used to discuss sports and household chores and is used in some very useful idiomatic expressions.

Chapter 14

Sightseeing

In This Chapter

- Typical tourist attractions
- Animals galore
- Making suggestions and plans
- Expressing your opinion
- Other countries
- The pronoun *y*

The weather in today's paper is calling for a mild and sunshiny day. It's perfect weather to have a *café au lait* at a sidewalk *café*, visit Notre Dame, and finally take a stroll down the Champs-Elysées. You've checked your guidebook to see what's open and at what times. Now it's time to take out your metro or bus map and plan your day so that you can leisurely enjoy the sights you long to see.

This chapter gives you a choice of things to do and interesting places to visit. You will become proficient in making suggestions and giving your opinions about things. And if you should decide to travel far and wide, you will be able to get there—in French.

The Sights to See

There's so much to do and so much to see in all the French-speaking countries. Are you in the mood for sightseeing or relaxing? Do you want to pack your day with activity, or do you prefer to proceed at a leisurely pace? The brochures you've picked up at your hotel or at the tourist office offer many suggestions. The following table gives you the words and phrases you need to talk about your choices.

Where to Go and What to Do

The Place	Le Lieu	Pronunciation
the aquarium	l'aquarium	*lah-kwah-ryuhm*
the church	l'église (*f.*)	*lay-gleez*
the night club	la boîte de nuit	*lah bwaht duh nwee*
the carnival	le carnaval	*luh kahr-nah-vahl*
the cathedral	la cathédrale	*lah kah-tay-drahl*
the castle	le château	*luh shah-to*
the circus	le cirque	*luh seerk*
the fair	la foire	*lah fwahr*
the fountain	la fontaine	*lah fohN-tehn*
the garden	le jardin	*luh zhahr-daN*
the flea market	le marché aux puces	*luh mahr-shay o pews*
the museum	le musée	*luh mew-zay*
the amusement park	le parc d'attractions	*luh pahrk dah-trahk-syohN*
the square	la place	*lah plahs*
the quay	le quai	*luh kay*

We Shall See

So will it be the exquisite paintings and sculptures of a particular museum, the stained glass windows of a cathedral, the luxurious rooms of a château, or perhaps a famous monument? To express what you would like to see or are going to see, you will need the irregular verb *voir* (to see). *Voir* is similar to a "shoe" verb in that the *nous* and *vous* forms change. These forms do not, however, look like the infinitive. In this case, the forms inside the shoe do! Consider *voir* a reverse shoe verb.

The Verb *Voir* (to See)

Conjugation	Pronunciation	Meaning
je vois	*zhuh vwah*	I see
tu vois	*tew vwah*	you see
il, elle, on voit	*eel, ehl, ohN vwah*	he, she, one sees
nous voyons	*noo vwah-yohN*	we see
vous voyez	*voo vwah-yay*	you see
ils, elles voient	*eel, ehl vwah*	they see

Are You an Animal Lover?

My friend Trudy stops to see the animals on every trip she takes. One of her biggest delights is going to a game farm to feed the baby animals. My son Michael has been partial to aquariums since his first experience years ago at the age of 4 months. And my husband, well, he's not an animal lover at all; his male ego falls for shirts with powerful animals sewn on the pockets.

Whether you want to visit a zoo or an aquarium, take a safari to Africa, or simply make a purchase with an animal design or logo, the names of the animals in the following table might come in handy.

Animals

Animal	L'animal	Pronunciation
bear	l'ours *m.*	*loors*
bird	l'oiseau *m.*	*lwah-zo*
cat	le chat	*luh shah*
chicken, hen	la poule	*lah pool*
cow	la vache	*lah vahsh*
dog	le chien	*luh shyaN*
dolphin	le dauphin	*luh do-faN*
elephant	l'éléphant	*lay-lay-fahN*
fish	le poisson	*luh pwah-sohN*
fox	le renard	*luh ruh-nard*
giraffe	le girafe	*luh zhee-rahf*

continues

Animals (continued)

Animal	L'animal	Pronunciation
goat	la chèvre	*lah shehvr*
gorilla	la gorille	*lah goh-reey*
horse	le cheval	*luh shuh-vahl*
leopard	le léopard	*luh lay-oh-pahr*
lion	le lion	*luh lee-ohN*
monkey	le singe	*luh saNzh*
panther	la panthère	*lah pahN-tehr*
pig	le cochon	*luh koh-shohN*
rabbit	le lapin	*luh lah-paN*
rhinoceros	le rhinocéros	*luh ree-noh-say-rohs*
shark	le requin	*luh ruh-kaN*
sheep	le mouton	*luh moo-tohN*
tiger	le tigre	*luh teegr*
whale	la baleine	*lah bah-lehn*

Take Me to the Zoo

Read the following ads for zoos and figure out which one is in Paris, which is closest to Paris, which is farthest from Paris, which is open all year, which are open every day, in which you can have a picnic, in which the animals roam free.

PARC ZOOLOGIQUE DU BOIS D'ATTILLY

OUVERTE TOUTE L'ANNÉE
GRAND PARC NATUREL
PIQUE-NIQUE
25 KM DE PARIS RN4

PARC ZOOLOGIQUE DE PARIS

Ouvert Tous les Jours
Restaurant—
Pique-Nique
Autobus 46—86—325
Consultez-nous sur le 11

PARC ZOOLOGIQUE DU CHATEAU DE THOIRY

800 Animaux en Liberté
Ouvert tous les jours
40 KM A 13 de Paris
11 -> consultez l'Annuaire Electronique

Making a Lot of Suggestions

You've always had your heart set on seeing the *Folies Bergères.* The glamorous ads, posters, and pictures you've seen have enticed you and piqued your curiosity. You don't know, however, how the others in your group feel about accompanying you. Live it up! Make the suggestion. There are two options in French that you'll find quite simple.

You can use the pronoun *on* + the conjugated form of the verb that explains what it is you want to do:

On va aux Folies Bergères?
ohN vah o foh-lee behr-zhehr
How about going to the Folies Bergères?

On fait une croisière?
ohN feh tewn krwah-zyehr
How about going on a cruise?

Another way to propose an activity is to use the command form that has *nous* as its understood subject:

Allons aux Folies Bergères!
ah-lohN zo foh-lee behr-zhehr
Let's go to the Folies Bergères!

Faisons une croisière!
fuh-zohN zewn krwah-zyehr
Let's go on a cruise!

When using the imperative (command) form, it is unnecessary to use the subject pronoun *nous.*

Memory Enhancer

The irregular verb *voir* is conjugated as follows:

je vois	nous voyons
tu vois	vous voyez
il, elle, on voit	ils, elles voient

Make suggestions about what to see or do by saying:

On + third-person singular form of the verb to express "How about …?"

The *nous* form of the verb without using the subject *nous* to express "Let's …."

Other Useful Phrases

If you're feeling rather confident with the language at this point, you might want to take a more sophisticated approach. There are a number of phrases you can use, all of which are followed by the infinitive of the verb. (The familiar *tu* forms are in parentheses.)

Ça vous (te) dit de (d') …?
sah voo (tuh) dee duh
Do you want to …?

Ça vous (t') intéresse de (d') …?
sah voo-zaN (taN)-tay-rehs duh
Are you interested in …?

Ça vous (te) plairait de (d') …?
sah voo (tuh) pleh-reh duh
Would it please you to …?

Vous voulez …? (Tu veux …?)
voo voo-lay (tew vuh)
Do you want to …?

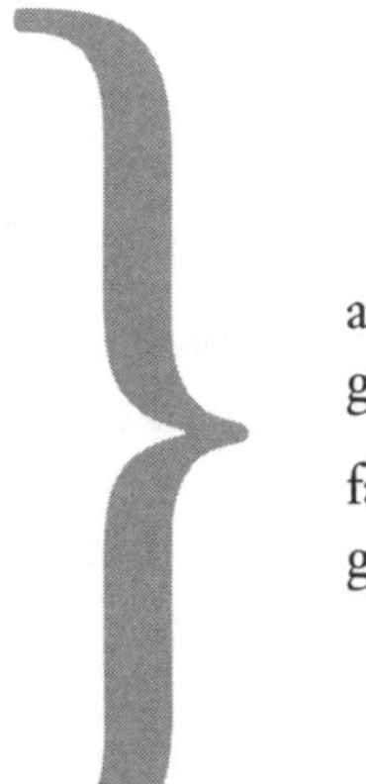

aller au cinéma?
going to the movies?

faire une croisière?
go on a cruise?

Any of the preceding phrases can be made negative by using *ne … pas:*

Ça *ne* te dit *pas* de (d') …?
Don't you want to …?

Ça *ne* t'intéresse *pas* de (d') …?
Aren't you interested in …?

Ça *ne* te plairait *pas* de (d') …?
Wouldn't it please you to …?

Tu *ne* veux *pas* …?
Don't you want to …?

aller au cinéma?
going to the movies?

faire une croisière?
go on a cruise?

Memory Enhancer

When answering a negative question in the affirmative, *si* is used instead of *oui*. When answering in the negative, *un*, *une*, and *des* become *de*.

Only petulant teenagers give abrupt yes or no answers to questions. Most of the rest of us say, "Yes, but …" or "No, because …." If you'd like to elaborate on your answer, here's what you'll have to do: Change the pronoun *vous* or *te* (*t'*) from the question to *me* (*m'*) in your answer.

<table>
<tr><td>Oui (Si), ça me dit de (d') …
Oui (Si), ça m'intéresse de (d')
Oui (Si), ça me plairait de (d')
Oui (Si), je veux.
Non, ça ne me dit pas de (d') …
Non, ça ne m'intéresse pas de (d')
Non ça ne me plairait pas de (d')
Non, je ne veux pas.</td><td>}</td><td>aller au cinéma.
faire **de** croisière.</td></tr>
</table>

What Do You Think?

How do you feel about a suggestion that was made to you? Does the activity appeal to you? If so, you would say:

J'aime la musique classique.
J'adore l'opéra.
Je suis fana de ballet.

When you do something or go somewhere new, different, exotic, or out of the ordinary, you're bound to have an opinion on whether or not you liked it. Was it fun? You had a good time? You were amused? Give your positive opinion by saying the following:

C'est (*seh*) …

… chouette (*shoo-eht;* great)!

… extra (*ehks-trah; terrific*)!

… formidable (*fohr-mee-dahbl;* great)!

… génial (*zhay-nyahl; great*)!

… fantastique (*fahN-tah-steek; fantastic*)!

… magnifique (*mah-nyee-feek; magnificent*)!

… merveilleux (*mehr-veh-yuh; marvelous*)!

… sensationnel (*sahN-sah-syoh-nehl; sensational*)!

… super (*sew-pehr; super*)!

… superbe (*sew-pehrb;* superb)!

Perhaps you don't like the suggestion presented. Maybe the activity bores you. You might say:

Je n'aime pas …	Je déteste …	Je ne suis pas fana de …
zhuh nehm pah …	*zhuh day-tehst …*	*zhuh nuh swee pah fah-nah duh …*
I don't like …	I hate …	I'm not a fan of …

Je n'aime pas la musique classique.
Je déteste l'opéra.
Je ne suis pas fana de ballet.

Just to be a good sport, you tried it anyway. It was just as you thought: not your cup of tea. To give your negative opinion about an activity, you could say:

C'est …

… affreux (*ah-fruh;* frightful, horrible)!

… la barbe (*lah bahrb;* boring)!

… dégoûtant (*day-goo-tahN;* disgusting)!

… désagréable (*day-zah-gray-ahbl*)!

… embêtant (*ahN-beh-tahN;* boring)!

… ennuyeux (*ahN-nwee-yuh;* boring)!

… horrible (*oh-reebl*)!

… ridicule (*ree-dee-kewl;* ridiculous)!

Your Sentiments Exactly

Are you one of those people who sees things as either black or white? Or do you see things in varying shades of gray? Personally, I'm a very opinionated person. I love it or I hate it. Rarely is there an in-between. I love the ballet because I like to picture myself as one of the dancers: beautiful, lean, and in the best of shape. I dislike the opera. It's just not my thing. The music is too loud, and I don't understand what they're saying. Don't be afraid to speak up and speak your mind. Tell how you feel about visiting the following attractions. Sample answers can be found in Appendix A.

1. (le Louvre) ______________________________.
2. (Notre-Dame de Paris) ______________________________.

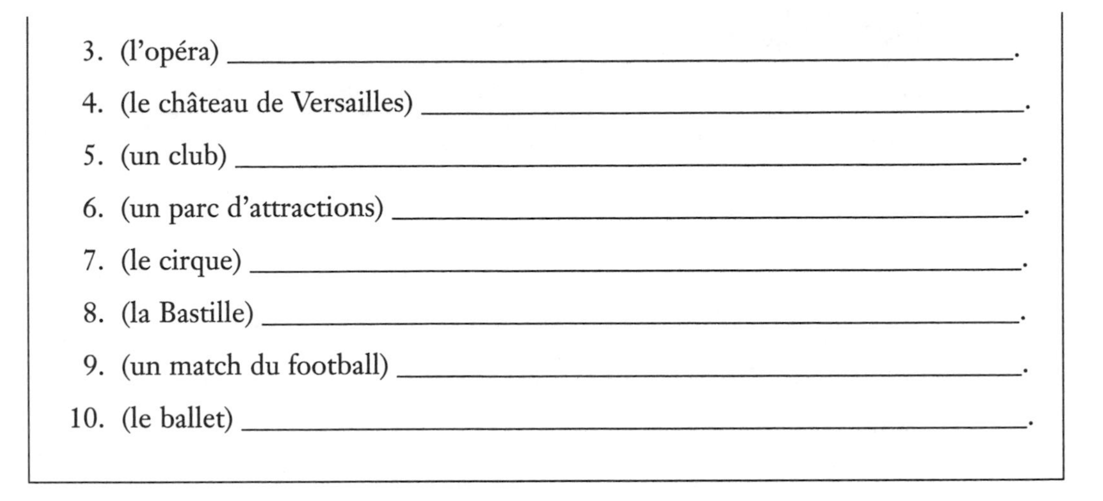

3. (l'opéra) ________________________________.
4. (le château de Versailles) ________________________________.
5. (un club) ________________________________.
6. (un parc d'attractions) ________________________________.
7. (le cirque) ________________________________.
8. (la Bastille) ________________________________.
9. (un match du football) ________________________________.
10. (le ballet) ________________________________.

Up, Up, and Away

Years ago, when my husband and I backpacked throughout Europe, we used our French in every single country we visited (except England, naturally). Since France borders Belgium, Luxembourg, Germany, Switzerland, Italy, and Spain, it is easy to see why French would be spoken and understood in all of those countries and why the people in France are familiar with those languages as well. Furthermore, due to France's importance in the European Union, French is spoken in all other European countries, too. Your travels may take you to many different places where French is spoken. It would prove quite helpful to learn the French names of the countries in the following table, especially those countries in Europe. If you look closely at the names of the feminine countries, you will notice that, except for Haïti (which is also the only country in the group that does not use a definite article: *la*, *l'*), they all end in *-e*. This makes them very easy to identify.

Countries

Country	Le Pays	Pronunciation
Feminine Countries		
Algeria	l'Algérie	*lahl-zhay-ree*
Austria	l'Autriche	*lo-treesh*
Belgium	la Belgique	*lah behl-zheek*
China	la Chine	*lah sheen*
Egypt	L'Egypt	*lay-geept*

continues

Countries (continued)

Country	Le Pays	Pronunciation
England	l'Angleterre	*lahN-gluh-tehr*
France	la France	*lah frahNs*
Germany	l'Allemagne	*lahl-mah-nyuh*
Greece	la Grèce	*lah grehs*
Haiti	Haïti	*ah-ee-tee*
India	l'Inde	*laNd*
Italy	l'Italie	*lee-tah-lee*
Norway	la Norvège	*lah nohr-vehzh*
Russia	la Russie	*lah rew-see*
Scotland	l'Écosse	*lay-kohs*
Spain	l'Espagne	*lehs-pah-nyuh*
Sweden	la Suède	*lah swehd*
Switzerland	la Suisse	*lah swees*
Masculine Countries		
Canada	le Canada	*luh kah-nah-dah*
Cambodia	le Cambodge	*luh kahN-bohdzh*
Denmark	le Danemark	*luh dahn-mahrk*
Israel	Israël	*eez-rah-ehl*
Japan	le Japon	*luh zhah-pohN*
Lebanon	le Liban	*luh lee-bahN*
Morocco	le Maroc	*luh mah-rohk*
Mexico	le Mexique	*luh mehk-seek*
Netherlands	les Pays-Bas	*lay pay-ee bah*
Portugal	le Portugal	*luh pohr-tew-gahl*
United States	les États-Unis	*lay zay-tah-zew-nee*
Zaire	le Zaïre	*luh zah-eer*

Three masculine countries end in *-e*. Israël and Haïti do not use any definite article.

Do your travels take you far and wide? Are you fortunate enough to be able to plan a trip to another continent? The names of six continents in the following table are all feminine. *L'Antarctique* (*lahN-tahrk-teek*, Antarctica), the seventh continent, is the only one that is masculine.

The Continents

Continent	Le Continent	Pronunciation
Africa	l'Afrique	*lah-freek*
Antarctica	l'Antarctique	*lahN-tahrk-teek*
Asia	l'Asie	*lah-zee*
Australia	l'Australie	*loh-strah-lee*
Europe	l'Europe	*lew-rohp*
North America	l'Amérique du Nord	*lah-may-reek dew nohr*
South America	l'Amérique du Sud	*lah-may-reek dew sewd*

Going

On your next trip to Europe, will you be going to Italy? Will you be staying with your relatives in Spain or Portugal? To express that you are going to or staying in another country, use the preposition *en* to express "to." Also use *en* to express "in" before the names of feminine countries, continents, provinces, islands, and states and before masculine countries starting with a vowel:

Je vais en Italie.
zhuh veh zahN nee-tah-lee
I am going to Italy.

Je reste en Espagne.
zhuh rehst ahN nehs-pah-nyuh
I'm staying in Spain.

Je vais voyager en Israël.
zhuh veh vwah-yah-zhay ahN neez-rah-ehl
I am going to travel to (in) Israel.

The preposition *au* (*aux* for plurals) is used to express "to" or "in" before the names of some masculine countries, islands, provinces, and states that start with a consonant:

Je vais au Japon.
zhuh veh zo zhah-pohN
I am going to Japan.

Je reste aux États-Unis.
zhuh rehst o zay-tah-zew-nee
I am staying in the United States.

Use *dans le* to express "to" or "in" before geographical names that are modified by an adjective:

Je vais dans le Dakota du Nord.
J'habite dans l'État de New Jersey.

Coming

Every traveler has an accent, albeit sometimes almost imperceptible, that alerts native speakers to the fact that he (or she) is from another region or country. My French nasal sounds give me away as a New Yorker. My consultant Roger's "th" that comes out "z" is typically French. The fact that my friend Carlos drops his final "s" is a dead giveaway that he's a native Hispanic. If your accent reveals your identity and you want to say that you are from (or coming from) a specific country, use the preposition *de* before the names of feminine countries, continents, provinces, islands, and states and before masculine countries starting with a vowel:

Je suis de France.
zhuh swee duh frahNs
I am from France.

Je suis d'Israël.
zhuh swee deez-rah-ehl
I am from Israel.

The preposition *de* + the definite article *(le, l', les)* is used before masculine countries and geographical names that are modified by an adjective:

Je suis du Canada.
zhuh swee dew kah-nah-dah
I am from Canada.

Je suis des États-Unis.
zhuh swee day-zay-tah-zew-nee
I am from the United States.

Je suis de la belle France.
zhuh swee duh lah behl frahNs
I am from beautiful France.

Je suis de l'Amérique du Nord.
zhuh swee duh lah-may-reek dew nohr
I am from North America.

Exactly Where Are You Going?

Start your sentence with *Je vais* (I'm going) and tell what country you are going to if you plan to see the following. Answers can be found in Appendix A.

1. (a bullfight) ________________________________.
2. (the Great Wall) ________________________________.
3. (Mexican jumping beans) ________________________________.
4. (the Moscow circus) ________________________________.
5. (the Leaning Tower of Pisa) ________________________________.
6. (Big Ben) ________________________________.
7. (the pyramids) ________________________________.

8. (the Eiffel Tower) ______________________________.
9. (Grand Canyon) ______________________________.
10. (home) ______________________________.

The French Pronoun *y*

The French pronoun *y* (*ee*) generally refers to or replaces previously mentioned places or locations and may also refer to things or ideas. The pronoun *y* usually replaces the preposition *à* (*au*, *à l'*, *à la*, *aux*) or other prepositions of location (shown in the following table) + a noun.

Prepositions of Location

Preposition	La Préposition	Pronunciation
at the house (business) of	chez	*shay*
against	contre	*kohNtr*
behind	derrière	*deh-ryehr*
between	entre	*ahNtr*
in	dans	*dahN*
in	en	*ahN*
in front of	devant	*duh-vahN*
on	sur	*sewr*
toward	vers	*vehr*
under	sous	*soo*

You received a letter today from your French friend. I, of course, would never open your mail, but I sure am curious about that letter. Is it on your desk? Are you going to answer it immediately? Are you going to go to France to visit your friend? Are you going to stay at your friend's house? Will your family say, "Go there and have a good time"? These questions can be answered in French by using the pronoun *y*.

Y means "there" when the place has already been mentioned, and it can also mean "it," "them," "in it/them," "to it/them," or "on it/them."

Il va à Paris.
Il *y* va.
He goes there.

Mon billet est dans ma poche.
Mon billet *y* est.
My ticket is in it (there).

Je réponds à la lettre.
J'*y* réponds.
I answer it.

The pronoun *y* is used to replace *de* + noun only when *de* is part of a prepositional phrase showing location:

La douane est *à côté des* bagages.
La douane *y* est.
Customs is there.

Sometimes *y* is used in French and is not translated into English:

La valise est sur la table?	Oui, elle *y* est.
Is the valise on the table?	Yes, it is.

Y is placed before the verb to which its meaning is tied. When there are two verbs, *y* is placed before the infinitive:

J'y vais. I am going there.	Je n'y vais pas. I'm not going there.
Je désire *y* aller. I want to go there.	N'*y* va pas. Don't go there.

Memory Enhancer

The familiar (*tu*) command forms of *-er* verbs (regular and irregular) retain the final *s* before *y*. Remember to put a liaison (link) between the final consonant and *y*.

In an affirmative command, *y* changes position. It is placed immediately after the verb and is joined to it by a hyphen:

Vas-*y*!	Allez-*y*!
vah zee	*ah-lay zee*
Go (there)! (familiar)	Go (there)! (polite)

Use the idiomatic French expression *Allons-y* when you want to express "Let's go" or "We're off."

Using *y*

Word has gotten out that you'll be going to Europe this summer. Your nosey next-door neighbor has heard the rumor and can't wait to pump you for information. Use *y* to efficiently answer her questions and make a rapid getaway. Sample responses can be found in Appendix A.

1. Vous allez en France?

   ____

2. Vous restez à Paris?

   ____

3. Vous passez vos vacances chez votre famille?

   ____

4. Vous allez descendre en ville?

   ____

5. Vous allez dîner dans des restaurants élégants?

   ____

6. Vous allez penser à votre travail?

   ____

Make a Suggestion

Let's say you are planning a trip with a group of friends. Your friends are spirited and lively—and none are shy about expressing an opinion about where the group should go. It's your turn to react to the various suggestions:

Example:
(aller en Italie) Allons-y! N'y allons pas!

1. (voyager en Grèce)

   ____

2. (aller à l'aquarium)

   ____

continues

continued

3. (rester dans un hôtel chic)

____

4. (passer la journée au carnaval)

____

5. (assister à une exposition d'art moderne)

____

The Least You Need to Know

- To suggest an activity use *on* + the conjugated verb or use the *nous* form conjugated without *nous*.
- Simple phrases can express your likes (*C'est super!*) and dislikes (*C'est la barbe!*).
- Countries that end in *-e* are usually feminine. The rest are masculine.
- The pronoun *y* can replace a preposition + a location. *Y* means "there."

Chapter 15

I Wanna Shop Till I Drop

In This Chapter

- Stores and what they sell
- Clothing, colors, sizes, materials, and designs
- All about *mettre*
- Getting what you like
- This, that, these, and those (a.k.a. demonstrative adjectives)

You've visited just about everything on your "must-see" list. For the time being, you've had your fill of sightseeing. Now you would like to pick up some souvenirs of your trip or those gifts you promised family and friends at home.

Are you particular about what you buy? Is it important that you pick out the perfect gift or memento? Do you spend time agonizing over the right color, size, material, and design? Or do you choose almost anything you feel will be appropriate? This chapter helps you make the shopping decisions that are best for you. Read and study all the information before you "shop till you drop."

Now That's My Kinda Store!

Today is a shopping day. Do you prefer to browse in a small boutique, or are you attracted to *un centre commercial* (*uhN sahNtr koh-mehr-syahl;* a large, elegant mall) such as *le Forum des Halles* in Paris or the underground *Place Bonaventure* in Montreal? The following table points you in the direction of stores that might interest you and the merchandise you can purchase in them.

Note: If you want to say that you are going to a store or that you'll be at a store, remember to use *à* (to, at) + the definite article (*au*, *à la*, *à l'*):

au grand magasin
à la parfumerie

Stores—*Les Magasins (lay mah-gah-zaN)*

The Store	Le Magasin	The Merchandise	La Marchandise
bookstore	la librairie *lah lee-breh-ree*	books	des livres *m.*
boutique	la boutique *lah boo-teek*	clothing	des vêtements *m.*
department store	le grand magasin *luh grahN mah-gah-zaN*	almost everything	presque tout
florist	le magasin de fleuriste *luh mah-gah-zaN duh fluh-reest*	flowers	des fleurs *f.*
jewelry store	la bijouterie *lah bee-zhoo-tree*	jewels rings bracelets watches earrings necklaces	des bijoux *m.* des bagues *f.* des bracelets *m.* des montres *f.* des boucles d'oreille *f.* des colliers *m.*
leather goods store	la maroquinerie *lah mah-roh-kaN-ree*	wallets pocket books suitcases briefcases	des portefeuilles *m.* des sacs *m.* des valises *f.* des serviettes *f.*

The Store	Le Magasin	The Merchandise	La Marchandise
newsstand	le kiosk à journaux *luh kee-ohsk ah zhoor-no*	newspapers magazines	des journaux *m.* des revues *f.*
perfume store	la parfumerie *lah par-fuhN-ree*	perfume	du parfum
record store	le magasin de disques *luh mah-gah-zaN duh deesk*	records cassettes compact discs	des disques *m.* des cassettes *f.* des C.D. *m.*
souvenir shop	le magasin de souvenirs *luh mah-gah-zaN duh soo-vuh-neer*	T-shirts posters miniatures paintings	des tee-shirt *m.* des posters *m.* des monuments en miniature *m.* des tableaux *m.*
tobacconist	le bureau de tabac *luh bew-ro duh tah-bah*	tobacco cigarettes pipes cigars matches lighters	du tabac des cigarettes *f.* des pipes *f.* des cigares *f.* des allumettes *f.* des briquets *m.*

Gems and Jewels

Some people feel, and rightfully so, that they can get a very good bargain when they purchase jewelry in a foreign country because they can avoid certain taxes and duties. Here's the living proof of that. In honor of our wedding anniversary, my husband purchased a beautiful watch for me during a trip to Saint Martin (the French side, of course). The watch, a well-known brand name, was double the price in a popular stateside store reputed far and wide to give the best deals on jewelry. He really got an incredible deal. If you know your prices and are a good shopper, or if you're simply in the mood to buy some jewelry, you can use the following table to get exactly what you want.

Jewels—*Les Bijoux (lay bee-zhoo)*

Jewel	French	Pronunciation
amethyst	une améthyste	*ewn ah-may-teest*
aquamarine	une aige-marine	*ewn ehg mah-reen*
diamond	un diamant	*uhN dee-ah-mahN*
emerald	une émeraude	*ewn aym-rod*
ivory	un ivoire	*uhN nee-vwahr*
jade	un jade	*uhN zhahd*
onyx	un onyx	*uhN noh-neeks*
pearls	des perles *f.*	*day pehrl*
ruby	un rubis	*uhN rew-bee*
sapphire	un saphir	*uhN sah-feer*
topaz	une topaze	*ewn toh-pahz*
turquoise	une turquoise	*ewn tewr-kwahz*

When buying jewelry, you might want to ask:

Est-ce en or?
ehs ahN nohr
Is it gold?

Est-ce en argent?
ehs ahN nahr-zhahN
Is it silver?

Clothing

It's simply impossible to take a trip to France, the fashion capital of the world, and not come home with at least one article of clothing. You want to have one French label so that you can brag that you are *dans le vent* (*dahN luh vahN*; in fashion). The following table will help you in your quest for something *au courant.*

Clothing—*Les Vêtements (lay veht-mahN)*

Clothing	Les Vêtements	Pronunciation
bathing suit	le maillot	*luh mah-yo*
string bikini	la ficelle	*lah fee-sehl*
belt	la ceinture	*lah saN-tewr*
boots	les bottes *f.*	*lay boht*
blouse	le chemisier	*luh shuh-meez-yay*

Clothing	Les Vêtements	Pronunciation
brassière	le soutien-gorge	*luh soo-tyaN gohrzh*
coat	le manteau	*luh mahN-to*
dress	la robe	*lah rohb*
gloves	les gants *m.*	*lay gahN*
hat	le chapeau	*luh shah-po*
jacket	la veste	*lah vehst*
jeans	le jean	*luh zheen*
jogging suit	le survêt	*luh sewr-veh*
pajamas	le pyjama	*luh pee-zhah-mah*
panties	la culotte	*lah kew-loht*
pants	le pantalon	*luh pahN-tah-lohN*
pantyhose (tights)	le collant	*luh koh-lahN*
pocketbook	le sac	*luh sahk*
pullover	le pull	*luh pewl*
raincoat	l'imperméable *m.*	*laN-pehr-may-ahbl*
robe	la robe de chambre	*lah rohb duh shahNbr*
sandals	les sandales *f.*	*lay sahN-dahl*
scarf	l'écharpe *f.* le foulard	*lay-shahrp,* *luh foo-lahr*
shirt (man-tailored)	la chemise	*lah shuh-meez*
shoes	les chaussures *f.*, les souliers *m.*	*lay sho-sewr;* *lay soo-lyay*
shorts	le short	*luh shohrt*
skirt	la jupe	*lah zhewp*
slip (half) (full)	le jupon la combinaison	*luh zhew-pohN* *lah kohN-bee-neh-zohN*
sneakers	les tennis	*lay tuh-nees*
socks	les chaussettes *f.*	*lay sho-seht*
stockings	les bas *m.*	*lay bah*
suit (men)	le complet le costume	*luh kohN-pleh* *luh kohs-tewm*
suit (women)	le tailleur	*luh tah-yuhr*
T-shirt	le tee-shirt	*luh tee-shehrt*
tie	la cravate	*lah krah-vaht*

continues

Clothing—*Les Vêtements (lay veht-mahN)* (continued)

Clothing	Les Vêtements	Pronunciation
umbrella	le parapluie	*luh pah-rah-plwee*
undershirt	le maillot de corps	*luh mah-yo duh kohr*
undershorts	le slip	*luh sleep*
underwear	les sous-vêtements *m.*	*lay soo-veht-mahN*
windbreaker	le blouson	*luh bloo-zohN*

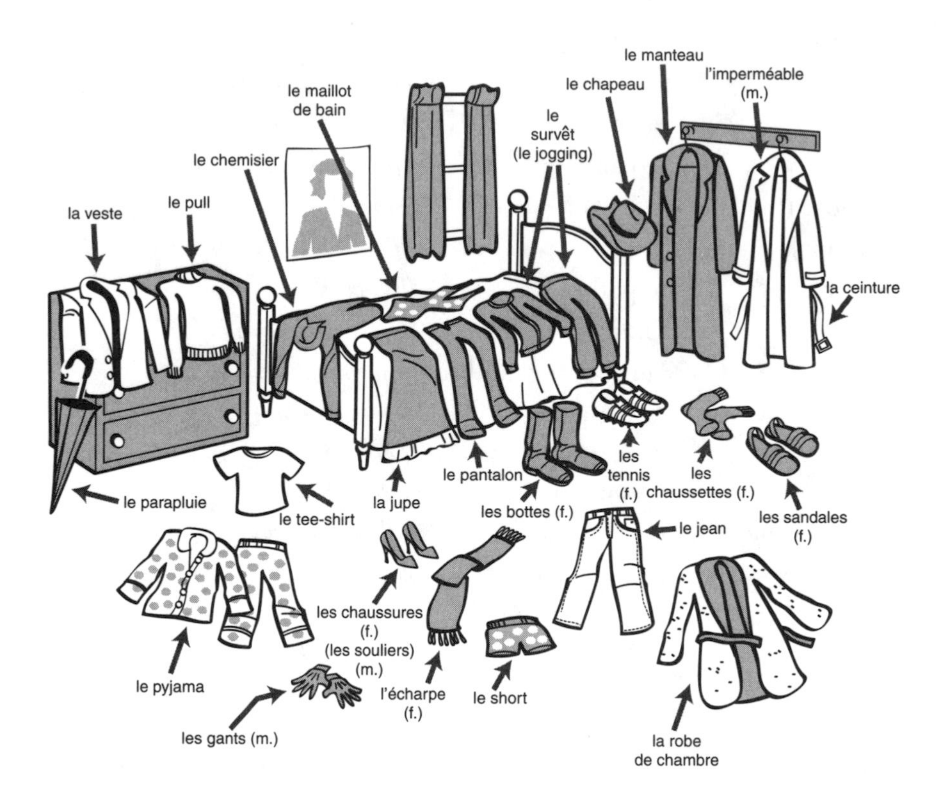

Because Europeans use the metric system, their sizes are different from ours. Look at the following conversion chart to determine the sizes you would wear:

Women

Shoes													
American	4	4½	5	5½	6	6½	7	7½	8	8½	9	9½	10
Continental	35	35	36	36	37	37	38	38	39	39	40	40	41

Dresses, suits						
American	8	10	12	14	16	18
Continental	36	38	40	42	44	46
Blouses, sweaters						
American	small		medium		large	
Continental	40	42	44	46	48	50

Men

Shoes										
American	7	7½	8	8½	9	9½	10	10½	11	11½
Continental	39	40	41	42	43	43	44	44	45	45
Suits, coats										
American	34	36	38	40	42	44	46	48		
Continental	44	46	48	50	52	54	56	58		
Shirts										
American	14	14½	15	15½	16	16½	17	17½		
Continental	36	37	38	39	40	41	42	43		

You want to make sure that you get your right size. Tell the salesperson:

Je porte du …	petit	moyen	grand
zhuh pohrt dew …	*puh-tee*	*mwah-yaN*	*grahN*
I wear …	small	medium	large
Ma taille est …	petite	moyenne	grande
ma tahy eh …	*puh-teet*	*mwah-yehn*	*grahNd*
My size is …	small	medium	large

For shoes, you would say:

Je chausse du (+ size).
zhuh shohs dew …
I wear shoe size …

Memory Enhancer

To describe a color as "light," add the word *clair*; to describe a color as "dark," add the word *foncé*. For example, "light blue" is *bleu clair*, and "dark green" is *vert foncé*.

Colors

My sister Susan, an *artiste*, has taught her seven-year-old son to describe things as chartreuse, teal, aubergine, and tangerine. I, on the other hand, see the world in primary colors. Whether you go for the *exotique* or the *ordinaire*, the following table will help you with the basic colors.

Note: Colors are adjectives and therefore must agree with the noun they are describing. For example, say:

un chemisier blanc a white blouse	une chemise blanche a white shirt

Colors—*Les Couleurs (lay koo-luhr)*

Color	La Couleur	Pronunciation	Color	La Couleur	Pronunciation
beige	beige	*behzh*	gray	gris(e)	*gree(z)*
black	noir(e)	*nwahr*	green	vert(e)	*vehr(t)*
blue	bleu(e)	*bluh*	orange	orange	*oh-rahNzh*
brown	brun(e)	*bruhN (brewn)*	pink	rose	*roz*
purple	mauve	*mov*	white	blanc(he)	*blahN(sh)*
red	rouge	*roozh*	yellow	jaune	*zhon*

Materials

While traveling, you might be tempted to make a clothing purchase. Do you find linen sexy? Do you love the feel of silk? Do you crave the coolness of cotton? Is leather a turn-on? Are you into wrinkle-free? We choose or reject different fabrics for a wide variety of reasons. The following table will help you pick the material you prefer for your special purchases.

Materials—*Les Tissus (lay tee-sew)*

Material	Le Tissu	Pronunciation
cashmere	cachemire	*kahsh-meer*
corduroy	velours côtelée	*vuh-loor koht-lay*
cotton	coton	*koh-tohN*

Material	Le Tissu	Pronunciation
denim	jean	*zheen*
flannel	flanelle	*flah-nehl*
knit	tricot	*tree-ko*
leather	cuir	*kweer*
linen	lin	*laN*
silk	soie	*swah*
suede	daim	*daN*
wool	laine	*lehn*

To express that an item of clothing is made out of a certain material, use the preposition *en* (*ahN*).

C'est une chemise en soie.
It's a silk shirt.

Read the Labels

Have you ever accidentally washed a "dry clean only" shirt? Or have you ever washed a 100 percent cotton pair of jeans, only to find that they've shrunk and can never be worn again? Make sure to read all labels carefully for the following information:

non-rétrécissable	lavable	en tissu infroissable
nohN-ray-tray-see-sahbl	*lah-vahbl*	*ahN tee-sew aN-frwah-sahbl*
nonshrinkable	washable	wrinkle-resistant

Designs

Designs are very important when selecting a garment. Horizontal stripes make a person appear heavier, whereas vertical stripes do the opposite. Plaids and polka dots also change the way we look. The following table will enable you to pick what's right for you.

Designs—*Le Dessin (luh deh-saN)*

Design	Le Dessin	Pronunciation
checked	à carreaux	*ah kah-ro*
in herringbone	à chevrons	*ah shuh-vrohN*

continues

Designs—*Le Dessin (luh deh-saN)* (continued)

Design	Le Dessin	Pronunciation
in plaid	en tartan	*ahN tahr-tahN*
with polka dots	à pois	*ah pwah*
in a solid color	uni(e)	*ew-nee*
with stripes	à rayures	*ah rah-yewr*

You're Putting Me On

Now that your wardrobe is full, you will have to decide what to put on. The verb *mettre* in the following table will help you say this. Because it is an irregular verb, you should probably memorize it.

The Verb *Mettre* (to Put [On])

Conjugation	Pronunciation	Meaning
je mets	*zhuh meh*	I put (on)
tu mets	*tew meh*	you put (on)
il, elle, on met	*eel, ehl, ohN meh*	he, she, one puts (on)
nous mettons	*noo meh-tohN*	we put (on)
vous mettez	*voo meh-tay*	you put (on)
ils, elles mettent	*eel, ehl meht*	they put (on)

Put It On

Does your lifestyle demand an extensive wardrobe, or are you strictly a jeans and T-shirt kind of person? Imagine you've found yourself in the following situations. Describe in detail (including jewelry) what you put on to go the following. Sample answers can be found in Appendix A.

1. (to work) ______________________________
2. (to the beach) ______________________________
3. (to a formal dinner party) ______________________________

4. (to a friend's house) ________________________________

5. (skiing) ________________________________

What Are You Looking For?

You're on a shopping spree, and everything looks so enticing. Say what you could buy in each of the following stores. Sample responses can be found in Appendix A.

Vivianne

VIVIANNE est la spécialiste de la grande taille (du 38 au 58). Elle vous propose les plus grandes marques du prêt-à-porter féminin et accessoires assortis (sacs, ceintures, chapeaux) pour vous séduire. Elle assure des retouches gratuites.

Madame Paris

Prestige de la France
Parfums, produits de beauté, bijoux, foulards, accessoires, maroquinerie.

VARIATIONS

100% pure mode, 100% pur charme, tout VARIATION en une boutique moderne pour l'homme et la femme. Pulls, polos, chemisiers, jupes, ensembles, dans une sélection des matières naturelles douces et chaudes vous permettront de créer des coordonnés aux couleurs de la mode; 100% laine vierge, angoras, mélanges, 100% coton. Alliez la mode avec le charme des choses qui durent.

The Object of My Affection

I have an absolutely fabulous red dress. Imagine I was telling you about it and said, "I put on my red dress to go to parties. I love my red dress. I wear my red dress very often." How tedious and boring! It sounds much better to say: "I put on my red dress to go to parties. I love it and wear it often."

What did I do to improve my conversation? I stopped repeating "my red dress" (a direct object noun) and replaced it with "it" (a direct object pronoun). Just what exactly are direct objects? Let's take a closer look.

Direct objects (which can be nouns or pronouns) tell "whom" or "what" the subject is acting upon and can refer to people, places, things, or ideas.

I see *the boy.*	I see *him.*
I like *the dress.*	I like *it.*
He pays *John and me.*	He pays *us.*

How do indirect objects differ from direct objects? Again, let's take a closer look.

Indirect object nouns can be replaced by indirect object pronouns. Take the story of my friend Georgette who is crazy about her new boyfriend, Paul. This is what she told me: "I write to Paul. Then I read my love letters to Paul. I buy presents for Paul. I make cakes for Paul. I cook dinners for Paul." To get to the point more efficiently, all she had to say was: "I write to Paul and then I read him (to him) my love letters. I buy him (for him) presents. I make him (for him) cakes and cook him (for him) dinners."

Memory Enhancer

Read the following two sentences:

I write (to) him love letters.

I buy (for) him presents.

Notice that the "to" and "for" are often understood but not used in English. So be careful in French when choosing a direct or indirect object pronoun. If the words "to" or "for" make sense in the sentence (even though they do not actually appear), use an indirect object pronoun.

Indirect objects answer the question "to whom" the subject is doing something or "for whom" the subject is acting. Indirect objects refer only to people or domesticated animals.

I speak *to the boys.*	I speak *to them.*
I buy a gift *for Mary.*	I buy a gift *for her.* (I buy her a gift.)

He gives *(to) me* a tie every Christmas.

We use direct and indirect pronouns automatically in English all the time to prevent the constant, monotonous repetition of a word and to allow our conversation to flow naturally. Direct and indirect object nouns in French can be replaced by the pronouns in the following table.

Object Pronouns

Direct Object Pronoun	Pronunciation	Meaning	Indirect Object Pronoun	Pronunciation	Meaning
me (m')	*muh*	me	me (m')	*muh*	(to) me
te (t')	*tuh*	you (familiar)	te (t')	*tuh*	(to) you (familiar)
le (l')	*luh*	he, it	lui	*lwee*	(to) him
la (l')	*lah*	her, it	lui	*lwee*	(to) her
nous	*noo*	us	nous	*noo*	(to) us
vous	*voo*	you (polite)	vous	*voo*	(to) you (polite)
les	*lay*	them	leur	*luhr*	(to) them

The clue to the correct usage of an indirect object is the French preposition *à* (*au, à la, à l', aux*) followed by the name of or reference to a person. Some verbs, such as *répondre (à)*, *téléphoner (à)*, and *ressembler (à)* are always followed by *à* + person and will therefore always take an indirect object pronoun.

As you can see, you should have little problem using the direct or indirect object pronouns for me (to me), you (to you), or us (to us) because these pronouns are all exactly the same. You must be careful, however, when expressing him, her, them, or to/for him, her, them, because there are now two sets of pronouns. Sometimes this does get a bit tricky. Remember to choose the pronoun that reflects the number and gender of the noun to which you are referring.

CAUTION

Attention!

Be careful! Some verbs, such as *écouter* (to listen to), *chercher* (to look for), *payer* (to pay for), and *regarder* (to look at), take direct objects in French.

Elle met le pantalon noir.	Elle le met.
Il met la chemise blanche.	Il la met.
Je mets mes gants bruns.	Je les mets.
Il téléphone *à Marie*.	Il *lui* téléphone.
Il téléphone *à Marie et à Luc*.	Il *leur* téléphone.

Position of Object Pronouns

Although we can automatically put object pronouns in their proper place in English, their correct placement in French does not follow English rules and requires some practice. Let's take a closer look.

Object pronouns are placed before the verb to which their meaning is tied (usually the conjugated verb). When there are two verbs, object pronouns are placed before the infinitive.

Je *la* mets.	Je *lui* parle.
Je ne *la* mets pas.	Je ne *lui* parle pas.
Je vais *la* mettre.	Je ne vais pas *lui* parler.
Ne *la* mets pas!	Ne *lui* parle pas!

Memory Enhancer

Direct and indirect object pronouns are generally placed before the conjugated verb:

Elle ne lui écrit pas.
She does not write to him.

When a conjugated verb is followed by an infinitive, the object pronoun is placed before the infinitive:

Ils vont le faire.
They are going to do it.

For affirmative commands only, the object pronoun is placed after the command and is attached to it with a hyphen, such as *finis-la* (finish it) but *ne la finis pas* (don't finish it).

In an affirmative command, object pronouns change position and are placed immediately after the verb and joined to it by a hyphen. *Me* becomes *moi* when it follows the verb.

Mets-*la*!	Parle-*lui*!
Mettez-*la*!	Parlez-*lui*!
	Donnez-*moi* la robe!

Direct objects tell you whom or what the subject is acting on and can refer to people, places, things, or ideas.

Indirect objects tell you to whom or for whom the subject is doing something. Indirect objects only refer to people.

Using Direct Object Pronouns

Imagine you are on a shopping spree in the *Samaritaine* department store in Paris, and your arms are loaded with all your "finds." A friend joins you and questions your choices. Answer his questions efficiently by using a direct object pronoun. Sample responses can be found in Appendix A.

1. Aimez-vous le pantalon bleu?

   ____

2. Prenez-vous les gants noirs?

   ____

3. Choisissez-vous la cravate rouge?

   ____

4. Regardez-vous les chaussucrs brunes?

   ____

5. Achetez-vous la chemise blanche?

   ____

6. Adorez-vous le blouson beige?

   ____

Using Indirect Object Pronouns

Your friend doesn't know what gifts to buy her friends and family members. Offer suggestions, following these examples:

Examples:

Paul/une radio	ses frères/une chemise
Offre-lui une radio.	Offre-leur une chemise.

1. Robert/une montre

   ____

2. ses parents/un tableau

   ____

3. Luc et Michel/des cravates

 ____

4. ses soeurs/des robes

 ____

5. son amie/un bracelet

 ____

6. sa grand-mère/un pull

 ____

You Want It? Ask for It!

Sometimes you just want to browse and resent having a salesperson hovering over you waiting to make a sale. At other times, you have specific wants and needs and require assistance. Here are some phrases to help you deal with most common situations.

When you enter a store, an employee might ask you:

Est-ce que je peux vous aider?
ehs-kuh zhuh puh voo zeh-day

Puis-je vous aider?
pweezh voo zeh-day

Vous désirez?
voo day-zee-ray

May I help you?

If you are just browsing, you would answer:

Non, merci, je regarde (tout simplement).
nohN mehr-see zhuh ruh-gahrd (too saN-pluh-mahN)
No, thank you, I am (just) looking.

If you want to see or buy something, you would answer:

Oui, je voudrais voir … s'il vous plaît.
wee zhuh voo-dreh vwahr … seel voo pleh
Yes, I would like to see … please.

Je cherche …
zhuh shehrsh …
I'm looking for …

And, of course, if you're a shopper like I am, you'd want to know the following:

Y a-t-il des soldes?
ee ah teel day sohld
Are there any sales?

Avez-vous cassé les prix?
ah-vay-voo kah-say lay pree
Have you slashed your prices?

Expressing Preferences

If the salesperson is going to help you, she or he has to understand your preferences:

> Quel pull est-ce que vous préférez?
> *kehl pewl esh-kuh voo pray-fay-ray*
> Which pullover do you prefer?

Memory Enhancer

Remember that the adjective *quel* (*quelle, quels, quelles*) must agree with the noun it modifies:

quel pantalon *quelle robe*
quels pantalons *quelles robes*

If you are deciding among different items, the salesperson would ask which one(s) you prefer by using one of the interrogative pronouns in the following table.

Interrogative Pronouns

	Masculine	Feminine
Singular	lequel (*luh-kehl*)	laquelle (*lah-kehl*)
Plural	lesquels (*lay-kehl*)	lesquelles (*lay-kehl*)

These interrogative pronouns must agree with the nouns to which they refer:

> Lequel de ces pulls est-ce que vous préférez?
> *luh-kehl duh say pewl ehs-kuh voo pray-fay-ray*
> Which one of these pullovers do you prefer?

> Lesquelles de ces robes est-ce que vous prenez?
> *lay-kehl duh say rohb ehs-kuh voo pruh-nay*
> Which ones of these dresses are you taking?

To express your preference (that is, to say "the … one" or "the … ones"), simply use the appropriate definite article plus an adjective that agrees. When speaking about the pullover, you might say:

> Je préfère le bleu clair.
> *zhuh pray-fehr luh bluh klehr*
> I prefer the light blue one.

> Je préfère le grand.
> *zhuh pray-fehr luh grahN*
> I prefer the big one.

When speaking about the dresses, you might say:

> Je prends les petites.
> *zhuh prahN lay puh-teet*
> I am taking the small ones.

> Je prends la rouge et la bleue.
> *zhuh prahN lah roozh ay lah bluh*
> I am taking the red one and the blue one.

Expressing Opinions

That shirt is you. You just love those pants. What a perfect jacket! When you are happy with an item, you will want to express your pleasure by saying one of the following phrases:

Ça me plaît.	*sah muh pleh*	I like it.
Ça me va.	*sah muh vah*	It suits (fits) me.
C'est agréable.	*seh tah-gray-ahbl*	It's nice.
C'est élégant(e).	*seh tay-lay-gahN*	It's elegant.
C'est pratique.	*seh prah-teek*	It's practical.

If you are unhappy with what you see, you might use the following:

Ça ne me plaît pas.	*sah nuh muh pleh pah*	I don't like it.
Ça ne me va pas.	*sah nuh muh vah pah*	It doesn't suit (fit) me.
Il (Elle) est abominable.	*eel (ehl) eh tah-boh-mee-nahbl*	It's horrible.
Il (Elle) est trop petit(e).	*eel (ehl) eh tro puh-tee(t)*	It's too small.
Il (Elle) est trop serré(e).	*eel (ehl) eh tro suh-ray*	It's too tight.
Il (Elle) est trop court(e).	*eel (ehl) eh tro koor(t)*	It's too short.
Il (Elle) est trop long(ue).	*eel (ehl) eh tro lohN(g)*	It's too long.
Il (Elle) est trop criard(e).	*eel (ehl) eh tro kree-ahr*	It's too loud.
Il (Elle) est trop étroit(e).	*eel (ehl) eh tro pay-trwaht*	It's too narrow.

If you're not satisfied and want something else, try saying:

Je cherche quelque chose de plus (moins) + adjective.
zhuh shehrsh kehl-kuh shooz duh plew (mwaN) …
I'm looking for something more (less) …

I'll Take This, That, One of These, and Some of Those

While considering a purchase, it's not uncommon to ask a friend or salesperson for an opinion of this suit, that shirt, these shoes, or those ties. A demonstrative adjective points out someone or something being referred to and allows you to be specific by expressing "this," "that," "these," and "those," as shown in the following list:

- The demonstrative pronoun used before a masculine singular nouns beginning with a consonant:

ce (*suh*)	ce sac	this (that) bag

- The demonstrative pronoun used before a masculine singular noun beginning with a vowel:

cet (*seht*)	cet imperméable	this (that) raincoat

- The demonstrative pronoun used before all feminine singular nouns:

cette (*seht*)	cette écharpe	this (that) scarf
	cette robe	this (that) dress

- The demonstrative pronoun used before all plural nouns:

ces (*say*)	ces sacs	these (those) bags
	ces écharpes	these (those) scarves

When using demonstrative adjectives, keep the following rules in mind:

- Demonstrative adjectives precede the nouns they modify and agree with them in number and gender. The special masculine form *cet* is used to prevent a clash of two vowel sounds together.
- Demonstrative adjectives are repeated before each noun:

  Ce pantalon et cette chemise sont formdables.

- The tags *-ci* (this, these) and *-là* (that, those) may be added to make further distinctions:

  Je préfère ce chemisier-ci.
  zhuh pray-fehr suh shuh-meez-yay see
  I prefer this blouse.

  Ce pantalon-là est trop grand.
  suh pahN-tah-lohN lah eh tro grahN
  That pair of pants is too big.

What Do You Think?

Look at the following articles of clothing and say how you feel about them. Give as much detail as possible. Sample responses can be found in Appendix A.

The Least You Need to Know

- To shop successfully in a French-speaking country, you must use the metric system.
- To make your conversation more fluid, use object pronouns to replace object nouns.
- Object pronouns are usually placed before the conjugated verb.
- When there are two verbs, the pronoun is placed before the infinitive.
- Object pronouns come after the verb in affirmative commands only.
- Demonstrative adjectives (*ce*, *cet*, *cette*, *ces*) agree in number and gender with the nouns they precede and describe.

Chapter 16

An Old-Fashioned, Home-Cooked Meal

In This Chapter

- Specialty food stores
- Selecting the right wine
- Quantities and amounts
- Using irregular *-ir* verbs
- A chocolate delight

In the preceding chapter you learned to shop for souvenirs, gifts, and some everyday odds and ends. You also picked out some fabulous French fashions and even managed, despite the metric system, to get the right size. Shopping is hard work, and you've really worked up an appetite. It's a bit early for dinner. What should you do next?

Your best bet is to stop in one of the local food stores to pick up a snack to tide you over until your next meal. You can grab *un sandwich* (*uhN sahNd-weesh;* a sandwich) made on *une baguette* (*ewn bah-geht;* a long loaf of French bread), *une pâtisserie* (*ewn pah-tees-ree;* a pastry), or just *du fromage* (*dew froh-mahzh;* a chunk of cheese). This chapter provides you with many alternatives and ensures that you get the right quantities—and at the end there's a special treat.

You'd Better Shop Around

I loved going on a class trip to Paris in 1990 with my youngest son, Michael. Like his mother, he's an incorrigible junk-food addict and truly appreciates the sweet things in life. It seems that there are pastry shops on every corner in Paris, and he and I enjoyed many an *éclair* together. Are you like us? Do you like to keep snacks in your hotel room just in case you get the midnight munchies? Or do you prefer to rent a condo or an apartment so you can do your own cooking? In any French-speaking country, you will be able to enjoy the culinary delights in the shops listed in the following table.

Food Shops

The Store	Le Magasin	Pronunciation
bakery	la boulangerie	*lah boo-lahNzh-ree*
butcher shop	la boucherie	*lah boosh-ree*
candy store	la confiserie	*lah kohN-feez-ree*
dairy store	la crémerie	*lah kraym-ree*
delicatessen	la charcuterie	*lah shahr-kew-tree*
fish store	la poissonnerie	*lah pwah-sohn-ree*
fruit store	la fruiterie	*la frwee-tree*
grocery (vegetable) store	l'épicerie	*lay-pees-ree*
liquor store	le magasin de vins	*luh mah-gah-zaN duh vaN*
pastry shop	la pâtisserie	*lah pah-tees-ree*
supermarket	le supermarché	*luh sew-pehr-mahr-shay*

Memory Enhancer

Many of the types of stores you will frequent end in *-erie*. Drop this ending and add *ier* (*ière*) to get the name of the male (female) person who works in the store: *l'épicier* (the male grocer); *l'épicière* (the female grocer).

Going Here and There

You've scouted out the shops in the area where you are staying, and now you're ready to venture out on your own and do some serious shopping. When it's time to stock up and you're ready to leave, use the verb *aller* and the preposition *à* + the appropriate definite article (*au*, *à la*, *à l'*) to indicate the store to which you are going:

Je vais à l'épicerie.	Je vais à la boulangerie.
I'm going to the grocery store.	I'm going to the bakery.

It is very common to use the preposition *chez* (to/at the house/business of) + the person to express where you are going:

Je vais chez l'épicier (épicière).

Je vais chez le (la) boulanger (boulangère).

Going Shopping

Try it. Tell your traveling companion where you are going to buy the following:

1. vegetables ____________
2. pastry ____________
3. meat ____________
4. fruit ____________
5. fish ____________
6. candy ____________
7. milk ____________
8. bread ____________

The delectable displays of food in the windows of various food stores across France just beckon you to enter and try something new and exotic. What foods (*aliments* m.) are among your favorites: fruits? vegetables? pastries? cheeses? Are you interested in trying different meat, poultry, game, or fish? Perhaps there's a wine that has caught your fancy. The following tables will help you enjoy the culinary experience of your choice.

At the Grocery Store

Vegetables	Les Légumes	Pronunciation
artichokes	les artichauts *m.*	*lay zahr-tee-sho*
asparagus	les asperges *f.*	*lay zahs-pehrzh*
beans (green)	les haricots verts *m.*	*lay zah-ree-ko vehr*
beets	les betteraves *m.*	*lay beht-rahv*
broccoli	le brocoli	*luh broh-koh-lee*
cabbage	le chou	*luh shoo*
carrot	la carotte	*lah kah-roht*
cauliflower	le chou-fleur	*luh shoo-fluhr*

continues

At the Grocery Store (continued)

Vegetables	Les Légumes	Pronunciation
corn	le maïs	*luh mah-ees*
cucumber	le concombre	*luh kohN-kohNbr*
eggplant	l'aubergine *f.*	*lo-behr-zheen*
lettuce	la laitue	*lah leh-tew*
mushroom	le champignon	*luh shahN-pee-nyohN*
onion	l'oignon *m.*	*loh-nyohN*
peas	les petits pois *m.*	*lay puh-tee pwah*
potato	la pomme de terre	*lah pohm duh tehr*
rice	le riz	*luh ree*
sauerkraut	la choucroute	*lah shoo-kroot*
spinach	les épinards *m.*	*lay zay-pee-nahr*
sweet potato	la patate douce	*lah pah-taht doos*
tomato	la tomate	*lah toh-maht*
turnip	le navet	*luh nah-veh*
zucchini	la courgette	*lah koor-zheht*

Fruits and Nuts

Fruits	Les Fruits	Pronunciation
apple	la pomme	*lah pohm*
apricot	l'abricot *m.*	*lah-bree-ko*
banana	la banane	*lah bah-nahn*
blueberry	la myrtille	*lah meer-tee-y*
cherry	la cerise	*lah suh-reez*
date	la datte	*lah daht*
grape	le raisin	*luh reh-zahN*
grapefruit	le pamplemousse	*luh pahNpl-moos*
lemon	le citron	*luh see-trohN*
lime	la limette	*lah lee-meht*
orange	l'orange *f.*	*loh-rahNzh*
peach	la pêche	*lah pehsh*
pear	la poire	*lah pwahr*

Fruits	Les Fruits	Pronunciation
pineapple	l'ananas *m.*	*lah-nah-nah*
plum	la prune	*lah prewn*
prune	le pruneau	*luh prew-no*
raisin	le raisin sec	*luh reh-zaN sehk*
raspberry	la framboise	*lah frahN-bwahz*
strawberry	la fraise	*lah frehz*
Nuts	**Les Noix**	**Pronunciation**
almond	l'amande *f.*	*lah-mahNd*
chestnut	le marron	*luh mah-rohN*
hazelnut	la noisette	*lah nwah-zeht*
walnut	la noix	*lah nwah*

At the Butcher or Delicatessen

Meats	Les Viandes	Pronunciation
bacon	le lard, le bacon	*luh lahr, luh bah-kohN*
beef	le boeuf	*luh buhf*
chopped meat	la viande hachée	*lah vyahNd ah-shay*
ham	le jambon	*luh zhahN-bohN*
lamb	l'agneau *m.*	*lah-nyo*
liver	le foie	*luh fwah*
pâté	le pâté	*luh pah-tay*
pork	le porc	*luh pohr*
roast beef	le rosbif	*luh rohs-beef*
sausage	les saucisses *f.*	*lay so-sees*
veal	le veau	*luh vo*
Fowl and Game	**La Volaille et le Gibier**	**Pronunciation**
chicken	le poulet	*luh poo-leh*
duck	le canard	*luh kah-nard*
goose	l'oie *f.*	*lwah*
quail	la caille	*lah kahy*
turkey	la dinde	*lah daNd*

At the Fish Store

Fish and Seafood	Le Poisson et les Fruits de Mer	Pronunciation
bass	la perche	*lah pehrsh*
clam	la palourde	*lah pah-loord*
codfish	la cabillaud	*lah kah-bee-yo*
crab	le crabe	*luh krahb*
flounder	le carrelet	*luh kahr-leh*
frogs' legs	les cuisses de grenouille *f.*	*lay kwees duh gruh-nuhy*
grouper	le mérou	*luh may-roo*
halibut	le flétan	*luh flay-tahN*
lobster	le homard	*luh oh-mahr*
mackerel	le maquereau	*luh mahk-roh*
monkfish	la lotte	*lah loht*
mussels	les moules *f.*	*lay mool*
oyster	l'huître *f.*	*lwee-truh*
red snapper	la perche rouge	*lah pehrsh roozh*
salmon	le saumon	*luh so-mohN*
sardines	les sardines *f.*	*lay sahr-deen*
scallops	les coquilles	*lay koh-kee*
sea bass	le bar	*luh bahr*
shrimp	la crevette	*lah kruh-veht*
snail	l'escargot *m.*	*lehs-kahr-go*
sole	la sole	*lah sohl*
swordfish	l'espadon *m.*	*lehs-pah-dohN*
trout	la truite	*lah trweet*
tuna	le thon	*luh tohN*

At the Dairy

Dairy Products	Les Produits Laitiers	Pronunciation
butter	le beurre	*luh buhr*
cheese	le fromage	*luh froh-mahzh*
cream	la crème	*lah krehm*
eggs	des oeufs *m.*	*day zuh*
yogurt	le yaourt	*luh yah-oort*

At the Bakery and Pastry Shop

Breads and Desserts	Les Pains et Les Desserts	Pronunciation
apple turnover	le chausson aux pommes	*luh sho-sohN o pohm*
bread	le pain	*luh paN*
brioche	la brioche	*lah bree-ohsh*
cake	le gâteau	*luh gah-to*
chocolate croissant	le pain au chocolat	*luh paN o shoh-koh-lah*
cookie	le biscuit	*luh bees-kwee*
cream puffs	les choux à la crème *m.*	*lay shoo ah lah krehm*
crescent roll	le croissant	*luh krwah-sahN*
danish	la danoise	*lah dah-nwahz*
doughnut	le beignet	*luh beh-nyeh*
loaf of French bread	la baguette	*lah bah-geht*
pie	la tarte	*lah tahrt*
roll	le petit pain	*luh puh-tee paN*

Beverages

Drinks	Les Boissons	Pronunciation
beer	la bière	*lah byehr*
champagne	le champagne	*luh shahN-pah-nyuh*
cider	le cidre	*luh seedr*
coffee	le café	*luh kah-fay*
juice	le jus	*luh zhew*
hot chocolate (cocoa)	le chocolat	*luh shoh-koh-laht*
lemonade	le citron pressé	*lun see-trohN preh-say*
milk	le lait	*luh leh*
mineral water	l'eau minérale *f.*	*lo mee-nay-rahl*
carbonated	gazeuse	*gah-zuhz*
noncarbonated	plate	*plaht*
soda	le soda	*luh soh-dah*
tea	le thé	*luh tay*
wine	le vin	*luh vaN*

If you want to be specific about a type of juice, use *de* + the name of the fruit:

le jus d'orange
orange juice

Serious Shopping

Tell what items you would purchase in the following stores. Begin your answers with: *J'achèterais* (I would buy). Sample responses can be found in Appendix A.

1. à la boucherie ______________________
2. à la pâtisserie ______________________
3. à la boulangerie ______________________
4. à l'épicerie ______________________
5. à la fruiterie ______________________
6. à la charcuterie ______________________

Your Likes and Dislikes

Do you cringe at the sight of broccoli but start to drool when you pick up the scent of ribs cooking on a grill? Are you a picky eater, or will you eat just about anything to stop your stomach from growling? For each of the following groups, tell what you love (*J'adore*), like (*J'aime*), and dislike (*Je déteste*). Sample responses can be found in Appendix A.

1. fruits ______________
2. vegetables ______________
3. meat ______________
4. fish ______________
5. bread ______________
6. cake ______________

What's That Wine?

Have you ever looked at a wine label and wondered what all the information meant? We've come to the rescue with a convenient key that will help you make sense of wine labels. Both French and American governments have strict rules concerning wine and labeling; in a nutshell, this is what you should know:

- The region where the wine was produced, such as Bourgogne (Burgundy), Bordeaux, Champagne.
- Product of France.
- The *appellation* of the wine (trademark) indicates the region in which the wine was produced and affirms that the grapes were grown, picked, fermented, and bottled according to strict government controls. Only better quality wines are marked with an *appellation*. Table wine is clearly marked as such and has no *appellation* since it is of a lesser quality. A champagne label merely states "Champagne."
- The quality of the wine (from the lowest to the highest):

  Vin de table: Ordinary table wine that has no vintage.

  Village wine: No vineyard is mentioned, which probably means that the wine is made from a variety of grapes from different vineyards.

  Premier cru and *grand cru:* These phrases indicate that the grapes used to produce the wine were of a superior quality because they were grown on the most fertile land and under the best climatic conditions. Although *premier cru* is considered the ultimate wine, many *connaisseurs* prefer the taste of *grand cru*. The ordinary palate would not be able to distinguish between the two.
- The town where the wine was bottled.
- The name and origin of the shipper. (For champagne, the champagne house is usually the shipper.)
- The net contents.
- The percentage of alcohol by volume.
- The name and address of the importer.

The following information may or may not be included on a wine label:

- The vintage (the year the wine was bottled)
- The brand or château name
- Whether the wine was "estate" or "château" bottled

Quantity Counts

You've decided to go on a picnic with a friend in the French countryside and stop by a *charcuterie* to purchase some sandwich meat. You figure that half a pound ought to be sufficient. But when you get to the counter to order, you find that no one understands how much you want. Why are you having this problem, and how will you get the right amount of meat? In France, the metric system is used for measuring quantities of food: Liquids are measured in liters, and solids are measured in kilograms or fractions thereof. Since most of us are used to dealing with ounces, pounds, pints, quarts, and gallons, I've included a conversion chart to help you out until the metric system becomes second nature.

Measuring Quantities of Food

Approximate Solid Measures	
1 oz. = 28 grams	¾ lb. = 375 grams
¼ lb. = 125 grams	1.1 lb. = 500 grams
½ lb. = 250 grams	2.2 lb. = 1,000 grams (1 kilogram)
Approximate Liquid Measures	
1 oz. = 30 milliliters	16 oz. (1 pint) = 475 milliliters
32 oz. (1 quart) = 950 milliliters (approximately 1 liter)	1 gallon = 3.75 liters

Not having been brought up on the metric system myself, I can understand that you might still be a bit confused. So I've made it even easier for you. Sometimes it's just easier to ask for a box, bag, or jar and to commit to memory the amounts we're accustomed to: a pound, a quart, and so on. Consult the following table to easily get the amount you want or need.

Getting the Right Amount

Amount	French	Pronunciation
2 pounds of	un kilo de	*uhN kee-lo duh*
a bag of	un sac de	*uhN sahk duh*
a bar of	une tablette de	*ewn tah-bleht duh*
a bottle of	une bouteille de	*ewn boo-tehy duh*
a box of	une boîte de	*ewn bwaht duh*

Amount	French	Pronunciation
a can of	une boîte de	*ewn bwaht duh*
a dozen	une douzaine de	*ewn doo-zehn duh*
a half pound of	deux cent cinquante grammes de	*duh sahN saN-kahNt grahm duh*
a jar of	un bocal de	*uhN boh-kahl duh*
a package of	un paquet de	*uhN pah-keh duh*
a pound of	un demi-kilo de, cinq cents grammes de	*uhN duh-mee kee-lo duh, saNk sahN grahm duh*
a quart of	un litre de	*uhN lee-truh duh*
a slice of	une tranche de	*ewn trahNsh duh*

You're on a diet, but you must have "just a taste" of the chocolate mousse that your French host spent hours preparing for you. He starts filling your bowl, and you try to motion "enough." Too bad, he just keeps heaping it on. Now there's really a lot of mousse on your plate. Finally, there's just too much. Don't allow yourself to get into this bind. Here are some expressions that will help you limit the quantity you receive.

Amounts

Amount	French	Pronunciation
a little	un peu de	*uhN puh duh*
a lot of	beaucoup de	*bo-koo duh*
enough	assez de	*ah-say duh*
too much	trop de	*tro duh*

All of these expressions of quantity include the word *de* (of). Before a vowel, *de* becomes *d'*. In all other instances, *de* never changes.

beaucoup de bonbons a lot of candies	une douzaine d'oeufs a dozen eggs

I'd Like ...

Someone will always be eager to help you in a small neighborhood store. Be prepared for the questions you might be asked and the proper way to give an answer that will get you what you want.

Vous désirez?
voo day-zee-ray
What would you like?

Est-ce que je peux vous aider?
ehs-kuh zhuh puh voo zeh-day
May I help you?

Your answer might begin:

Je voudrais …
zhuh voo-dreh …
I would like …

Pourriez-vous me donner …?
poo-ryay voo muh doh-nay …
Could you give me …?

S'il vous plaît …
sweel voo pleh …
Please …

You might then be asked:

Et avec ça?
ay ah-vehk sah
And with that?

C'est tout?
seh too
Is that all?

An appropriate response would be to either give additional items that you want or to answer as follows:

Oui, c'est tout, merci.
wee seh too mehr-see
Yes, that's all, thank you.

-ir Verb Irregularities

Snacking is fine, but now you're in the mood for a good dinner. Imagine walking along the port in Martinique and smelling the aromas emanating from the various restaurants. Of course, you want to know what type of cuisine is being served. Let's take a closer look at these verbs and some other similar ones. The verb *servir* (to serve) and a few others that end in *-ir*—*dormir* (to sleep), *partir* (to leave), *sentir* (to feel, smell), and *sortir* (to go out)—do not follow the pattern of present tense conjugation for *-ir* verbs that has already been studied. They drop the consonant before the *-ir* of the infinitive in the singular forms and retain that consonant in the plural forms.

The Verb *Dormir* (to Sleep)

Conjugation	Pronunciation	Meaning
je dors	*zhuh dohr*	I sleep
tu dors	*tew dohr*	you sleep
il, elle, on dort	*eel, ehl, ohN dohr*	he, she, one sleeps
nous dor**m**ons	*noo dohr-mohN*	we sleep
vous dor**m**ez	*voo dohr-may*	you sleep
ils, elles dor**m**ent	*eel, ehl dohrm*	they sleep

The Verb *Partir* (to Leave)

Conjugation	Pronunciation	Meaning
je pars	*zhuh pahr*	I leave
tu pars	*tew pahr*	you leave
il, elle, on part	*eel ehl, ohN pahr*	he, she, one leaves
nous par**t**ons	*noo pahr-tohN*	we leave
vous par**t**ez	*voo pahr-tay*	you leave
ils, elles par**t**ent	*eel, ehl pahrt*	they leave

The Verb *Sentir* (to Smell, Feel)

Conjugation	Pronunciation	Meaning
je sens	*zhuh sahN*	I smell, feel
tu sens	*tew sahN*	you smell, feel
il, elle, on sent	*eel, ehl, ohN sahN*	he, she, one smells, feels
nous sen**t**ons	*noo sahN-tohN*	we smell, feel
vous sen**t**ez	*voo sahN-tay*	you smell, feel
ils, elles sen**t**ent	*eel, ehl sahNt*	they smell, feel

The Verb *Servir* (to Serve)

Conjugation	Pronunciation	Meaning
je sers	*zhuh sehr*	I serve
tu sers	*tew sehr*	you serve
il, elle, on sert	*eel, ehl, ohN sehr*	he, she, one serves
nous servons	*noo sehr-vohN*	we serve
vous servez	*voo sehr-vay*	you serve
ils, elles servent	*eel, ehl sehrv*	they serve

The Verb *Sortir* (to Go Out)

Conjugation	Pronunciation	Meaning
je sors	*zhuh sohr*	I go out
tu sors	*tew sohr*	you go out
il, elle, on sort	*eel, ehl, ohN sohr*	he, she, one goes out
nous sortons	*noo sohr-tohN*	we go out
vous sortez	*voo sohr-tay*	you go out
ils, elles sortent	*eel, ehl sohrt*	they go out

The Treat's on Me

Why not impress your friends with a treat from *Bon Appétit* magazine: chocolate mousse! It's delicious, easy to prepare, and freezes beautifully. You will need:

8 oz. semi-sweet chocolate bits
1 square unsweetened chocolate
2 TB. butter
2 eggs, separated
1 pint heavy cream
1 TB. very strong black instant coffee
1 TB. Grand Marnier

In a microwave oven set on medium heat, melt semi-sweet chocolate, unsweetened chocolate, and butter. Stir. Let the mixture cool slightly. While the mixture is cooling, beat egg whites until stiff and cream until whipped but not stiff.

Add coffee, Grand Marnier, and egg yolks to the chocolate mixture. Stir.

Slowly fold in egg whites. Add whipped cream. Mix slowly so that cream remains fluffy.

Spoon into individual dessert cups and let chill for at least 4 hours. Serve with additional whipped cream (serves 12).

It's a Puzzle to Me

Do you want to make sure you have all these verb forms down pat? Practice can make perfect in a fun way. Complete the crossword puzzle with the correct forms of all the verbs.

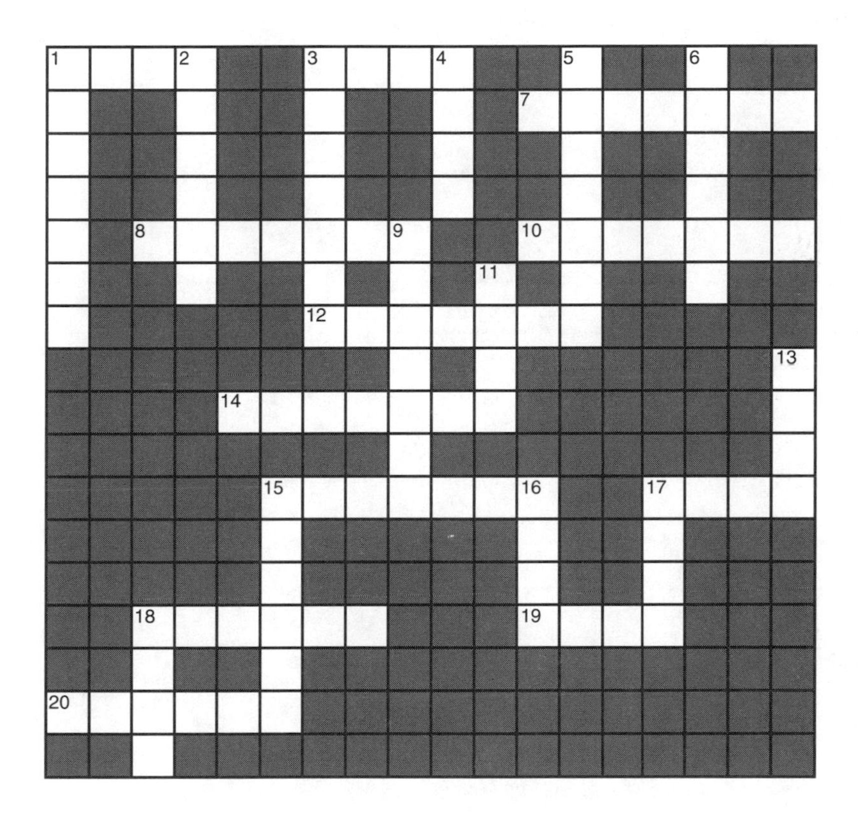

Horizontalement

1. (leave) je
3. (sleep) you
7. (serve) ils
8. (serve) nous
10. (sleep) elles
12. (go out) nous
14. (feel) ils
15. (leave) nous
17. (serve) il
18. (feel) vous
19. (serve) tu
20. (sleep) vous

Verticalement

1. (leave) elles
2. (go out) vous
3. (sleep) nous
4. (feel) il
5. (feel) nous
6. (serve) vous
9. (go out) ils
11. (sleep) il
13. (leave) elle
15. (leave) vous
16. (feel) je
17. (go out) tu
18. (go out) elle

The Least You Need to Know

- Use the verb *aller* + *à* + the definite article to express where you are going.
- Purchasing the correct amount of food in France requires knowledge of the metric system.
- Ask for a box or a jar of something if you are not familiar with the metric system.
- Certain *-ir* verbs follow a different pattern of conjugation and should be memorized.

Chapter 17

Eating Out

In This Chapter

- How to order in a restaurant
- Getting exactly what you want
- Special diets
- Exclamations

Let's say you're in Paris, the city of lights. Alas, it is neither lunch nor dinner time, but using the lessons from the last chapter, you've managed to grab a snack to tide you over until your next real meal. Or maybe you've stocked your hotel room refrigerator and are lying around your room snacking on *biscuits*, *fromage*, and *citronnade*. Your new knowledge of the metric system helped you when ordering the right amount of cheese.

But now you are really hungry; it's time to head out and find a place for dinner. The French are fanatical about food, and their haute cuisine is considered to be the finest and most sophisticated in the world. Indeed, when Americans started taking food more seriously, they turned to France for guidance and inspiration. (Remember, Boston's own Julia Child built her reputation around teaching French cooking.)

With all the French cooking terms that have crept into our culture, there are plenty of places at home to practice gastromic French—from menus to cookbooks and magazines. By the end of this chapter, you will be a pro at ordering from a French menu, even if you have certain dietary needs or restrictions. And if, perchance, you are dissatisfied with your meal, you will be able to send it back and get what you want.

Select a Place You'd Like

Wherever you decide to eat, France offers a wide variety of eating establishments to suit your hunger and your pocketbook. Are you going out for breakfast (*le petit déjeuner, luh puh-tee day-zhuh-nay*), lunch (*le déjeuner, luh day-zhuh-nay*), dinner (*le dîner, luh dee-nay*), or an early afternoon snack (*le goûter, luh goo-tay*)? If you're not in the mood for a formal restaurant, why not try one of the following:

- Une auberge (*ewn o-behrzh*) An inn
- Un bistro (*uhN bees-tro*) A small, informal neighborhood pub or tavern
- Une brasserie (*ewn brahs-ree*) A large café serving quick meals
- Un cabaret (*uhN kah-bah-reh*) A nightclub
- Un café (*uhN kah-fay*) A small, neighborhood restaurant where residents socialize
- Une cafétéria (*ewn kah-fay-tay-ryah*) A self-service restaurant
- Une casse-croûte (*ewn kahs-kroot*) A restaurant serving sandwiches
- Une crêperie (*ewn krehp-ree*) A stand or restaurant serving *crâpes* (filled pancakes)
- Un fast-food (*uhN fahst-food*) A fast-food chain restaurant
- *Un self* (*uhN sehlf*) A self-service restaurant

Which Restaurant Do You Prefer?

You've opened a tourist magazine and found ads for restaurants. Now you have to decide what you are in the mood for this evening. Explore the ads and determine what you would expect to get in each of these restaurants. Answers can be found in Appendix A.

NOTRE SELECTIONS DE RESTAURANTS

Noms	Spécialités	N°P
LE SAINT-NICOLAS	CUISINE FINE TRADITONNELLE	4
LES QUATRES SAISONS (Abela Hôtel Monaco)	CUISINE FRANÇAISE SPECIALITES LIBANAISES	5
LE SAINT-BENOIT	CUISINE DE LA MER	6
TIP TOP BAR	SPECIALITES ITALIENNES	7
FLASHMAN'S	RESTAURATION ANGLAISE	13
STARS'N'BARS	CUISINE AMERICAINE MUSIQUE TOUS LES SOIRS	13
LE METROPOLE PALACE	CUISINE FRANÇAISE	15
LES AMBASSADEURS (Hôtel Métropole)	SPECIALITES LIBANAISES ET FRANÇAISES	15
LA PORTE D'OR	SPECIALITES VIETNAMIENNES ET CHINOISES	16
LE CHINA TOWN	SPECIALITES VIETNAMIENNES ET CHINOISES	16
CAFE MOZART	BUFFET CHAUD & FROID, GLACES, PATISSERIES	82
RESTAURANT DU PORT	POISSONS, SPECIALITES ITALIENNES	24
LA CANTINELLA	SPECIALITES ITALIENNES	Plan
SASS' CAFE	PIANO BAR	Plan
LE PARADISE	RESTAURANT GLACIER	56
L'ESCALE	SPECIALITES DE POISSONS	55
HARRY'S BAR	MENU HOMMES D'AFFAIRES	12

A Table, Please

If you've chosen to dine in a restaurant, it might be necessary to reserve a table. When you call, make sure to include all the pertinent information:

Je voudrais réserver une table …
zhuh voo-dreh ray-sehr-vay ewn tahbl …
I would like to reserve a table …

pour ce soir	pour demain soir
poor suh swahr	*poor duh-maN swahr*
for this evening	for tomorrow evening

pour samedi soir
poor sahm-dee swahr
for Saturday night

pour deux personnes
poor duh pehr-sohn
for two people

à huit heures et demie
ah wee tuhr ay duh-mee
at 8:30 P.M.

sur (à) la terrasse, s'il vous plaît
sewr (ah) lah teh-rahs seel voo pleh
on the terrace, please (outdoors)

We're Dining Out

Let's say you do not reserve a table and just show up at a restaurant unannounced. The maître d' will most certainly ask:

Une table pour combien de personnes?
ewn tahbl poor kohN-byaN duh pehr-sohn
A table for how many?

Your response should contain all the necessary information:

Une table pour quatre personnes, s'il vous plaît.
ewn tahbl poor kahtr pehr-sohn seel voo pleh
A table for four, please.

Un, Deux, Trois

Label all the different things you put on your dinner table. Study the names carefully for a few days. When you feel confident, remove the labels and name as many items as you can.

You've now been seated. You look around and are delighted with the fine china, the crystal, the linen napkins, and the crisp white tablecloth. But wait! Madam's place has not been properly set. The following table gives you the vocabulary you need when asking the waiter for cutlery, as well as other terms that will come in handy.

A Table Setting

Item	French	Pronunciation
bowl	le bol	*luh bohl*
carafe	la carafe	*lah kah-rahf*
cup	la tasse	*lah tahss*
dinner plate	l'assiette *f.*	*lah-syeht*
fork	la fourchette	*lah foor-sheht*
glass	le verre	*luh vehr*
knife	le couteau	*luh koo-to*
menu	le menu, la carte	*luh muh-new, lah kahrt*

Item	French	Pronunciation
napkin	la serviette	*lah sehr-vyeht*
pepper shaker	le poivrier	*leh pwah-vree-yay*
place setting	le couvert	*luh koo-vehr*
salt shaker	la salière	*lah sahl-yehr*
saucer	la soucoupe	*lah soo-koop*
soup dish	l'assiette à soupe *f.*	*lah-syeht ah soop*
tablecloth	la nappe	*lah nahp*
teaspoon	la cuillère	*lah kwee-yehr*
tablespoon	la cuillère à service	*lah kwee-yehr ah sehr-vees*
waiter	le garçon	*luh gahr-sohN*
waitress	la serveuse	*lah sehr-vuhz*
wine glass	le verre à vin	*luh vehr ah vaN*

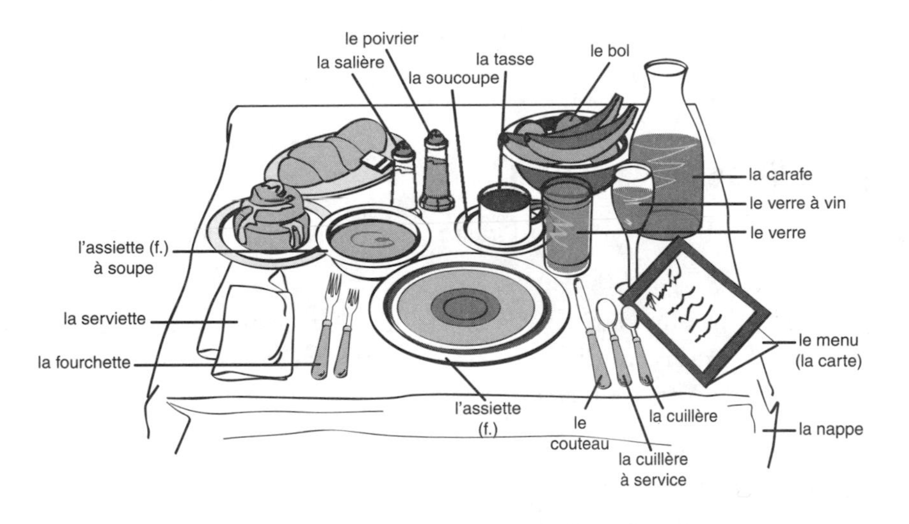

If you find that something is missing from your table or you need to make a request of the staff, the following phrases will help you get want you want:

- Use an indirect object pronoun:

Il me faut	*eel muh foh*	I need
Il te faut	*eel tuh foh*	You need
Il lui faut	*eel lui foh*	He/she needs
Il nous faut	*eel noo foh*	We need
Il vous faut	*eel voo foh*	You need
Il leur faut	*eel leur foh*	They need

- Use the expression *avoir besoin de* (to need):

J'ai besoin de	*zhay buh-zwaN duh*	I need
Tu as besoin de	*tew ah buh-zwaN duh*	You need
Il a besoin de	*eel ah buh-zwaN duh*	He needs
Elle a besoin de	*ehl ah buh-zwaN duh*	She needs
Nous avons besoin de	*noo zah-vohN buh-zwaN duh*	We need
Vous avez besoin de	*voo sah-vay buh-zwaN duh*	You need
Ils ont besoin de	*eel zohN buh-zwaN duh*	They need
Elles ont besoin de	*ehl zohN buh-zwaN duh*	They need

Oh, Waiter!

Now use what you've learned to tell your server that you need the following:

1. a salt shaker ____________________
2. a napkin ____________________
3. a fork ____________________
4. a knife ____________________
5. a plate ____________________
6. a spoon ____________________

Garçon, What Do You Recommend?

It's time to order. It's always a good idea to get the server's recommendations before ordering:

Quel est le plat du jour?
kehl eh luh plah dew zhoor
What is today's specialty?

Qu'est-ce que vous recommandez?
kehs-kuh voo ruh-koh-mahN-day
What do you recommend?

Quelle est la spécialité de la maison?
kehl eh lah spay-see-ah-lee-tay duh lah meh-zohN
What is the house specialty?

The waiter has come to give you a menu and see if you'd like a drink before dinner. You can use the following to order both drinks and food:

Je voudrais …
zhuh voo-dreh …
I would like …

Je prendrai …
zhuh prahN-dray …
I'll have …

Apportez-moi, s'il vous plaît …
ah-pohr-tay mwah seel voo pleh …
Please bring me …

un apéritif
uhN nah-pay-ree-teef
a before-dinner drink

un cocktail
uhN kohk-tehl
a cocktail

Rien pour moi.
ryaN poor mwah.
Nothing for me.

This Menu Is Greek to Me

A French menu can be confusing and overwhelming unless you know certain culinary terms. If you are a novice to the French language, you might feel that it is too embarrassing or pointless to ask about a dish because you know that you probably won't understand the waiter's explanation! The following table gives you the terms you need to interpret sauce names and other items on a French menu.

What's on the Menu?

Dish Served	Pronunciation	Description
aïoli	*ah-yoh-lee*	mayonnaise flavored with garlic
à la bonne femme	*ah lah bohn fahm*	a white wine sauce with vegetables
béarnaise	*bay-ahr-nehz*	a butter-egg sauce flavored with wine, shallots, and tarragon
bercy	*behr-see*	a meat or fish sauce
blanquette	*blahN-keht*	a creamy egg and white wine sauce usually served with stew
crécy	*kray-see*	carrots
daube	*dohb*	a stew, usually beef, with red wine, onions, and garlic
farci(e)	*fahr-see*	a stuffing
florentine	*floh-rahN-teen*	spinach
forestière	*foh-rehs-tyehr*	wild mushrooms
hollandaise	*oh-lahN-dehz*	an egg yolk butter sauce with lemon juice or vinegar
jardinière	*zhahr-dee-nyehr*	vegetables
maître d'hôtel	*mehtr do-tehl*	a butter sauce with parsley and lemon juice
mornay	*mohr-nay*	a white sauce with cheese
parmentier	*pahr-mahN-tyay*	potatoes
périgourdine	*pay-ree-goor-deen*	mushrooms (truffles)
provençale	*proh-vahN-sahl*	a vegetable garnish
rémoulade	*ray-moo-lahd*	mayonnaise flavored with mustard
véronique	*vay-rohN-neek*	grapes
vol-au-vent	*vohl-o-vahN*	puff pastry with creamed meat

Now you should feel somewhat confident to order. The following tables will help you get from the appetizer through the main course. If you have any problems with the names of various types of meat or fish, refer to Chapter 16.

(Dinner in France is a light meal and is generally served after 7 P.M. Don't be surprised to see eggs or pizza on a dinner menu.)

Appetizers—*Les Hors-d'oeuvres (lay zohr-duhvr)*

Les Hors-d'oeuvres	Pronunciation	Description
crudités variées	*krew-dee-tay vah-ryay*	sliced raw vegetable usually in a vinaigrette sauce
escargots	*ehs-kahr-go*	snails
foie gras	*fwah grah*	fresh, sometimes uncooked, goose liver, served with toasted French bread
pâté	*pah-tay*	pureed liver or other meat served in a loaf
quiche lorraine	*keesh loh-rehn*	egg custard tart served with meat (bacon or ham)
quenelles	*kuh-nehl*	dumplings
rillettes	*ree-yeht*	pork mixture served as a spread

Soups—*Les Soupes (lay soop)*

Les Soupes	Pronunciation	Description
la bisque	*lah beesk*	creamy soup made with crayfish
la bouillabaise	*lah boo-yah-behs*	seafood stew
le consommé	*luh kohN-soh-may*	clear broth
la petite marmite	*lah puh-teet mahr-meet*	rich consommé served with vegetables and meat
le potage	*luh poh-tahzh*	thick soup made of pureed vegetables
la soupe à l'oignon	*lah soop ah loh-nyohN*	onion soup served with bread and cheese
velouté	*vuh-loo-tay*	creamy soup

Meats—*Les Viandes (lay vyahnd)*

Les Viandes	Pronunciation	Meats
le bifteck	*luh beef-tehk*	steak
l'entrecôte *f.*	*lahNtr-koht*	sirloin steak
l'escalope *f.*	*leh-skah-lohp*	scallopine, cutlet
la côte de boeuf	*lah koht duh buhf*	prime rib
la poitrine de …	*lah pwah-treen duh*	breast of …
le carré d'agneau	*luh kah-ray dah-nyo*	rack of lamb
le chateaubriand	*luh shah-to-bree-yahN*	a porterhouse steak
le foie	*luh fwah*	liver
le gigot d'agneau	*luh zhee-go dah-nyo*	leg of lamb
le pot-au-feu	*luh poh-to-fuh*	boiled beef
le rosbif	*luh rohs-beef*	roast beef
le tournedos	*luh toor-nuh-do*	small fillets of beef
les côtes de porc *f.*	*lay koht duh pohr*	pork chops
les côtes de veau *f.*	*lay koht duh vo*	veal chops
les médaillons de… *m.*	*lay may-dah-yohN duh*	small rounds of
les saucisses *f.*	*lay so-sees*	sausages

I'm Hungry—Let's Eat!

Even if you know how to order your hamburger or veal chops, you want to be certain that your entrée is cooked to your specifications. The waiter might ask:

Vous le (la, les) voulez comment?
voo luh (lah, lay) voo-lay koh-mahN
How do you want it (them)?

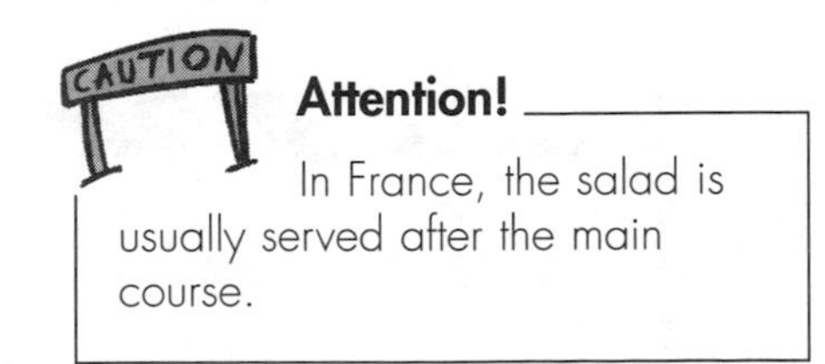

Attention!

In France, the salad is usually served after the main course.

Remember to use the appropriate direct object pronoun to refer to the noun you are using:

Vous recommandez *le gigot*?
Vous *le* recommandez?

The following table will help you express your wants and needs.

How Would You Like It Prepared?

Meats and Vegetables—*Viandes et Légumes* (*vee-yahNd ay lay-gewm*)					
baked	cuit au four	*kwee to foor*	broiled	rôti	*ro-tee*
boiled	bouilli	*boo-yee*	browned	gratiné	*grah-tee-nay*
fried	frit	*free*	sautéed	sauté	*so-tay*
grilled	grillé	*gree-yay*	steamed	à la vapeur	*ah lah vah-puhr*
in its natural juices	au jus	*o zhew*	stewed	en cocotte	*ahN koh-koht*
mashed	en purée	*ahN pew-ray*	very rare	bleu	*bluh*
poached	poché	*poh-shay*	rare	saignant	*seh-nyahN*
pureed	en pureé	*ahN pew-ray*	medium	à point	*ah pwaN*
roasted	rôti	*ro-tee*	well-done	bien cuit	*byaN kwee*
with sauce	en sauce	*ahN sos*			

Eggs—*Des Oeufs* (*day zuh*)		
fried	au plat	*o plah*
hard-boiled	durs	*dewr*
medium-boiled	mollets	*moh-leh*
omelette	une omelette	*ewn nohm-leht*
plain omelette	une omelette nature	*ewn nohm-leht nah-tewr*
poached	pochés	*poh-shay*
scrambled	brouillés	*broo-yay*
soft-boiled	à la coque	*ah lah kohk*

Culture Capsule

Keep in mind that a French chef has a different interpretation of the terms "rare," "medium," and "well-done" than an American chef. In French cooking, "rare" means almost alive, "medium" is a tiny bit more cooked than our rare, and "well-done" is a bit more than our medium. What the chef thinks is burned is what we mean by well done. He may prepare it well done, but don't expect a smile when it is served.

Hot and Spicy

The French use a lot of herbs, spices, seasonings, and condiments to flavor their foods. Knowing the words in the following table will help you determine the ingredients of your dish or will enable you to ask for a seasoning you prefer.

Herbs, Spices, and Condiments

French	Pronunciation	English
le basilic	*luh bah-zee-leek*	basil
la feuille de laurier	*lah fuhy duh loh-ryay*	bay leaf
le beurre	*luh buhr*	butter
les câpres *m.*	*lay kahpr*	capers
la ciboulette	*lah see-boo-leht*	chives
l'aneth *m.*	*lah-neht*	dill
l'ail *m.*	*lahy*	garlic
le gingembre	*luh zhaN-zhahNbr*	ginger
le miel	*luh myehl*	honey
le raifort	*luh reh-fohr*	horseradish
la confiture	*lah kohN-fee-tewr*	jam, jelly
le ketchup	*luh keht-chuhp*	ketchup
le citron	*luh see-trohN*	lemon
le sirop d'érable	*luh see-roh day-rahbl*	maple syrup
la mayonnaise	*lah mah-yoh-nehz*	mayonnaise
la menthe	*lah mahNt*	mint
la moutarde	*lah moo-tahrd*	mustard
l'huile *f.*	*lweel*	oil
l'origan *m.*	*loh-ree-gahN*	oregano
le persil	*luh pehr-seel*	parsley
le poivre	*luh pwahvr*	pepper
le sel	*luh sehl*	salt
le sucre	*luh sewkr*	sugar
l'estragon *m.*	*lehs-trah-gohN*	tarragon
le vinaigre	*luh vee-nehgr*	vinegar

Diet Do's and Don'ts

If you have specific likes, dislikes, or dietary restrictions that you would like to make known, keep the following phrases handy:

I am on a diet.	Je suis au régime.	*zhuh swee zo ray-zheem*
I'm a vegetarian.	Je suis végétarien(ne).	*zhuh swee vay-zhay-tah-ryaN (ryen)*
I can't have …	Je ne tolére …	*zhuh nuh toh-lehr …*
any dairy products	aucun produit laitier	*o-kuhN proh-dwee leh-tyay*
any alcohol	aucun produit alcoolique	*o-kuhN proh-dwee ahl-koh-leek*
any saturated fats	aucune matière grasse animale	*o-kewn mah-tyehr grahs ah-nee-mahl*
any shellfish	aucun fruit de mer	*o-kuhN frweed mehr*
I'm looking for a dish …	Je cherche un plat …	*zhuh shehrsh uhN plah …*
high in fiber	riche en fibre	*reesh ahN feebr*
low in cholesterol	léger en cholestérol	*lay-zhay ahN koh-lehs-tay-rohl*
low in fat	léger en matières grasses	*lay-zhay ahN mah-tyehr grahs*
low in sodium	léger en sodium	*lay-zhay ahN sohd-yuhm*
nondairy	non-laitier	*nohN-leh-tyay*
salt-free	sans sel	*sahN sehl*
sugar-free	sans sucre	*sahN sewkr*
without artificial coloring	sans colorant	*sahN koh-loh-rahN*
without preservatives	sans conservateurs	*sahN kohN-sehr-vah-tuhr*

Back to the Kitchen

Certainly there are times, even in France, when the cooking or table setting is just not up to your standards. The following table presents some problems you might run into.

Possible Problems

Problem	French	Pronunciation
… is cold	… est froid(e)	*eh frwah(d)*
… is too rare	… n'est pas assez cuit(e)	*neh pah zah-say kwee(t)*
… is overcooked	… est trop cuit(e)	*eh tro kwee(t)*
… is tough	… est dur(e)	*eh dewr*
… is burned	… est brûlé(e)	*eh brew-lay*
… is too salty	… est trop salé(e)	*eh tro sah-lay*
… is too sweet	… est trop sucré(e)	*eh tro sew-kray*
… is too spicy	… est trop épicé(e)	*eh tro ay-pee-say*
… is spoiled	… est tourné(e)	*eh toor-nay*
… tastes like …	… a le goût de …	*ah luh goo duh*
… is dirty	… est sale	*eh sahl*

Fancy Finales

In France, it is traditional to have *une salade* (*ewn sah-lahd*) followed by *des fromages variés* (*day froh-mahzh vah-ryay*; cheeses). Popular cheeses include *boursin*, *brie*, *camembert*, *chèvre*, *munster*, *port-salut*, and *roquefort*.

When choosing a cheese, you might want to ask:

Is it …	Est-il …	eh-teel …
mild	maigre	*mehgr*
sharp	piquant	*pee-kahN*
hard	fermenté	*fehr-mahN-tay*
soft	à pâte molle	*ah paht mohl*

Attention!

It is quite customary in France to serve a plate of cheese as dessert, but feel free to ask for something else.

Finally, it's time for dessert, but there are so many French specialties from which to choose. The following table will help you make a decision.

Divine Desserts

Dessert	Pronunciation	Description
une bavaroise	*ewn bah-vahr-wahz*	Bavarian cream
des beignets	*day beh-nyeh*	fruit doughnuts

continues

Divine Desserts (continued)

Dessert	Pronunciation	Description
une bombe	*ewn bohNb*	ice cream with many flavors
une charlotte	*ewn shahr-loht*	sponge cake and pudding
une crème caramel	*ewn krehm kah-rah-mehl*	egg custard served with caramel sauce
une gaufre	*ewn gohfr*	waffle
des oeufs à la neige	*day zuh ah lah nehzh*	meringues in a custard sauce
une omelette norvégienne	*ewn nohm-leht nohr-vay-zhyehn*	baked Alaska
des poires belle hélène	*day pwahr behl ay-lehn*	poached pears with vanilla ice cream and chocolate sauce
des profiteroles	*day proh-fee-trohl*	cream puffs with chocolate sauce

If you are ordering ice cream, the following terms will help you get the type and flavor (*le parfum; luh pahr-fuhN*) you prefer:

an ice cream	une glace	*ewn glahs*
a yogurt	un yaourt	*uhN yah-oort*
a cone	un cornet	*uhN kohr-neh*
a cup	une coupe	*ewn koop*
chocolate	au chocolat	*o shoh-koh-lah*
vanilla	à la vanille	*ah lah vah-nee-y*
strawberry	aux fraises	*o frehz*

Drink to Me Only

The French usually drink wine with dinner. The wines you might order include the following:

red wine	le vin rouge	*luh vaN roozh*
rosé wine	le vin rosé	*luh vaN ro-zay*
white wine	le vin blanc	*luh vaN blahN*
sparkling wine	le vin mousseux	*luh vaN moo-suh*
champagne	le champagne	*luh shahN-pah-nyuh*

Perhaps you do not indulge in alcohol or prefer something else to drink with your meal. During the course of a meal, you might even wish to have several different drinks: juice, water, soda, coffee, or tea. Other beverages you might enjoy during or after dinner are presented in the following table.

Beverages

Drink	French	Pronunciation
coffee	un café	*uhN kah-fay*
with milk (morning)	au lait	*o leh*
espresso	express	*ehks-prehs*
with cream	crème	*krehm*
black	noir	*nwahr*
iced	glacé	*glah-say*
decaffeinated	décaféiné	*day-kah-fay-ee-nay*
tea	un thé	*uhN tay*
with lemon	au citron	*o see-trohN*
with sugar	sucré	*sew-kray*
herbal	une tisane	*ewn tee-zahn*
mineral water	de l'eau minérale	*duh lo mee-nay-rahl*
carbonated	gazeuse	*gah-zuhz*
noncarbonated	plate	*plaht*

Culture Capsule

The French do not load their drinks with ice cubes (*des glaçons; day glah-sohN*) the way many Americans do. In fact, "on the rocks" is not even an option in some places. You might even have to pay extra for ice since it's a rare commodity.

I'm Dying of Thirst

You've spent a long and tiring day sightseeing, and you feel that it's time to stop and pause for a moment. You'd like to rest your weary feet, and you need a quick pick-me-up. You see a French café and realize that it's the perfect place to stop, grab a nice cool drink, and people-watch. If you're thirsty, learning the irregular verb *boire* (to drink) in the following table will help you order what you like. *Boire* is similar to a "shoe verb" in that the *nous* and *vous* forms change. They do not, however, look like the infinitive. The forms for the other subject pronouns do.

The Verb *Boire* (to Drink)

Conjugation	Pronunciation	Meaning
je bois	*zhuh bwah*	I drink
tu bois	*tew bwah*	you drink
il, elle, on boit	*eel, ehl, ohN bwah*	he, she, one drinks
nous buvons	*noo bew-vohN*	we drink
vous buvez	*voo bew-vay*	you drink
ils, elles boivent	*eel, ehl bwahv*	they drink

The cost of a drink or meal in a French café depends on where it is consumed. The same soft drink is cheapest if purchased at the indoor counter (because you have to stand), is more expensive at an indoor table (because the scenery isn't terribly exciting), and is most expensive at a table on the outside terrace (where you can take in everything that is going on). Don't be surprised to pay $3 for a 6-ounce bottle of soda!

You Can't Have It All

The food is delicious, even better than you expected. *Pâtisseries* beckon on every corner. Temptations lurk everywhere. You do not, however, want to return from vacation 20 pounds heavier. Don't eat it all; share some with a companion.

The partitive is used in French to express part of a whole or an indefinite quantity, and it is equivalent to the English "some" or "any."

Partitive	Used Before
du (de + le)	Masculine singular nouns beginning with a consonant
de la	Feminine singular nouns beginning with a consonant
de l'	Any singular noun beginning with a vowel
des (de + les)	All plural nouns

In a negative sentence or before an adjective preceding a plural noun, the partitive is expressed by *de*. (No definite article is used.)

Nous n'avons pas de ragout.
noo nah-vohN pah duh rah-goo
We don't have (any) stew.

Elle prépare de bons gâteaux.
ehl pray-pahr duh bohN gah-to
She prepares good cakes.

Breakfast in Bed

Did you ever just feel like lounging around your hotel room and being lazy, perhaps after several days of intensive sightseeing? Order the breakfast of your choice.

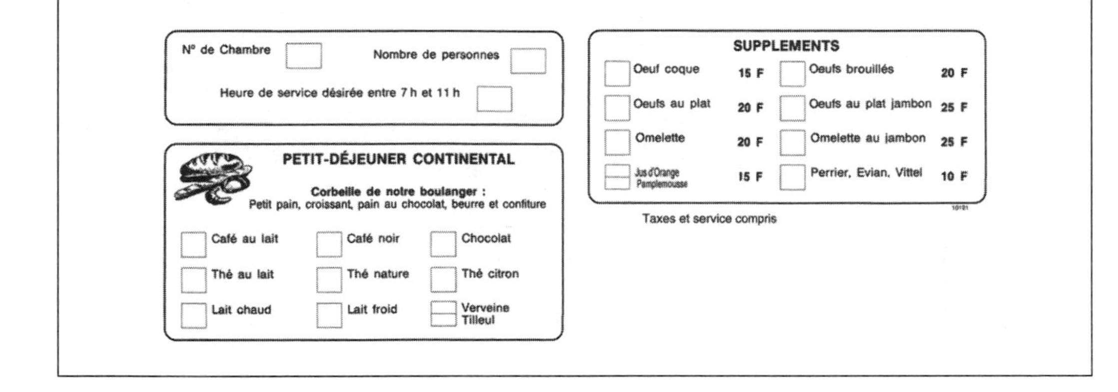

Nº de Chambre

Nombre de personnes

Heure de service désirée entre 7 h et 11 h

PETIT-DÉJEUNER CONTINENTAL

Corbeille de notre boulanger :
Petit pain, croissant, pain au chocolat, beurre et confiture

Café au lait	Café noir	Chocolat
Thé au lait	Thé nature	Thé citron
Lait chaud	Lait froid	Verveine Tilleul

SUPPLEMENTS

Oeuf coque	15 F	Oeufs brouillés	20 F
Oeufs au plat	20 F	Oeufs au plat jambon	25 F
Omelette	20 F	Omelette au jambon	25 F
Jus d'Orange Pamplemousse	15 F	Perrier, Evian, Vittel	10 F

Taxes et service compris

The Pronoun *en*

Imagine you've spent the whole day out on the town with a friend and now you'd like to go eat. You reach into your pocket, and lo and behold, you find that you've exhausted your cash supply. You turn to your companion and ask the logical question, "Do you have any money?" He wants to answer you in French and say, "Yes, I do." He can't use the verb *faire* (to do), however, because *faire* cannot stand alone. If he said, "Je fais de l'argent," that would mean he is making money—not something he'd want to admit. The way around this predicament is to use the pronoun *en*, a handy word that, when used properly, will prove to be extremely helpful.

The pronoun *en* refers to previously mentioned things or places. *En* usually replaces *de* + noun and can mean "some or any of it/them," "about it/them," "from it/them," or "from there":

Il veut *des biscuits*.
Il *en* veut.
eel ahN vuh
He wants some (of them).

Je ne veux pas *de salade*.
Je n'*en* veux pas.
zhuh nahN vuh pah
I don't want any (of it).

Nous parlons *du restaurant.*	Elles sortent *du café.*
Nous *en* parlons.	Elles *en* sortent.
noo zahN pahr-lohN	*ehl zahN sohrt*
We speak about it.	They leave (it) from there.

En is always expressed in French even though it may have no English equivalent or is not expressed in English:

As-tu *de l'argent?*	Oui, j'*en* ai.
Do you have any money?	Yes, I do.
J'ai besoin *d'un couteau.*	J'*en* ai besoin.
I need a knife.	I need one.

En is used to replace a noun (*de* + noun) after a number or a noun or adverb of quantity:

Il prépare *dix sandwiches.*	Il *en* prépare dix.
He is preparing 10 sandwiches.	He is preparing 10 (of them).
Il prépare une tasse *de thé.*	Il *en* prépare une tasse.
He is preparing a cup of tea.	He is preparing a cup of it.
Il prépare beaucoup *de tartes.*	Il *en* prépare beaucoup.
He is preparing a lot of pies.	He is preparing a lot (of them).

Attention!

En never refers to people.

En is placed before the verb to which its meaning is tied, usually before the conjugated verb. When there are two verbs, *en* is placed before the infinitive:

J'*en* prends.	Je n'*en* prends pas.
I take (eat) some.	I don't take (eat) any.

In an affirmative command, *en* changes position and is placed immediately after the verb and joined to it by a hyphen. The familiar command forms of *-er* verbs (regular and irregular) retain their final *s* before *en.* This is to prevent the clash of two vowel sounds together. Remember to put a liaison (linking) between the final consonant and *en:*

Manges-*en*! (*mahNzh zahN*)	Mangez-*en*! (*mahN-zhay zahN*)
Eat some! (familiar)	Eat some! (polite)

Yes or No?

You've returned from a fabulous trip only to discover that you can't buckle your belt and you ripped your jeans as you bent over. You want to lose weight, but temptations abound everywhere. What does your conscience dictate?

Example:
Je mange du chocolat? des fruits?
Du chocolat? N'en mange pas. Des fruits? Manges-en.

1. Je mange des bonbons? des légumes? ________________
2. Je prépare de la salade? de la mousse? ____________
3. Je prends du poisson? des saucisses? __________________
4. Je choisis de la glace? du yaourt? ____________________
5. J'achète de l'eau minérale? du soda? __________

Délicieux!

I'm interested in your opinion. What did you think of your meal? Was it just average, or did you give it a rave review? If you thought it was truly exceptional, you might want to exclaim your pleasure by using the adjective *quel* in the following table to express "What a ...!"

Quel and *Quelle*

	Masculine	Feminine
Singular	quel	quelle
Plural	quels	quelles

Make sure to put the adjective in its proper position:

Quel repas formidable!
kehl ruh-pah fohr-mee-dahbl
What a great meal!

Quels desserts délicieux!
kehl deh-sehr day-lee-syuh
What delicious desserts!

Quelle mousse excellente!
kehl moos ehk-seh-lahNt
What an excellent mousse!

Quelles bonnes omelettes!
kehl bohn zohm-leht
What good omelettes!

Merci Beaucoup

I knew you'd love French food. Now you want to tell me just how much you enjoyed it. Use the correct form of *quel* to express how you felt about what you ate and drank: soup, steak, wine, salad, cheese, and mousse.

Don't forget to ask for the check at the end of your meal:

> L'addition, s'il vous plaît.
> *lah-dee-syohN, seel voo pleh*
> The check, please.

The Least You Need to Know

- To get what you want in a restaurant, learn the terms for the foods you like to eat and the way you like them prepared.
- Use the partitive (*de*, *du*, *de la*, *de l'*, *des*) to express "some."
- The pronoun *en* expresses "some" and may replace the partitive.
- To make an exclamation, use *quel* + noun. When using an adjective, make sure to put it in its proper position.

Chapter 18

Fun and Games

In This Chapter

- Fun things to do
- The irregular verbs *vouloir* (to want) and *pouvoir* (to be able to)
- Extending, accepting, and refusing invitations
- Using adverbs to describe abilities

You've seen the sights, collected mementos, and purchased souvenirs and designer clothing. You feel much better, too, now that you have eaten. Now it's time to have fun and enjoy yourself or simply take a pause and relax.

Are you heading off to the sea to engage in water sports, up to the mountains for skiing or hiking, onto the links for a round of golf, or onto the courts for a brisk tennis match? Are you a film buff or a theater-goer? Do you enjoy a lively opera or an elegant ballet? Perhaps the game's the thing, and you'll spend some time with a one-armed bandit in a luxurious casino. This chapter helps you do it all, invite someone to accompany you, and describe your abilities.

Sports Are My Life

My husband loves to golf; his clubs have seen nearly as many countries as we have! I adore the beach and like nothing better than to feel the sand between my toes as I gaze out at the ocean. Whether you're a sports fanatic or a beach lover, you'll need some specific phrases and terms to make your preferences known. The following table provides a list of sports and outdoor activities.

Use the verb *faire* when talking about engaging in a sport:

Je fais du volley-ball.
I play volleyball.

Sports

Sport	Le Sport	Pronunciation
aerobics	de l'aérobic *m.*	*duh lahy-roh-beek*
baseball	du base-ball	*dew bays-bohl*
basketball	du basket-ball	*dew bahs-keht bohl*
bicycling	du vélo	*dew vay-lo*
boating	du canotage	*dew kah-noh-tahzh*
bodybuilding	de la musculation	*duh lah mew-skew-lah-syohN*
canoeing	du canoë	*dew kah-noh-ay*
cycling	du cyclisme	*dew see-kleez-muh*
deep-sea fishing	de la pêche sous-marine	*duh la pehsh soo-mah-reen*
diving	du plongeon	*dew plohN-zhohN*
fishing	de la pêche	*duh lah pehsh*
football	du football américain	*dew foot-bohl ah-may-ree-kaN*
golf	du golf	*dew gohlf*
hockey	du hockey	*dew oh-kee*
horseback riding	de l'équitation *f.*	*duh lay-kee-tah-syohN*
hunting	de la chasse	*duh lah shahs*
jogging	du jogging	*dew zhoh-geeng*
mountain climbing	de l'alpinisme *m.*, de l'escalade *f.*	*duh lahl-pee-neez-muh,* *duh lehs-kah-lahd*
parasailing	du parachutisme	*dew pah-rah-shew-teez-muh*
roller skating	du patin à roulettes	*dew pah-taN ah roo-leht*
sailing	du bateau à voiles	*dew bah-to ah vwahl*

Sport	Le Sport	Pronunciation
scuba diving	de la plongée sous-marine	*duh lah plohN-zhay soo-mah-reen*
skating	du patin	*dew pah-taN*
skiing	du ski	*dew skee*
soccer	du football	*dew foot-bohl*
surfing	du surf	*dew sewrf*
swimming	de la natation	*duh lah nah-tah-syohN*
tennis	du tennis	*dew tuh-nees*
volleyball	du volley-ball	*dew voh-lee bohl*
waterskiing	du ski nautique	*dew skee no-teek*
windsurfing	de la planche à voile	*duh lah plahNsh ah vwahl*

- Use *du* (*de* + *le*) before the name of a masculine singular sport that begins with a consonant.
- Use *de l'* before the name of any sport that begins with a vowel.
- Use *de la* before the name of any feminine, singular sport.

Want to Join Me?

It really isn't much fun to play alone. Why not ask someone to join you? To extend an invitation, you can use the irregular verbs *vouloir* (to want) and *pouvoir* (to be able to) in the following tables. Both verbs have similar conjugations. They are similar to "shoe verbs" in that their *nous* and *vous* forms begin like the infinitive, whereas their other forms undergo a change.

The Verb *Vouloir* (to Want)

Conjugation	Pronunciation	Meaning
je veux	*zhuh vuh*	I want
tu veux	*tew vuh*	you want
il, elle, on veut	*eel, ehl, ohN vuh*	he, she, one wants
nous voulons	*noo voo-lohN*	we want
vous voulez	*voo voo-lay*	you want
ils, elles veulent	*eel, ehl vuhl*	they want

The Verb *Pouvoir* (to Be Able to [Can])

Conjugation	Pronunciation	Meaning
je peux	*zhuh puh*	I am able to (can)
tu peux	*tew puh*	you are able to (can)
il, elle, on peut	*eel, ehl, ohN puh*	he, she, one is able to (can)
nous pouvons	*noo poo-vohN*	we can
vous pouvez	*voo poo-vay*	you can
ils, elles peuvent	*eel, ehl puhv*	they can

To invite someone to do something, you would ask:

Vous voulez (Tu veux) + infinitive of the verb
Do you want to …?

Vous voulez (Tu veux) faire du ski?
Do you want to go skiing?

or

Vous pouvez (Tu peux) + infinitive of the verb
Can you …?

Vous pouvez (Tu peux) aller à la pêche?
Can you go fishing?

Each sport has its own particular playing field or milieu. When you're ready for some exercise, look at the following table to choose the place where you would go to participate in the sport or activity.

Where to Go

Place	Le Lieu	Pronunciation
beach	la plage	*lah plahzh*
course (golf)	le parcours	*luh pahr-koor*
court	le court	*luh koort*
court (jai alai)	le fronton	*luh frohN-tohN*
field	le terrain	*luh teh-raN*
gymnasium	le gymnase	*luh zheem-nahz*
mountain	la montagne	*lah mohN-tah-nyuh*

Place	Le Lieu	Pronunciation
ocean	l'océan *m.*	*loh-see-ahN*
park	le parc	*luh pahrk*
path	le sentier	*luh sahN-tyay*
pool	la piscine	*lah pee-seen*
rink	la patinoire	*lah pah-tee-nwahr*
sea	la mer	*lah mehr*
slope	la piste	*lah peest*
stadium	le stade	*luh stahd*
track	la piste	*lah peest*

I'll Meet You There

Various traveling companions have been invited for a day of sports. Say that the given subjects can engage in the following sports and say where they want to go.

Example:
je (swimming)
Je peux faire de la natation.
Je veux aller à la plage.

1. tu (tennis) ______________________________

   ____

2. nous (golf) ______________________________

   ____

3. vous (fishing) ______________________________

   ____

4. elle (baseball) ______________________________

   ____

5. ils (skating) ______________________________

   ____

The Necessary Equipment

You probably don't want to lug your sports equipment with you on vacation. You certainly wouldn't want it to get lost in the shuffle. So if you were interested in borrowing or renting equipment, you would say:

Il me faut …	J'ai besoin de …	Pourriez-vous me prêter (louer) …
eel muh foh …	*zhay buh-zwaN duh …*	*poor-yay voo muh preh-tay (loo-ay) …*
I need …	I need …	Could you lend (rent) me …

s'il vous plaît
seel voo pleh
please

Refer to the following table for more examples.

Sports Equipment—*L'équipement Sportif (lay-keep mahN spohr-teef)*

Equipment	L'équipement	Pronunciation
ball		
football, soccer	un ballon	*uhN bah-lohN*
baseball, tennis	une balle	*ewn bahl*
bat	une batte	*ewn baht*
bicycle	un vélo, une bicyclette	*uhN vay-lo, ewn bee-see-kleht*
boat	un bateau	*uhN bah-to*
boots (ski)	des chaussures de ski *f.*	*day sho-sewr duh skee*
fishing rod	une canne à pêche	*ewn kahn ah pehsh*
golf clubs	des club de golf *m.*	*day klewb duh gohlf*
helmet (diver's)	un casque de scaphandre	*uhN kahsk duh skah-fahNdr*
net	un filet	*uhN fee-leh*
poles (ski)	des bâtons *m.*	*day bah-tohN*
puck	une rondelle (Canada), un palet (France)	*ewn rohN-dehl, uhN pah-leh*
racket	une raquette	*ewn rah-keht*
sailboard	une planche à voile	*ewn plahNsh ah vwahl*
skateboard	une planche à roulettes	*ewn plahNsh ah roo-leht*

Equipment	L'équipement	Pronunciation
skates	des patins *m.*	*day pah-taN*
ice	à glace	*ah glahs*
roller	à roulettes	*ah roo-leht*
ski bindings	des fixations de ski	*day feek-sah-syohN duh skee*
skis (water)	des skis *m.* (nautiques)	*day skee (no-teek)*
stick (hockey)	une crosse	*ewn krohs*
surfboard	une planche de surf	*ewn plahNsh duh sewrf*

Doing the Inviting

Tomorrow's forecast is perfect for the sports-minded individual. Pick up the phone and invite someone to go with you to the proper place so that you can go: hiking, skiing, jogging, skating, mountain climbing, or scuba diving. Sample responses can be found in Appendix A.

Memorize the irregular verbs *vouloir* (to want) and *pouvoir* (to be able to) so that you can easily extend an invitation.

____

____

____

____

A Polite Yes

Whether you've been invited to participate in a sport or outing, visit a museum, or just stay at someone's home, the phrases in the following table will allow you to graciously accept any invitation extended to you.

Acceptance

Phrase	French	Pronunciation
With pleasure.	Avec plaisir.	*ah-vehk pleh-zeer*
Of course.	Bien entendu.	*byaN nahN-tahN-dew*

continues

Acceptance (continued)

Phrase	French	Pronunciation
Of course.	Bien sûr.	*byaN sewr*
That's a good idea.	C'est une bonne idée.	*seh tewn bohn ee-day*
Great!	Chouette!	*shoo-eht*
Okay. (I agree.)	D'accord.	*dah-kohr*
And how! You bet!	Et comment!	*ay koh-mahN*
There's no doubt about it.	Il n'y a pas d'erreur.	*eel nyah pah deh-ruhr*
Why not?	Pourquoi pas?	*poor-kwah pah*
If you want to.	Si tu veux (vous voulez)	*see tew vuh (voo voo-lay)*
Gladly.	Volontiers!	*voh-lohN-tyay*

A Polite Refusal and an Excuse

What if you really can't go to an event because of some prior engagement or commitment? Or perhaps you just feel like being alone. You can cordially refuse any invitation without hurting anyone's feelings by expressing your regrets or giving an excuse. You might use an expression from the following table.

Regrets and Excuses

Phrase	French	Pronunciation
It's impossible.	C'est impossible.	*seh taN-poh-seebl*
Not again!	Encore!	*ahN-kohr*
I don't feel like it.	Je n'ai pas envie.	*zhuh nay pah zahN-vee*
I can't.	Je ne peux pas.	*zhuh nuh puh pah*
I'm not free.	Je ne suis pas libre.	*zhuh nuh swee pah leebr*
I don't want to.	Je ne veux pas.	*zhuh nuh vuh pah*
I'm sorry.	Je regrette. Je suis désolé(e).	*zhuh ruh-greht* *zhuh swee day-zoh-lay*
I'm tired.	Je suis fatigué(e).	*zhuh swee fah-tee-gay*
I'm busy.	Je suis occupé(e).	*zhuh swee zoh-kew-pay*

I Really Don't Care

We all have days when we're very wishy-washy. One minute we're gung-ho about an idea and the next we don't even contemplate it. If you can't make up your mind or are indifferent to an idea, you might use one of the phrases from the following table.

Expressing Indifference and Indecision

Phrase	French	Pronunciation
It depends.	Ça dépend.	*sah day-pahN*
It's all the same to me.	Ça m'est égal.	*sah meh tay-gahl*
Whatever you want.	Comme tu veux (vous voulez).	*kohm tew vuh (voo voo-lay)*
I really don't know.	Je ne sais pas trop.	*zhuh nuh seh pah tro*
Perhaps. Maybe.	Peut-être.	*puh-tehtr*

Other Things to Do

Perhaps sports aren't part of your agenda. There are plenty of other activities you can pursue to have a good time. The phrases in the following table will give you the tools to make many other intriguing suggestions.

Places to Go and Things to Do

Place	Le Lieu	Activity	L'activité
ballet	aller au ballet	see the dancers	voir les danseurs
beach	aller à la plage	swim, sunbathe	nager, prendre un bain de soleil
casino	aller au casino	gamble	jouer
concert	aller au concert	listen to the orchestra	écouter l'orchestre
disco	aller à une discothèque	dance	danser
hike	faire une randonnée	see the sights	voir les sites pittoresques
mall	aller au centre commercial	go window shopping	faire du lèche-vitrines

continues

Places to Go and Things to Do (continued)

Place	Le Lieu	Activity	L'activité
movies	aller au cinéma	see a film	voir un film
opera	aller à l'opéra	listen to the singers	écouter les chanteurs
stay in one's room	rester dans sa chambre	play cards	jouer aux cartes

Will You Be Joining Us?

Let's say you've received a ton of invitations. One friend would like you to go window-shopping, while another is urging you to go surfing. You also have conflicting plans for the evening: Your husband wants to go to the movies, but your daughter is eager to go to a disco. And, if that isn't enough, business colleagues have even asked you to spend the evening at the opera! Fashion a reply to all these invitations using the phrases you've learned so far. Sample responses can be found in Appendix A.

1. shopping ______
2. surfing ______
3. movies ______
4. discotheque ______
5. opera ______

At the Shore

Did you ever arrive at the pool or the beach only to realize that you forgot to bring your suntan lotion or some other essential item? Your day could be ruined unnecessarily. Remember to pack the following items for a pleasant day in the sun.

Beach Stuff

Item	L'article	Pronunciation
beach ball	un ballon de plage	*uhN bah-lohN duh plahzh*
beach chair	une chaise longue	*ewn shehz lohNg*

Item	L'article	Pronunciation
beach towel	un drap de bain	*uhN drah dbaN*
sunglasses	des lunettes de soleil *f.*	*day lew-neht duh soh-lehy*
suntan lotion	la lotion solaire, la crème solaire	*lah loh-syohN soh-lehr, lah krehm soh-lehr*
suntan oil	l'huile solaire	*lweel soh-lehr*

At the Movies and on TV

Do you crave some quiet relaxation? Is the weather bad? Do you feel like getting away from everyone and everything? There's always a movie or TV. It seems that cable has invaded the planet and can accommodate anyone who needs a few carefree hours in the room. So, if you want to be entertained, consult the following table for the possibilities.

On passe quel genre de film?
ohN pahs kehl zhahNr duh feelm
What kind of film are they showing?

Qu'est-ce qu'il y a à la télé?
kehs keel yah ah lah tay-lay
What's on TV?

Movies and Television Programs

Genre	Le Genre	Pronunciation
adventure film	un film d'aventure	*uhN feelm dah-vahN-tewr*
cartoon	un dessin animé	*uhN deh-saN ah-nee-may*
comedy	un film comique	*uhN feelm koh-meek*
documentary	un documentaire	*uhN doh-kew-mahN-tehr*
drama	un drame	*uhN drahm*
game show	un jeu	*uhN zhuh*
horror movie	un film d'horreur	*uhN feelm doh-ruhr*
love story	un film d'amour	*uhN feelm dah-moor*
mystery	un mystère	*uhN mees-tehr*
news	les informations *f.*	*lay zaN-fohr-mah-syohN*
police story	un film policier	*uhN feelm poh-lee-syay*
science-fiction film	un film de science-fiction	*uhN feelm duh see-ahNs-feek-syohN*
soap opera	un feuilleton (mélodramatique)	*uhN fuhy-tohN (may-loh-drah-mah-teek)*
spy movie	un film d'espionnage	*uhN feelm dehs-pee-yoh-nazh*
talk show	une causerie	*ewn koz-ree*
weather	la météo	*lah may-tay-o*
western	un western	*uhN wehs-tehrn*

The abbreviations in the following table will help you when choosing a movie or theater.

Movie Abbreviations

Abbreviation	French	Meaning
INT-18 ans	Interdit aux moins de 18 ans	Forbidden for those under 18
V.O.	Version originale	Original version, subtitled
V.F.	Version française	Dubbed in French
T.R.	Tarif réduit	Reduced rate
C.V.	Carte vermeille	"Red" senior citizens' card

What Did You Think?

Use the following phrases to express your enjoyment of a film or program.

I love it!	J'adore!	*zhah-dohr*
It's a good movie.	C'est un bon film.	*seh tuhN bohN feelm*
It's amusing!	C'est amusant!	*seh tah-mew-zahN*
It's great!	C'est génial!	*seh zhay-nyahl*
It's moving!	C'est émouvant!	*seh tay-moo-vahN*
It's original!	C'est original!	*seh toh-ree-zhee-nahl*

If you are less than thrilled with the show, try these phrases:

I hate it!	Je déteste!	*zhuh day-tehst*
It's a bad movie.	C'est un mauvais film.	*seh tuhN mo-veh feelm*
It's a loser!	C'est un navet!	*seh tuhN nah-veh*
It's garbage!	C'est bidon!	*seh bee-dohN*
It's the same old thing!	C'est toujours la même chose!	*seh too-zhoor lah mehm shohz*
It's too violent!	C'est trop violent!	*seh tro vee-oh-lahN*

I Think ...

Using the phrases you've learned, give your opinion of the following types of movies. Sample responses can be found in Appendix A.

1. a love story ______________________________
2. a science-fiction film ______________________________
3. a horror film ______________________________
4. a police film ______________________________
5. a mystery ______________________________
6. a cartoon ______________________________

Take a Hike

With so much emphasis today on physical fitness and staying in shape, many people find it rewarding to go for a long walk. The following table will help you identify the things you see along the way, whether you take a leisurely hike, a stroll in the country, or a tour of the city.

Nature Calls

English	French	Pronunciation
bridge	le pont	*luh pohN*
farm	la ferme	*lah fehrm*
fields	les champs *m.*	*lay shahN*
flowers	les fleurs *f.*	*lay fluhr*
forest	la forêt	*lah foh-reh*
lake	le lac	*luh lahk*
landscape	le paysage	*luh pay-ee-sahzh*
moon	la lune	*lah lewn*
mountains	les montagnes *f.*	*lay mohN-tah-nyuh*
ocean	l'océan *m.*	*loh-say-ahN*
sky	le ciel	*luh syehl*
stars	les étoiles *f.*	*lay zay-twahl*
stream	le ruisseau	*luh rwee-so*
trees	les arbres *m.*	*lay zahrbr*
valley	la vallée	*lah vah-lay*
view	la vue	*lah vew*
village	le village	*luh vee-lahzh*
waterfall	la cascade	*lah kahs-kahd*
woods	les bois *m.*	*lay bwah*

At a Concert

A friend has invited you to L'Opéra in Paris, but you feel a little hesitant about going. Although you're familiar with some French composers and their works (Bizet's *Carmen* is your personal favorite), you're afraid you won't be able to hold up your end of the conversation. The names of the instruments in the following table should assist you in expressing your ideas.

Musical Instruments

Instrument	L'instrument	Pronunciation
cello	le violoncelle	*luh vee-oh-lohN-sehl*
clarinet	la clarinette	*lah klah-ree-neht*
drum	le tambour	*luh tahN-boor*
drums	la batterie	*lah bah-tree*
flute	la flûte	*lah flewt*
guitar	la guitare	*lah gee-tahr*
harp	la harpe	*lah ahrp*
oboe	le hautbois	*luh o-bwah*
piano	le piano	*luh pyah-no*
piccolo	le piccolo	*luh pee-koh-lo*
saxophone	le saxophone	*luh sahk-soh-fohn*
trombone	le trombone	*luh trohN-bohn*
trumpet	la trompette	*lah trohN-peht*
violin	le violon	*luh vee-oh-lohN*

Jouer à vs. *Jouer de*

In English, we use the verb "to play" whether we are referring to the playing of an instrument or the playing of a sport. The French, however, make a distinction. The verb *jouer* means to play. When followed by the preposition *de* + a definite article (*du, de la, de l', des*), *jouer* refers to the playing of musical instruments.

Il joue du piano.
eel zhoo dew pyah-no
He plays the piano.

Elle joue de la flûte.
ehl zhoo duh lah floot
She plays the flute.

When referring to sports or to games (such as card or board games), *jouer* is followed by *à* + a definite article (*au, à la, à l', aux*):

Ils jouent au tennis.
eel zhoo o teh-nees
They play tennis.

Elles jouent aux cartes.
ehl zhoo o kahrt
They play cards.

Let's Play

Would you use *jouer à* or *jouer de* to complete the following sentences? Answers can be found in Appendix A.

1. Nous _______________ football.
2. Vous _______________ flûte.
3. Tu _______________ guitare.
4. Ils _______________ tennis.
5. Je _______________ piano.
6. Elle _______________ cartes.

Just How Good Are You?

Adverbs are often used to describe how well you do something, such as "He plays the cello *beautifully*." (In English, most adverbs end in *-ly*.) In French, adverbs are used for the same purpose, and they generally end in *-ment*.

Adverbs are formed by adding *-ment* to the masculine singular form of adjectives that end in a vowel. If the masculine form of the adjective ends in a consonant, first change it to the feminine form and then add *-ment*. This works quite well as long as you look for the proper letter at the end of the adjective and remember the feminine forms. The following tables show you just how easy this is.

Adverbs Formed from Masculine Adjectives

Masculine Adjective	Adverb	Meaning
facile *fah-seel*	facilement *fah-seel-mahN*	easily
passionné *pah-syoh-nay*	passionnément *pah-syoh-nay-mahN*	enthusiastically
probable *proh-bahbl*	probablement *proh-bahbl-mahN*	probably
rapide *rah-peed*	rapidement *rah-peed-mahN*	rapidly, quickly
sincère *saN-sehr*	sincèrement *saN-sehr-mahN*	sincerely
vrai *vreh*	vraiment *vreh-mahN*	truly, really

Adverbs Formed from Feminine Adjectives

Masculine Adjective	Feminine Adjective	Adverb	Meaning
lent *lahN*	lente *lahNt*	lentement *lahNt-mahN*	slowly
certain *sehr-taN*	certaine *sehr-tehn*	certainement *sehr-tehn-mahN*	certainly
seul *suhl*	seule *suhl*	seulement *suhl-mahN*	only
actif *ahk-teef*	active *ahk-teev*	activement *ahk-teev-mahN*	actively
complet *kohN-pleh*	complète *kohN-pleht*	complètement *kohN-pleht-mahN*	completely
continuel *kohN-tee-new-ehl*	continuelle *kohN-tee-new-ehl*	continuellement *kohN-tee-new-ehl-mahN*	continuously
doux *doo*	douce *doos*	doucement *doos-mahN*	gently
fier *fyehr*	fière *fyehr*	fièrement *fyehr-mahN*	proudly
franc *frahN*	franche *frahNsh*	franchement *frahNsh-mahN*	frankly
sérieux *say-ree-yuh*	sérieuse *say-ree-uhz*	sérieusement *say-ree-uhz-mahN*	seriously

The following table lists two irregular adverb formations.

Irregular Adverbs

Masculine Adjective	Feminine Adjective	Adverb	Meaning
bref *brehf*	brève *brehv*	brièvement *bree-ehv-mahN*	briefly
gentil *zhahN-tee*	gentille *zhahN-tee*	gentiment *zhahN-tee-mahN*	gently

Exceptions to the Rule

Life would be so easy if there were no exceptions to the rules. This, however, is not the case with French adverbs. Fortunately, the irregularities are easy to understand and should present no difficulties in adverb formation.

As shown in the following table, some adverbs are formed by changing a silent *e* from the adjective to *é* before the adverbial *-ment* ending.

When forming adverbs, watch out for irregular adjectives.

More Irregular Adverbs

Adjective	Adverb	Meaning
énorme *ay-nohrm*	énormément *ay-nohr-may-mahN*	enormously
intense *aN-tahNs*	intensément *aN-tahN-say-mahN*	intensely
précis *pray-see*	précisément *pray-see-zay-mahN*	precisely
profond *proh-fohN*	profondément *proh-fohN-day-mahN*	profoundly

Adjectives ending in *-ant* and *-ent* have adverbs ending in *-amment* and *-emment*, respectively, as shown in the following table.

Even More Irregular Adverbs

Adjective	Adverb	Meaning
constant *kohN-stahN*	constamment *kohN-stah-mahN*	constantly
courant *koo-rahN*	couramment *koo-rah-mahN*	fluently
différent *dee-fay-rahN*	différemment *dee-fay-reh-mahN*	differently
évident *ay-vee-dahN*	évidemment *ay-vee-deh-mahN*	evidently
récent *ray-sahN*	récemment *ray-seh-mahN*	recently

Be careful with the adverbs in the following table; they have distinct forms from adjectives.

Very Irregular Adverbs

Adjective	Adverb
bon (*bohN*) good	bien (*byaN*) well
mauvais (*moh-veh*) bad	mal (*mahl*) badly
meilleur (*meh-yuhr*) better	mieux (*myuh*) better
petit (*puh-tee*) little	peu (*puh*) little

Elle est petite et elle mange peu.
ehl eh puh-teet ay ehl mahNzh puh
She is little, and she eats little.

Ils sont de bons musiciens et ils jouent bien de la guitare.
eel sohN duh bohN mew-zee-syaN ay eel zhoo byaN duh lah gee-tahr
They are good musicians, and they play the guitar well.

Memory Enhancer

If you can't think of the adverb or one does not exist, use the phrases *d'une façon* (*dewn fah-sohN*) or *d'une manière* (*dewn mah-nyehr*), both of which express "in a way," "in a manner," or "in a fashion."

Some adverbs and adverbial expressions are not formed from adjectives at all and therefore do not end in *-ment*. The following table gives the most common adverbs that follow this rule. These familiar, high-frequency words are extremely useful in everyday conversation.

Adverbs and Adverbial Expressions Not Formed from Adjectives

Adverb	Pronunciation	Meaning
alors	*ah-lohrs*	then
après	*ah-preh*	afterward
aussi	*o-see*	also, too
beaucoup	*bo-koo*	much
bientôt	*byaN-to*	soon
comme	*kohm*	as
d'habitude	*dah-bee-tewd*	usually, generally
déjà	*day-zhah*	already

continues

Adverbs and Adverbial Expressions Not Formed from Adjectives (continued)

Adverb	Pronunciation	Meaning
encore	*ahN-kohr*	still, yet, again
enfin	*ahN-faN*	finally, at last
ensemble	*ahN-sahNbl*	together
ensuite	*ahN-sweet*	then, afterwards
ici	*ee-see*	here
là	*lah*	there
loin	*lwaN*	far
longtemps	*lohN-tahN*	a long time
maintenant	*maNt-nahN*	now
même	*mehm*	even
moins	*mwaN*	less
parfois	*pahr-fwah*	sometimes
plus	*plew*	more
près	*preh*	near
presque	*prehsk*	almost
puis	*pwee*	then
quelquefois	*kehl-kuh-fwah*	sometimes
si	*see*	so
souvent	*soo-vahN*	often
tard	*tahr*	late
tôt	*to*	soon, early
toujours	*too-zhoor*	always, still
tout	*too*	quite, entirely
tout à coup	*too tah koo*	suddenly
tout à fait	*too tah feh*	entirely
tout de suite	*toot sweet*	immediately
très	*treh*	very
trop	*tro*	too much
vite	*veet*	quickly

Position of Adverbs

Adverbs generally are placed after the verb they modify. Sometimes, however, the position of the adverb varies, and the adverb is placed where we would logically put an English adverb.

D'habitude il joue bien au football.
dah-bee-tewd eel zhoo byaN o foot-bohl
Usually he plays soccer well.

Il joue très bien au football.
eel zhoo treh byaN o foot-ball
He plays soccer very well.

What Do You Do Well?

How's your cooking? Can you carry a tune? Are you light on your feet, or do you stomp on your partner's toes on the dance floor? We each perform according to our own individual abilities. Express how you fare at the following activities by using adverbs. Sample responses can be found in Appendix A.

Example: parler anglais   Je parle anglais couramment.

1. parler français ____________________
2. jouer du piano ____________________
3. jouer au golf ____________________
4. cuisiner (cook) ____________________
5. penser (think) ____________________
6. travailler ____________________
7. voyager ____________________
8. chanter ____________________
9. danser ____________________
10. nager ____________________

The Least You Need to Know

- The verb *faire* is used to express participation in a sport.
- *Vouloir* (to want) or *pouvoir* (to be able) + a verb infinitive can be used to propose, accept, and refuse invitations.
- *Jouer* + *à* + a definite article (*au*, *à la*, *à l'*, *aux*) is used to discuss playing a sport or game. *Jouer* + *de* + a definite article is used to discuss playing a musical instrument.
- Many adverbs are formed by adding *-ment* to adjectives ending in a vowel.

Part 4

Time Out: Problems

No one likes to encounter problems, especially when traveling in a foreign country. Unfortunately, life's little annoyances tend to crop up at the most inopportune times. In Part 4, you'll learn how to deal with the bothersome inconveniences that interfere with your daily routine and threaten to ruin the best of times.

The minor problems—forgetting your toothbrush, tearing an item of clothing, running out of film, wearing down the soles of your shoes, needing to make a phone call or send a letter or package—are easy to deal with. Other situations are more serious and require a more extensive knowledge of the language to get fast attention: an illness, a torn contact lens, broken glasses, or a forgotten prescription.

Part 4 discusses a multitude of possible problems and covers the phrases you'll need to deal with them as effortlessly and quickly as possible.

Chapter 19

Bad Hair? Torn Jacket? Broken Glasses? Personal Services

In This Chapter

- Personal services
- Problems and solutions
- Using stress pronouns
- Making comparisons

You've been traveling and having a wonderful time. All of a sudden, there is a problem that just can't wait: Your roots have surfaced in record time, you've spilled mustard on your new white silk shirt, your contact lens has torn, you've broken a heel on your shoe, or your five-year-old has dropped your camera, smashing the lens. You're not home, and you're very hesitant about what to do. Ask the concierge of your hotel or consult *les pages jaunes* (*lay pahzh zhon*), the yellow pages. Don't worry, the French have competent, expert technicians; all you have to do is know what to say to get the job done. This chapter will make that task easy.

I'm Having a Bad Hair Day

You're on vacation and feeling quite carefree; the sky's the limit. You pass by a salon and are struck by a sudden whim to return home with a brand new look. Why not be daring? You're in Paris, the world-famous center of *haute couture* (high style and fashion). You want a more tantalizing "you," and this is the place to get it.

In the past, men went *chez le coiffeur* (to the barber's), while women were accustomed to going *au salon de beauté* (to the beauty parlor). Today, these establishments have become more or less unisex, with men and women demanding more or less the same services. To get what you want, simply ask:

Pourriez-vous me donner …?	Je voudrais …	S'il vous plaît
poo-ryay voo muh doh-nay …	*zhuh voo-dreh …*	*seel voo pleh*
Could you give me …?	I would like …	Please

Today's salons provide the services listed in the following table.

Hair Care

Phrase	French	Pronunciation
a blunt cut	une coupe en carré	*ewn koop ahN kah-ray*
a coloring (vegetable)	une teinture (végétale)	*ewn taN-tewr (vay-zhay-tahl)*
a facial	un massage facial	*uhN mah-sahzh fah-syahl*
a haircut	une coupe de cheveux	*ewn koop duh shuh-vuh*
highlights	des reflets *m.*	*day ruh-fleh*
layers	une coupe dégradée	*ewn koop day-grah-day*
a manicure	une manucure	*ewn mah-new-kewr*
a pedicure	une pédicurie	*ewn pay-dee-kew-ree*
a permanent	une permanente	*ewn pehr-mah-nahNt*
a rinse	un rinçage colorant	*uhN raN-sahzh koh-loh-rahN*
a set	une mise en plis	*ewn mee zohN plee*
a shampoo	un shampooing	*uhN shahN-pwaN*
a trim	une coupe	*ewn koop*
a waxing	une épilation	*ewn ay-pee-lah-syohN*

The following table gives you the phrases you need to get other services. Use the following phrase to preface your request:

Pourriez-vous …, s'il vous plaît?
poo-ryay voo …, seel voo pleh
Could you please …?

Other Services

Service	French	Pronunciation
blow dry my hair	me donner un brushing	*muh doh-nay uhN bruh-sheeng*
curl my hair	me friser les cheveux	*muh free-zay lay shuh-vuh*
shave my beard, my mustache	me raser la barbe, la moustache	*muh rah-zay lah bahrb, lah moo-stahsh*
straighten my hair	me défriser les cheveux	*muh day-free-zay lay shuh-vuh*
trim my bangs	me rafraîchir la frange	*muh rah-freh-sheer lah frahNzh*
trim my beard, sideburns	me rafraîchir la barbe, les pattes	*muh rah-freh-sheer, lah bahrb lay paht*

Just a Trim, Please

It's hard enough getting the haircut and style you want when there is no language barrier. Imagine the disasters that could befall your poor head in a foreign country! The following phrases will help you make your styling and coloring preferences clear:

Je préfère mes cheveux …
zhuh pray-fehr may shuh-vuh …
I prefer my hair …

long	longs	*lohN*
medium	mi-longs	*mee-lohN*
short	courts	*koor*
curly	bouclés	*boo-klay*
straight	raides (lissés)	*rehd (lee-say)*
wavy	frisés	*free-zay*
auburn	auburn, châtain clair	*oh-bewrn, shah-taN klehr*
black	noir	*nwahr*
blond	blond	*blohN*

brunette	brun	*bruhN*
chestnut brown	châtain	*shah-taN*
red	roux	*roo*
a darker color	une teinte plus foncée	*ewn taNt plew fohN-say*
a lighter color	une teinte plus claire	*ewn taNt plew klehr*
the same color	la même couleur	*lah mehm koo-luhr*

Are you allergic to any products or specific chemicals? Are you sensitive to smells? Do you hate it when your hair feels like cardboard? If you don't like certain hair-care products, don't be shy. Tell the hairdresser:

Ne mettez pas de (d') …, s'il vous plaît.
nuh meh-tay pah duh …, seel voo pleh
Don't put any … please.

gel	gel coiffant *m.*	*zhehl kwah-fahN*
hairspray	laque *f.*	*lahk*
lotion	lotion *f.*	*loh-syohN*
mousse	mousse coiffante *f.*	*moos kwah-fahNt*
shampoo	shampooing *m.*	*shahN-pwaN*
conditioner	après-shampooing, shampooing démelant	*ah-preh shahN-pwaN, shahN-pwaN day-muh-lahN*

Problems and Then Some

There are phrases that will come in handy when you are seeking certain services or are trying to have something repaired. Use the following phrases at the dry cleaner, the shoemaker, the optometrist, the jeweler, or the camera store.

Vous êtes ouvert à quelle heure?
voo zeh too-vehr ah kehl uhr
At what time do you open?

Vous fermez à quelle heure?
voo fehr-may ah kehl uhr
At what time do you close?

Vous êtes ouvert (vous fermez) quels jours?
voo zeht oo-vehr (voo fehr-may) kehl zhoor
What days are you open? Closed?

Pouvez-vous me réparer …?
poo-vay voo muh ray-pah-ray …
Can you fix … for me?

Pouvez-vous le (la, l', les) réparer aujourd'hui?
poo-vay voo luh (lah, lay) ray-pah-ray o-zhoor-dwee
Can you fix it (them) today?

Puis-je avoir un reçu?
pweezh ah-vwahr uhN ruh-sew
May I have a receipt?

Pouvez-vous le (la, l', les) réparer provisoirement (pendant que j'attends)?
poo-vay voo luh (lah, lay) ray-pah-ray proh-vee-zwahr-mahN (pahN-dahN kuh zhah-tahN)
Can you fix it (them) temporarily (while I wait)?

At the Dry Cleaner's—*à la Teinturerie*

You've unpacked. Your blue pants look like you slept in them, and your tan jacket has an ugly stain on the sleeve that you hadn't noticed when you packed it. Don't fret. Your stains, spots, tears, and wrinkles can be taken care of if you know how to explain your problem and ask for the necessary service.

Quel est le problème? Il y a …
kehl eh luh proh-blehm? eel yah …
What's the problem? There is (are) …

a hole	un trou	*uhN troo*
a missing button	un bouton qui manque	*uhN boo-tohN kee mahNk*
a spot	une tache	*ewn tahsh*
a tear	une déchirure	*ewn day-shee-rewr*

Now that you've explained the problem, state what you'd like done about it:

Vous pouvez me nettoyer (à sec) ce (cette, cet, ces) …?
voo poo-vay muh neh-twah-yay ah sehk suh (seht, seht, say) …
Can you (dry) clean this (these) … for me?

Vous pouvez me faire recoudre ce (cette, cet, ces) …?
voo poo-vay muh fehr ruh-koodr suh (seht, seht, say) …
Can you mend this (these) … for me?

Vous pouvez me repasser (réparer) ce (cette, cet, ces) …?
voo poo-vay muh ruh-pah-say (ray-pah-ray) suh (seht, seht, say) …
Can you press (repair) this (these) … for me?

Vous pouvez m'amidonner ce (cette, cet, ces) …?
voo poo-vay mah-mee-doh-nay suh (seht, seht, say) …
Can you starch this (these) … for me?

Vous pouvez me tisser ce (cette, cet, ces)…?
voo poo-vay muh tee-say suh (seht, seht, say) …
Can you weave this (these) … for me?

Vous faites le stoppage?
voo feht luh stoh-pahzh
Do you do invisible mending?

If you'd like a service performed for someone else, use the appropriate indirect object: *te* (for you), *lui* (for him, her), *nous* (for us), *vous* (for you), *leur* (for them).

Vous pouvez *lui* tisser ce manteau?
Can you please weave this coat for him (her)?

Use the verb *faire* (to make, do) before an infinitive to say that you want something done for yourself.

Je voudrais faire nettoyer à sec mon costume.
I would like to have my suit dry cleaned.

At the Laundry—*à la Blanchisserie* or *à la Laverie Automatique*

If your laundry has piled up and you don't mind doing it yourself, you might try to seek out a laundromat. Use the following phrases to get the information you need:

J'ai beaucoup de lessive.
zhay bo-koo duh leh-seev
I have a lot of dirty laundry.

Je voudrais laver mes vêtements.
zhuh voo-dreh lah-vay may veht-mahN
I'd like to wash my clothes.

Je voudrais faire laver mes vêtements.
zhuh voo-dreh fehr lah-vay may veht-mahN
I'd like to have my clothes washed.

So you're embarrassed to have anyone see your dirty laundry, or perhaps you're afraid that your beautiful new silk shirt will get ruined by an amateur. If you want to do the job yourself, the following phrases might serve you well:

Y a-t-il une machine à laver (un séchoir) libre?
ee ah-tee ewn mah-sheen ah lah-vay (uhN saysh-wahr) leebr
Is there a free washing machine (dryer)?

Où puis-je acheter de la lessive en poudre?
oo pweezh ahsh-tay duh lah leh-seev ahN poodr
Where can I buy soap powder?

At the Shoemaker's—*Chez le Cordonnier*

Let's say you've walked so much that you've worn your soles down. Or perhaps you've broken a shoelace on your dress shoes or would just like a shine. The following phrases will help you describe your problem:

Pouvez-vous me réparer …?
poo-vay voo muh ray-pah-ray …
Can you repair … for me?

ces chaussures *say sho-sewr* these shoes	ces bottes *say boht* these boots
ce talon *suh tah-lohN* this heel	cette semelle *seht suh-mehl* this sole
Vendez-vous des lacets? *vahN-day-voo day lah-seh* Do you sell shoelaces?	Je voudrais un cirage. *zhuh voo-dreh zuhN see-rahzh* I'd like a shoeshine.

These Boots Were Made for Walking

You've got an unexpected, important business meeting to attend, and your walking shoes are inappropriate attire. Your dress shoes are in need of repair, and you need them in a hurry. What service does this shoemaker provide? The answer can be found in Appendix A.

CV, CORDONNERIE,
VARTAN
Prend et Livre à domicile
83, r. de Longchamp
765016 PARIS

____

____

____

At the Optometrist's—*Chez l'Opticien*

What could be more annoying than losing or tearing a contact lens or breaking or losing a pair of glasses while away from home? For those of us who depend on these optical necessities, the following phrases could one day prove useful:

Le verre (la monture) est cassé(e).
luh vehr (lah mohN-tewr) eh kah-say
The lens (the frame) is broken.

Pouvez-vous me réparer ces lunettes?
poo-vay voo muh ray-pah-ray say lew-neht
Can you repair these glasses for me?

Pouvez-vous remplacer cette lentille (ce verre) de contact?
poo-vay voo rahN-plah-say seht lahN-tee-y (suh vehr) duh kohN-tahkt
Can you replace this contact lens?

Avez-vous des verres progressifs?
ah-vay-voo day vehr proh-greh-seef
Do you have progressive lenses?

Vendez-vous des lunettes de soleil?
vahN-day voo day lew-neht duh soh-lehy
Do you sell sunglasses?

I Can't See Without Them

Individuals with very poor vision may have eyeglasses with lenses as thick as coke bottles that distort the size and shape of their eyes. Because of the strength of their prescription, these same people may have trouble finding replacement lenses in an emergency. What two services does the following optometrist offer? The answer can be found in Appendix A.

OPTIQUE, ANTOINE

S.O.S. LUNETTES, EN 1 HEURE, RENSEIGNEZ-VOUS, SPÉCIAL MYOPES
verres de fortes correction, ne déformant plus le visage
37 bd St Germain, 75005 PARIS

____

____

____

At the Jeweler's—*Chez le Bijoutier*

If your watch has stopped or isn't working as it should, you might find it necessary to have it repaired before returning home.

Pouvez-vous réparer cette montre?
poo-vay voo ray-pah-ray seht mohNtr
Can you repair this watch?

Ma montre ne marche pas.
mah mohNtr nuh mahrsh pah
My watch doesn't work.

Ma montre avance (retarde).
ma mohNtr ah-vahNs (ruh-tahrd)
My watch is fast (slow).

Vendez-vous des bandes (des piles)?
vahN-day voo day bahnd (day peel)
Do you sell bands (batteries)?

At the Camera Shop—*au Magasin de Photographie*

For many people, a vacation is not a vacation unless they capture it on film. If you need to visit a camera shop or film store in a French-speaking country, the following words will come in handy:

un appareil-photo
uhN nah-pah-rahy foh-to
a camera

un appareil vidéo
uhN nah-pah-rahy vee-day-o
a video camera

If you have special needs, you might ask the following:

Vendez-vous des pellicules de vingt (trente-six) en couleur (noir et blanc)?
vahN-day voo day peh-lee-kewl duh vaN (trahNt-sees) ahN koo-luhr (nwahr ay blahN)
Do you sell rolls of 20 (36) exposure film in color (black and white)?

Vendez-vous des pellicules pour diapositives?
vahN-day voo day peh-lee-kewl poor dee-ah-poh-zee-teev
Do you sell film for slides?

Je voudrais faire développer ce film.
zhuh voo-dreh fehr day-vloh-pay suh feelm
I would like to have this film developed.

Do You Get the Picture?

Are you dissatisfied with the pictures you've been taking? Perhaps you just want something a bit more modern that's easier to use. What services would you expect to receive at this photo-supply store?

PHOTO-EXPERT, TOUTES LES GRANDES MARQUES

Vente-Achat-Échange, Réparation

Vente au plus bas prix, Achat au plus haut cours

____

____

____

Other Services

In addition to the shoemaker, the camera store, and the hairdresser, you may need other special services from time to time. For instance, you may need to find your consulate to report a lost passport. Or perhaps your handbag has been stolen and you'd like to file a police report. You may even want a translator to make sure you don't get into deeper trouble. The following phrases should help:

Où est …
oo eh …
Where is …

… le commissariat de police?
… luh koh-mee-sah-ryah duh poh-lees
… the police station?

… le consulat américain?
… luh kohN-sew-lah ah-may-ree-kaN
… the American consulate?

… l'ambassade américaine?
… lahN-bah-sahd ah-may-ree-kehn
… the American embassy?

J'ai perdu …
zhay pehr-dew …
I lost …

…mon passeport.
… mohN pahs-pohr
… my passport.

… mon portefeuille.
… mohN pohr-tuh-fuhy
… my wallet.

Aidez-moi, s'il vous plaît.
eh-day mwah, seel voo pleh
Help me, please.

Il me faut un interprète.
eel muh fo tuhN naN-tehr-preht
I need an interpreter.

Y a-t-il quelqu'un qui parle anglais?
ee ah teel kehl kuhN kee pahrl ahN-gleh
Does anyone here speak English?

Under Stress

Stress pronouns are so named because you use them to emphasize a certain fact. Stress pronouns may highlight or replace certain nouns or pronouns, or they are used after prepositions. Whereas in English we tend to add stress with our voices ("*I'm* leaving"), the French tend to add stress by adding a pronoun ("*Moi, je pars.*") This concept sounds more confusing than it is. The following table shows subject pronouns with their corresponding stress pronouns.

Stress Pronouns

Subject Pronoun	Stress	Meaning	Subject Pronoun	Stress	Meaning
	Singular			***Plural***	
(je)	moi (*mwah*)	I, me	(nous)	nous (*noo*)	we, us
(tu)	toi (*twah*)	you (fam.)	(vous)	vous (*voo*)	you (pl. pol.)
(il)	lui (*lwee*)	he, him	(ils)	eux (*uh*)	they, them
(elle)	elle (*ehl*)	she, her	(elles)	elles (*ehl*)	they, them
(on)	soi (*swah*)	oneself			

Stress Pronouns at Work

Stress pronouns are used in the following situations:

- When you want to emphasize the subject:

  Moi, je veux parler au propriétaire.
  mwah, zhuh vuh pahr-lay o proh-pree-ay-tehr
  Me, I want to speak to the owner.

  Lui, il a fait une faute.
  lwee, eel ah feh tewn foht
  He made a mistake.

- After *ce* + *être* (it is):

Qui est-ce? C'est moi.	C'est lui qui répare les montres.
kee ehs? seh mwah	*seh lwee kee ray-pahr lay mohNtr*
Who is it? It is I.	He (It is he who) repairs watches.

- When the pronoun has no verb:

  Qui est la propriétaire? Elle.
  kee eh lah proh-pree-ay-tehr? ehl
  Who is the owner? She (is).

- In compound subjects:

  Anne et eux vont chez le coiffeur.
  ahn ay uh vohN shay luh kwah-fuhr
  Anne and they are going to the hairdresser.

If one of the stress pronouns is *moi*, the subject pronoun *nous* is used in summary (because someone + me = we) but does not have to appear in the sentence:

Henri et moi, nous allons chez l'opticien.
Henri et moi allons chez l'opticien.
Henry and I go to the optometrist.

If one of the stress pronouns is *toi*, the subject *vous* is used in summary (because someone + you [singular] = you [plural]) but does not have to appear in the sentence:

Guy et toi, vous allez chez le cordonnier.
Guy et toi allez chez le cordonnier.
Guy and you go to the shoemaker.

- Stress pronouns are used after a preposition when referring to a person or persons:

Je vais chez toi.	Ne pars pas sans lui.
zhuh veh shay twah	*nuh pahr pah sahN lwee*
I'm going to your house.	Don't leave without him.

- Stress pronouns are used after certain verbs that do not use a direct object:

avoir affaire à	*ah-vwahr ah-fehr ah*	to have business with
être à	*ehtr ah*	to belong to
penser à	*pahN-say ah*	to think about (of)
se fier à	*suh fee-ay ah*	to trust
s'intéresser à	*saN-tay-reh-say ah*	to be interested in

J'ai affaire à lui.
zhay ah-fehr ah lwee
I have business with him.

Cette montre est à moi.
seht mohNtr eh tah mwah
That watch is mine.

Stress Relief

If you want to speak like a native, make sure you use stress pronouns correctly. Here are some examples of the different types of sentences that require them. Fill in the appropriate pronoun. The answers can be found in Appendix A.

1. (us) Il a affaire à __________.
2. (he, I) __________ et __________ allons à l'ambassade.
3. (you [familiar]) __________, tu vas chez le coiffeur?
4. (she) __________, elle répare bien les vêtements.
5. (they [masculine]) Je ne peux pas partir sans __________.
6. (you [polite]) C'est __________ qui allez m'accompagner.

Comparison Shopping

Which shop offers the least expensive merchandise? Which merchant is the most honest? Who is the most reliable? When shopping for goods or services, we often compare cost, reputation, and the goods or services themselves before making a choice. The following table gives you the phrases and adjectives you need when making comparisons.

Comparison of Adjectives—Inequality

	Adjective	Pronunciation	Meaning
Positive	honnête	*oh-neht*	honest
Comparative	plus honnête, moins honnête	*plew zoh-neht, mwaN zoh-neht*	more honest, less honest
Superlative	le (la, les) plus honnête(s), le (la, les) moins honnête(s)	*luh (lah) (lay) plew zoh-neht, luh (lah) (lay) mwaN zoh-neht*	the most honest, the least honest

Que may or may not be used after the comparative. When used, *que* expresses "than." *Que* becomes *qu'* before a vowel or vowel sound.

Qui est plus charmant(e)?

Roger est plus charmant (que Lucien).

Sylvie est plus chamante (qu'Anne).

The preposition *de* + definite article (*du, de la, de l', des*) can be used to express "in/of the":

Ce cordonnier est honnète.
Ce cordonnier est plus honnète que lui.
Ce cordonnier est le plus honnète (de la ville).

Ces coiffeuses sont aimables.
Ces coiffeuses sont les plus aimables.
Ces coiffeuses sont les moins aimables (du salon).

When I prepare my special recipe for French pot roast, everyone gathers around the table in eager anticipation. My son Eric eats the slowest and savors every morsel. My husband eats with gusto. But my son Michael eats the fastest of all. His reasoning is "More for me!" Whether it's eating, working, or running, the different ways in which people do things can be compared. The following table shows how to make comparisons using adverbs.

Comparison of Adverbs—Inequality

	Adjective	Pronunciation	Meaning
Positive	rapidement	*rah-peed-mahN*	rapidly
Comparative	plus rapidement, moins rapidement	*plew rah-peed-mahN, mwaN rah-peed-mahN*	more rapidly, less rapidly
Superlative	le plus rapidement, le moins rapidement	*luh plew rah-peed-mahN, luh mwaN rah-peed-mahN*	the most rapidly, the least rapidly

That's Highly Irregular

Beware of irregular comparisons. Never use *plus* or *mauvais* with the adjective *bon* or with the adverb *bien*. There are special comparative forms that express "better" and "best":

bon(ne)(s)	meilleur(e)(s)	le (la, les) meilleur(e)(s)
good	better	the best
bien	mieux	le mieux
well	better	the best

Comparisons of Equality

You've spent the day visiting museums in Paris. The Louvre is vast and contains treasures from antiquity, while the Picasso museum is very modern. Did you find these museums equally appealing, or did you prefer one to the other? Did you spend equal amounts of time in each, or did one visit last longer than the other? If everything was equal, you can express this equality by using the following:

aussi + adjective or adverb + *que*
as … as

Il est aussi charmant qu'eux.
eel eh to-see shahr-mahN kuh
He is as charming as they.

Elle travaille aussi dur que nous.
ehl trah-vahy o-see dewr kuh noo
She works as hard as we do.

Memory Enhancer

The tags *-ci* (this, these) and *-là* (that, those) can be joined to nouns to help differentiate between two things or actions being compared: *Ce coiffeur-ci est plus sympathique que ce coiffeur-là.* (This hairdresser is nicer than that hairdresser.)

You Compare

How do you compare to those you know? Are you shorter? Thinner? More charming? Do you dance better? Work more seriously? Listen more patiently? Use what you've learned to compare yourself to friends or family members. Sample answers can be found in Appendix A.

____

____

____

The Least You Need to Know

- You can solve your problems and get the services you need in a foreign country with a few simple phrases.
- Stress pronouns are used for emphasis after *c'est* and *ce sont*, in compound subjects, after prepositions and certain verbs, alone when there is no verb, or in comparisons.
- Use *plus* (more) or *moins* (less) before adjectives or adverbs to make comparisons or to state the superlative.
- Use *aussi … que* (as … as) before adjectives and adverbs to express that things are equal.

Chapter 20

I Need a Doctor ... Now!

In This Chapter

- Your body
- Symptoms, complaints, and illnesses
- Explaining "how long"
- The irregular verb *dire* (to say, tell)
- All about reflexive verbs

In the preceding chapter, you learned how to take care of minor problems and repairs. With just a few simple sentences, you can readily deal with life's petty annoyances. In this chapter, you'll learn the key words and phrases you'll need should you become sick while abroad.

Falling ill while you're away from home is hard enough, but the situation is even tougher if you can't communicate what is wrong. In this chapter, you will learn how to explain your ailments and how long you've been experiencing the symptoms.

It Hurts Right Here

I feel especially well suited to writing this chapter since my family seems to have spent an inordinate amount of time in foreign hospitals while we were supposed to be on vacation! For instance, one year my uncle arrived in France for a holiday only to be hit with a gall bladder attack. He spent the rest of his vacation flat on his back recovering from surgery for gallstones. Or take my son, who, while vacationing in the Dominican Republic, was rushed to a hospital after he smashed his tooth against a toilet bowl. And then there was the year that my husband and I were nearly leveled by jet lag while backpacking through Europe. After going without sleep for 10 days, we finally got sleeping medication from a Parisian doctor. But by the end of our trip, I wound up in a hospital in Leeds, England, with severe gastroenteritis.

> **Attention!**
>
> Jet lag is an annoying disturbance that upsets the body's biological clock. To minimize it, wear loose clothing, drink 8 ounces of water for every hour in flight, eat lightly, and get plenty of exercise.

While I hope your luck isn't like ours, it pays to be prepared if illness strikes. To begin with, familiarize yourself with the parts of the body in the following table.

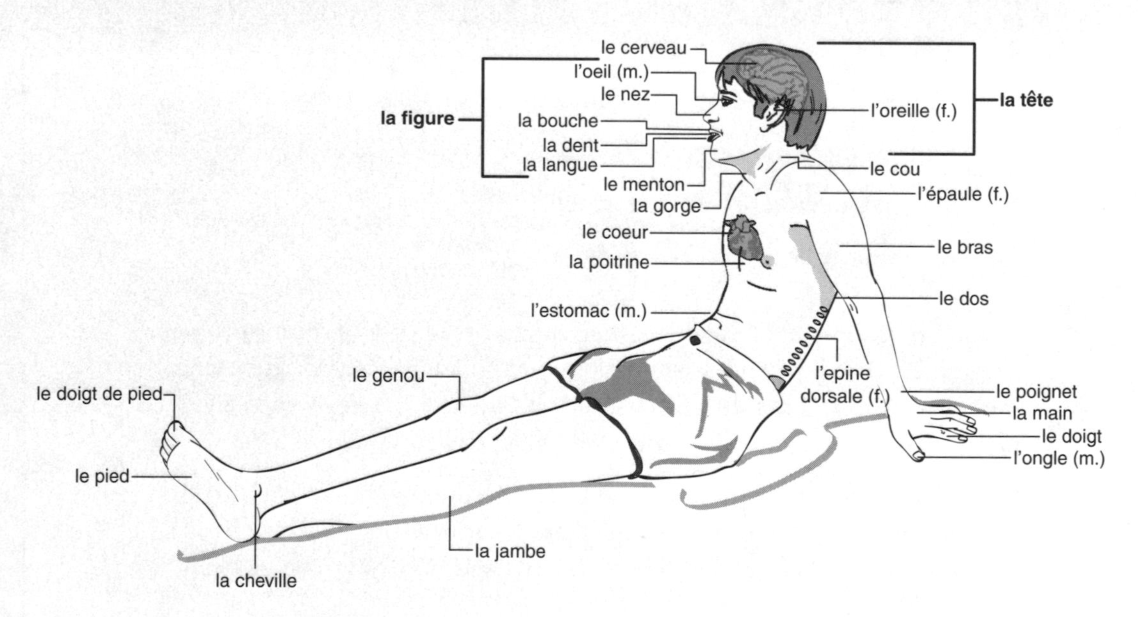

Parts of the Body

Body Part	French	Pronunciation
ankle	la cheville	*lah shuh-vee-y*
arm	le bras	*luh brah*
back	le dos	*luh do*
body	le corps	*luh koor*

Body Part	French	Pronunciation
brain	le cerveau, la cervelle	*luh sehr-vo, lah sehr-vehl*
chest	la poitrine	*lah pwah-treen*
chin	le menton	*luh mahN-tohN*
ear	l'oreille *f.*	*loh-rehy*
elbow	le coude	*luh kood*
eye	l'oeil *m.*	*luhy*
eyes	les yeux	*lay zyuh*
face	la figure, le visage	*lah fee-gewr, luh vee-zahzh*
finger	le doigt	*luh dwah*
foot	le pied	*luh pyay*
hand	la main	*lah maN*
head	la tête	*lah teht*
heart	le coeur	*luh kuhr*
knee	le genou	*luh zhuh-noo*
leg	la jambe	*lah zhahNb*
lip	la lèvre	*lah lehvr*
liver	le foie	*luh fwah*
lung	le poumon	*luh poo-mohN*
mouth	la bouche	*lah boosh*
nail	l'ongle *m.*	*lohNgl*
neck	le cou	*luh koo*
nose	le nez	*luh nay*
shoulder	l'épaule *f.*	*lay-pohl*
skin	la peau	*lah po*
spine	l'épine dorsale *f.*, la colonne vertébrale	*lay-peen dohr-sahl, lah koh-lohn vehr-tay-brahl*
stomach	l'estomac *m.*, le ventre	*leh-stoh-mah, luh vahNtr*
throat	la gorge	*lah gohrzh*
toe	l'orteil *m.*	*lohr-tehy*
tongue	la langue	*lah lahNg*
tooth	la dent	*lah dahN*
wrist	le poignet	*luh pwah-nyeh*

You Give Me a Pain in the ...

Do you want to avoid a trip to the doctor while on vacation? The soundest piece of advice anyone can give you is this: If you don't have a cast-iron stomach, don't drink the tap water when you travel. But let's say you forgot this warning and ate salad greens that were washed with tap water. Or you ordered a drink on the rocks, ignorant of the future gastrointestinal effects of the ice cubes. You've spent too much time in *les toilettes* and now find it necessary to go to the doctor. The obvious first question will be, "What's the matter with you?" (*"Qu'est-ce que vous avez?"*; *kehs-kuh voo zah-vay*) To say what hurts or bothers you, the expression *avoir mal à* + definite article is used:

Un, Deux, Trois

Keep a full-length picture of someone in your special French corner. Point to the different parts of the body and practice naming them in French.

J'ai mal au ventre.
zhay mahl o vahNtr
I have a stomachache.

Ils ont mal aux pieds.
eel zohN mahl o pyay
Their feet hurt.

Another way of talking about your symptoms is to use the expression *faire mal à*, which means "to hurt." (This requires an indirect object for *à* + person). Use the appropriate indirect object pronoun to refer to the person who might be in pain, such as *me* (to me), *te* (to you), *lui* (to him or her), *nous* (to us), *vous* (to you), *leur* (to them). Remember, too, to use the correct form of the possessive adjective that refers to the person in question (*mon, ma, mes; ton, ta, tes; son, sa, ses; notre, nos; votre, vos; leur, leurs*).

Mon ventre me fait mal.
mohN vahNtr muh feh mahl
My stomach hurts (me).

Ses pieds lui font mal.
say pyay lwee fohN mahl
His (Her) feet hurt (him, her).

Ouch! That Hurts!

Let's say your symptoms are more specific than a vague ache or pain. The following table gives a list of symptoms that will come in handy if you need to describe a problem. Use the phrase *J'ai* (*zhay;* I have) to preface your complaint.

Attention!

The verb *faire* must agree with the subject. If you are talking about symptoms, *faire* must agree with the body part that is ailing you.

Remember to conjugate the verb *avoir* so that it agrees with the subject. Although the French use *avoir* to express what's bothering them, our English may not include the word "have":

Elle a mal aux yeux.
Her eyes hurt.

If you have to go to the dentist, use the expression *avoir mal aux dents* (to have a toothache) or *avoir une rage* (pronounced *ewn rahzh*) *de dents* (to have a very bad toothache):

J'ai mal aux dents.
I've got a toothache.

Other Symptoms

Symptom	Le Symptôme	Pronunciation
blister	une ampoule	*ewn nahN-pool*
bruise	une contusion	*ewn kohN-tew-zyohN*
bump	une bosse	*ewn bohs*
burn	une brûlure	*ewn brew-lewr*
chills	des frissons	*day free-sohN*
cough	une toux	*ewn too*
cramps	des crampes	*day krahNp*
cut	une coupure	*ewn koo-pewr*
diarrhea	de la diarrhée	*dun lah dee-ah-ray*
fever	de la fièvre	*duh lah fyehvr*
fracture	une fracture	*ewn frahk-tewr*
indigestion	une indigestion	*ewn naN-dee-zhehs-tyohN*
infection	une infection	*ewn aN-fehk-syohN*
lump	une grosseur	*ewn groh-sewr*
migraine	une migraine	*ewn mee-grehn*
pain	une douleur	*ewn doo-luhr*
rash	une éruption	*ewn nay-rewp-syohN*
sprain	une foulure	*ewn foo-lewr*
swelling	une enflure	*ewn nahN-flewr*
wound	une blessure	*ewn bleh-sewr*

Other useful phrases include:

Je tousse.
zhuh toos
I'm coughing.

J'éternue.
zay-tehr-new
I'm sneezing.

Je saigne.
zhuh seh-nyuh
I'm bleeding.

Je suis constipé(e).
zhuh swee kohN-stee-pay
I'm constipated.

J'ai des nausées.
zhay day no-zay
I'm nauseous.

Je me sens mal.
zhuh muh sahN mahl
I feel bad.

Je n'en peux plus.
zhuh nahN puh plew
I'm exhausted.

J'ai du mal à dormir.
zhay dew mahl ah dohr-meer
I have trouble sleeping.

J'ai mal partout.
zhay mahl pahr-too
I hurt everywhere.

What's Wrong?

Now use all that you've learned so far to describe your symptoms and complaints to a doctor. Pretend you have the following health problems. Sample responses can be found in Appendix A.

1. flu-like symptoms ______________________________
2. an allergy ______________________________
3. a sprained ankle ______________________________
4. a migraine ______________________________

And the Diagnosis Is …

Obviously, you won't be the only one doing the talking when you visit the doctor. You will also be asked to fill out forms, disclose any medications you are taking, and answer other questions about your symptoms and general health. The doctor or nurse may ask you about the medical problems listed in the following table.

Avez-vous subi (eu) …?
ah-vay voo sew-bee (ew) …
Have you had …?

Souffrez-vous de (d') …?
soo-fray voo duh …
Do you suffer from …?

Medical Problems

Problem	French	Pronunciation
allergic reaction	une réaction allergique	*ewn ray-ahk-syohN ah-lehr-zheek*
angina	une angine	*ewn nahN-zheen*

Problem	French	Pronunciation
appendicitis	l'appendicite *f.*	*lah-pahN-dee-seet*
asthma	l'asthme *m.*	*lahz-muh*
bronchitis	la bronchite	*lah brohN-sheet*
cancer	le cancer	*luh kahN-sehr*
cold	un rhume	*uhN rewm*
diabetes	le diabète	*luh dee-ah-beht*
dizziness	le vertige	*luh vehr-teezh*
exhaustion	l'épuisement *m.*	*lay-pweez-mahN*
flu	la grippe	*lah greep*
hay fever	le rhume des foins	*luh rewm day fwaN*
heart attack	une crise cardiaque	*ewn kreez kahr-dyahk*
hepatitis	l'hépatite *f.*	*lay-pah-teet*
pneumonia	la pneumonie	*lah pnuh-moh-nee*
stroke	une attaque d'apoplexie	*ewn nah-tahk dah-poh-plehk-see*
sunstroke	une insolation	*ewn naN-soh-lah-syohN*

How Long Have You Felt This Way?

Your doctor will probably ask how long you've been experiencing your symptoms. The phrases in the following table suggest the number of ways you may hear the question posed and the ways in which to answer the question. The phrases vary in difficulty but all mean the same thing. If you need to ask "how long," the first expression is the easiest one to use.

How Long Have Your Symptoms Lasted?

Question	English	Answer	English
Depuis quand ... (*duh-pwee kahN*)	Since when ...	Depuis ... (*duh-pwee*)	Since ...
Depuis combien de temps ... (*duh-pwee kohN-byaN duh tahN*)	How long has (have) ... been	Depuis ... (*duh-pwee*)	For ...

continues

How Long Have Your Symptoms Lasted? (continued)

Question	English	Answer	English
Combien de temps y a-t-il que … (*kohN-byaN duh tahN ee ah-teel kuh*)	How long has (have) … been	Il y a + time + que … (*eel yah* + time + *kuh*)	For …
Ça fait combien de temps que … (*sah feh kohN-byaN duh tahN kuh*)	How long has (have) … been	Ça fait + time + que … (*sah feh* + time + *kuh*), Voilà + time + que … (*vwah-lah* + time + *kuh*)	For …

Depuis combien de temps souffrez-vous?
duh-pwee kohN-byaN duh tahN soo-fray voo
How long have you been suffering?

Depuis deux jours.
duh-pwee duh zhoor
For two days

Depuis quand souffrez-vous?
duh-pwee kahN soo-fray voo
Since when have you been suffering?

Depuis hier.
duh-pwee yehr
Since yesterday.

Combien de temps y a-t-il que vous souffrez?
kohN-byaN duh tahN ee ah-teel kuh voo soo-fray
How long have you been suffering?

Il y a un jour.
eel yah uhN zhoor
For one day.

Ça fait combien de temps que vous souffrez?
sah feh kohN-byaN duh tahN kuh voo soo-fray
How long have you been suffering?

Ça fait une semaine.
sah feh tewn suh-mehn
It's been a week.

Voilà une semaine.
vwah-lah ewn suh-mehn
For a week.

Me? A Hypochondriac?

Now use all these variations to explain how long you've been suffering. Talk about a cough you've had for two weeks, a headache that has hung on for three days, or the stomachache that has been bugging you for nearly a month.

1. cough ______________________________

____

2. headache ______________________________

____

3. stomachache ______________________________

____

Tell It Like It Is

What do you say when someone asks how you are? Do you say that you are fine, or do you describe every little ache and pain you've been experiencing? When you want to express what you say or tell someone, use the irregular verb *dire* (to tell, say), as shown in the following table.

The Verb *Dire* (to Say, Tell)

Conjugation	Pronunciation	Meaning
je dis	*zhuh dee*	I say, tell
tu dis	*tew dee*	you say, tell
il, elle, on dit	*eel, ehl, ohN dee*	he, she, onc says, tells
nous disons	*noo dee-zohN*	we say, tell
vous dites	*voo deet*	you say, tell
ils, elles disent	*eel, ehl deez*	they say, tell

What Are You Doing to Yourself?

If you want to express how you feel, you can use the irregular verb *se sentir*. As you can see, *se sentir* is not just an ordinary verb because it has a special pronoun before it. This pronoun, which can act as either a direct or indirect object pronoun, is called a reflexive pronoun. A reflexive pronoun shows that the subject is performing an action upon itself. The subject and the reflexive pronoun refer to the same person(s) or thing(s): She hurt herself. They enjoy themselves. Sometimes, as with the verb *se sentir*, it is unclear from the English that the verb is reflexive. The following table demonstrates how to conjugate a reflexive verb using the correct reflexive pronouns.

Memory Enhancer

To say "that" after *dire* use *que*, as in *"On dit que je ne suis pas gravement malade."* ("They say that I'm not very sick.")

The Verb *Se Sentir* (to Feel)

Conjugation	Pronunciation	Meaning
je **me** sens	*zhuh muh sahN*	I feel
tu **te** sens	*tew tuh sahN*	you feel
il, elle, on **se** sent	*eel, ehl, ohN suh sahN*	he, (she, one) feels
nous **nous** sentons	*noo noo sahN-tohN*	we feel
vous **vous** sentez	*voo voo sahN-tay*	you feel
ils, elles **se** sentent	*eel, ehl suh sahNt*	they feel

Now you can express how you feel:

Je me sens bien.
zhuh muh sahN byaN
I feel well.

Je me sens mal.
zhuh muh sahN mahl
I feel bad.

Je me sens mieux.
zhuh muh sahN myuh
I feel better.

Je me sens pire.
zhuh muh sahN peer
I feel worse.

You're on your way out the door, but not before paying the bill (*la note;* pronounced *lah noht*) and asking the following question:

Puis-je avoir une quittance pour mon assurance maladie, s'il vous plaît?
pweezh ah-vwahr ewn kee-tahNs poor mohN nah-sew-rahNs mah-lah-dee seel voo pleh
May I please have a receipt for my medical insurance?

Is It Reflexive?

Of course you know the feeling of returning home from a trip with a suitcase packed full of gifts for family members and friends. But do you treat yourself right, too? Do you cast aside all financial concerns and treat yourself to that special souvenir you wanted? In French, when you perform an action upon or for yourself, that action (verb) is reflexive and requires a reflexive pronoun. In many instances, you can use the same verb without the reflexive pronoun and perform the action upon or for someone else. In these cases, an object pronoun (direct or indirect) is used.

Je *me* lave.	Je lave mon chien.	Je *le* lave.
I wash myself.	*I wash my dog.*	*I wash* him.

In the last example, the direct object pronoun *le* expresses "him."

Je *m'*achète un sac.
I buy myself *a bag.*

J'achète un sac à Anne.
I buy a bag for Anne.

Je *lui* achète un sac.
I buy (for) her *a bag.*

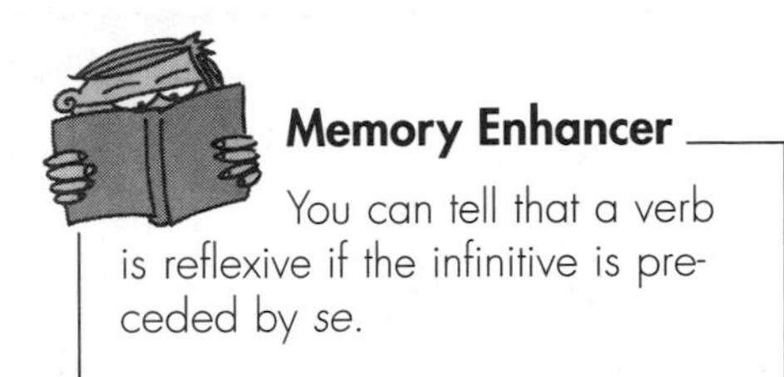

Memory Enhancer

You can tell that a verb is reflexive if the infinitive is preceded by *se*.

In this last example, the indirect object pronoun *lui* expresses "for her."

Some verbs are usually or always used reflexively. The following table provides a list of the most common reflexive verbs.

Common Reflexive Verbs

Problem	Pronunciation	Meaning
s'appeler*	*sah-play*	to be named, called
s'approcher de	*sah-proh-shay duh*	to approach
s'arrêter de	*sah-ruh-tay duh*	to stop
se baigner	*suh beh-nyay*	to bathe
se blesser	*suh bleh-say*	to hurt oneself
se brosser	*suh broh-say*	to brush
se casser	*suh kah-say*	to break
se coiffer	*suh kwah-fay*	to do one's hair
se coucher	*suh koo-shay*	to go to bed
se demander	*suh duh-mahN-day*	to wonder
se dépêcher	*suh day-peh-shay*	to hurry
se déshabiller	*suh day-zah-bee-yay*	to undress
se détendre	*suh day-tahNdr*	to relax
s'endormir	*sahN-dohr-meer*	to go to sleep
se fâcher (contre)	*suh fah-shay (kohNtr)*	to get angry (with)
s'habiller	*sah-bee-yay*	to dress
s'inquiéter de*	*saN-kee-ay-tay duh*	to worry about
se laver	*suh lah-vay*	to wash
se lever*	*suh luh-vay*	to get up
se maquiller	*suh mah-kee-yay*	to apply makeup

continues

Common Reflexive Verbs (continued)

Problem	Pronunciation	Meaning
se mettre à	*suh mehtr ah*	to begin
s'occuper de	*soh-kew-pay duh*	to take care of
se peigner	*suh peh-nyay*	to comb
se promener*	*suh proh-mnay*	to take a walk
se rappeler*	*suh rah-play*	to recall
se raser	*suh rah-zay*	to shave
se reposer	*suh ruh-poh-zay*	to rest
se réunir	*suh ray-ew-neer*	to meet
se réveiller	*suh ray-veh-yay*	to wake up
se servir de	*suh sehr-veer duh*	to use
se tromper	*suh trohN-pay*	to make a mistake

** Remember that these verbs are "shoe verbs." They all have spelling changes and must be conjugated accordingly. Refer to Chapter 12 to refresh your memory.*

Suppose you are telling someone all the things you do in the morning to prepare yourself for work or school. You might say, "I brush my teeth. I shave my mustache. I wash my hair." Since you use the word "my," you don't have to finish the sentence with "for myself." It's understood. In French, however, the opposite is done. The reflexive pronoun *me* (for myself) is used. It then becomes unnecessary to use the possessive adjective "my" (*mon*, *ma*, *mes*) when referring to parts of the body because the action is obviously being performed on the subject, and so the definite article is used instead.

Memory Enhancer

Verbs that are not ordinarily reflexive can be made reflexive simply by adding a reflexive pronoun, providing the sentence makes sense: *Je parle.* (I speak.) *Je me parle.* (I talk to myself.)

Je me brosse les dents.	Il se rase la barbe.
zhuh muh brohs lay dahN	*eel suh rahz lah bahrb*
I brush my teeth.	He shaves his beard.

Position of Reflexive Pronouns

No matter what language you study, it is not uncommon to find that word orders differ from one language to the next. In English, we generally put reflexive pronouns after verbs. You might tell a friend, "I always look *at myself* in the mirror before I go out." In French, this is not the case. The reflexive pronoun is placed in the same position as the other pronouns you have studied (direct, indirect, *y* and *en*)—that is, before the verb to which its meaning is tied (usually the conjugated verb). When there are two verbs, the pronoun is placed before the infinitive.

Je *me* lave.	I wash (myself).
Je ne *me lave* pas.	I don't wash (myself).
Je vais *me* laver.	I'm going to wash (myself).
Ne *te* lave pas!	Don't wash (yourself).

In an affirmative command, reflexive pronouns change position and are placed immediately after the verb, joined to it by a hyphen. *Te* becomes *toi* when it follows the verb.

Lave-*toi!* Lavez-*vous!*

Attention!

Te becomes *toi* in an affirmative command.

Using Reflexive Verbs

Use what you've learned so far to describe all the things you do before leaving the house in the morning. (*Je me lave.*) Then talk about the things you are going to do before going to bed at night. (*Je vais me laver.*)

1. Morning: ______________________________

   ____

2. Night: ______________________________

   ____

You're In Command

You're traveling in a group and are sharing a room with a few friends. You're all getting ready to go out on the town. Practice using reflexive verbs by telling a friend (and then a group of friends) to do and not to do the following.

Example:
Brush your hair.
Brosse-toi les cheveux!
Ne te brosse pas les cheveux!
Brossez-vous les cheveux!
Ne vous brossez pas les cheveux!

continues

continued

1. Take a bath. ______________________________

____

2. Hurry up. ______________________________

____

3. Shave. ______________________________

____

4. Get dressed. ______________________________

____

5. Brush your teeth. ______________________________

____

6. Have fun. ______________________________

____

The Least You Need to Know

- If you fall ill in another country, you need to know how to name the different parts of the body as well as your symptoms and feelings.
- To ask how long something has lasted, use *depuis quand …*, *depuis combien de temps …*, *combien de temps y a-t-il que …*, or *ça fait combien de temps que …*.
- Reflexive verbs, identified by the reflexive pronouns that accompany them, are used to show that the subject is acting upon itself.

Chapter 21

Oops, I Forgot to Pack My Toothbrush!

In This Chapter

- Large and small drugstore and medical items
- The irregular verb *venir* (to come)
- Speaking in the past

Chapter 20 helped you express how you feel. You learned to communicate good health as well as aches and pains. Whether you need just a few aspirins or a prescription drug, you'll want to take a trip to the drugstore. When you get there, you'll be amazed at all the other things you can purchase.

On the last trip we took, both my husband and I forgot to pack our toothbrushes, toothpaste, and a hairbrush. Imagine our dismay when we realized our blunder. We laughed it off, however, and simply went to the nearest drugstore. In France, we had the choice of going to *une pharmacie* (*ewn fahr-mah-see*), *une droguerie* (*ewn drohg-ree*), or *un drugstore* (*uhN druhg-stohr*). Confused? Don't worry, this chapter guides you to the correct spot where you can find all your toiletry needs as well as any medication. In addition, you'll learn how to express yourself in the past tense.

I Need an Aspirin

Whether you are trying to obtain medication or a bottle of shampoo, you want to be sure you're in the right place in France.

- *Une pharmacie*, which is easily identified by a green cross above the door, sells prescription drugs, over-the-counter medications, items intended for personal hygiene, and some cosmetics. If the pharmacy is closed, there will usually be a sign on the door telling customers where they can locate a neighboring pharmacy that is open all night (*une pharmacie de garde*).
- *Une droguerie* sells chemical products, paints, household cleansers and accessories (mops, brooms, buckets), and some hygiene and beauty products, but it does not dispense prescriptions.
- *Un drugstore* resembles a small department store. You can expect to find varied sections selling personal hygiene items, books, magazines, newspapers, records, maps, guides, gifts, and souvenirs but no prescription medicine. Additionally, you may find fast-food restaurants, a bar, and even a movie theater.

If you are indeed trying to fill a prescription, you can say to the druggist:

Il me faut des médicaments.
eel muh fo day may-dee-kah-mahN
I need medication.

Pourriez-vous exécuter (tout de suite) cette ordonnance, s'il vous plaît?
poo-ryay voo ehg-zay-kew-tay (toot sweet) seht ohr-doh-nahNs, seel voo pleh
Could you please fill this prescription (immediately)?

If you're simply looking for something over-the-counter, the following table will help you find it. Begin by saying the following to a clerk:

Je cherche …
zhuh shersh …
I'm looking for …

Drugstore Items

English	French	Pronunciation
For Men and Women		
alcohol	de l'alcool *m.*	*duh lahl-kohl*
antacid	un anti-acide	*uhN nahN-tee ah-seed*

English	French	Pronunciation
For Men and Women		
antihistamine	un antihistaminique	*uhN nahn-tee-ees-tah-mee-neek*
antiseptic	un antiseptique	*uhN nahN-tee-sehp-teek*
aspirins	des aspirines	*day zah-spee-reen*
bandages (wound)	des pansements *m.*	*day pahNs-mahN*
bobby pins	des épingles à cheveux *f.*	*day zay-paNgl ah shuh-vuh*
brush	une brosse	*ewn brohs*
cleansing cream	de la crème démaquillante	*duh lah krehm day-mah-kee-yahNt*
condoms	des préservatifs *m.*	*day pray-zehr-vah-teef*
cotton (absorbent)	du coton de l'ouate	*dew koh-tohN duh lwaht*
cough drops	des pastilles *f.*	*day pah-stee-y*
cough syrup	le sirop contre la toux	*luh see-roh kohNtr lah too*
deodorant	du déodorant	*dew day-oh-doh-rahN*
eye drops	les gouttes pour les yeux *f.*, du collyre	*lay goot poor lay zyuh, dew koh-leer*
eye liner	du traceur à paupières	*dew trah-suhr ah po-pyehr*
eye shadow	du fard à paupières	*dew fahr ah po-pyehr*
eyebrow pencil	un crayon pour les yeux	*uhN kreh-yohN poor lay zyuh*
laxative (mild)	un laxatif (léger)	*uhN lahk-sah-teef (lay-zhay)*
lipstick	du rouge à lèvres	*dew roozh ah lehvr*
mascara	du mascara	*dew mahs-kah-rah*
mirror	un miroir	*uhN meer-wahr*
moisturizer	de la crème hydratante	*duh lah krehm ee-drah-tahNt*
mouthwash	un dentifrice	*uhN dahN-tee-frees*
nail file	une lime à ongles	*ewn leem ah ohNgl*
nail polish	du vernis à ongles	*dew vehr-nee ah ohNgl*
nail polish remover	du dissolvant	*dew dee-sohl-vahN*
nose drops	des gouttes nasales *f.*	*day goot nah-zahl*
powder	de la poudre	*duh lah poodr*
razor (electric)	un rasoir (électrique)	*uhN rah-zwahr (ay-lehk-treek)*
razor blades	des lames de rasoir *f.*	*day lahm duh rah-zwahr*
safety pins	des épingles de sûreté *f.*	*day zay-paNgl duh sewr-tay*
sanitary napkins	des serviettes hygiéniques *f.*	*day sehr-vyeht ee-zhyay-neek*

continues

Drugstore Items (continued)

English	French	Pronunciation
For Men and Women		
scissors	des ciseaux *m.*	*day see-zo*
shampoo (antidandruff)	du shampooing (anti-pellicules)	*dew shahN-pwaN (ahN-tee peh-lee-kewl)*
shaving cream	de la crème à raser	*duh lah krehm ah rah-zay*
sleeping pills	des somnifères *m.*	*day sohm-nee-fehr*
soap (bar)	une savonette	*ewn sah-voh-neht*
suntan lotion	de la lotion solaire	*duh lah loh-syohN soh-lehr*
talcum powder	du talc	*dew tahlk*
tampons	des tampons périodiques *m.*	*day tahN-pohN pay-ree-oh-deek*
thermometer	un thermomètre	*uhN tehr-mo-mehtr*
tissues	des mouchoirs en papier *m.*	*day moosh-wahr ahN pah-pyay*
toothbrush	une brosse à dents	*ewn brohs ah dahN*
toothpaste	de la pâte dentifrice	*duh lah paht dahN-tee-frees*
tweezers	une pince à épiler	*ewn paNs ah ay-pee-lay*
vitamins	des vitamines *f.*	*day vee-tah-meen*
For Babies		
bottle	un biberon	*uhN beeb-rohN*
diapers (disposable)	des couches (disponibles) *m.*	*day koosh dees-poh-neebl*
pacifier	une sucette	*ewn sew-seht*

What Do You Need?

You're away on vacation and are not feeling quite up to par. Ask the clerk for everything you need for the following situations. Begin each sentence with *Il me faut* … (I need …)

1. You have a cold. ____

   ____

2. You have a headache. ____

   ____

3. You got a cut. ____

____

4. Your stomach is upset. ____

____

5. You forget shaving equipment/makeup. ________________________________

____

6. Your baby is crying a lot. ____

____

Special People, Special Needs

A pharmacy that specializes in *la location d'appareils médiaux* (*lah loh-kah-syohn dah-pah-rehy may-dee-ko*)—the rental of medical appliances—would either sell or have information concerning the items for the physically challenged featured in the following table.

Où puis-je obtenir ...?
oo pweezh ohb-tuh-neer ...
Where can I get ...?

Special Needs

Equipment	L'equipment	Pronunciation
cane	une canne	*ewn kahn*
crutches	des béquilles	*day bay-kee*
hearing aid	un audiophone	*uhN no-dyoh-fohn*
walker	un déambulateur	*uhN day-ahN-bew-lah-tuhr*
wheelchair	un fauteuil roulant	*uhN fo-tuhy roo-lahN*

Come Along

If you called a pharmacy to locate a certain product, you would use the verb *venir* to inform the pharmacist of when you would be coming to pick it up. The following table provides the forms of this irregular verb, which is similar to a shoe verb in that the *nous* and *vous* forms look like the infinitive, whereas the forms for the other subject pronouns do not.

Use *venir* + *de* (*d'* before a vowel or vowel sound) + infinitive for something that has just happened.

Je viens d'arriver.
I just arrived.

The Verb *Venir* (to Come)

Conjugation	Pronunciation	Meaning
je viens	*zhuh vyaN*	I come
tu viens	*tew vyaN*	you come
il, elle, on vient	*eel, ehl, ohN vyaN*	he, she, one comes
nous venons	*noo vuh-nohN*	we come
vous venez	*voo vuh-nay*	you come
ils, elles viennent	*eel, ehl vyehn*	they come

You Must Be Living in the Past

"Oh, no!" you exclaim to yourself. It seems you've misplaced your eye drops or can't find your shaving cream. One reason you might go to a *pharmacie* or a *droguerie* is because you forgot something at home that you really need. To express what you did or did not do, you must use the past tense. In French, this tense is called the *passé composé*—the compound past. The word "compound" is a key word because it implies that the past tense is made up of more than one part. Two elements are needed to form the *passé composé:* a helping verb, which expresses that something has taken place, and a past participle, which expresses exactly what the action was. In English, we most often use only the past participle and not the helping verb, although it is implied. We'd say, "Oh, no! I forgot my toothbrush." (We probably wouldn't say, "Oh no! I have forgotten my toothbrush.") In French, the helping verb must be used: *"Zut! J'ai oublié ma brosse à dents."*

The Helping Verb *Avoir*

Since *avoir* means "to have," it is quite logical that it would serve as a helping verb. Because it is the first verb to follow the subject, the verb *avoir* must be conjugated. Then you must add a past participle.

Forming the Past Participle of Regular Verbs

All regular *-er*, *-ir*, and *-re* verbs form their past participles differently, as shown in the following table. There are no changes made to the past participles of shoe verbs (*-cer*, *-ger*, *-yer*, *e* + consonant + *-er*, and *é* + consonant + *-er* verbs). The past participle remains the same for every subject: *J'ai dansé*, *Tu as dansé*, and so on.

Past Participle Formation

-er Verbs	*-ir* Verbs	*-re* Verbs
voyag**er** voyag**é**	chois**ir** chois**i**	répondre répond**u**

Tu as oublié les aspirines.
tew ah oo-blee-yay lay zah-spee-reen
You forgot the aspirins.

Ils ont rendu le rasoir.
eel zohN rahN-dew luh rah-zwahr
They returned the razor.

Le docteur a réfléchi avant d'agir.
luh dohk-tuhr ah ray-flay-shee ah-vahN dah-zheer
The doctor thought before acting.

It Didn't Happen That Way

Since the helping verb is conjugated, it is the verb that is used to form the negative and questions. *Ne* and *pas* are placed around it.

Tu *n'*as *pas* oublié les aspirines.
tew nah pah zoo-bee-yay lay zah-spee-reen
You didn't forget (You haven't forgotten) the aspirins.

Le docteur *n'*a *pas* réfléchi avant d'agir.
luh dohk-tuhr nah pas ray-flay-shee ah-vahN dah-zheer
The doctor didn't think before acting.

Ils *n'*ont *pas* rendu le rasoir.
eel nohN pah rahN-dew luh rah-zwahr
They didn't return (They haven't returned) the razor.

Memory Enhancer

Some short adverbs may be placed before the past participle. For example: *Elle a trop mangé.* (She ate too much.)

Memory Enhancer

All negatives are placed around the helping verb. For example: *Il n'a pas agi.* (He didn't act.) *Je n'ai jamais joué au golf.* (I never played golf.)

You Didn't, Did You?

A trip to the doctor is often necessary and rarely pleasant when one isn't feeling up to par. To get well, one should cooperate. Some patients, as we all know, are very stubborn. Tell what each person did and didn't do in the past.

Example:
je/parler à l'infirmière
J'ai parlé à l'infirmière.
Je n'ai pas parlé à l'infirmière.

1. je/remplir le formulaire ______________________
2. tu/répondre franchement ______________________
3. tu/obéir au docteur ______________________
4. nous/acheter nos médicaments ______________________
5. elle/chercher ses pilules ______________________
6. ils/attendre le pharmacien ______________________

Asking About the Past

You can make a question by using intonation, *est-ce que*, or *n'est-ce pas:*

Ils ont rendu le rasoir?
eel zohN rahN-dew luh rah-zwahr
They returned the razor?

Est-ce qu'ils ont rendu le rasoir?
ehs-keel zohN rahN-dew luh rah-zwahr
Did they return the razor?

Ils ont rendu le rasoir, n'est-ce pas?
eel zohn rahN-dew luh rah-zwahr nehs pah
They returned the razor, didn't they?

To use inversion, simply invert the subject pronoun and the conjugated helping verb.

As-tu oublié les aspirines?
ah-tew oo-blee-yay lay zah-spee-reen
Did you forget (Have you forgotten) the aspirins?

Le docteur, a-t-il réfléchi avant d'agir?
luh dohk-tuhr ah-teel ray-flay-shee ah-vahN dah-zheer
Did the doctor think before acting?

A-t-il rendu le rasoir?
ah-teel rahN-dew luh rah-zwahr
Did he return (Has he returned) the razor?

Asking About the Past Negatively

This is relatively easy without inversion:

Ils *n'ont pas* rendu le rasoir?
eel nohN pah rahN-dew luh rah-zwahr
They didn't return the raser?

*Est-ce qu'*ils *n'ont pas* rendu le rasoir?
ehs-keel nohN pah rahN-dew luh rah-zwahr
Haven't they returned (Didn't they return) the razor?

Forming a negative question with inversion is a bit trickier. *Ne* and *pas* are placed around the inverted pronoun and verb.

*N'*as-tu *pas* oublié les aspirines?
nah-tew pah zoo-blee-yay lay zah-spee-reen
Did*n't* you forget (Have*n't* you forgotten) the aspirins?

Le docteur, *n'*a-t-il *pas* réfléchi avant d'agir?
luh dohk-turh nah-teel pah ray-flay-shee ay-vahN dah-zheer
Did*n't* the doctor think before acting?

*N'*ont-ils *pas* rendu le rasoir?
nohN-teel pah rahN-dew luh rah-zwahr
Did*n't* they return (Have*n't* they returned) the razor?

Your Past Is in Question

What makes a person get sick? Eating too much? Working too hard? Not following the doctor's orders? Ask both affirmative and negative questions in the past about each of these subjects.

Example:
il/trop crier
A-t-il trop crié?
N'a-t-il pas trop crié?

continues

continued

1. nous/travailler trop dur ____________________
2. elle/obéir au docteur ____________________
3. ils/perdre conscience ____________________
4. vous/trop maigrir ____________________
5. tu/trop manger ____________________
6. il/attendre dehors longtemps ____________________

Past Participles of Irregular Verbs

Those verbs not belonging to the *-er*, *-ir*, or *-re* family have irregular past participles shown in the following table. We have studied some of these verbs in depth in previous chapters; others will appear in subsequent chapters as noted.

To make a sentence in the past negative, put the negative phrase around the conjugated helping verb.

Il n'a jamais fumé.

Irregular Past Participles

Infinitive	Past Participle	Pronunciation
avoir (to have)	eu	*ew*
boire (to drink)	bu	*bew*
connaître (to be acquainted with, *Chapter 23)	connu	*koh-new*
devoir (to have to, *Chapter 22)	dû	*dew*
dire (to say, tell)	dit	*dee*
écrire (to write, *Chapter 23)	écrit	*ay-kree*
être (to be)	été	*ay-tay*
faire (to make, do)	fait	*feh*
lire (to read, *Chapter 23)	lu	*lew*
mettre (to put [on])	mis	*mee*
pouvoir (to be able to)	pu	*pew*
prendre (to take)	pris	*pree*

Infinitive	Past Participle	Pronunciation
recevoir (to receive)	reçu	*ruh-sew*
savoir (to know, *Chapter 23)	su	*sew*
voir (to see)	vu	*vew*
vouloir (to want)	voulu	*voo-lew*

These verbs form the *passé composé* in the same way as regular verbs.

Il a été au cinéma.

Il n'a pas été au cinéma.

A-t-il été au cinéma?

N'a-t-il pas été au cinéma?

The Helping Verb *Être*

A few common verbs use *être* instead of *avoir* as the helping verb. Most of these verbs show some kind of motion involving either going up, down, in, out, or staying at rest.

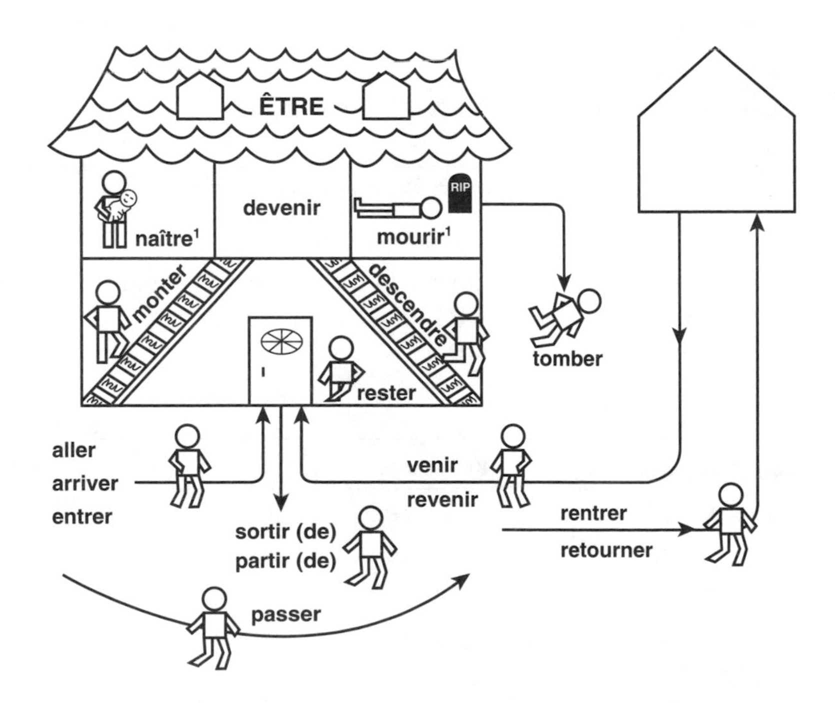

To help remember which verbs use *être*, think of the house in the previous figure as being inhabited by DR and MRS VANDERTRAMPP.

	Infinitive	Past Participle	Pronunciation
D	devenir (to become)	devenu*	*duh-vuh-new*
R	revenir (to come back)	revenu*	*ruh-vuh-new*
M	mourir (to die)	mort*	*mohr*
R	retourner (to return)	retourné	*ruh-toor-nay*
S	sortir (to go out)	sorti	*sohr-tee*
V	venir (to come)	venu*	*vuh-new*
A	arriver (to arrive)	arrivé	*ah-ree-vay*
N	naître (to be born)	né*	*nay*
D	descendre (to descend, go down)	descendu	*deh-sahN-dew*
E	entrer (to enter)	entré	*ahN-tray*
R	rentrer (to return)	rentré	*rahN-tray*
T	tomber (to fall)	tombé	*tohN-bay*
R	rester (to remain, stay)	resté	*rehs-tay*
A	aller (to go)	allé	*ah-lay*
M	monter (to go up, mount)	monté	*mohN-tay*
P	partir (to leave)	parti	*pahr-tee*
P	passer (to pass by [without a direct object])	passé	*pah-say*

**All past participles are irregular and must be memorized. All reflexive verbs use* être *as their helping verb. They will be discussed in the next chapter.*

Notice what happens, however, when we add the past participle in the following table. (The * indicates that the subject may be singular or plural.)

The Past Tense with *Être*

Masculine Subjects	Feminine Subjects
je suis allé	je suis allée
tu es allé	tu es allée
il est allé	elle est allée
nous sommes allés	nous sommes allées
vous êtes allé(s)*	vous êtes allée(s)*
ils sont allés	elles sont allées

As you can see, the past participles of all verbs conjugated with *être* agree in gender (masculine or feminine [add *e*]) and number (singular or plural [add *s*]) with the subject. For a mixed group, always use the masculine forms. If the masculine past participle ends in an unpronounced consonant, the consonant will be pronounced for the feminine singular and plural forms.

Il est resté. *eel eh reh-stay* He stayed.	Elle est restée. *ehl eh reh-stay* She stayed.	Ils sont restés. *eel sohN reh-stay* They stayed.
Il est venu tôt. *eel eh vuh-new to* He came early.	Elle est venue tôt. *ehl eh vun-new to* She came early.	Ils sont venus tôt. *eel sohN vuh-new to* They came early.
Il est mort. *eel eh mohr* He died.	Elle est morte. *ehl eh mohrt* She died.	Elles sont mortes. *ehl sohN mohrt* They died.

Negatives and questions are formed in the same way with *être* as the helping verb as with *avoir:*

Elle est arrivée.	Est-elle arrivée?
Elle *n'*est *pas* arrivée.	*N'*est-elle *pas* arrivée?

Who Did What?

Yesterday was Saturday, and most people were free to do as they wished. Did they go out or hang out around the house? Tell what each person did using the correct helping verb (*avoir* or *être*) and the past participle.

1. il/faire du football ______________________________
2. nous/être en ville ______________________________
3. tu/voir ce film ______________________________
4. je/pouvoir finir le travail ______________________________
5. elles/prendre une grande décision ______________________________
6. vous/lire un livre ______________________________
7. ils/avoir un rendez-vous ______________________________
8. elle/faire des courses ______________________________

continues

continued

9. je (*f.*)/arriver chez un ami ________________
10. nous (*m.*)/revenir du Canada ________________
11. ils/rester à la maison ________________
12. tu (*f.*)/partir à la campagne ________________
13. vous (*m. plural*)/aller ________________
14. elle/sortir avec des amies à la plage ________________
15. ils/descendre en ville ________________
16. elles/rentrer tard ________________

The Least You Need to Know

- To get prescription drugs, you must go to *une pharmacie* not *un drugstore*.
- Use the irregular verb *venir* to express "to come." *Venir* + *de* + the infinitive means "to have just."
- The past tense in French is made up of two parts: a helping verb (*avoir* or *être*) and a past participle.

Chapter 22

Phone Home ... or Anywhere Else

In This Chapter

- Making a phone call
- Proper telephone etiquette
- When there's a problem
- The irregular verb *devoir* (to have to)
- Using reflexive verbs in the past tense

Your medicinal problems and toiletry needs were taken care of in the preceding chapter. You feel great and would like to let your family and friends know that everything is all right; it's time to phone home.

Placing a long-distance telephone call from a foreign country is always a bit of a challenge. It is often necessary to speak with an operator, and most people don't realize how difficult it is to communicate by telephone with someone who speaks a different language. The luxury of relying on reading someone's body language or watching his or her lips for clues disappears once a telephone is introduced. This chapter helps you place a call within or outside the country you are visiting, prepares you for dealing with busy signals, wrong numbers, and other phone mishaps, and teaches you how to use reflexive verbs in the past tense.

Making a Call

If you plan to call long distance from a foreign country, expect that someone will have to explain to you how to use the phone system. It is also likely that the procedures for making local calls will be different from the ones you are used to back home. One thing you will want to make sure to do is correctly express the type of call you wish to make. The following table provides some options.

Types of Phone Calls

Type of Call	French	Pronunciation
collect call	la communication en P.C.V.	*lah koh-mew-nee-kah-syohN ahN pay-say-vay*
credit-card call	la communication par carte de crédit	*lah koh-mew-nee-kah-syohN pahr kahrt duh kray-dee*
local call	la communication locale	*lah koh-mew-nee-kah-syohN loh-kahl*
long-distance call	la communication interurbaine	*lah koh-mew-nee-kah-syohN aN-tehr-ewr-behn*
out-of-the-country call	la communication à l'étranger	*lah koh-mew-nee-kah-syohN ah lay-trahN-zhay*
person-to-person call	la communication avec préavis	*lah koh-mew-nee-kah-syohN ah-vehk pray-ah-vee*

In case you have problems using a telephone, you should familiarize yourself with the different parts of the phone featured in the following table.

The Telephone

English	French	Pronunciation
booth	la cabine téléphonique	*lah kah-been tay-lay-foh-neek*
button	le bouton	*luh boo-tohN*
coin return button	le bouton de remboursement	*luh boo-tohN duh rahN-boors-mahN*
cordless phone	le poste sans cordon	*luh pohst sahN kohr-dohN*
portable phone	le téléphone portatif	*luh tay-lay-fohn pohr-tah-teef*
dial	le cadran	*luh kah-drahN*

English	French	Pronunciation
keypad	le clavier à touches	*luh klah-vyay ah toosh*
phone card	la télécarte	*lah tay-lay-kahrt*
public phone	le téléphone public	*luh tay-lay-fohn pew-bleek*
receiver	le combiné, le récepteur	*luh kohN-bee-nay, luh ray-sehp-tuhr*
slot	la fente	*lah fahNt*
speaker telephone	le poste mains libres	*luh pohst maN leebr*
telephone	le téléphone	*luh tay-lay-fohn*
telephone book	l'annuaire *m.*	*lah-new-ehr*
telephone number	le numéro de téléphone	*luh new-may-ro duh tay-lay-fohn*
touch-tone phone	le poste à clavier (à touches)	*luh pohst ah klah-vyay (ah toosh)*

You are now ready to place a call. Be prepared for your hotel to charge exorbitant rates; that's usually the case. In France, it's an excellent idea to purchase a *télécarte* (available at post offices, cafés, and convenience stores), which enables you to buy 50 or 120 message units of calls. The number of message units required for the call depends on the total speaking time and the area phoned. More message units are necessary to call a farther distance or to speak for a longer period of time. A magnetic strip on the *télécarte*, similar to the one on a credit card, enables you to use French phones. Because the pictures on these cards vary and change over time, some of the *télécartes* will one day be collector's items. The following table explains how to complete your call using a *télécarte.*

Keep track of your *télécarte.* If you lose it, anyone can use it since there is no means of identifying the owner.

Making a Phone Call

Phrase	French	Pronunciation
to call back	rappeler, retéléphoner	*rah-play, ruh-tay-lay-fohn-nay*
to dial	composer (faire) le numéro	*kohN-po-zay (fehr) luh new-may-ro*
to hang up (the receiver)	raccrocher, quitter	*rah-kroh-shay, kee-tay*
to insert the card	introduire la carte	*aN-troh-dweer lah kahrt*

continues

Making a Phone Call (continued)

Phrase	French	Pronunciation
to know the area code	savoir l'indicatif, du pays (country), de la ville (city)	*sah-vwahr laN-dee-kah-teef dew pay-ee, duh lah veel*
to leave a message	laisser un message	*leh-say uhN meh-sahzh*
to listen for the dial tone	attendre la tonalité	*ah-tahNdr lah toh-nah-lee-tay*
to pick up (the receiver)	décrocher	*day-kroh-shay*
to telephone	téléphoner, donner un coup de fil	*tay-lay-foh-nay, doh-nay uhN koo duh feel*

Calling from Your Hotel Room

POUR TÉLÉPHONER

Pour vos communications locales	Faites le 1
Pour vos communications interurbaines	Faites le 1 + 16
Pour vos communications à l'étranger	Faites le 1 + 19
Pour parler à une autre chambre	Faites le 2 suivi par le n° de la chambre
Pour commander un repas	Faites le 3
Réception	Faites le 4
Concierge (bagages, réveil, restaurant)	Faites le 5
Bar (à partir de 16 h.)	Faites le 6
Service de blanchissage	Faites le 7

This card was by the phone in your hotel room. What number(s) would you call for each of the following? The answers can be found in Appendix A.

1. To get something to drink?

   ____

2. To get your laundry done?

   ____

3. To make a long-distance call?

   ____

4. To make a local call?

   ____

5. To make a call abroad?

 ____

6. To speak to a friend in another room?

 ____

7. To place a wake-up call?

 ____

8. To speak to the front desk?

 ____

In English, to say that someone is going to do something again, we use the prefix *re-*, as in "redial" or "recall." The French add the same prefix, as in *recomposer* (to redial). Drop the *e* from *re-* before a vowel, as in *rappeler* (to call back).

Please Phone Home

The front of the French yellow pages, *les pages jaunes* (*lay pahzh zhon*), provides a tremendous amount of information. What choices are given if you want to phone home? The answers can be found in Appendix A.

30 TELECOM

ETRANGER

COMMENT OBTENIR VOTRE CORRESPONDANT

Automatique

décrochez | tonalité | 19 | tonalité | indicatif du pays (p.32) | indicatif de zone (p.34) | numéro demandé

Par l'intermédiaire d'un agent de FRANCE TELECOM

- Communications à destination des pays autres que ceux obtenus par l'automatique.
- Communications à destination des réseaux non encore automatisés des pays atteints par voie automatique.
- Communications spéciales (cartes Pastel, etc.).

décrochez | tonalité | 19 | tonalité | 33 | indicatif du pays (p.32) | vous obtenez un agent de FRANCE TELECOM à qui vous formulez votre demande

____

____

____

____

Special Needs

Many telephone products are available for those with limited visual, auditory, and motor skills. Read the following description of items available to the physically challenged. Can you figure out what kinds of products can be obtained? (Answers below.)

> Pour aider les personnes handicapées qui ont des difficultés à utiliser le téléphone, cinq produits de base concernant les déficients auditifs, visuels et moteurs, sont proposés:
>
> —le combiné téléphonique à écoute amplifiée réglable
>
> —l'avertisseur lumineux d'appel téléphonique
>
> —le poste téléphonique simplifié à 2 numéros préenregistrés
>
> —la bobine (reel) magnétique pour capsule téléphonique
>
> —les couronnes (rings, rims) à gros chiffres, à repères (with marks) ou en braille adaptables sur un poste téléphonique à cadran

Did you say an adjustable, amplified receiver? A special light informing the user that a call was made? A simplified phone with two preregistered numbers? A close-captioned telephone? An outer ring with large numbers? A telephone dial written in Braille? Good for you!

Culture Capsule

The gray, open, public phone booths in France use the 50 or 120 *Unités Télécom* phone cards. These cards are on sale at tobacconists, post offices, and in any location with a sign that reads *"Télécarte en vente ici."*

To call the United States or Canada, dial 19 + 1 + area code + number.

Attention!

Allô is used only on the telephone in France. To greet someone in person, use *bonjour, bonsoir* (in the evening only), or *salut* (to be more friendly).

Hello? Who's Calling?

Telephone conversations are a lot more difficult to conduct than face-to-face ones since you're not able to observe a person's facial expressions and gestures. In addition, telephones tend to distort voices and sounds. Familiarize yourself with the words used to make and answer a phone call. The following table shows you how to begin a telephone conversation.

Phone Conversations

Calling	English	Answering	English
Allô *(ah-lo)*	Hello	Allô *(ah-lo)*	Hello
Je suis bien chez ...? *(zhuh swee byaN shay)*	Is this the ... residence?	Qui est à l'appareil? *(kee eh tah lah-pah-rehy)*	Who's calling?
C'est ... *(seh)*	It's ...	Ici ... *(ee-see)*	This is ...
... est là? *(eh lah)*	Is ... in (there)?		
Je voudrais parler à ... *(zhuh voo-dreh pahr-lay ah)*	I would like to speak to ...	Ne quittez (quitte) pas. *(nuh kee-tay [keet] pah)*	Hold on.
		Un moment *(uhN moh-mahN)*	Just a moment.
		Il (Elle) n'est pas là. *(eel [ehl] neh pah lah)*	He (She) is not in.
Quand sera-t-il (elle) de retour? *(kahN suh-rah-teel [tehl] duh ruh-toor)*	When will he (she) be back?	Voulez-vous (veux-tu) laisser un message? *(voo-lay voo [vuh-tew] leh-say uhN meh-sahzh)*	Do you want to leave a message?
Je vais rappeler plus tard. *(zhuh veh rah-play plew tahr)*	I'll call back later.		

Sorry, Wrong Number

You can run into many problems when making a phone call: a wrong number, a busy signal, a hang up. Here are some examples of phrases you might say or hear should you run into any difficulties.

Vous demandez quel numéro?
voo duh-mahN-day kehl new-may-ro
What number are you calling?

C'est une erreur.
seh tewn eh-ruhr
It's a mistake.

J'ai/Vous avez le mauvais numéro.
zhay/voo zah-vay luh moh-veh new-may-ro
I/You have the wrong number.

On nous a coupés.
ohN noo zah koo-pay
We got cut off (disconnected).

Recomposez le numéro, s'il vous plaît.
ruh-kohN-poh-zay luh new-may-ro seel voo pleh
Please redial the number.

Le téléphone est en panne (hors de service).
luh tay-lay-fohn eh tahN pahn (tohr dsehr-vees)
The telephone is out of order.

J'entends mal.
zhahN-tahN mahl
I can't hear you.

Je ne peux pas vous (t') entendre.
zhuh nuh puh pah voo zahN-tahNdr (tahN-tahNdr)
I can't hear you.

Rappelez-moi (Rappelle-moi) plus tard.
rah-play (rah-pehl)-mwah plew tahr
Call me back later.

What Are Your Obligations?

Perhaps you are very busy and do not have time to talk on the phone today. The irregular verb *devoir*, shown in the following table, enables you to express what you have to do instead. This verb resembles a shoe verb in that the *nous* and *vous* forms look like the infinitive, whereas the other forms do not.

The Verb *Devoir* (to Have To)

Conjugation	Pronunciation	Meaning
je dois	*zhuh dwah*	I have to
tu dois	*tew dwah*	you have to
il, elle, on doit	*eel (ehl, ohN) dwah*	he (she, one) has to
nous devons	*noo duh-vohN*	we have to
vous devez	*voo duh-vay*	you have to
ils, elles doivent	*eel (ehl) dwahv*	they have to

Since the verb *devoir* is followed by another verb, *devoir* is conjugated while the second verb remains in the infinitive.

Je dois raccrocher.
zhuh dwah rah-kroh-shay
I have to hang up.

Ils doivent se reposer.
eel dwahv suh ruh-po-zay
They have to rest.

Nous devons téléphoner à notre famille.
noo duh-vohN tay-lay-foh-nay ah nohtr fah-mee-y
We have to call our family.

I Can't Talk Now

We've all had experiences in which the phone has started ringing just as we've gotten one foot out the door or when we're up to our elbows in grease. Sometimes we're in too much of a hurry to turn around and pick it up. Tell why each of these people can't speak on the phone right now by using *devoir* (conjugated) + infinitive.

1. elle/réparer sa voiture ____________________
2. nous/aller en ville ____________________
3. tu/sortir ____________________
4. vous/faire des courses ____________________
5. ils/travailler ____________________
6. je/partir tout de suite ____________________

What Did You Do to Yourself?

Other reasons why you can't talk on the phone may involve a reflexive verb in the past tense. All reflexive verbs use *être* as a helping verb in the *passé composé:*

Je me suis endormi(e).	Nous nous sommes endormi(e)s.
Tu t'es endormi(e).	Vous vous êtes endormi(e)(s).
Il s'est endormi.	Ils se sont endormis.
Elle s'est endormie.	Elles se sont endormies.

In the negative and in questions, the reflexive pronoun stays before the conjugated helping verb.

Elle ne *s'est* pas réveillée à temps.	She didn't wake up in time.
S'est-elle réveillée à temps?	Did she wake up in time?
Ne *s'est*-elle pas réveillée à temps?	Didn't she wake up in time?

There is no agreement of the past participle if the reflexive pronoun is used as an indirect object. This happens only rarely.

Elle *s*'est lavée.
She washed *herself*.

"Herself" is the direct object. Since *s'* is a preceding direct object, the past participle *lavée* must agree with the preceding feminine direct object pronoun *s'*.

> Elle *s'*est lavé les cheveux.
> She washed her hair *herself.*

The implied "(for) herself" is the indirect object. "Hair" is the direct object. Since *s'* is a preceding indirect object and the direct object (*les cheveux*) comes after the verb, there is no agreement of the past participle *lavé* with the preceding indirect object pronoun *s'*.

Making Excuses

Tell why each person didn't get to make the phone call he or she was supposed to make.

1. je (*f.*)/se casser le bras ____________________
2. elle/se réveiller tard ____________________
3. nous (*m.*)/s'occuper d'autre chose ____________________
4. ils/se mettre à travailler ____________________
5. vous (*f. plural*)/se lever à midi ____________________
6. tu (*f.*)/se coucher tôt ____________________

The Least You Need to Know

- Use the information in the front of the French yellow pages to help you make the most of your phone calls.
- A *télécarte* enables you to use most French telephones.
- Reflexive verbs use *être* as their helping verb in the past tense.

Chapter 23

Please, Mr. Postman

In This Chapter

- Sending and receiving mail
- The irregular verbs *écrire* (to write) and *lire* (to read)
- The difference between *savoir* and *connaître*
- Comparing the *passé composé* and the imperfect

In the preceding chapter you learned how to make a phone call, begin a telephone conversation, explain any difficulties with the line, and use proper phone etiquette. You also learned that public telephones are readily available in French post offices—and that's where we are off to next.

Chances are you won't go to a post office to make a phone call, but you will visit one to send letters, postcards, and packages to family and friends. You'll learn how to send registered and special-delivery letters as well as letters via air mail so that you can be assured your mail gets to its destination—and gets there fast. In your correspondence, you'll be able to express facts you learned and people you became acquainted with as well as all the activities you participated in from the time of your arrival.

Sending Your Mail

You've just visited the Musée du Louvre, dined at La Tour d'Argent, and shopped at Chanel, and now you can't wait to share your experiences with your friends and family. Any letter sent through the mail usually arrives at its destination. The real question is how soon it will get there. If it's speed you want, postage rates will be higher. It costs about 3 euros to send a first-class, local letter in France. At an exchange rate of approximately 1 euro to the American dollar, postage in the United States is a bargain. You cannot mail a letter or package, of course, without a few mail essentials such as envelopes and stamps. The following table provides the vocabulary you need to send your mail.

Mail and Post Office Terms

Term	French	Pronunciation
address	l'addresse *f.*	*lah-drehs*
addressee	le destinataire	*luh dehs-tee-nah-tehr*
air letter	l'aérogramme *m.*	*lahy-roh-grahm*
envelope	l'enveloppe *f.*	*lahN-vlohp*
letter	la lettre	*lah lehtr*
mailbox	la boîte aux lettres	*lah bwaht o lehtr*
money order	le mandat-poste	*luh mahN-dah pohst*
package	le paquet	*luh pah-keh*
parcel	le colis	*luh koh-lee*
postcard	la carte postale	*lah kahrt pohs-tahl*
postage	l'affranchissement *m.*	*lah-frahN-shees-mahN*
postal code	le code postal (régional)	*luh kohd pohs-tahl (ray-zhoh-nahl)*
postal worker	le facteur *m.*, la factrice *f.*	*luh fahk-tuhr, lah fahk-trees*
rate	le tarif	*luh tah-reef*
sender	l'expéditeur *m.*, l'expéditrice *f.*	*lehks-pay-dee-tuhr, lehks-pay-dee-trees*
sheet of stamps	la feuille de timbres	*lah fuhy duh taNbr*
stamp	le timbre	*luh taNbr*
window	le guichet	*luh gee-sheh*

Culture Capsule

In France, the P.T.T. (postes, télégraphes, et téléphones) regulates the post office as well as the telephone system. Many post offices open as early as 8 A.M. and close as late as 7 P.M., but they may take a two-hour lunch break! The main branch in Paris is always open. You can purchase stamps at some cafés, *bureaux de tabac,* and hotels. If you don't want to take a trip to the post office, look for a yellow mailbox.

Service with a Smile

So you've written your letter, folded it, and sealed it in an envelope. Now all you need to do is find a post office or a mailbox. If you don't know where one is located, simply ask:

Où se trouve (est) le bureau de poste (la boîte aux lettres) le (la) plus proche?
oo suh troov (eh) luh bew-ro duh pohst (lah bwaht o lehtr) luh (lah) plew prohsh
Where is the nearest post office (mailbox)?

Different types of letters and packages require special forms, paperwork, and postage rates. It is important to know how to ask for the type of service you need.

Quel est le tarif de l'affranchissement …?
kehl eh luh tah-reef duh lah-frahN-shees-mahN …
What is the postage rate …?

… pour les États-Unis	*poor lay zay-tah zew-nee*	… for the United States
… pour une lettre envoyée par avion	*poor ewn lehtr ahN-vwah-yay pahr ah-vyohN*	… for an air mail letter
… pour une lettre recommandée	*poor ewn lehtr ruh-koh-mahN-day*	… for a registered letter
… pour une lettre par exprès	*poor ewn lehtr pahr ehks-preh*	… for a special-delivery letter

Je voudrais envoyer cette lettre (ce paquet) par courrier régulier (par avion, par exprès).
zhuh voo-dreh zahN-vwah-yay seht lehtr (suh pah-keh) pahr koo-ryay ray-gew-lyay (pahr ah-vyohN, pahr ehks-preh)
I would like to send this letter (this package) by regular mail (by air mail, special delivery).

Je voudrais envoyer ce paquet livrable contre remboursement (payable à l'arrivée).
zhuh voo-dreh zahN-vwah-yay suh pah-keh lee-vrahbl kohNtr rahN-boors-mahN (peh-yahbl ah lah-ree-vay)
I would like to send this package C.O.D.

Combien pèse cette lettre (ce paquet)?
kohN-byaN pehz seht lehtr (suh pah-keh)
How much does this letter (package) weigh?

Quand arrivera-t-il (elle)? Quand arriveront-ils (elles)?
kahN tah-ree-vrah teel (tehl)? kahN tah-ree-vrohN teel (tehl)
When will it arrive? When will they arrive?

What Should I Write?

As you fill out different kinds of paperwork, you will be asked to write down a variety of information. Familiarize yourself with the irregular verb *écrire* (to write) in the following table. Notice that it is necessary to add a *v* before the ending in all the plural forms. The past participle of *écrire* is *écrit* (*ay-kree*).

The Verb *Écrire* (to Write)

Conjugation	Pronunciation	Meaning
j'écris	*zhay-kree*	I write
tu écris	*tew ay-kree*	you write
il, elle, on écrit	*eel, ehl, ohN nay-kree*	he, she, one writes
nous écrivons	*noo zay-kree-vohN*	we write
vous écrivez	*voo zay-kree-vay*	you write
ils, elles écrivent	*eel, ehl zay-kreev*	they write

I Love to Read

You will be doing a lot of reading in French, whether it's forms, signs, menus, magazines, or newspapers. The irregular verb *lire* (to read) is presented in the following table. It is necessary to add an *s* before the ending in all the plural forms. The past participle of *lire* is *lu* (pronounced *lew*).

The Verb *Lire* (to Read)

Conjugation	Pronunciation	Meaning
je lis	*zhuh lee*	I read
tu lis	*tew lee*	you read
il, elle, on lit	*eel, ehl, ohN lee*	he, she, one reads
nous lisons	*noo lee-zohN*	we read
vous lisez	*voo lee-zay*	you read
ils, elles lisent	*eel, ehl leez*	they read

Do French magazines intrigue you? Are you interested in catching up on the news? Is there a sign you don't understand? I'll never forget the time I saw a sign that read "EAU NON-POTABLE." Although I was a French major, I had never come across this phrase; "potable" was an unfamiliar English cognate to me. I knew that *eau* was water, but that was all I understood. It's a good thing I didn't take a drink. When I later looked up the phrase, I found that it meant that the water was unfit to drink. The following table features items that you might read while in France.

Things to Read

English	French	Pronunciation
ad	une annonce publicitaire	*ewn nah-nohNs pew-blee-see-tehr*
book	un livre	*uhN leevr*
magazine	un magazine, une revue	*uhN mah-gah-zeen, ewn ruh-vew*
menu	la carte, le menu	*lah kahrt, luh muh-new*
newspaper	un journal	*uhN zhoor-nahl*
novel	un roman	*uhN roh-mahN*
pamphlet	une brochure	*ewn broh-shewr*
receipt	le reçu	*luh ruh-sew*
sign	un écriteau	*uhN nay-kree-to*
warning	un avertissement	*uhN nah-vehr-tees-mahN*

Do You Know Anything About This?

Do you know the name of a great French restaurant? You do? Do you know where it's located? How about the phone number? You know the owner, too? He's your second cousin, and he really knows how to prepare a mean bouillabaisse? That's great.

To express certain facts, information, relationships, and abilities, you will need the two French verbs that express "to know": *savoir* in this table and *connaître* in the table that follows it.

The Verb *Savoir* (to Know) (Past Participle: *Su*)

Conjugation	Pronunciation	Meaning
je sais	*zhuh seh*	I know
tu sais	*tew seh*	you know
il, elle, on sait	*eel, ehl, ohN seh*	he, she, one knows
nous savons	*noo sah-vohN*	we know
vous savez	*voo sah-vez*	you know
ils, elles savent	*eel, ehl sahv*	they know

The Verb *Connaître* (to Know) (Past Participle: *Connu*)

Conjugation	Pronunciation	Meaning
je connais	*zhuh koh-neh*	I know
tu connais	*tew koh-neh*	you know
il, elle, on connaît	*eel, ehl, ohN koh-neh*	he, she, one knows
nous connaissons	*noo koh-neh-sohN*	we know
vous connaissez	*voo koh-neh-say*	you know
ils connaissent	*eel koh-nehs*	they know

Know the Difference?

If there are two ways to express "to know," how are you supposed to know when to use each one? The important thing to remember is that the French differentiate between knowing facts and how to do things (*savoir*) and knowing (being acquainted with) people, places, things, and ideas (*connaître*).

Savez-vous l'adresse?
sah-vay voo lah-drehs
Do you know the address?

Sait-il faire du ski?
seh-teel fehr dew skee
Does he know how to ski?

The verb *connaître* shows familiarity with a person, place, or thing. If you can replace "to know" with "to be acquainted with," use the verb *connaître.*

Connaissez-vous Marie?
koh-neh-say-voo mah-ree
Do you know Marie?
(Are you acquainted with her?)

Connais-tu cette chanson?
koh-neh-tew seht shahN-sohN
Do you know that song?
(Have you heard the song but you don't know the words?)

Notice the difference between:

Je sais ce poème.
I know this poem (by heart).

Je connais ce poème.
I know this poem. (I'm familiar with it.)

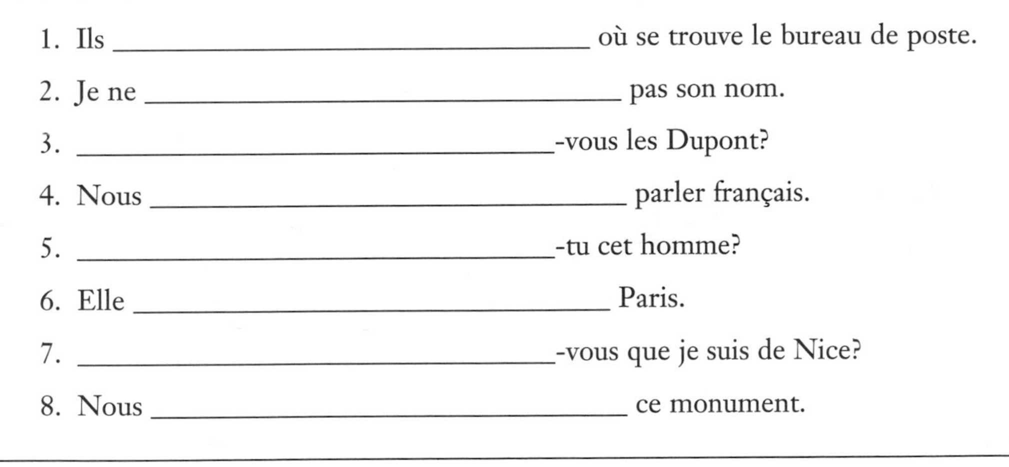

Using *Savoir* and *Connaître*

If you keep the differences between the two verbs in mind, you will quickly learn to use them properly. Show that you've gotten the hang of it by filling in the blanks with the correct form of *savoir* or *connaître.*

1. Ils ______________________ où se trouve le bureau de poste.
2. Je ne ______________________ pas son nom.
3. ______________________-vous les Dupont?
4. Nous ______________________ parler français.
5. ______________________-tu cet homme?
6. Elle ______________________ Paris.
7. ______________________-vous que je suis de Nice?
8. Nous ______________________ ce monument.

What Was Going On?

I **was sitting** idly at a club on the boulevard St. Germain, sipping a Cointreau and watching everyone else have a good time. **I didn't know** anyone, and **I was getting bored.** All of a sudden, the music *started up* and I *became* intrigued by a sexy Frenchman who **could dance** up a storm. I'm not shy so I *went over* to him and *asked* him for the next dance. I **couldn't** believe he *said* yes. We *danced* and *talked* all night and I *wound up* having a very pleasant evening. He even *asked me* for my number.

It happened recently but nonetheless in the past. In English, we speak or write easily in the past. In French, however, it's not as simple because there are two different past tenses: the *passé composé* and the imperfect ***(l'imparfait)***, as shown in the preceding paragraph. This tends to make speaking in the past a bit confusing. If you mistake one for the other, you'll still be understood. Sometimes either tense is correct. What's the difference? The *passé composé* expresses specific actions or events that were completed in the past, whereas the imperfect expresses an uncompleted action or a continuing state in the past.

Formation of the Imperfect

Before going into a more detailed explanation, let's see how the imperfect is formed. For regular and irregular verbs, the imperfect tense is formed by dropping the *-ons* ending from the *nous* form of the present tense and adding the following endings:

je	*-ais*	nous	*-ions*
tu	*-ais*	vous	*-iez*
il, elle, on	*-ait*	ils, elles	*-aient*

Memory Enhancer

The imperfect is different from the *passé composé* in that the imperfect doesn't require a helping verb.

The following table shows how easy this is.

The Imperfect

-er **Verbs**	***-ir*** **Verbs**	***-re*** **Verbs**
nous parl**ons**	nous finiss**ons**	nous répond**ons**
je parlais *zhuh pahr-leh*	je finissais *zhuh fee-nee-seh*	je répondais *zhuh ray-pohN-deh*
tu parlais *tew pahr-leh*	tu finissais *tew fee-nee-seh*	tu répondais *tew ray-pohN-deh*
il, elle, on parlait *eel, ehl, ohN pahr-leh*	il, elle, on finissait *eel, ehl, ohN fee-nee-seh*	il, elle, on répondait *eel, ehl, ohN ray-pohN-deh*
nous parlions *noo pahr-lyohN*	nous finissions *noo fee-nee-syohN*	nous répondions *noo ray-pohN-dyohN*
vous parliez *voo pahr-lyay*	vous finissiez *voo fee-nee-syay*	vous répondiez *voo ray-pohN-dyay*
ils, elles parlaient *eel, ehl pahr-leh*	ils, elles finissaient *eel, ehl fee-nee-seh*	ils, elles répondaient *eel, ehl ray-pohN-deh*

The only verb that is irregular in the imperfect is *être:*

j'étais *zay-teh*	nous étions *noo zay-tyohN*
tu étais *tew ay-teh*	vous étiez *voo zay-tyay*
il, elle, on était *eel, ehl, ohN ay-teh*	ils, elles étaient *eel, ehl zay-teh*

Memory Enhancer

Verbs ending in *-ions* in the present tense have an *i* before the *-ions* and *-iez* imperfect tense endings: *nous vérifions, nous vérifiions.*

For all other irregular verbs in the present tense, you must know the correct *nous* form of the present tense to form the imperfect.

Imperfect Redux

How good is your memory? Fill in the *nous* form of the present tense for the irregular verbs in the following table and then supply the correct form of the imperfect for the subject given.

Infinitive	Nous Form of Present	Imperfect
avoir (to have)	nous ________	elle ________
boire (to drink)	nous ________	je ________
connaître (to be acquainted with)	nous ________	vous ________
devoir (to have to)	nous ________	tu ________
dire (to say, tell)	nous ________	ils ________
dormir (to sleep)	nous ________	nous ________
écrire (to write)	nous ________	elles ________
faire (to make, do)	nous ________	vous ________
lire (to read)	nous ________	je ________
mettre (to put [on])	nous ________	nous ________
partir (to leave)	nous ________	tu ________
pouvoir (to be able to)	nous ________	elle ________
prendre (to take)	nous ________	ils ________
recevoir (to receive)	nous ________	vous ________
savoir (to know)	nous ________	elles ________
sentir (to feel, smell)	nous ________	il ________

continues

continued

servir (to serve)	nous ________	elle ________
sortir (to go out)	nous ________	tu ________
voir (to see)	nous ________	elles ________
vouloir (to want)	nous ________	je ________

Imperfect and Spelling Changes

Certain shoe verbs have spelling changes:

- *-cer* verbs

  Verbs ending in *-cer* change *c* to *ç* before *a* or *o* to maintain the soft *c* sound. These changes occur within the shoe:

j'avançais	nous avancions
tu avançais	vous avanciez
il, elle, on avançait	ils, elles avançaient

Memory Enhancer

The imperfect is for past events that occurred over a period of time (a wavy line) and the *passé composé* is for past events that occurred in an instant (a dot).

- *-ger* verbs

  Verbs ending in *-ger* insert a silent *e* between *g* and *a* or *o* to keep the soft *g* sound. These changes occur within the shoe:

je mangeais	nous mangions
tu mangeais	vous mangiez
il, elle, on mangeait	ils, elles mangeaient

The *Passé Composé* vs. the Imperfect

Which should you use and when? The *passé composé* expresses an action that was completed at a specific time in the past. Think of a camera. The *passé composé* represents an action that could be captured by an instamatic; the action happened and was completed.

The imperfect expresses an action that continued in the past over an indefinite period of time. Think again of a camera. The imperfect represents an action that could be captured by a video camera; the action continued to flow, it *was* happening, *used to* happen, or *would* (meaning *used to*) happen. The imperfect is a descriptive tense. The following table provides a more in-depth look at the differences between the two tenses.

Comparison of the *Passé Composé* and the Imperfect

Passé Composé	Imperfect
1. Events that were started and completed at a definite time in the past (even if the time isn't mentioned): *J'ai parlé au directeur.* (I spoke to the director.)	1. Continuous events in the past (that may or may not have been completed): *Je parlais au directeur.* (I was speaking to the director.)
2. A specific event that occurred at a specific point in time: *Hier il est sorti à midi.* (Yesterday he went out at noon.)	2. Repeated events that took place in the past: *D'habitude il sortait à midi.* (He usually went out at noon.)
3. A specific event that was repeated a stated number of times: *Ils sont allés au cinéma six fois.* (They went to the movies six times.)	3. Describing a person, place, thing, or state of mind: *Nous étions contents.* (We were happy.) *La mer était calme.* (The sea was calm.) *La porte était ouverte.* (The door was open.) *Je voulais partir.* (I wanted to leave.)

Passé Composé or *Imparfait*?

The weather was beautiful, and I went on a picnic with a friend. Something unforeseen happened that almost ruined our day. Complete this story with the correct form of the verb in the *passé composé* or in the imperfect:

C'(être) _________ une belle journeé de printemps. Le ciel (être) _________ bleu et les oiseaux (chanter) _________. Je ne (faire) _________ pas grand-chose quand tout à coup le téléphone (sonner) _________. C'(être) _________ mon amie Barbara. Elle me (m') (demander) _________ si je (vouloir) _________ faire un pique-nique dans les bois. Je (J') (dire) _________ "Oui, volontiers!" Alors je (partir) _________ la chercher à 10 h chez elle et nous (aller) _________ au parc en voiture. En route, nous (s'arrêter) _________ à la charcuterie pour acheter des sandwiches et des boissons. À 11 h nous (arriver) _________ au parc. Le soleil (briller) _________ et il (faire) _________ si beau. Nous (trouver) _________ vite un endroit pour nous installer. Nous (commencer) _________ à manger nos sandwiches quand tout à coup une abeille (attaquer) _________ Barbara. Elle (crier) _________ mais elle (s'échapper) _________. Nous (passer) _________ le reste de la journée à parler de nos amis et à nous amuser. L'après-midi (être) _________ magnifique.

The Least You Need to Know

- *Savoir* means to know a fact or how to do something. *Connaître* means to be acquainted with a person, place, or thing.
- The imperfect is used to describe what the subject was doing. The *passé composé* states what the subject did.
- The imperfect is usually formed by adding appropriate endings to the *nous* form (minus the *-ons* ending) of the verb.

Part 5

It's Time for Business

Today, more than ever, businesses seek bilingual personnel who can communicate effectively in our ever-expanding, multilingual world. Knowing a foreign language can be the key to a very successful career.

Part 5 is for readers whose jobs and businesses require more than a cursory knowledge of French. Our modern, high-tech society demands a knowledge of current computer terms and phrases, as well as the vocabulary necessary to fax and photocopy important documents. Business and banking expressions are also a must. And for travelers who are constantly on the go or who like to combine business with pleasure, alternatives to the traditional hotel stay are presented.

By the time you've completed Part 5, if you've worked diligently, ambitiously, and conscientiously, you'll be ready to face any situation that you might encounter in French. I know you can do it on your own!

Chapter 24

For the Businessperson

In This Chapter

- Stationery store supplies
- Photocopies, faxes, and computers
- Business talk
- The future tense

Chapter 23 helped you find a mailbox and a post office, purchase stamps, envelopes, and other mail essentials, and inquire about postal rates. It also explained how to express in French what you wish to read or write, facts and people you know, and activities you carried out in the past.

Now that you're a pro at letter writing, you might make an attempt to conduct some business in French. To do so, you'll need office supplies and a knowledge of the fax, photocopy, and computer phrases presented in this chapter. You'll learn some key phrases that all good businesspeople use and how to express your future business plans.

I Need Supplies

To carry out any kind of business, you'll need to purchase some necessary tools of the trade. One important stop would be *à la papeterie* (*ah lah pah-puh-tree;* at the stationery store), where you'll find the business items listed in the following table. Begin your transaction by saying:

Je voudrais acheter …
zhuh voo-dreh zahsh-tay …
I would like to buy …

At the Stationery Store

Item	French	Pronunciation
ball-point pen	un stylo (à bille)	*uhN stee-lo (ah beey)*
calculator (solar)	une calculette (solaire)	*ewn kahl-kew-leht (soh-lehr)*
envelopes	des envelopes *f.*	*day zahN-vlohp*
eraser	une gomme	*ewn gohm*
glue	de la colle	*duh lah kohl*
notebook	un cahier	*uhN kah-yay*
paper	du papier	*dew pah-pyay*
paper clips	des agrafes *f.*, des pinces *f.*	*day ah-grahf, day paNs*
pencil sharpener	un taille-crayon	*uhN tahy-kreh-yohN*
pencils	des crayons *m.*	*day kreh-yohN*
post-its	des billets *m.*	*day bee-yeh*
ruler	une règle	*ewn rehgl*
scotch tape	une bande adhésive, un scotch	*ewn bahNd ahd-ay-seev, uhN skohtch*
stapler	une agrafeuse	*ewn ah-grah-fuhz*
stationery	du papier à lettres	*dew pah-pyay ah lehtr*
string	de la ficelle	*duh lah fee-sehl*
wrapping paper	du papier d'emballage	*dew pah-pyay dahN-bah-lahzh*
writing pad	un bloc	*uhN blohk*

Photocopies, Faxes, and Computers

Today, most businesses require three essential items to help facilitate and expedite business projects: faxes, photocopy machines, and computers.

Photocopying

Imagine that your firm has sent you to France on a business trip. You have a generous expense account for which you must submit receipts. Your wallet is quite full of them, and you'd like a backup copy in case one or two get lost in your travels. A wise idea would be to have photocopies made as soon as possible. Here's what you might have to say:

Je voudrais faire une photocopie de ce papier (ce document).
zhuh voo-dreh fehr ewn foh-to-koh-pee duh suh pah-pyay (suh doh-kew-mahN)
I would like to make a photocopy of this paper (this document).

Je voudrais faire faire une photocopie de ce papier (ce document).
zhuh voo-dreh fehr fehr ewn foh-to-koh-pee duh suh pah-pyay (suh doh-kew-mahN)
I would like to have a photocopy made of this document.

Quel est le prix par page?
kehl eh luh pree pahr pahzh
What is the cost per page?

Pouvez-vous l'élargir (de cinquante pour cent)?
poo-vay voo lay-lahr-zheer (duh saN-kahNt poor sahN)
Can you enlarge it (by 50 percent)?

Pouvez-vous le réduire (de vingt-cinq pour cent)?
poo-vay vous luh ray-dweer (duh vaN-saNk poor sahN)
Can you reduce it (by 25 percent)?

Pouvez-vous en faire une copie en couleurs?
poo-vay voo ahN fehr ewn koh-pee ahN koo-luhr
Can you make a color copy?

Attention!

Although the verb *faxer* is often used informally, its use is frowned upon by purists, who regard it as nothing more than *franglais.*

Faxing

Businesses have come to realize that faxing information and documents is an extremely convenient service. Being able to transmit and receive information in a matter of seconds or minutes speeds up the time it takes to transact business, and that translates into extra dollars and euros. If you are conducting business in France, you will want to be fax literate:

Avez-vous un télécopieur?
ah-vay voo uhN tay-lay-kohp-yuhr
Do you have a fax machine?

Quel est le numéro de votre télécopieur?
kehl eh luh new-may-ro duh vohtr tay-lay-kohp-yuhr
What is your fax number?

Je voudrais transmettre une télécopie.
zhuh voo-dreh trahNz-mehtr ewn tay-lay-koh-pee
I'd like to send a fax.

Puis-je transmettre cette télécopie, s'il vous plaît?
pweezh trahNz-mehtr seht tay-lay-koh-pee, seel voo pleh
May I fax this, please?

Puis-je vous transmettre une télécopie de cette lettre (de ce document)?
pweezh voo trahNz-mehtr ewn tay-lay-koh-pee duh seht lehtr (duh suh doh-kew-mahN)
May I fax this letter (document) to you?

Envoyez-m'en (Envoie-m'en) une télécopie.
ahN-vwah-yay mahN (ahN-vwah mahN) ewn tay-lay-koh-pee
Fax me a copy of it.

Je n'ai pas reçu votre télécopie.
zhuh nay pah ruh-sew vohtr tay-lay-koh-pee
I didn't get your fax.

Avez-vous reçu ma télécopie?
ah-vay voo ruh-sew mah tay-lay-koh-pee
Did you receive my fax?

Votre télécopie n'est pas lisible.
vohtr tay-lay-koh-pee neh pah lee-zeebl
Your fax is illegible.

Veuillez la transmettre de nouveau.
vuh-yay lah trahNz-mehtr duh noo-vo
Please send it again.

Computing

In today's fast-paced world, you must have some computer knowledge to conduct business. It's important to know what system, programs, and peripherals other businesses are using. Will your word processors and spreadsheets be compatible? Can you network? The following phrases will help you even if you're not a computer geek. Don't worry. You'll be able to get by using the terms in the following table.

Quel système (type, genre) d'ordinateur avez-vous?
kehl sees-tehm (teep, zhahNr) dohr-dee-nah-tuhr ah-vay-voo
What kind of computer do you have?

Quel système opérant employez-vous?
kehl sees-tehm oh-pay-rahN ahN-plwah-yay-voo
What operating system are you using?

Quel système de traitement de texte employez-vous?
kehl sees-tehm duh treht-mahN duh tehkst ahN-plwah-yay-voo
What word processing program are you using?

Quel tableur employez-vous?
kehl tah-bluhr ahN-plwah-yay-voo
What spreadsheet program are you using?

Quels périphériques avez-vous?
kehl pay-ree-fay-reek ah-vay-voo
What peripherals do you have?

Nos systèmes, sont-ils compatibles?
no sees-tehm sohN teel kohN-pah-teebl
Are our systems compatible?

Avez-vous …?
ah-vay voo …
Do you have …?

Employez-vous …?
ahN-plwah-yay-voo …
Do you use …?

Mini-Dictionary for Computer Users

Word	French	Pronunciation
access	l'accès *m.*	*lahk-seh*
bar graph	l'histogramme *m.*	*lees-toh-grahm*
(to) boot	démarrer	*day-mah-ray*
brand name	la marque	*lah mahrk*

continues

Mini-Dictionary for Computer Users (continued)

Word	French	Pronunciation
bug	la bogue	*lah bohg*
byte	le byte	*luh beet*
cable	le câble	*luh kahbl*
cartridge (laser, ink jet)	la cartouche (laser, jet d'encre)	*lah kahr-toosh (lah-zehr, zheh dahNkr)*
CD-ROM disc	le disque optique numérique	*luh deesk ohp-teek new-may-reek*
chip	la puce	*lah pews*
(to) click	cliquer	*klee-kay*
clipboard	le presse-papiers	*luh prehs-pah-pyay*
computer	l'ordinateur *m.*	*lohr-dee-nah-tuhr*
computer science	l'informatique *f.*	*laN-fohr-mah-teek*
connection	le raccordement	*luh rah-kohrd-mahN*
connector	le connecteur	*luh koh-nehk-tuhr*
CPU	l'unité centrale *f.*	*lew-nee-tay sahN-trahl*
cursor	le curseur	*luh kuhr-suhr*
database	la base de données	*lah bahz duh doh-nay*
(to) debug	déboguer	*day-boh-gay*
debugger (software)	le débogueur	*luh day-boh-guhr*
desktop computer	l'ordinateur *m.*	*lohr-dee-nah-tuhr*
diskette (3½ in.)	la disquette (de trois pouces et demi)	*lah dees-keht (duh trwah poos ay duh-mee)*
disk drive	le lecteur de disques	*luh lehk-tuhr duh deesk*
DOS	le disque système opérant	*luh deesk sees-tehm oh-pay-rahN*
(to) download	décharger	*day-shahr-zhay*
drop-down menu	le menu-déroulant	*luh muh-new day-roo-lahN*
e-mail	la messagerie électronique, le courrier électronique	*lah meh-sahzh-ree ay-lehk-troh-neek, luh koor-yay ay-lehk-troh-neek*
field	la zone	*lah zon*
filter	le filtre écran	*luh feeltr ay-krahN*
freeware	le graciel	*luh grah-syehl*

Word	French	Pronunciation
function key	la touche de fonction	*lah toosh duh fohNk-syohN*
graphics card (high resolution)	la carte graphique (haute résolution)	*lah kahrt grah-feek (ot ray-zoh-lew-syohN)*
hacker	le pirate	*luh pee-raht*
hard disk	le disque dur	*luh deesk dewr*
hardware	le matériel	*luh mah-tay-ryehl*
(to) insert	introduire, insérer	*aN-troh-dweer, aN-say-ray*
Internet	l'Internet	*laN-tehr-neht*
joystick	la manette de jeux	*lah mah-neht duh zhuh*
key	la touche	*lah toosh*
keyboard	le clavier	*luh klah-vyay*
laptop computer	l'ordinateur portable *m.*	*lohr-dee-nah-tuhr pohr-tahbl*
mail merge	le mailing, le publipostage	*luh meh-leeng, luh pew-blee-pohs-tahzh*
memory	la mémoire	*lah may-mwahr*
memory card	la carte d'extension de mémoire	*lah kahrt dehk-stahN-syohN duh may-mwahr*
modem	le modem	*luh moh-dehm*
monitor	le moniteur	*luh moh-nee-tuhr*
motherboard	la carte-mère	*lah kahrt mehr*
mouse	la souris	*lah soo-ree*
network	le réseau	*luh ray-zo*
operating system	le système opérant	*luh sees-tehm oh-pay-rahN*
peripherals	les périphériques *m.*	*lay pay-ree-fay-reek*
power surge	le parasite violent	*luh pah-rah-seet vee-oh-lahN*
public domain	le domaine publique	*luh doh-mehn pew-bleek*
(to) reboot	redémarrer	*ruh-day-mah-ray*
(to) scan	scanner, digitaliser	*skah-nay, dee-zhee-tah-lee-zay*
screen	l'écran *m.*	*lay-krahN*
software	le logiciel	*luh loh-zhee-syehl*
speed	la vitesse	*lah vee-tehs*
spell checker	le correcteur orthographique	*luh koh-rehk-tuhr ohr-toh-grah-feek*

continues

Mini-Dictionary for Computer Users (continued)

Word	French	Pronunciation
spreadsheet	le tableur	*luh tah-bluhr*
system	le système	*luh sees-tehm*
thesaurus	le thesaurus	*luh tuh-so-rews*
user	l'utilisateur *m.*	*lew-tee-lee-zah-tuhr*
word processor	le système de traitement de texte	*luh sees-tehm duh treht-mahN duh tehkst*

Surfing the Net

Whenever I need some help and can't seem to find anyone around, I just go down to the den. Chances are my husband or one of my sons is there, face glued to the computer screen, eyes fixed on the monitor, fingers poised on the keyboard. Everyone's passion these days seems to be surfing the Internet. You can spend hours traveling to different countries and collecting information about every subject imaginable for a minimal fee. If you would like, you can do so in French! It's so simple that I did it myself in a matter of minutes. Here's what you do:

1. Go to the location box on your web browser.
2. Type www.yahoo.com.
3. Click Enter.
4. Scroll down to "Local Yahoo!s."
5. Select France.
6. You can search for subjects you like and practice everything you've learned so far.

Do You Know Your Computer?

Let's say you want to communicate via computer with a business associate in France. You will have to be able to give certain facts about your system to facilitate the transmission. Can you answer these questions about your computer? Sample responses can be found in Appendix A.

1. Quel système d'ordinateur employez-vous?

   ____

2. Quels périphériques employez-vous?

   ____

3. Votre système a combien de megabytes de mémoire?

   ____

4. Quelle est la vitesse de votre système?

   ____

5. Quels logiciels employez-vous?

   ____

Being a Good Businessperson

If you are planning to export or ship goods to a French firm that uses French as its primary language, the key words in the following table ought to provide what the average businessperson might need.

Mini-Dictionary for Businesspeople

Word	French	Pronunciation
accountant	le comptable	*luh kohN-tahbl*
activity	le mouvement d'affaires	*luh moov-mahN dah-fehr*
amount	le montant	*luh mohN-tahN*
(to) appraise	évaluer	*ay-vah-lew-ay*
assets	l'actif *m.*	*lahk-teef*
(to) authorize	autoriser	*o-to-ree-zay*
balance sheet	le bilan	*luh bee-lahN*
bankruptcy	la faillite	*lah fah-yeet*
bill	la facture de paiement	*lah fahk-tewr duh peh-mahN*
bill of exchange	la lettre de change	*lah lehtr duh shahNzh*
bill of lading	le connaissement	*luh koh-nehs-mahN*

continues

Mini-Dictionary for Businesspeople (continued)

Word	French	Pronunciation
bill of sale	la lettre de vente	*lah lehtr duh vahNt*
bookkeeping	la comptabilité	*lah kohN-tah-bee-lee-tay*
business	l'affaire *f.*	*lah-fehr*
(to) buy	acheter	*ahsh-tay*
(to) buy for cash	payer comptant	*peh-yay kohN-tahN*
(to) cash a check	toucher un chèque	*too-shay uhN shehk*
compensation for damage	le dédommagement	*luh day-doh-mahzh-mahN*
competitive price	le prix de concurrence	*luh pree duh kohN-kew-rahNs*
consignee	le destinataire	*luh dehs-tee-nah-tehr*
consumer	le consommateur	*lun kohN-soh-mah-tuhr*
contract	le contrat	*luh kohN-trah*
cost price	le prix de revient	*luh pree duh ruh-vyaN*
credit	le crédit	*luh kray-dee*
date of maturity	l'écheance *f.*	*lay-shay-ahNs*
debit	le débit	*luh day-bee*
(to) deliver	livrer	*lee-vray*
discount	l'exonération *f.*, la réduction, le rabais	*lehk-zoh-nay-rah-syohN,* *lah ray-dewk-syohN,* *luh rah-beh*
due	échu	*ay-shew*
expenses	les frais *m.*	*lay freh*
(to) export	exporter	*ehks-pohr-tay*
foreign trade	le commerce extérieur	*luh koh-mehrs ehks-tay-ryuhr*
goods	les produits *m.*, les biens *m.*	*lay proh-dwee,* *lay byaN*
(to) import	importer	*aN-pohr-tay*
interest rates	les intérêts *m.*	*lay zaN-tay-reh*
invoice	la facture	*lah fahk-tewr*
lawsuit	le procès	*luh proh-seh*
lawyer	l'avocat *m.*	*lah-voh-kah*
liabilities	le passif	*luh pah-seef*

Word	French	Pronunciation
mail-order business	l'établissement de vente par correspondance *m.*	*lay-tah-blees-mahN duh vahNt pahr koh-rehs-pohN-dahNs*
management	la gestion	*lah zhehs-tyohN*
manager	le gérant	*luh zhay-rahN*
merchandise	la marchandise	*lah mahr-shahN-deez*
middleman	l'intermédiaire *m.*	*laN-tehr-mayd-yehr*
money	l'argent *m.*	*lahr-zhahN*
office	le bureau	*luh bew-ro*
outlay	la mise de fonds	*lah meez duh fohN*
overhead expenses	les frais généraux *m.*	*lay freh zhay-nay-ro*
owner	le propriétaire	*luh proh-pree-yay-tehr*
(to) package	emballer	*ahN-bah-lay*
partner	l'associé *m.*	*lah-soh-syay*
past due	arriéré, en retard	*ah-ryay-ray, ahN ruh-tahr*
payment	le versement	*luh vehrs-mahN*
percent	pour cent	*poor sahN*
producer	le producteur	*luh proh-dewk-tuhr*
property	la propriété	*lah proh-pree-yay-tay*
purchase	l'achat *m.*	*lah-shah*
recession	la crise	*lah kreez*
retailer	le détaillant	*luh day-tah-yahN*
running expenses	les frais d'exploitation *m.*	*lay freh dehks-plwah-tah-syohN*
sale	la vente	*lah vahNt*
sample	l'échantillon *m.*	*lay-shahN-tee-yohN*
(to) sell for cash	vendre au comptant	*vahNdr o kohN-tahN*
selling price	le prix de vente	*luh pree duh vahNt*
(to) send	envoyer, adresser	*ahN-vwah-yay, ah-dreh-say*
(to) send back	renvoyer	*rahN-vwah-yay*
(to) send C.O.D.	envoyer payable à l'arrivée	*ahN-vwah-yay peh-yahbl ah lah-ree-vay*
(to) settle	régler	*ray-glay*

continues

Mini-Dictionary for Businesspeople (continued)

Word	French	Pronunciation
shipment	l'expédition *f.*	*lehks-pay-dee-syohN*
shipper	l'expéditeur *m.*	*lehks-pay-dee-tuhr*
supply and demand	l'offre *m.* et la demande	*lohfr ay lah duh-mahNd*
tax	l'impôt *m.*	*laN-po*
tax-exempt	exempt d'impôts	*ehg-zahN daN-po*
trade	le commerce	*luh koh-mehrs*
transact business	faire des affaires	*fehr day zah-fehr*
(to) transfer	transférer	*trahNz-fay-ray*
value added tax	la taxe sur la valeur ajoutée	*lah tahks sewr lah vah-luhr ah-zhoo-tay*
wholesaler	le grossiste	*luh groh-seest*
(to) wrap	emballer	*ahN-bah-lay*
(to) yield a profit	rendre un bénéfice	*rahNdr uhN bay-nay-fees*

There's Hope for the Future

An optimistic businessperson tends to look to the future and prepare wisely for it. In French, the future can be expressed in one of two ways: by using *aller* (to go) + an infinitive or by using the future tense.

Aller + Infinitive

Since the verb *aller* means "to go," it is understandable that it is used to express what the speaker *is* going to do. Since "to go" will be the first verb used, it will have to be conjugated.

Memory Enhancer

Refresh your memory.

Here's the irregular verb *aller* (to go):

je vais	*nous allons*
tu vas	*vous allez*
il, elle, on va	*ils, elles vont*

Je vais aller en ville.
zhuh veh zah-lay ahN veel
I'm going to go into the city.

Ils vont envoyer la lettre.
eel vohN tahN-vwah-yay lah lehtr
They are going to send the letter.

The Future Tense

The future can also be expressed by changing the verb to the future tense. The future tense tells what the subject will do or what action will take place in future time. The future of regular verbs is formed by adding endings to the infinitive of the verb, as shown in the following table. Notice that the endings for the future resemble the conjugation of the verb *avoir*, except for the *nous* and *vous* forms, where the *av-* (*nous avons*, *vous avez*) beginning is dropped.

For *-re* verbs, drop the final *e* from the infinitive before adding the appropriate ending:

Il m'attendra à midi.
He will wait for me at noon.

Attention!

The future can be implied by using the present tense: *J'arrive dans dix minutes.* (I'll arrive in 10 minutes.)

The Future

-er Verbs	*-ir* Verbs	*-re* Verbs
travailler—to work	choisir—to choose	vendre—to sell
will work	*will choose*	*will sell*
je travailler**ai** *zhuh trah-vahy-ray*	je choisir**ai** *zhuh shwah-zee-ray*	je vendr**ai** *zhuh vahN-dray*
tu travailler**as** *tew trah-vahy-rah*	tu choisir**as** *tew shwah-zee-rah*	tu vendr**as** *tew vahN-drah*
il, elle, on travailler**a** *eel, ehl, ohN trah-vahy-rah*	il, elle, on choisir**a** *eel, ehl, ohN shwah-zee-rah*	il, elle, on vendr**a** *eel, ehl, ohN vahN-drah*
nous travailler**ons** *noo trah-vahy-rohN*	nous choisir**ons** *noo shwah-zee-rohN*	nous vendr**ons** *noo vahN-drohN*
vous travailler**ez** *voo trah-vahy-ray*	vous choisir**ez** *voo shwah-zee-ray*	vous vendr**ez** *vous vahN-dray*
ils, elles travailler**ont** *eel, ehl trah-vahy-rohN*	ils, elles choisir**ont** *eel, ehl shwah-zee-rohN*	ils, elles vendr**ont** *eel, ehl vahN-drohN*

The Future Tense of Shoe Verbs

Only certain shoe verbs use the changes within the shoe to form every form of the future tense. The other shoe verbs form the future tense as described in the preceding section.

- Verbs ending in *-yer* change *y* to *i* in all forms of the future. There is no more shoe since all verb forms are using *i* instead of *y*. Verbs ending in *-ayer* may or may not change *y* to *i*. Both *je paierai* and *je payerai* are acceptable:

j'emplo**i**erai *zhahN-plwah-ray*	nous emplo**i**erons *noo zahN-plwah-rohN*
tu emplo**i**eras *tew ahN-plwah-rah*	vous emplo**i**erez *voo zahN-plwah-ray*
il, elle, on emplo**i**era *eel, ehl, ohN ahN-plwah-rah*	ils, elles emplo**i**eront *eel, ehl ahN-plwah-rohN*

- Verbs ending in *e* + consonant + *er* (but not *é* + consonant + *er*) change silent *e* to *è* in the future. Once again, there will be no more shoe since changes are made in all forms:

j'ach**è**terai *zhah-sheht-ray*	nous ach**è**terons *noo zah-sheht-rohN*
tu ach**è**teras *tew ah-sheht-rah*	vous ach**è**terez *voo zah-sheht-ray*
il, elle, on ach**è**tera *eel, ehl, ohN ah-sheht-rah*	ils, elles ach**è**teront *eel, ehl zah-sheht-rohN*

- The verbs *appeler* and *jeter* double their consonants in the shoe in the present tense. They do the same in all forms of the future tense:

j'appe**ll**erai *zhah-pehl-ray*	nous appe**ll**erons *noo zah-pehl-rohN*
tu appe**ll**eras *tew ah-pehl-rah*	vous appe**ll**erez *voo zah-pehl-ray*
il, elle, on appe**ll**era *eel, ehl, ohN ah-pehl-rah*	ils, elles appe**ll**eront *eel, ehl zah-pehl-rohN*

je je**tt**erai *zhuh zheht-ray*	nous je**tt**erons *noo zheht-rohN*
tu je**tt**eras *tew zheht-rah*	vous je**tt**erez *voo zheht-ray*
il, elle, on je**tt**era *eel, ehl, ohN zheht-rah*	ils, elles je**tt**eront *eel, ehl zheht-rohN*

Verbs Irregular in the Future

The verbs in the following table have irregular stems in the future tense. Simply add the future endings to these stems to get the correct future form. Complete the chart with the correct form of the future tense. Answers can be found in Appendix A.

Infinitive	Stem	Future
avoir (to have)	aur- (*ohr*)	tu __________
devoir (to have to)	devr- (*duhv*)	nous __________
envoyer (to send)	enverr- (*ahN-vuhr*)	il __________
être (to be)	ser- (*sehr*)	elles __________
faire (to make, do)	fer- (*fuhr*)	je __________
pouvoir (to be able to)	pourr- (*poor*)	vous __________
recevoir (to receive)	recevr- (*ruh-suhv*)	nous __________
savoir (to know)	saur- (*sohr*)	ils __________
venir (to come)	viendr- (*vyaNdr*)	tu __________
voir (to see)	verr- (*vuhr*)	je __________
vouloir (to want)	voudr- (*voodr*)	elle __________

Predicting the Future

Do you wish had a crystal ball to look into the future, or would you rather not know? If you're curious, consult your horoscope to see what's in store for you. What does the horoscope predict for each sign? Answers can be found in Appendix A.

Bélier (21 mars–20 avril)
Des opportunités financières exceptionnelles se présenteront.

Taureau (21 avril–20 mai)
Vous passerez un mois très agréable.

Gémeaux (21 mai–20 juin)
Vous aurez des tensions et des disputes avec des collègues.

continues

continued

Cancer (21 juin–22 juillet)
Vous serez en très bonne forme.

Lion (23 juillet–21 août)
Vous vous concentrerez sur vos affaires financières.

Vierge (22 août–22 septembre)
Vous prendrez une décision importante concernant votre avenir professionnel.

Balance (23 septembre–22 octobre)
Vous serez en harmonie avec vos amis.

Scorpion (23 octobre–22 novembre)
Votre ambition vous servira.

Sagittaire (23 novembre–20 décembre)
Vous aurez des discussions importantes avec des membres de votre famille.

Capricorne (21 décembre–20 janvier)
Tout ira bien pour vous.

Verseau (21 janvier–19 février)
Vous ferez la connaissance d'une personne importante.

Poissons (20 février–20 mars)
Votre agenda sera tous les soirs plein et les propositions de week-end afflueront.

The Least You Need to Know

- To conduct business abroad, it is essential to become familiar with certain technological terms for items such as photocopiers, fax machines, and computers.
- To express that an action will take place in the near future, use the correct conjugated form of the verb *aller* + the infinitive of the action that is going to take place.
- The future tense usually is formed by adding the following endings to the infinitive: *-ai*, *-as*, *-a*, *-ons*, *-ez*, *-ont*. A few irregular verbs must be memorized.

Chapter 25

Buying and Renting Property

In This Chapter

- Apartments and houses
- Rooms, furniture, appliances, and amenities
- The conditional

Although you love the luxury of a well-appointed hotel, this might not prove to be cost efficient in the long run. You could be better off purchasing or renting an apartment, house, or condominium or even buying into a time-sharing property. This chapter explains how to get the facilities you want and need and how to express what you would do in certain circumstances.

Rent a *Château*

Renting a *château* might be a stretch to the pocketbook, but renting or buying a piece of property in a French-speaking country is not at all uncommon today. If you're even considering such a move, read Peter Mayle's *A Year in Provence*. Not only is the book an enjoyable, light read, it may convince you to live in the south of France. So if you've decided that it's time to get daring and buy a home of your own, you will want to be able to read and understand the ads in the papers and to ask an agent or seller what is being offered. Whether you want a fireplace, huge closets, or central heating, the following table will help you decipher what features a house or apartment offers. Use the phrase *"Il me faut …"* (*eel muh fo;* "I need … ") to express your needs.

The House, the Apartment, the Rooms

Term	French	Pronunciation
air conditioning (central)	la climatisation (centrale)	*lah klee-mah-tee-zah-syohN (sahN-trahl)*
apartment	l'appartement *m.*	*lah-par-tuh-mahN*
apartment building	l'immeuble *m.*	*lee-muhbl*
attic	le grenier	*luh gruh-nyay*
backyard	le jardin	*luh zhahr-daN*
balcony	le balcon	*luh bahl-kohN*
basement	le sous-sol	*luh soo-sohl*
bathroom	la salle de bains, le toilettes	*lah sahl duh baN, lay twah-leht*
bedroom	la chambre (à coucher)	*lah shahNbr (ah koo-shay)*
closet	la penderie, la garde-robe	*lah pahN-dree, lah gahrd-rohb*
courtyard	la cour	*lah koor*
cupboard	le placard	*luh plah-kahr*
den	la salle de séjour, le living	*lah sahl duh say-zhoor, luh lee-veeng*
dining room	la salle à manger	*lah sahl ah mahN-zhay*
door	la porte	*lah pohrt*
elevator	l'ascenseur *m.*	*lah-sahN-suhr*
entrance	l'entrée *f.*	*lahN-tray*
fireplace	la cheminée	*lah shuh-mee-nay*
floor	le plancher	*luh plahN-shay*
floor (story)	l'étage *m.*	*lay-tahzh*
garage	le garage	*luh gah-rahzh*
ground floor	le rez-de-chaussée	*luh rayd-sho-say*
hallway	le couloir, le vestibule	*luh koo-lwahr, luh vehs-tee-bewl*
heating	le chauffage	*luh sho-fahzh*
electric	électrique	*ay-lehk-treek*
gas	au gaz	*o gahz*

Term	French	Pronunciation
house	la maison	*lah meh-zohN*
key	la clef	*lah klay*
kitchen	la cuisine	*lah kwee-zeen*
laundry room	la buanderie	*lah bwahN-dree*
lawn	la pelouse	*lah pluh-looz*
lease	le bail	*luh bahy*
living room	le salon	*luh sah-lohN*
maintenance	l'entretien *m.*	*lahNtr-tyaN*
owner	le propriétaire	*luh proh-pree-yay-tehr*
private road	l'allée privée *f.*	*lah-lay pree-vay*
rent	le loyer	*luh lwah-yay*
roof	le toit	*luh twah*
room	la pièce, la salle	*lah pyehs,* *lah sahl*
security deposit	la caution	*lah ko-syohN*
shower	la douche	*lah doosh*
stairs	l'escalier *m.*	*lehs-kah-lyay*
storage room	le débarras	*luh day-bah-rah*
tenant	le locataire	*luh loh-kah-tehr*
terrace	la terrasse	*lah teh-rahs*
wall	le mur	*luh mewr*
window	la fenêtre	*lah fuh-nehtr*

Home Sweet Home

You simply must have a double oven so that you can impress your French business associates with your repertoire of *nouvelle cuisine.* A microwave oven is a must. How about a dishwasher? What about furniture, a television, and a washer and dryer? What furniture and appliances come with the property you have purchased or rented? Consult the following table for a complete list of just about everything there is. Use *"Y a-t-il ...?" (ee ah-teel;* "Is [Are] there ...?") to ask your questions.

Furniture and Accessories

Item	French	Pronunciation
armchair	un fauteuil	*uhN fo-tuhy*
bed	un lit	*uhN lee*
bookcase	une étagère	*ewn nay-tah-zhehr*
carpet	un tapis	*uhN tah-pee*
chair	une chaise, un siège	*ewn shehz, uhN syehzh*
clock	une pendule	*ewn pahN-dewl*
curtains	des rideaux *m.*	*day ree-do*
dishwasher	un lave-vaisselle	*uhN lahv veh-sehl*
dresser	une commode	*ewn koh-mohd*
dryer	un séchoir, un sèche-linge	*uhN say-shwahr,* *uhN sehsh-laNzh*
food processor	un robot ménager	*uhN roh-bo may-nah-zhay*
freezer	un congélateur	*uhN kohN-zhay-lah-tuhr*
furniture	des meubles *m.*	*day muhbl*
lamp	une lampe	*ewn lahNp*
microwave oven	un four à micro-ondes	*uhN foor ah mee-kro-ohNd*
mirror	un miroir	*uhN meer-wahr*
oven	un four	*uhN foor*
picture	un tableau	*uhN tah-blo*
refrigerator	un réfrigérateur	*uhN ray-free-zhay-rah-tuhr*
rug	un tapis	*uhN tah-pee*
shades	des stores *m.*	*day stohr*
sofa	un canapé, un divan	*uhN kah-nah-pay, uhN dee-vahN*
stereo	une chaîne stéréo	*ewn shehn stay-ray-o*
stove	une cuisinière	*ewn kwee-zee-nyehr*
table night	une table de nuit	*ewn tahbl* *duh nwee*
television large screen	une télévision à grand écran	*ewn tay-lay-vee-zyohN* *ah grahN day-krahN*
VCR	un magnétoscope	*uhN mah-nyay-toh-skohp*
wardrobe	une armoire *f.*	*ewn nahr-mwahr*
washing machine	une machine à laver	*ewn mah-sheen ah lah-vay*

Purchasing Furniture

Suppose you've rented or purchased an unfurnished place. What are some services you'd expect a furniture store to provide?

Read the following ad to find out what attractive offers you could expect from the company. A general translation can be found in Appendix A.

MOBILIER DE CANNES UNE VALEUR SÛRE

Nous vous garantissons gratuitement (free) vos meubles pendant 5 ans et le revêtement de sièges pendant 2 ans contre tout défaut de fabrication.

Nous nous déplaçons gratuitement chez vous pour prendre des mesures, établir des devis (estimates), et vous conseiller.

Nous vous offrons une garantie tous risques, gratuitement, pendant un an.

Nous reprenons vos vieux meubles lors de l'achat de meubles neufs.

Nous assurons ces services et garanties, sans supplément de prix, dans tous nos magasins, partout en France continentale.

Should You Buy or Rent?

Whether you buy or rent, there are bound to be certain preferences you'd like to express or particular questions you have. Use the following phrases and expressions to help you get exactly what you want.

Je cherche …
zhuh shersh …
I'm looking for …

… la publicité immobilière
… lah pew-blee-see-tay ee-moh-bee-lyehr
… the real-estate advertising section

… les petites annonces
… lay puh-tee tah-nohNs
… the classified ads

… une agence immobilière
… ewn nah-zhahNs ee-moh-bee-lyehr
… a real estate agency

Je voudrais louer (acheter) …
zhuh voo-dreh loo-ay (ahsh-tay) …
I would like to rent (buy) …

… un appartement
… uhN nah-pahr-tuh-mahN
… an apartment

… un condominium
… uhN kohN-doh-mee-nyuhm
… a condominium

… une maison
… ewn meh-zohN
… a house

Est-ce de haute prestation?
ehs duh ot prehs-tah-syohN
Is it luxurious?

Y a-t-il des cambriolages?
ee ah-teel day kahN-bree-oh-lahzh
Are there break-ins?

Y a-t-il le partage du temps?
ee ah-teel luh pahr-tahzh dew tahN
Is there time-sharing?

Quel est le loyer?
kehl eh luh lwah-yay
What is the rent?

Ça coûte combien l'entretien de l'appartement (de la maison)?
sah koot kohN-byaN lahNtr-tyan duh lah-pahr-tuh-mahN (duh lah meh-zohN)
How much is the maintenance of the apartment (house)?

… est compris(e)?
… eh kohN-pree(z)
Is … included?

l'électricité *f.*
lay-lehk-tree-see-tay
the electricity

le chauffage
luh sho-fahzh
the heat

le gaz
luh gahz
the gas

la climatisation
lah klee-mah-tee-zah-syohN
the air conditioning

À combien sont les paiements mensuels?
ah kohN-byaN sohN lay peh-mahN mahN-swehl
How much are the monthly payments?

Dois-je payer une caution?
dwahzh peh-yay ewn ko-syohN
Do I have to leave a deposit?

Je voudrais prendre une hypothèque.
zhuh voo-dreh prahNdr ewn nee-poh-tehk
I'd like to take out a mortgage.

Je vais à la banque.
zhuh veh zah lah bahnk
I'm going to the bank.

Cracking the Code

Armed with a pencil and a cup of coffee, you've decided to begin reading the real estate ads. Instantly, you frown and become exasperated at all the unfamiliar jargon. The following list will help you decode the abbreviations so you can determine what is really being offered.

1 **À Vendre**

MAISON DE CARACTERE, dans village 2 kms mer, 8 kms Montpellier, 150m2 habitable, 20m2 patio grand séjour avec cheminée, 4 chambres, mezannine, chauffage électrique, 140.000 euros $140.000. 19 bis, allée du bas Vaupereux Verrière le Buisson 91370 Villeneuve-les-Maguelonne France. Tél.

How to Read a Real Estate Ad

1. *À vendre*—For sale.
2. *maison de caractère*—A house with character.
3. *2 kms mer*—Two kilometers from the sea.
4. *8 kms Montpellier*—Eight kilometers from the city of Montpellier.
5. *150m² habitable*—Living space of 150 square meters.
6. *20m² patio*—A patio that measures 20 square meters.
7. *grand séjour avec cheminée*—A large living room with a fireplace.
8. *4 chambres*—Four bedrooms.
9. *mezannine*—A landing between the ground and first floors.
10. *chauffage électrique*—Electric heat.
11. *140.000 euros*—The price of the house in new French currency.
12. *19 bis*—This street has a #19 and then a second #19 called *19 bis.* This is the equivalent of an address that reads 19 followed by a second address that reads 19A.
13. *allée du bas Vaupereux Verrière le Buisson*—The street on which the house is located.
14. *91370*—A regional code.
15. *Villeneuve-les-Maguelonne France*—The city or village in which the house is located.
16. *tél*—The telephone number to call if you are interested.

Here Are the Conditions

Would you like a big or small house? Would you like it furnished or unfurnished? How about a swimming pool? The conditional is a mood in French that expresses what the speaker would do or what would happen under certain circumstances. The conditional of the verb *vouloir* or *aimer* is frequently used to express what the speaker would like.

> Je voudrais (J'aimerais) louer un appartement.
> *zhuh voo-dreh (zhehm-ray) loo-ay uhN nah-pahr-tuh-mahN*
> I would like to rent an apartment.

Attention!

Because they look so much alike, you will have to look carefully at the endings tacked onto the infinitive stems of verbs to differentiate between the future (what the subject will do) and the conditional (what the subject would do).

Formation of the Conditional

The conditional is formed with the same stem that is used to form the future, whether you are using a regular, irregular, or shoe verb. The endings for the conditional, however, are different. They are exactly the same as the endings for the imperfect. In other words, to form the conditional, start with the future stem and add the imperfect endings, as shown in the following table. For *-re* verbs, drop the final *e* from the infinitive before adding the appropriate ending.

The Conditional of Regular Verbs

-er **Verbs**	***-ir*** **Verbs**	***-re*** **Verbs**
travailler (to work) *would work*	choisir (to choose) *would choose*	vendre (to sell) *would sell*
je travaillerais *zhuh tra-vahy-reh*	je choisirais *zhuh shwah-zee-reh*	je vendrais *zhuh vahN-dreh*
tu travaillerais *tew trah-vahy-reh*	tu choisirais *tew shwah-zee-reh*	tu vendrais *tew vahN-dreh*
il, elle, on travaillerait *eel, ehl, ohN trah-vahy-reh*	il, elle, on choisirait *eel, ehl, ohN shwah-zee-reh*	il, elle, on vendrait *eel, ehl, ohN vahN-dreh*
nous travaillerions *noo trah-vahy-ryohN*	nous choisirions *noo shwah-zee-ryohN*	nous vendrions *noo vahN-dryohN*
vous travailleriez *voo trah-vahy-ryay*	vous choisiriez *voo shwah-zee-ryay*	vous vendriez *voo vahN-dryay*
ils, elles travailleraient *eel, ehl trah-vahy-reh*	ils, elles choisiraient *eel, ehl shwah-zee-reh*	ils, elles vendraient *eel, ehl vahN-dreh*

The Conditional of Shoe Verbs

Only certain shoe verbs use the changes within the shoe to form all forms of the conditional. All other shoe verbs follow the rules for conditional formation previously listed.

- Verbs ending in *-yer* change *y* to *i* in all forms of the conditional. There is no more shoe since all verb forms are using *i* instead of *y*. Verbs ending in *-ayer* may or may not change *y* to *i*. Both *je paierais* and *je payerais* are acceptable:

  j'emplo*i*erais
  zhahN-plwah-reh

  nous emplo*i*erions
  noo zahN-plwah-ryohN

  tu emplo*i*erais
  tew ahN-plwah-reh

  vous emplo*i*eriez
  voo zahN-plwah-ryay

  il, elle, on emplo*i*erait
  eel, ehl, ohN ahN-plwah-reh

  ils, elles emplo*i*eraient
  eel, ehl ahN-plwah-reh

- Verbs ending in *e* + consonant + *er* (but not *é* + consonant + *er*) change silent *e* to *è* in the conditional. Once again, there will be no more shoe since changes are made in all forms:

  j'achèterais
  zhah-sheh-treh

  nous achèterions
  noo zah-sheht-ryohN

  tu achèterais
  tew ah-sheh-treh

  vous achèteriez
  voo zah-sheht-ryay

  il, elle, on achèterait
  eel, ehl, ohN ah-sheh-treh

  ils, elles achèteraient
  eel, ehl ah-sheh-treh

- The verbs *appeler* and *jeter* double their consonants in the shoe in the present and do the same in all forms of the conditional:

  j'appellerais
  zhah-pehl-reh

  nous appellerions
  noo zah-pehl-ryohN

  tu appellerais
  tew ah-pehl-reh

  vous appelleriez
  voo zah-pehl-ryay

  il, elle, on appellerait
  eel, ehl, ohN ah-pehl-reh

  ils, elles appelleraient
  eel, ehl ah-pehl-reh

  je jetterais
  zhuh zheh-treh

  nous jetterions
  noo zheht-ryohN

  tu jetterais
  tew zheh-treh

  vous jetteriez
  voo zheht-ryay

  il, elle, on jetterait
  eel, ehl, ohN zheh-treh

  ils, elles jetteraient
  eel, ehl zheh-treh

Irregular Verbs in the Conditional

The verbs in the following table have irregular stems in the conditional. To complete the chart, simply add the conditional endings to these stems to get the correct conditional form. The answers can be found in Appendix A.

Infinitive	**Stem**	**Conditional**
avoir (to have)	aur- (*ohr*)	tu ___________
devoir (to have to)	devr- (*duhv*)	nous ___________
envoyer (to send)	enverr- (*ahN-vuhr*)	il ___________
être (to be)	ser- (*sehr*)	elles ___________
faire (to make, do)	fer- (*fuhr*)	je ___________
pouvoir (to be able to)	pourr- (*poor*)	vous ___________
recevoir (to receive)	recevr- (*ruh-suhvr*)	nous ___________
savoir (to know)	saur- (*sohr*)	ils ___________
venir (to come)	viendr- (*vyaNdr*)	tu ___________
voir (to see)	verr- (*vuhr*)	je ___________
vouloir (to want)	voudr- (*voodr*)	elle ___________

The Least You Need to Know

- Learning the correct vocabulary will help you get the living accommodations you want and need.
- The conditional is formed by using the future stem (usually the infinitive) and the imperfect endings: *-ais, -ais, -ait, -ions, -iez, -aient.*
- As always, a few irregular verbs must be memorized.

Chapter 26

Money Is the Issue

In This Chapter

- Banking terms
- The subjunctive

Chapter 25 prepared you for an extended stay in a French-speaking country. You learned the words and phrases you would need if you wanted to rent an apartment or condominium or even buy a house. You know how to describe the features you need to live comfortably, whether that includes a gourmet kitchen with a breakfast nook or a living room with cathedral ceilings.

This final chapter is for anyone who must make a trip to the bank: a tourist who wants to change money, a businessperson with financial obligations, an investor with monetary concerns, or someone who is interested in purchasing real estate or a business. You will also learn how to express your specific, personal needs by using the subjunctive.

At the Bank

There are many reasons for a person to stop into a bank in a foreign country. The most common reason is to exchange money. (Banks do give a very favorable rate of exchange.) But perhaps you have greater goals. Maybe you want to purchase real estate, set up a business, make investments, dabble in the stock market, or stay a while and open a savings or checking account. If so, you will need to familiarize yourself with the phrases in the following table.

Mini-Dictionary of Banking Terms

Term	French	Pronunciation
automatic teller machine	un distributeur automatique de billets, un guichet automatique de banque	*uhN dee-stree-bew-tuhr o-to-mah-teek duh bee-yeh, uhN gee-sheh o-to-mah-teek duh bahNk*
balance	le solde	*luh sohld*
bank	la banque	*lah bahNk*
bank book	le livret d'épargne	*luh lee-vreh day-pahr-nyuh*
bill	le billet, la coupure	*luh bee-yeh, lah koo-pewr*
(to) borrow	emprunter	*ahN-pruhN-tay*
branch	la succursale	*lah sew-kewr-sahl*
cash	l'argent liquide *m.*	*lahr-zhahN lee-keed*
(to) cash	toucher, encaisser	*too-shay, ahN-keh-say*
cashier	la caisse	*lah kehs*
change (coins)	la monnaie	*lah moh-neh*
check	le chèque	*luh shehk*
checkbook	le carnet de chèques, le chéquier	*luh kahr-neh duh shehk, luh shay-kyay*
checking account	le compte-chèques	*luh kohNt shehk*
coin	la pièce	*lah pyehs*
credit	le crédit	*luh kray-dee*
currency	la monnaie	*lah moh-neh*
customer	le (la) client(e)	*luh (lah) klee-yahN(t)*
debt	la dette	*lah deht*
deposit	le dépôt, le versement	*luh day-po, luh vehrs-mahN*
(to) deposit	déposer, verser	*day-po-zay, vehr-say*
employee	l'employé(e)	*lahN-plwah-yay*
(to) endorse	endosser	*ahN-doh-say*
(to) exchange	échanger	*ay-shahN-zhay*

Term	French	Pronunciation
exchange rate	le cours du change	*luh koor dew shahNzh*
guarantee	la caution	*lah ko-syohN*
installment payment	le versement échelonné	*luh verhs-mahN aysh-loh-nay*
interest (compound)	l'intérêt *m.* (composé)	*laN-tay-reh (kohN-po-zay)*
interest rate	le taux d'intérêt	*luh to daN-tay-reh*
(to) invest	placer	*plah-say*
investment	le placement	*luh plahs-mahN*
(to) take out a loan	faire un emprunt	*fehr uhN nahN-pruhN*
long term	à long terme	*ah lohN tehrm*
(to) manage	gérer	*zhay-ray*
money exchange bureau	le bureau de change	*luh bew-ro duh shahNzh*
monthly statement	le relevé mensuel	*luh ruh-lvay mahN-swehl*
mortgage	l'hypothèque *f.*	*lee-poh-tehk*
overdraft	le découvert	*luh day-koo-vehr*
overdrawn check	le chèque sans provision	*luh shehk sahN proh-vee-zyohN*
(to) pay cash	payer comptant	*peh-yay kohN-tahN*
payment	le versement, le paiement	*luh vehrs-mahN, luh peh-mahN*
percentage	le pourcentage	*luh poor-sahN-tahzh*
purchase	l'achat *m.*	*lah-shah*
receipt	le reçu, la quittance	*luh ruh-sew, lah kee-tahNs*
revenue	le revenu	*luh ruhv-new*
safe	le coffre-fort	*luh kohfr-fohr*
sale	la vente	*lah vahNt*
(to) save	économiser, épargner	*ay-koh-noh-mee-zay, ay-pahr-nyay*
savings account	le compte d'épargne	*luh kohNt day-pahr-nyuh*
short term	à court terme	*ah koor tehrm*
(to) sign	signer	*see-nyay*
signature	la signatue	*lah see-nyah-tewr*
sum	la somme	*lah sohm*

continues

Mini-Dictionary of Banking Terms (continued)

Term	French	Pronunciation
teller	le caissier, la caissière	*luh keh-syay,* *lah keh-syehr*
total	le montant	*luh mohN-tahN*
transfer	le virement	*luh veer-mahN*
traveler's check	le chèque de voyage	*luh shehk duh vwah-yahzh*
void	annulé	*ah-new-lay*
window	le guichet	*luh gee-sheh*
(to) withdraw	retirer	*ruh-tee-ray*
withdrawal	le retrait	*luh ruh-treh*

Money can also be exchanged at *un bureau de change*. These money exchanges can be found all over the streets of Paris and all over the world. Some offer excellent rates, while others charge exorbitant commissions. It is always wise to investigate a few first.

Services I Need

If you're planning a trip to the bank, the following phrases will be most helpful in common, everyday banking situations: making deposits and withdrawals, opening a checking account, or taking out a loan.

Attention!

Before you take a trip, it's a wise idea to change at least $50 into foreign currency. Generally, the exchange rate at airports is not to your advantage.

CAUTION

Attention!

If you travel with traveler's checks, make sure to keep the numbers of the checks in a separate place—just in case. Also make sure you fully understand how traveler's checks are used.

Quelles sont les heures d'ouverture et de fermeture?
kehl sohN lay zuhr doo-vehr-tewr ay duh fehr-muh-tewr
What are the banking hours?

Je voudrais …
zhuh voo-dreh …
I would like …

… faire un dépôt (un versement)
… *fehr un day-po (uhN vehrs-mahN)*
… to make a deposit

… faire un retrait
… *fehr uhN ruh-treh*
… to make a withdrawal

… faire un paiement (un versement)
… *fehr un peh-mahN (uhN vehrs-mahN)*
… to make a payment

… faire un emprunt
… *fehr uhN nahN-pruhN*
… to take out a loan

… toucher un chèque
… *too-shay uhN shehk*
… to cash a check

... ouvrir un compte
... oo-vreer uhN kohNt
... to open an account

... fermer un compte
... fehr-may uhN kohNt
... to close an account

... changer de l'argent
... shahN-zhay duh lahr-zhahN
... to change some money

Est-ce que je recevrai un relevé mensuel?
ehs-kuh zhuh ruh-sehv-ray uhN ruh-lvay mahN-swehl
Will I get a monthly statement?

Quel est le cours du change aujourd'hui?
kehl eh luh koor dew shahNzh o-zhoor-dwee
What is today's exchange rate?

Avez-vous un distributeur (guichet) automatique de billets?
ah-vay voo uhN dee-stree-bew-tuhr (gee-sheh) o-to-mah-teek duh bee-yeh
Do you have an automatic teller machine?

Comment s'en sert-on?
kohN-mahN sahN sehr-tohN
How does one use it?

Je voudrais prendre un emprunt personnel.
zhuh voo-dreh prahNdr uhN nahN-pruhN pehr-soh-nehl
I'd like to make a personal loan.

Je voudrais prendre une hypothèque.
zhuh voo-dreh prahNdr ewn nee-poh-tehk
I'd like to take out a mortgage.

Quelle est la période d'amortissement?
kehl eh lah pay-ryohd dah-mohr-tees-mahN
What is the time period of the loan?

À combien sont les paiements mensuels?
ah kohN-byaN sohN lay peh-mahN mahN-swehl
How much are the monthly payments?

Quel est le taux d'intérêt?
kehl eh luh to daN-tay-reh
What is the interest rate?

Quand faut-il commencer à faire des paiements?
kahN fo-teel koh-mahN-say ah fehr day peh-mahN
When is it necessary to start making payments?

These Are My Needs

Everyone needs more money. It seems that the more you have, the more you want. In Chapter 20, you learned that the verb *devoir* followed by an infinitive could be used to express need. Another way of expressing that someone needs to or must do something is to use the expression *il faut que …* (*eel fo kuh;* it is necessary that). *Il faut que* and other expressions showing necessity are followed by a special verb form called the subjunctive.

The subjunctive is a mood, not a tense, and it expresses wishing, wanting, emotion, and doubt. It is used after many phrases showing uncertainty and after certain conjunctions as well. Those applications will not be discussed in this book.

Since the subjunctive is not a tense (a verb form indicating time), the present subjunctive can be used to refer to actions in the present or the future. The past subjunctive will not be discussed in this book since its use is limited.

To use the subjunctive, certain conditions must be met:

- Two different clauses must exist with two different subjects.
- The two clauses must be joined by *que.*
- One of the clauses must show need, necessity, emotion, or doubt.

Here are some examples showing when you would use the subjunctive:

Il faut que je travaille dur.
eel fo kuh zhuh trah-vahy dewr
I (I'll) have to work hard.

Il faut que nous téléphonions à notre agent.
eel fo kuh noo tay-lay-fohn-yohN ah nohtr ah-zhahN
We (We'll) have to call our agent.

Il faut qu'ils se reposent.
eel fo keel suh ruh-poz
They (They'll) have to rest.

Formation of the Present Subjunctive

To form the present subjunctive of regular verbs and some irregular verbs, as shown in the following table, drop the *-ent* ending from the *ils/elles* form of the present and add these endings:

je	*-e*	nous	*-ions*
tu	*-es*	vous	*-iez*
il, elle, on	*-e*	ils, elles	*-ent*

The Present Subjunctive of Regular Verbs

-er Verbs	*-ir* Verbs	*-re* Verbs
parler	finir	attendre
ils parl**ent**	ils finiss**ent**	ils attend**ent**
… que je parle … *kuh zhuh pahrl*	… que je finisse … *kuh zhuh fee-nees*	… que j'attende … *kuh zhah-tahNd*
… que tu parles … *kuh tew pahrl*	… que tu finisses … *kuh tew fee-nees*	… que tu attendes … *que tew ah-tahNd*
… qu'il parle … *keel pahrl*	… qu'il finisse … *keel fee-nees*	… qu'il attende … *keel ah-tahNd*
… que nous parlions … *kuh noo pahr-lyohN*	… que nous finissions … *kuh noo fee-nee-syohN*	… que nous attendions … *kuh noo zah-tahN-dyohN*
… que vous parliez … *kuh voo pahr-lyay*	… que vous finissiez … *kuh voo fee-nee-syay*	… que vous attendiez … *kuh voo zah-tahN-dyay*
… qu'ils parlent … *keel pahrl*	… qu'ils finissent … *keel fee-nees*	… qu'ils attendent … *keel zah-tahNd*

Shoe Verbs

As shown in the following table, shoe verbs and verbs that are conjugated like shoe verbs follow the shoe rule when forming the subjunctive.

The Subjunctive of Shoe Verbs

Boire	Ils Boivent
… que je boive	**… que nous buvions**
… que tu boives	**… que vous buviez**
… qu'il boive	… qu'ils boivent

continues

The Subjunctive of Shoe Verbs (continued)

Prendre	**Ils Prennent**
… que je prenne	**… que nous prenions**
… que tu prennes	**… que vous preniez**
… qu'il prenne	… qu'ils prennent
Manger	**Ils Mangent**
… que je mange	**… que nous mangions**
… que tu manges	**… que vous mangiez**
… qu'il mange	… qu'ils mangent
Envoyer	**Ils Envoient**
… que je envoie	**… que nous envoyions**
… que tu envoies	**… que vous envoyiez**
… qu'il envoie	… qu'ils envoient
Acheter	**Ils Achetent**
… que je achète	**… que nous achetions**
… que tu achètes	**… que vous achetiez**
… qu'il achète	… qu'ils achètent
Préférer	**Ils Préfèrent**
… que je préfère	**… que nous préférions**
… que tu préfères	**… que vous préfériez**
… qu'il préfère	… qu'ils préfèrent
Appeler	**Ils Appellent**
… que j'appelle	**… que nous appelions**
… que tu appelles	**… que vous appeliez**
… qu'il appelle	… qu'ils appellent

Verbs Irregular in the Subjunctive

Some verbs follow no rules and must be memorized. The following table lists the verbs that will prove to be most useful.

Note: There are no changes to *-cer* shoe verbs in the subjunctive because *c* followed by *e* or *i* always produces a soft sound.

… que je commen*ce* … que nous commen*ci*ons

Irregular Subjunctives

Aller	
… que j'aille (*ahy*)	**… que nous allions** (*ah-lyohN*)
… que tu ailles (*ahy*)	**… que vous alliez** (*ah-lyay*)
… qu'il aille (*ahy*)	… qu'ils aillent (*ahy*)

Vouloir	
… que je veuille (*vuhy*)	**… que nous voulions** (*voo-lyohN*)
… que tu veuilles (*vuhy*)	**… que vous vouliez** (*voo-lyay*)
… qu'il veuille (*vuhy*)	… qu'ils veuillent (*vuhy*)

Faire	
… que je fasse (*fahs*)	… que nous fassions (*fah-syohN*)
… que tu fasses (*fahs*)	… que vous fassiez (*fah-syay*)
… qu'il fasse (*fahs*)	… qu'ils fassent (*fahs*)

Pouvoir	
… que je puisse (*pwees*)	… que nous puissions (*pwee-syohN*)
… que tu puisses (*pwees*)	… que vous puissiez (*pwee-syay*)
… qu'il puisse (*pwees*)	… qu'ils puissent (*pwees*)

Savoir	
… que je sache (*sahsh*)	… que nous sachions (*sah-shyohN*)
… que tu saches (*sahsh*)	… que vous sachiez (*sah-shyay*)
… qu'il sache (*sahsh*)	… qu'ils sachent (*sahsh*)

Avoir	
… que j'aie (*ay*)	… que nous ayons (*ay-yohN*)
… que tu aies (*ay*)	… que vous ayez (*ay-yay*)
… qu'il ait (*ay*)	… qu'ils aient (*ay*)

Être	
… que je sois (*swah*)	… que nous soyons (*swah-yohN*)
… que tu sois (*swah*)	… que vous soyez (*swah-yay*)
… qu'il soit (*swah*)	… qu'ils soient (*swah*)

There's So Much to Do

Do you have a million things to do this afternoon? Me, too. There's no escaping the necessary hassles and chores of our daily routine. Express what these people have to do using *il faut que* + subjunctive.

Example:
il/travailler Il faut qu'il travaille.

1. nous/préparer le dîner ______
2. elle/finir son travail ______
3. ils/attendre un coup de téléphone ______
4. je/téléphone à mon bureau ______
5. vous/accomplir beaucoup ______
6. tu/descendre en ville ______
7. je/se lever de bonne heure ______
8. il/aller à la banque ______
9. vous/être en ville à midi ______
10. tu/acheter un cadeau ______
11. elles/prendre un taxi ______
12. nous/faire les courses ______

Other Expressions of Need That Take the Subjunctive

Il faut que is a very common expression used with the subjunctive. There are, however, many other expressions that require the subjunctive. To speak properly, you should familiarize yourself with them, as shown in the following table.

Other Expressions Requiring the Subjunctive

Expression	French	Pronunciation
It is imperative that …	Il est impératif que …	*eel eh taN-pay-rah-teef kuh …*
It is important that …	Il est important que …	*eel eh taN-pohr-tahN kuh …*
It is necessary that …	Il est nécessaire que …	*eel eh nay-seh-sehr kuh …*
It is preferable that …	Il est préférable que …	*eel eh pray-fay-rahbl kuh …*
It is urgent that …	Il est urgent que …	*eel eh tewr-zhahN kuh …*
It is better that …	Il vaut mieux que …	*eel vo myuh kuh …*

The Least You Need to Know

- French banks are modern and efficient and provide the same services as banks in the United States.
- Use *devoir* (conjugated) + infinitive to express that the subject needs or has to do something.
- The subjunctive is used to express needs, wants, emotions, and doubts.
- To form the present subjunctive of most verbs, drop the *-ent* ending from the third person plural (*ils*) form and add the subjunctive endings: *-e*, *-es*, *-e*, *-ions*, *-iez*, *-ent*.

Appendix A

Answer Key

Chapter 2

Wow Them with Your Accent

1. *ay-reek luh pahrk*
2. *koh-leht lah-pyehr*
3. *mee-shehl luh-shyaN*
4. *ah-laN luh-shah*
5. *ah-nyehs luh-loo*
6. *roh-lahN lah-moosh*
7. *pah-treek luh-buhf*
8. *soh-lahNzh lah-foh-reh*

Chapter 3

You Understand So Much Already!

1. The blouse is orange.
2. The service is horrible.
3. The sandwich is immense.
4. The chef is excellent.

1. The pullover is rose (pink).
2. The film is important.
3. The question is unique.
4. The trip is urgent.

You've Got It!

1. The doctor helps the baby.
2. Mom prepares soup and salad.
3. The family watches television.
4. The tourist reserves the room.
5. The child adores modern music.

What Do You Think?

1. Le jardin est splendide.
2. La fontaine est superbe.
3. L'artiste est populaire.
4. La musique est splendide.
5. Le restaurant est élégant.
6. L'hôtel est élégant.

Special Tricks

hôtesse; hostess
île; isle (island)
pâte; paste (also an English word pâte)
intérêt; interest
état; state
étrange; strange
étude; study
répondre; to respond

French Awareness

1. on the regular menu
2. that's life
3. free rein
4. stylish
5. government takeover
6. cream of the crop
7. something already seen
8. team spirit
9. accomplished task
10. awkward mistake
11. love of life
12. art object
13. best part
14. answer, please
15. meeting

You Are Well Read

1. *The Human Comedy*
2. *The Stranger*
3. *The Infernal Machine*
4. *Terrible Children*
5. *The Sentimental Education*
6. *The Miserable People*
7. *Dangerous Affairs*
8. *The Human Condition*
9. *The Hypochondriac*
10. *Nausea*

Chapter 4

Using Your Idioms I

1. au revoir
2. tout de suite
3. en retard
4. de bonne heure
5. tout à l'heure
6. de temps en temps (de temps à autre)
7. du matin au soir
8. à demain

Using Your Idioms II

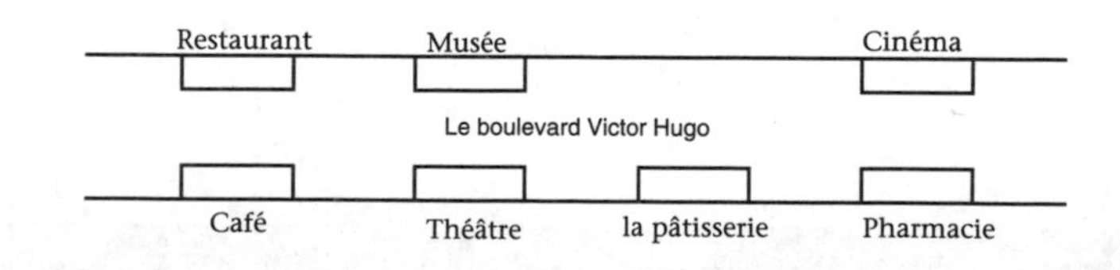

Using Your Idioms III

1. J'ai sommeil.
2. J'ai chaud.
3. J'ai faim.
4. J'ai soif.
5. J'ai tort.
6. J'ai trente ans.
7. J'ai raison.
8. J'ai froid.

Using Your Idioms IV

Sample responses:

1. mauvais
2. du soleil
3. doux
4. mauvais
5. frais

Chapter 5

Just Look It Up

1. feu
2. renvoyer, congédier
3. lumière
4. allumer
5. terre
6. atterrir
7. mieux
8. meilleur

Chapter 6

Mark Your Nouns

1. le 2. le 3. le 4. la 5. le 6. la 7. le 8. la

Mark More Nouns

1. une 2. un 3. un 4. un 5. une 6. une 7. un 8. un

What's Their Line?

1. avocate
2. dentiste
3. coiffeuse
4. facteur
5. bouchère
6. étudiant
7. chef
8. infirmière
9. pompier
10. patron
11. mannequin
12. pâtissier
13. médecin
14. ouvrier

More Than One

1. Je vois les boutiques.
2. Je vois les automobiles.
3. Je vois les croix.
4. Je vois les tapis.
5. Je vois les restaurants.
6. Je vois les magazines.
7. Je vois les palais.
8. Je vois les autobus.

Practice with Plurals

1. les châteaux
2. les lunettes
3. les gens
4. les journaux
5. les colis
6. les palais
7. les ciseaux
8. les joujoux

Chapter 7

Tu or Vous?

doctor—vous
cousin—tu
friend—tu
salesman—vous
woman—vous
two friends—vous
policeman—vous
group of friends—vous

Who's Who?

Charles—il
Lucie et Sylvie—elles
Berthe—elle
Pierre—il
Luc et Henri—ils
Robert et Suzette—ils
Janine, Charlotte, Michèle, et Roger—ils
Paul, Roland, et Annick—ils
La fête—elle
Le bal costumé—il
La musique et le décor—ils
Les vêtements—ils
Le travail et le coût—ils
La cuisine et la nourriture—elles
L'ambiance—elle
L'hôte et l'hôtesse—ils

Conjugation 101

1. traverse
2. demandent
3. cherchons
4. accompagne
5. louez
6. présentent
7. réserve
8. montes
9. parle
10. posent

Conjugation 102

1. finissons
2. réfléchit
3. jouissent
4. applaudis
5. réussit
6. choisis
7. agissez
8. remplissent

Conjugation 103

1. attends
2. descendent
3. perdons
4. répondez
5. entend
6. rends

Ask Me—I Dare You

1. Nous parlons trop?
   Nous parlons trop, n'est-ce pas?
   Est-ce que nous parlons trop?
   Parlons-nous trop?

2. Il descend souvent en ville?
   Il descend souvent en ville, n'est-ce pas?
   Est-ce qu'il descend souvent en ville?
   Descend-il souvent en ville?

3. Vous accomplissez beaucoup?
   Vous accomplissez beaucoup, n'est-ce pas?
   Est-ce que vous accomplissez beaucoup?
   Accomplissez-vous beaucoup?

4. Marie téléphone toujours à sa famille?
   Marie téléphone toujours à sa famille, n'est-ce pas?
   Est-ce que Marie téléphone toujours à sa famille?
   Marie téléphone-t-elle toujours à sa famille?

5. Tu attends toujours les autres?
   Tu attends toujours les autres, n'est-ce pas?
   Est-ce que tu attends toujours les autres?
   Attends-tu toujours les autres?

6. Les garçons jouent au tennis?
   Les garçons jouent au tennis, n'est-ce pas?
   Est-ce que les garçons jouent au tennis?
   Les garçons jouent-ils au tennis?

7. Elles écoutent le guide.
   Elles écoutent le guide, n'est-ce pas?
   Est-ce qu'elles écoutent le guide?
   Écoutent-elles le guide?

8. Luc et Anne semblent heureux?
   Luc et Anne semblent heureux, n'est-ce pas?
   Est-ce que Luc et Anne semblent heureux?
   Luc et Anne semblent-ils heureux?

It's All About You

Sample responses:

1. Je ne fume jamais.
2. Je ne crie pas.
3. Je ne joue plus au tennis.
4. Je ne danse pas bien.
5. Je parle français.
6. Je bavarde avec des amis.
7. Je ne dîne pas tôt.
8. J'aime réussir.

Your Trip Awaits

1. Voyages de la Jeunesse
2. Loisirs et Vacances
3. Maison de Voyages
4. Sports et Loisirs

Chapter 8

Using *Être*

1. suis en train de
2. sommes d'accord
3. sont sur le point d'
4. est à
5. êtes de retour

An Introductory Conversation

Sample responses:

1. Bonjour! Ça va?
2. Je m'appelle …
3. Três bien, merci. Et vous?
4. Je suis de …
5. Je suis professeur.

Getting the Scoop

Sample responses:

A. Robert est d'où? Il voyage avec qui? Il voyage où? Comment est-ce qu'il voyage? Ils passent combien de mois en France? Où est-ce qu'ils passent deux mois? Qu'est-ce qu'ils désirent visiter? Quand retournent-ils à Pittsburgh?

B. Tu t'appelles comment? Tu es d'où? Qu'est-ce que tu cherches? Pourquoi cherches-tu une correspondante américaine? Tu désires pratiquer quoi? Quand parles-tu anglais? Qu'est-ce que tu adores? Comment es-tu?

Chapter 9

A Sense of Belonging

1. La mère de Michael
2. Le père d'André et de Marie
3. Les grands-parents des jeunes filles
4. L'oncle du garçon
5. Le grand-père de la famille
6. Le frère de l'enfant

It's a Matter of Preference

Sample responses:

1. Mes actrices favorites sont ….
2. Ma chanson favorite est ….
3. Mes restaurants favoris sont ….
4. Mon sport favori est ….
5. Ma couleur favorite est ….
6. Mon film favori est ….

Totally Possessed

1. leur
2. sa
3. ton
4. mon
5. vos
6. son
7. ses
8. leur
9. son
10. notre

Using *Avoir*

1. as le temps
2. a l'habitude de
3. avez de la chance
4. ont l'occasion de
5. ai l'intention de
6. a lieu

Creative Descriptions

Sample responses:

1. grande, magnfique
2. bons, intéressants
3. jeune, intelligent
4. belles, extraordinaires
5. grand, superbe

Chapter 10

Airline Advice

1. For your comfort and security, take only one carry-on suitcase into the cabin. Any dangerous articles will be removed from it at the security check.
2. Choose sturdy bags that lock. Place identification on the outside and inside of all bags. Don't put anything of value in your bags that will be placed in the hold. Carry on anything important.

Airport Signs

1. c
2. e
3. a
4. f
5. b
6. d

Where To?

1. allons
2. va
3. vas
4. vont
5. vais
6. allez

Ask for It

1. Les toilettes, s'il vous plaît.
   Où sont les toilettes?
2. Le contôle des passeports, s'il vous plaît.
   Où est le contrôle des passeports?
3. La douane, s'il vous plaît.
   Où est la douane?
4. Les ascenseurs, s'il vous plaît.
   Où sont les ascenseurs?
5. La sortie, s'il vous plaît.
   Où est la sortie?
6. Le bureau de change, s'il vous plaît.
   Où est le bureau de change?

Giving Commands

Verb	Tu	Vous	Meaning
aller	Va!	Allez!	Go!
continuer	Continue!	Continuez!	Continue!
descendre	Descends!	Descendez!	Go down!
marcher	Marche!	Marchez!	Walk!
monter	Monte!	Montez!	Go Up!
passer	Passe!	Passez!	Pass!
prendre (Chapter 11)	Prends!	Prenez!	Take!
tourner	Tourne!	Tournez!	Turn!
traverser	Traverse!	Traversez!	Cross!

Chapter 11

Using *Quel*

1. Quel train?
2. Quelle couleur?
3. Quelles blouses?
4. Quels journaux?
5. Quelle voiture?
6. Quelles cassettes?
7. Quel match?
8. Quels plats?

Off You Go

Make reservations 24 hours in advance. You must rent for 1 day. Rental is based on a 24-hour period. You have unlimited kilometers. You can drop off your car at a sister agency. You are only liable for 300 euros in case of damage. There is an additional small fee in case of theft. There's 24-hour road service. You must pay for your own gas. Prices are subject to change.

Your Number's Up?

1. Quarante-cinq, soixante-sept, quatre-vingt-neuf, soixante-dix-sept
2. Quarante-huit, vingt et un, quinze, cinquante et un
3. Quarante-six, seize, quatre-vingt-dix-huit, treize
4. Quarante-trois, onze, soixante-douze, quatre-vingt-quatorze

Chapter 12

Hotel Amenities

The amenities include a bar, a sauna, a luxury room, special dinner, a beach, conference rooms, a casino, spa services, and transportation.

Using *-cer* Verbs

1. commence
2. renonçons
3. remplaces
4. avance
5. annoncent

Using *-ger* Verbs

1. range
2. déranges
3. partageons
4. nagez
5. arrangent

Using *-yer* Verbs

1. paies (payes)
2. emploie
3. ennuyez
4. nettoie
5. essaie (essaye)

Using *e* + Consonant + *-er* Verbs

1. promène
2. appelez
3. enlève
4. jette
5. amenons

Using *é* + Consonant + *-er* Verbs

1. célèbre
2. Répétez
3. protégeons
4. espèrent
5. possède

Chapter 13

What's the Date?

1. le cinq août
2. le quatorze août
3. le vingt-deux août
4. le huit août
5. le six août
6. le trente et un juillet

Using *Faire*

1. font un voyage
2. faites la queue
3. fais venir
4. faisons une promenade
5. fait la connaissance de
6. fais des achats (emplettes)
7. fait attention
8. font une partie de

Chapter 14

Take Me to the Zoo

In Paris—Parc Zoologique de Paris

Closest to Paris—Parc Zoologique du Bois d'Attily

Farthest from Paris—Parc Zoologique du Château de Thoiry

Open all year—Parc Zoologique du Bois d'Attily

Open every day—Parc Zoologique du Château de Thoiry, Parc Zoologique de Paris

Picnic—Parc Zoologique de Paris

Animals roam free—Parc Zoologique du Château de Thoiry

Your Sentiments Exactly

Sample responses:

1. C'est chouette.
2. C'est extra.
3. C'est embêtant.
4. C'est merveilleux.
5. C'est formidable.
6. Je déteste.
7. C'es génial.
8. C'est ennuyeux.
9. C'est la barbe.
10. C'est sensationnel.

Exactly Where Are You Going?

1. Je vais en Espagne.
2. Je vais en Chine.
3. Je vais au Mexique.
4. Je vais en Russie.
5. Je vais en Italie.
6. Je vais en Angleterre.
7. Je vais en Égypte.
8. Je vais en France.
9. Je vais aux États-Unis.
10. Je vais aux États-Unis.

Using *y*

Sample responses:

1. J'y vais.
2. J'y reste.
3. Je n'y passe pas mes vacances.
4. Je vais y descendre.
5. Je vais y dîner.
6. Je ne vais pas y penser.

Make a Suggestion

1. Voyageons-y! N'y voyageons pas!
2. Allons-y! N'y allons pas!
3. Restons-y! N'y restons pas!
4. Passons-y la journée! N'y passons pas la journée!
5. Assistons-y! N'y assistons pas!

Chapter 15

Put It On

Sample responses:

Work—Je mets une robe, des bas, des chaussures, un bracelet, une montre, une bague, et un collier.

Beach—Je mets un bikini et dcs sandales.

Dinner party—Je mets une robe du soir, des bas, des chaussures, et des bijoux.

Friend's house—Je mets un jean, une chemise, des chaussettes, des tennis, et une montre.

Skiing—Je mets un pantalon, un pull, des chaussettes, des chaussures, un manteau, un chapeau, et des gants.

What Are You Looking For?

Sample responses:

Madame Paris—perfumes, beauty products, jewelry, scarfs, accessories, and leather goods

Vivianne—large-size, ready-to-wear clothing for women and assorted accessories

Variations—Men and women's clothing: sweaters, polos, blouses, skirts, and ensembles

Using Direct Object Pronouns

Sample responses:

1. Je l'aime.
2. Je ne les prends pas.
3. Je la choisis.
4. Je les regarde.
5. Je ne l'achète pas.
6. Je ne l'adore pas.

Using Indirect Object Pronouns

1. Offre-lui une montre.
2. Offre-leur un tableau.
3. Offre-leur des cravates.
4. Offre-leur des robes.
5. Offre-lui un bracelet.
6. Offre-lui un pull.

What Do You Think?

1. Cette large cravate à rayures est laide.
2. Ce short en tartan est trop criard.
3. Cette chemise à pois est abominable.
4. Ce petit tee-shirt à rayures est trop serré.

Chapter 16

Going Shopping

Je vais à l'épicerie.
Je vais à la pâtisserie.
Je vais à la boucherie.
Je vais à la fruiterie.
Je vais à la poissonerie.
Je vais à la confiserie.
Je vais à la crémerie.
Je vais à la boulangerie.

Serious Shopping

Sample responses:

1. De la viande—du jambon, du rosbif, du poulet
2. Des pâtisseries—des éclairs, des choux à la crême, un gâteau
3. Du pain—des croissants, des brioches
4. Des légumes—des carottes, des haricots verts, des asperges
5. Des fruits—des pommes, des poires, des raisins
6. De la charcuterie—du pâté, du lard, de la mortadelle

Your Likes and Dislikes

Sample responses:

1. Je déteste les fruits.
2. J'adore les légumes.
3. J'aime la viande.
4. J'adore le poisson.
5. J'aime le pain.
6. J'adore le gâteau.

It's a Puzzle to Me

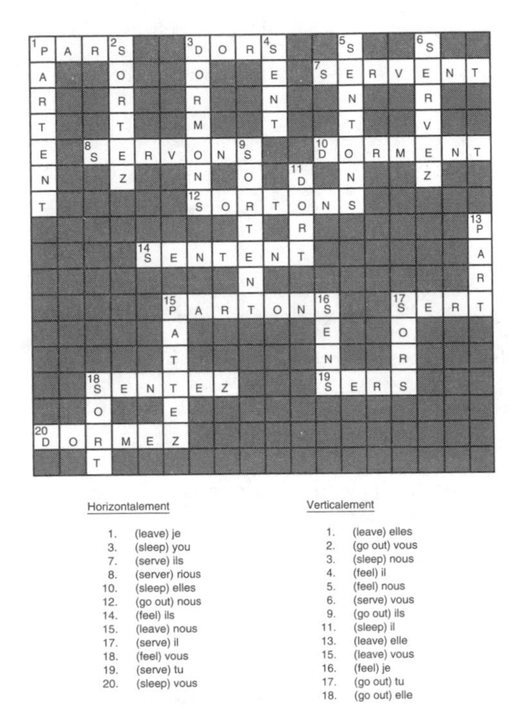

Chapter 17

Which Restaurant Do You Prefer?

1. Fine, traditional cooking
2. French cooking and Lebanese specialties
3. Seafood
4. Italian specialties
5. English food
6. American food, music every evening
7. French food
8. Lebanese and French specialties
9. Vietnamese and Chinese specialties
10. Vietnamese and Chinese specialities
11. Hot and cold buffet, ice cream, and pastries
12. Fish, Italian specialties
13. Italian specialties
14. Drinks and music
15. Ice cream
16. Seafood
17. Businessman's special

Oh, Waiter

Il me faut

1. une salière
2. une serviette
3. une fourchette
4. un couteau
5. une assiette
6. une cuiller

Yes or No?

1. N'en mange pas. Manges-en.
2. Prépares-en. N'en prépare pas.
3. Prends-en. N'en prends pas.
4. N'en choisis pas. Choisis-en.
5. Achètes-en. N'en achète pas.

Chapter 18

I'll Meet You There

1. Tu peux faire du tennis. Tu veux aller au court.
2. Nous pouvons faire du golf. Nous voulons aller au parcours.
3. Vous pouvez faire de la pêche. Vous voulez aller à la mer.
4. Elle peut faire du base-ball. Elle veut aller au stade.
5. Ils peuvent faire du patin. Ils veulent aller à la patinoire.

Doing the Inviting

1. Tu veux aller à la montagne?
2. Vous voulez aller à la piste de ski?
3. On va au sentier?
4. Allons à la patinoire.
5. Allons à la montagne.
6. Ça te dit d'aller à la mer?

Will You Be Joining Us?

Sample responses:

C'est chouette.
Je n'ai pas envie.
C'est une bonne idée.
Ça dépend.
Je regrette.

I Think …

Sample responses:

C'est émouvant.
Je déteste.
C'est bidon.
C'est un bon film.
C'est amusant.
C'est toujours la même chose.

Let's Play

1. jouons au
2. jouez de la
3. joues de la
4. jouent au
5. joue du
6. joue aux

What Do You Do Well?

Sample responses:

1. Je parle français courramment.
2. Je joue mal du piano.
3. Je joue bien au golf.
4. Je cuisine parfaitement bien.
5. Je pense sérieusement.
6. Je travaille dur.
7. Je voyage souvent.
8. Je chante beaucoup.
9. Je danse assez bien.
10. Je nage peu.

Chapter 19

These Boots Were Made for Walking

He picks up and then delivers repaired shoes.

I Can't See Without Them

The optometrist promises to have your glasses ready in an hour and to sell special high-correction lenses that don't deform your face.

Do You Get the Picture?

It buys (at the highest rate), sells (at the lowest rate), trades, and repairs the most famous brand cameras.

Stress Relief

1. nous 2. lui/moi 3. toi 4. elle 5. eux 6. vous

You Compare

Sample responses:

Ma soeur est plus grande que moi.
Ma mère cuisine mieux que moi.
Moi, je travaille plus dur que mon mari.
Mon mari, lui, il est plus patient que moi.

Chapter 20

What's Wrong?

Sample responses:

1. Je tousse. J'éternue. J'ai des frissons. J'ai de la fièvre.
2. J'éternue. J'ai une migraine.

3. J'ai mal à la cheville. J'ai de la douleur.
4. J'ai mal à la tête. J'ai du mal à dormir. J'ai de la douleur.

Me? A Hypochondriac?

1. Je tousse depuis deux semaines. Ça fait deux semaines que je tousse. Il y a deux semaines que je tousse. Voilà deux semaines que je tousse.
2. J'ai mal à la tête depuis trois jours. Ça fait trois jours que j'ai mal à la tête. Il y a trois jours que j'ai mal à la tête. Voilà trois jours que j'ai mal à la tête.
3. J'ai mal au ventre depuis un mois. Ça fait un mois que j'ai mal au ventre. Il y a un mois que j'ai mal au ventre. Voilà un mois que j'ai mal au ventre.

Using Reflexive Verbs

Sample responses:

1. Je me réveille. Je me lève. Je me déshabille. Je me lave. Je me baigne. Je m'habille. Je me coiffe. Je me maquille. (Je me rase.) Je me regarde dans la glace. Je me prépare.
2. Je vais me déshabiller. Je vais me laver. Je vais m'habiller. Je vais me coucher. Je vais m'endormir.

You're In Command

1. Baigne-toi. Ne te baigne pas. Baignez-vous. Ne vous baignez pas.
2. Dépêche-toi. Ne te dépêche pas. Dépêchez-vous. Ne vous dépêchez pas.
3. Rase-toi. Ne te rase pas. Rasez-vous. Ne vous rasez pas.
4. Habille-toi. Ne t'habille pas. Habillez-vous. Ne vous habillez pas.
5. Brosse-toi les dents. Ne te brosse pas les dents. Brossez-vous les dents. Ne vous brossez pas les dents.
6. Amuse-toi. Ne t'amuse pas. Amusez-vous. Ne vous amusez pas.

Chapter 21

What Do You Need?

Sample responses:

1. Il me faut des aspirines et des gouttes nasales.
2. Il me faut des aspirines.
3. Il me faut un antiseptique et des pansements.
4. Il me faut du lait de magnésie.
5. Il me faut un rasoir, des lames de rasoir, et de la crème à raser.
6. Il me faut un biberon et une sucette.

You Didn't, Did You?

1. J'ai rempli … Je n'ai pas rempli …
2. Tu as répondu … Tu n'as pas répondu …
3. Tu as obéi … Tu n'as pas obéi …
4. Nous avons acheté … Nous n'avons pas acheté …
5. Elle a cherché … Elle n'a pas cherché …
6. Ils ont attendu … Ils n'ont pas attendu …

Your Past Is in Question

1. Avons-nous travaillé …? N'avons-nous pas travaillé …?
2. A-t-elle obéi …? N'a-t-elle pas obéi …?
3. Ont-ils perdu …? N'ont-ils pas perdu …?
4. Avez-vous trop maigri …? N'avez-vous pas trop maigri …?
5. As-tu trop mangé …? N'as-tu pas trop mangé …?
6. A-t-il attendu …? N'a-t-il pas attendu …?

Who Did What?

1. Il a fait …
2. Nous avons été …
3. Tu as vu …
4. J'ai pu …
5. Elles ont pris …
6. Vous avez lu …
7. Ils ont eu …
8. Elle a fait …
9. Je suis arrivée …
10. Nous sommes revenus …
11. Ils sont restés …
12. Tu es partie …
13. Vous êtes allés …
14. Elle est sortie …
15. Ils sont descendus …
16. Elles sont rentrées …

Chapter 22

Calling from Your Hotel Room

1. 6
2. 7
3. 1 + 16
4. 1
5. 1 + 19
6. 2 + room number
7. 5
8. 4

Please Phone Home

Automatically—Lift the receiver. When you get a dial tone, dial 19; you'll get another tone. Give the area code for the country you are calling, the area code of the zone you are calling, and then dial the number.

With the help of a France *télécom* agent—Lift the receiver. When you get a dial tone, dial 19; you'll get another dial tone. Then dial 33 followed by the code for the country you are calling. A French operator will pick up.

I Can't Talk Now

1. Elle doit réparer …
2. Nous devons aller …
3. Tu dois sortir …
4. Vous devez faire …
5. Ils doivent travailler.
6. Je dois partir …

Making Excuses

1. Je me suis cassé le bras.
2. Elle s'est réveillée tard.
3. Nous nous sommes occupés d'autre chose.
4. Ils se sont mis à travailler.
5. Vous vous êtes levées à midi.
6. Tu t'es couchée tôt.

Chapter 23

Using *Savoir* and *Connaître*

1. savent
2. sais
3. connaissez
4. savons
5. connais
6. connaît
7. savez
8. connaissons

Imperfect Redux

avoir (to have)	nous avons	elle avait
boire (to drink)	nous buvons	je buvais
connaître (to be acquainted with)	nous connaissons	vous connaissiez
devoir (to have to)	nous devons	tu devais
dire (to say, tell)	nous disons	ils disaient
dormir (to sleep)	nous dormons	nous dormions
écrire (to write)	nous écrivons	elles écrivaient
faire (to make, do)	nous faisons	vous faisiez
lire (to read)	nous lisons	je lisais
mettre (to put [on])	nous mettons	nous mettions
partir (to leave)	nous partons	tu partais
pouvoir (to be able to)	nous pouvons	elle pouvait
prendre (to take)	nous prenons	ils prenaient
recevoir (to receive)	nous recevons	vous receviez
savoir (to know)	nous savons	elles savaient

sentir (to feel, smell)	nous sentons	il sentait
servir (to serve)	nous servons	elle servait
sortir (to go out)	nous sortons	tu sortais
voir (to see)	nous voyons	elles voyaient
vouloir (to want)	nous voulons	je voulais

Passé Composé or *Imparfait*?

1. était
2. était
3. chantaient
4. faisais
5. a sonné
6. était
7. a demandé
8. voulais
9. ai dit
10. suis parti(e)
11. sommes allé(e)s
12. nous sommes arrêté(e)s
13. sommes arrivé(e)s
14. brillait
15. faisait
16. avons trouvé
17. commencions
18. a attaqué
19. a crié
20. s'est échappée
21. avons passé
22. était

Chapter 24

Do You Know Your Computer?

Sample responses:

1. J'ai un P.C.
2. J'emploie un modem, une souris, et un scanneur.
3. Il a cent megabytes de mémoire.
4. La vitesse est ….
5. J'emploie un programme de traitement de texte et une feuille de calcul.

Verbs Irregular in the Future

Future
tu auras
nous devrons
il enverra
elles seront
je ferai
vous pourrez
nous recevrons

continues

Verbs Irregular in the Future (continued)

Future
ils sauront
tu viendras
je verrai
elle voudra

Predicting the Future

Aries Exceptional financial opportunities will present themselves.

Taurus You will have a very good month.

Gemini You will have tension and arguments with your colleagues.

Cancer You will be in good shape.

Leo You will concentrate on your financial affairs.

Virgo You will make an important decision concerning your professional future.

Libra You will be in harmony with your friends.

Scorpio Your ambition will serve you.

Sagittarius You will have important discussions with family members.

Capricorn Everything will go well for you.

Aquarius You will meet an important person.

Pisces You will be busy every night and will have many weekend plans.

Chapter 25

Purchasing Furniture

Your furniture will be guaranteed for five years and you will be guaranteed for recovering for two years should there be any problem with the manufacturing.

They will give a free decorating consultation and will come to give free estimates and take measurements.

You will be given a guarantee against all risks for one year.

Your old furniture will be removed.

All guarantees are free throughout continental France.

Irregular Verbs in the Conditional

Conditional
tu aurais
nous devrions
il enverrait
elles seraient
je ferais
vous pourriez
nous recevrions
ils sauraient
tu viendrais
je verrais
elle voudrait

Chapter 26

There's So Much to Do

Il faut que …

1. nous préparions …
2. elle finisse …
3. ils attendent …
4. je téléphone …
5. vous accomplissiez …
6. tu descendes …
7. je me lève …
8. il aille …
9. vous soyez …
10. tu achètes …
11. elles prennent …
12. nous fassions …

Appendix B

Verb Charts

Regular Verbs

-*er* Verbs

PARLER **to speak** Past participle: parl**é** Commands: Parle! Parlons! Parlez!

Subject	Present	Imperfect	Future	Conditional	Subjunctive
je	parl**e**	parl**ais**	parler**ai**	parler**ais**	parl**e**
tu	parl**es**	parl**ais**	parler**as**	parler**ais**	parl**es**
il	parl**e**	parl**ait**	parler**a**	parler**ait**	parl**e**
nous	parl**ons**	parl**ions**	parler**ons**	parler**ions**	parl**ions**
vous	parl**ez**	parl**iez**	parler**ez**	parler**iez**	parl**iez**
ils	parl**ent**	parl**aient**	parler**ont**	parler**aient**	parl**ent**

-ir Verbs

FINIR **to finish** Past participle: fini Commands: Finis! Finissons! Finissez!

Subject	Present	Imperfect	Future	Conditional	Subjunctive
je	finis	finissais	finirai	finirais	finisse
tu	finis	finissais	finiras	finirais	finisses
il	finit	finissait	finira	finirait	finisse
nous	finissons	finissions	finirons	finirions	finissions
vous	finissez	finissiez	finirez	finiriez	finissiez
ils	finissent	finissaient	finiront	finiraient	finissent

-re Verbs

VENDRE **to sell** Past Participle: vendu Commands: Vends! Vendons! Vendez!

Subject	Present	Imperfect	Future	Conditional	Subjunctive
je	vends	vendais	vendrai	vendrais	vende
tu	vends	vendais	vendras	vendrais	vendes
il	vend	vendait	vendra	vendrait	vende
nous	vendons	vendions	vendrons	vendrions	vendions
vous	vendez	vendiez	vendrez	vendriez	vendiez
ils	vendent	vendaient	vendront	vendraient	vendent

-er Verbs with Spelling Changes

-cer Verbs

PLACER **to place** Past Participle: placé Commands: Place! Plaçons! Placez!

Subject	Present	Imperfect	Future	Conditional	Subjunctive
je	parle	plaçais	placerai	placerais	place
tu	places	plaçais	placeras	placerais	places
il	place	plaçait	placera	placerait	place
nous	plaçons	placions	placerons	placerions	placions
vous	placez	placiez	placerez	placeriez	placiez
ils	placent	plaçaient	placeront	placeraient	placent

-ger Verbs

MANGER **to eat** Past participle: mang**é** Commands: Mange! Mangeons! Mangez!

Subject	Present	Imperfect	Future	Conditional	Subjunctive
je	mang**e**	mang**eais**	manger**ai**	manger**ais**	mang**e**
tu	mang**es**	mang**eais**	manger**as**	manger**ais**	mang**es**
il	mang**e**	mang**eait**	manger**a**	manger**ait**	mang**e**
nous	mang**eons**	mang**ions**	manger**ons**	manger**ions**	mang**ions**
vous	mang**ez**	mang**iez**	manger**ez**	manger**iez**	mang**iez**
ils	mang**ent**	mang**eaient**	manger**ont**	manger**aient**	mang**ent**

-yer Verbs

EMPLOYER **to use** Past participle: employ**é** Commands: Emploie! Employons! Employez!

Subject	Present	Imperfect	Future	Conditional	Subjunctive
je	emploi**e**	employ**ais**	emploier**ai**	emploier**ais**	emploi**e**
tu	emploi**es**	employ**ais**	emploier**as**	emploicr**ais**	emploi**es**
il	emploi**e**	employ**ait**	emploier**a**	emploier**ait**	emploi**e**
nous	employ**ons**	employ**ions**	emploier**ons**	emploier**ions**	employ**ions**
vous	employ**ez**	employ**iez**	emploier**ez**	emploier**iez**	employ**iez**
ils	emploi**ent**	employ**aient**	emploier**ont**	emploier**aient**	emploi**ent**

-e + Consonant + *-er* Verbs

ACHETER **to speak** Past participle: achet**é** Commands: Achète! Achetons! Achetez!

Subject	Present	Imperfect	Future	Conditional	Subjunctive
je	achète	achet**ais**	achèter**ai**	achèter**ais**	achète
tu	achèt**es**	achet**ais**	achèter**as**	achèter**ais**	achèt**es**
il	achète	achet**ait**	achèter**a**	achèter**ait**	achète
nous	achet**ons**	achet**ions**	achèter**ons**	achèter**ions**	achet**ions**
vous	achet**ez**	achet**iez**	achèter**ez**	achèter**iez**	achet**iez**
ils	achèt**ent**	achet**aient**	achèter**ont**	achèter**aient**	achèt**ent**

-*er* Verbs with Double Consonants

APPELER **to speak** Past participle: appel**é** Commands: Appelle! Appelons! Appelez!

Subject	Present	Imperfect	Future	Conditional	Subjunctive
je	appell**e**	appel**ais**	appeller**ai**	appeller**ais**	appell**e**
tu	appell**es**	appel**ais**	appeller**as**	appeller**ais**	appell**es**
il	appell**e**	appel**ait**	appeller**a**	appeller**ait**	appell**e**
nous	appel**ons**	appel**ions**	appeller**ons**	appeller**ions**	appel**ions**
vous	appel**ez**	appel**iez**	appeller**ez**	appeller**iez**	appel**iez**
ils	appell**ent**	appel**aient**	appeller**ont**	appeller**aient**	appell**ent**

JETER **to throw** Past participle: jet**é** Commands: Jette! Jetons! Jetez!

Subject	Present	Imperfect	Future	Conditional	Subjunctive
je	jett**e**	jet**ais**	jetter**ai**	jetter**ais**	jett**e**
tu	jett**es**	jet**ais**	jetter**as**	jetter**ais**	jett**es**
il	jett**e**	jet**ait**	jetter**a**	jetter**ait**	jett**e**
nous	jet**ons**	jet**ions**	jetter**ons**	jetter**ions**	jet**ions**
vous	jet**ez**	jet**iez**	jetter**ez**	jetter**iez**	jet**iez**
ils	jett**ent**	jet**aient**	jetter**ont**	jetter**aient**	jett**ent**

-*é* + Consonant + -*er* Verbs

RÉPÉTER **to repeat** Past participle: répét**é** Commands: Répète! Répétons! Répétez!

Subject	Present	Imperfect	Future	Conditional	Subjunctive
je	répèt**e**	répét**ais**	répéter**ai**	répéter**ais**	répèt**e**
tu	répèt**es**	répét**ais**	répéter**as**	répéter**ais**	répèt**es**
il	répèt**e**	répét**ait**	répéter**a**	répéter**ait**	répèt**e**
nous	répét**ons**	répét**ions**	répéter**ons**	répéter**ions**	répét**ons**
vous	répét**ez**	répét**iez**	répéter**ez**	répéter**iez**	répét**ez**
ils	répèt**ent**	répét**aient**	répéter**ont**	répéter**aient**	répèt**ent**

Irregular Verbs

Verbs conjugated with *être* in the past tense are indicated by an asterisk (*).

ALLER* **to go** Past participle: allé Commands: Va! Allons! Allez!

Subject	Present	Imperfect	Future	Conditional	Subjunctive
je	**vais**	allais	irai	irais	**aille**
tu	**vas**	allais	iras	irais	**ailles**
il	**va**	allait	ira	irait	**aille**
nous	**allons**	allions	irons	irions	**allions**
vous	**allez**	alliez	irez	iriez	**alliez**
ils	**vont**	allaient	iront	iraient	**aillent**

AVOIR **to have** Past participle: eu Commands: Aie! Ayons! Ayez!

Subject	Present	Imperfect	Future	Conditional	Subjunctive
j'	**ai**	avais	aurai	aurais	**aie**
tu	**as**	avais	auras	aurais	**aies**
il	**a**	avait	aura	aurait	**ait**
nous	**avons**	avions	aurons	aurions	**allions**
vous	**avez**	aviez	aurez	auriez	**alliez**
ils	**ont**	avaient	auront	auraient	**aillent**

BOIRE **to drink** Past participle: bu Commands: Bois! Buvons! Buvez!

Subject	Present	Imperfect	Future	Conditional	Subjunctive
je	**bois**	buvais	boirai	boirais	boive
tu	**bois**	buvais	boiras	boirais	boives
il	**boit**	buvait	boira	boirait	boive
nous	**buvons**	buvions	boirons	boirions	**buvions**
vous	**buvez**	buviez	boirez	boiriez	**buviez**
ils	**boivent**	buvaient	boiront	boiraient	boivent

CONNAITRE **to know** Past participle: connu Commands: Connais! Connaissons! Connaissez!

Subject	Present	Imperfect	Future	Conditional	Subjunctive
je	**connais**	connaiss**ais**	connaîtr**ai**	connaîtr**ais**	connaiss**e**
tu	**connais**	connaiss**ais**	connaîtr**as**	connaîtr**ais**	connaiss**es**
il	**connaît**	connaiss**ait**	connaîtr**a**	connaîtr**ait**	connaiss**e**
nous	**connaissons**	connaiss**ions**	connaîtr**ons**	connaîtr**ions**	connaiss**ions**
vous	**connaissez**	connaiss**iez**	connaîtr**ez**	connaîtr**iez**	connaiss**iez**
ils	**conaissent**	connaiss**aient**	connaîtr**ont**	connaîtr**aient**	connaiss**ent**

DEVOIR **to have to** Past participle: dù Commands: Dois! Devons! Devez!

Subject	Present	Imperfect	Future	Conditional	Subjunctive
je	**dois**	dev**ais**	devr**ai**	devr**ais**	doiv**e**
tu	**dois**	dev**ais**	devr**as**	devr**ais**	doiv**es**
il	**doit**	dev**ait**	devr**a**	devr**ait**	doiv**e**
nous	**devons**	dev**ions**	devr**ons**	devr**ions**	**devions**
vous	**devez**	dev**iez**	devr**ez**	devr**iez**	**deviez**
ils	**doivent**	dev**aient**	devr**ont**	devr**aient**	doiv**ent**

DIRE **to say, tell** Past participle: dit Commands: Dis! Disons! Dites!

Subject	Present	Imperfect	Future	Conditional	Subjunctive
je	**dis**	dis**ais**	dir**ai**	dir**ais**	dis**e**
tu	**dis**	dis**ais**	dir**as**	dir**ais**	dis**es**
il	**dit**	dis**ait**	dir**a**	dir**ait**	dis**e**
nous	**disons**	dis**ions**	dir**ons**	dir**ions**	dis**ions**
vous	**dites**	dis**iez**	dir**ez**	dir**iez**	dis**iez**
ils	**disent**	dis**aient**	dir**ont**	dir**aient**	dis**ent**

DORMIR **to sleep** Past participle: dormi Commands: Dors! Dormons! Dormez!

Subject	Present	Imperfect	Future	Conditional	Subjunctive
je	**dors**	dorm**ais**	dormir**ai**	dormir**ais**	dorm**e**
tu	**dors**	dorm**ais**	dormir**as**	dormir**ais**	dorm**es**
il	**dort**	dorm**ait**	dormir**a**	dormir**ait**	dorm**e**

Subject	Present	Imperfect	Future	Conditional	Subjunctive
nous	**dormons**	dorm**ions**	dormir**ons**	dormir**ions**	dorm**ions**
vous	**dormez**	dorm**iez**	dormir**ez**	dormir**iez**	dorm**iez**
ils	**dorment**	dorm**aient**	dormir**ont**	dormir**aient**	dorm**ent**

ÉCRIRE **to write** Past participle: écrit Commands: Écris! Écrivons! Écrivez!

Subject	Present	Imperfect	Future	Conditional	Subjunctive
j'	**écris**	écriv**ais**	écrir**ai**	écrir**ais**	écriv**e**
tu	**écris**	écriv**ais**	écrir**as**	écrir**ais**	écriv**es**
il	**écrit**	écriv**ait**	écrir**a**	écrir**ait**	écriv**e**
nous	**écrivons**	écriv**ions**	écrir**ons**	écrir**ions**	écriv**ions**
vous	**écrivez**	écriv**iez**	écrir**ez**	écrir**iez**	écriv**iez**
ils	**écrivent**	écriv**aient**	écrir**ont**	écrir**aient**	écriv**ent**

ÊTRE **to be** Past participle: été Commands: Sois! Soyons! Soyez!

Subject	Present	Imperfect	Future	Conditional	Subjunctive
je	**suis**	ét**ais**	ser**ai**	ser**ais**	**sois**
tu	**es**	ét**ais**	ser**as**	ser**ais**	**sois**
il	**est**	ét**ait**	ser**a**	ser**ait**	**soit**
nous	**sommes**	ét**ions**	ser**ons**	ser**ions**	**soyons**
vous	**êtes**	ét**iez**	ser**ez**	ser**iez**	**soyez**
ils	**sont**	ét**aient**	ser**ont**	ser**aient**	**soient**

FAIRE **to make, do** Past participle: fait Commands: Fais! Faisons! Faites!

Subject	Present	Imperfect	Future	Conditional	Subjunctive
je	**fais**	fais**ais**	fer**ai**	fer**ais**	**fasse**
tu	**fais**	fais**ais**	fer**as**	fer**ais**	**fasses**
il	**fait**	fais**ait**	fer**a**	fer**ait**	**fasse**
nous	**faisons**	fais**ions**	fer**ons**	fer**ions**	**fassions**
vous	**faites**	fais**iez**	fer**ez**	fer**iez**	**fassiez**
ils	**font**	fais**aient**	fer**ont**	fer**aient**	**fassent**

LIRE **to read** Past participle: lu Commands: Lis! Lisons! Lisez!

Subject	Present	Imperfect	Future	Conditional	Subjunctive
je	**lis**	lis**ais**	lir**ai**	lir**ais**	lis**e**
tu	**lis**	lis**ais**	lir**as**	lir**ais**	lis**es**
il	**lit**	lis**ait**	lir**a**	lir**ait**	lis**e**
nous	**lisons**	lis**ions**	lir**ons**	lir**ions**	lis**ions**
vous	**lisez**	lis**iez**	lir**ez**	lir**iez**	lis**iez**
ils	**lisent**	lis**aient**	lir**ont**	lir**aient**	lis**ent**

METTRE **to put** Past participle: mis Commands: Mets! Mettons! Mettez!

Subject	Present	Imperfect	Future	Conditional	Subjunctive
je	**mets**	mett**ais**	mettr**ai**	mettr**ais**	mett**e**
tu	**mets**	mett**ais**	mettr**as**	mettr**ais**	mett**es**
il	**met**	mett**ait**	mettr**a**	mettr**ait**	mett**e**
nous	**mettons**	mett**ions**	mettr**ons**	mettr**ions**	mett**ions**
vous	**mettez**	mett**iez**	mettr**ez**	mettr**iez**	mett**iez**
ils	**mettent**	mett**aient**	mettr**ont**	mettr**aient**	mett**ent**

OUVRIR **to open** Past participle: ouvert Commands: Ouvre! Ouvrons! Ouvrez!

Subject	Present	Imperfect	Future	Conditional	Subjunctive
je	**ouvre**	ouvr**ais**	ouvrir**ai**	ouvrir**ais**	ouvr**e**
tu	**ouvres**	ouvr**ais**	ouvrir**as**	ouvrir**ais**	ouvr**es**
il	**ouvre**	ouvr**ait**	ouvrir**a**	ouvrir**ait**	ouvr**e**
nous	**ouvrons**	ouvr**ions**	ouvrir**ons**	ouvrir**ions**	ouvr**ions**
vous	**ouvrez**	ouvr**iez**	ouvrir**ez**	ouvrir**iez**	ouvr**iez**
ils	**ouvrent**	ouvr**aient**	ouvrir**ont**	ouvrir**aient**	ouvr**ent**

PARTIR* **to leave** Past participle: parti Commands: Pars! Partons! Partez!

Subject	Present	Imperfect	Future	Conditional	Subjunctive
je	**pars**	part**ais**	partir**ai**	partir**ais**	part**e**
tu	**pars**	part**ais**	partir**as**	partir**ais**	part**es**
il	**part**	part**ait**	partir**a**	partir**ait**	part**e**

Subject	Present	Imperfect	Future	Conditional	Subjunctive
nous	**partons**	part**ions**	partir**ons**	partir**ions**	part**ions**
vous	**partez**	part**iez**	partir**ez**	partir**iez**	part**iez**
ils	**partent**	part**aient**	partir**ont**	partir**aient**	part**ent**

POUVOIR **to be able to, can** Past participle: pu

Subject	Present	Imperfect	Future	Conditional	Subjunctive
je	**peux puis**	pouv**ais**	pourr**ai**	pourr**ais**	**puisse**
tu	**peux**	pouv**ais**	pourr**as**	pourr**ais**	**puisses**
il	**peut**	pouv**ait**	pourr**a**	pourr**ait**	**puisse**
nous	**pouvons**	pouv**ions**	pourr**ons**	pourr**ions**	**puissions**
vous	**pouvez**	pouv**iez**	pourr**ez**	pourr**iez**	**puissiez**
ils	**peuvent**	pouv**aient**	pourr**ont**	pourr**aient**	**puissent**

PRENDRE **to take** Past participle: pris Commands: Prends! Prenons! Prenez!

Subject	Present	Imperfect	Future	Conditional	Subjunctive
je	**prends**	pren**ais**	prendr**ai**	prendr**ais**	prenn**e**
tu	**prends**	pren**ais**	prendr**as**	prendr**ais**	prenn**es**
il	**prend**	pren**ait**	prendr**a**	prendr**ait**	prenn**e**
nous	**prenons**	pren**ions**	prendr**ons**	prendr**ions**	pren**ions**
vous	**prenez**	pren**iez**	prendr**ez**	prendr**iez**	pren**iez**
ils	**prennent**	pren**aient**	prendr**ont**	prendr**aient**	prenn**ent**

RECEVOIR **to receive** Past participle: reçu Commands: Reçois! Recevons! Recevez!

Subject	Present	Imperfect	Future	Conditional	Subjunctive
je	**reçois**	recev**ais**	recevr**ai**	recevr**ais**	reçoiv**e**
tu	**reçois**	recev**ais**	recevr**as**	recevr**ais**	reçoiv**es**
il	**reçoit**	recev**ait**	recevr**a**	recevr**ait**	reçoiv**e**
nous	**recevons**	recev**ions**	recevr**ons**	recevr**ions**	**recevions**
vous	**recevez**	recev**iez**	recevr**ez**	recevr**iez**	**receviez**
ils	**reçoivent**	recev**aient**	recevr**ont**	recevr**aient**	reçoiv**ent**

SAVOIR **to know** Past participle: su Commands: Sache! Sachons! Sachiez!

Subject	Present	Imperfect	Future	Conditional	Subjunctive
je	sais	savais	saurai	saurais	sache
tu	sais	savais	sauras	saurais	saches
il	sait	savait	saura	saurait	sache
nous	savons	savions	saurons	saurions	sachions
vous	savez	saviez	saurez	sauriez	sachiez
ils	savent	savaient	sauront	sauraient	sachent

SENTIR **to feel, smell** Past participle: senti Commands: Sens! Sentons! Sentez!

Subject	Present	Imperfect	Future	Conditional	Subjunctive
je	sens	sentais	sentirai	sentirais	sente
tu	sens	sentais	sentiras	sentirais	sentes
il	sent	sentait	sentira	sentirait	sente
nous	sentons	sentions	sentirons	sentirions	sentions
vous	sentez	sentiez	sentirez	sentiriez	sentiez
ils	sentent	sentaient	sentiront	sentiraient	sentent

SERVIR **to serve** Past participle: servi Commands: Sers! Servons! Servez!

Subject	Present	Imperfect	Future	Conditional	Subjunctive
je	sers	servais	servirai	servirais	serve
tu	sers	servais	serviras	servirais	serves
il	sert	servait	servira	servirait	serve
nous	servons	servions	servirons	servirions	servions
vous	servez	serviez	servirez	serviriez	serviez
ils	servent	servaient	serviront	serviraient	servent

SORTIR* **to go out** Past participle: sorti Commands: Sors! Sortons! Sortez!

Subject	Present	Imperfect	Future	Conditional	Subjunctive
je	sors	sortais	sortirai	sortirais	sorte
tu	sors	sortais	sortiras	sortirais	sortes
il	sort	sortait	sortira	sortirait	sorte

Subject	Present	Imperfect	Future	Conditional	Subjunctive
nous	**sortons**	sort**ions**	sortir**ons**	sortir**ions**	sort**ions**
vous	**sortez**	sort**iez**	sortir**ez**	sortir**iez**	sort**iez**
ils	**sortent**	sort**aient**	sortir**ont**	sortir**aient**	sort**ent**

VENIR* **to come** Past participle: venu Commands: Viens! Venons! Venez!

Subject	Present	Imperfect	Future	Conditional	Subjunctive
je	**viens**	ven**ais**	viendr**ai**	viendr**ais**	vienn**e**
tu	**viens**	ven**ais**	viendr**as**	viendr**ais**	vienn**es**
il	**vient**	ven**ait**	viendr**a**	viendr**ait**	vienn**e**
nous	**venons**	ven**ions**	viendr**ons**	viendr**ions**	**venions**
vous	**venez**	ven**iez**	viendr**ez**	viendr**iez**	**veniez**
ils	**viennent**	ven**aient**	viendr**ont**	viendr**aient**	vienn**ent**

VOIR **to see** Past participle: vu Commands: Vois! Voyons! Voyez!

Subj.	Present	Imperfect	Future	Conditional	Subjunctive
je	**vois**	voy**ais**	verr**ai**	verr**ais**	voi**e**
tu	**vois**	voy**ais**	verr**as**	verr**ais**	voi**es**
il	**voit**	voy**ait**	verr**a**	verr**ait**	voi**e**
nous	**voyons**	voy**ions**	verr**ons**	verr**ions**	**voyions**
vous	**voyez**	voy**iez**	verr**ez**	verr**iez**	**voyiez**
ils	**voient**	voy**aient**	verr**ont**	verr**aient**	voi**ent**

VOULOIR **to want** Past participle: voulu Commands: Veuille! Veuillons! Veuillez!

Subject	Present	Imperfect	Future	Conditional	Subjunctive
je	**veux**	voul**ais**	voudr**ai**	voudr**ais**	**veuille**
tu	**veux**	voul**ais**	voudr**as**	voudr**ais**	**veuilles**
il	**veut**	voul**ait**	voudr**a**	voudr**ait**	**veuille**
nous	**voulons**	voul**ions**	voudr**ons**	voudr**ions**	**voulions**
vous	**voulez**	voul**iez**	voudr**ez**	voudr**iez**	**vouliez**
ils	**veulent**	voul**aient**	voudr**ont**	voudr**aient**	**veuillent**

Appendix

Dictionaries

French to English

à   to, at

à côté (de)   next to, beside

à droite (de)   to the right (of)

à gauche (de)   to the left (of)

à quelle heure   at what time

à tout à l'heure   see you later

à travers   across, through

agneau *m.*   lamb

ail *m.*   garlic

aimer   to like, love

aliments *m.*   food

Allemagne *f.*   Germany

aller   to go

alors   then

ambassade *f.*   embassy

ami *m.*   friend (male)

an *m.*   year

ananas *m.*   pineapple

anchois *m.*   anchovy

Angleterre *f.*   England

année *f.*   year

annuaire *m.*   telephone book

août *m.*   August

appareil-photo *m.*   camera

apporter   to bring

après   after, afterward

après-demain *m.*   day after tomorrow

argent *m.*   silver, money

ascenseur *m.*   elevator

assez de   enough

assiette *f.*   dinner plate

atelier *m.*   studio

attendre   to wait (for)

atterrissage *m.*   landing

au bas de   at the bottom of

au bout (de)   at the end (of), after

au fond (de)   at the bottom (back)of

au haut (de)   in (at) the top (of)

au lieu (de)   instead (of)

au loin   in the distance

au milieu (de)   in the middle (of)

au revoir   good-bye

aujourd'hui *m.*   today

aussi   also, too

avant   before

avant-hier   day before yesterday

averse *f.*   shower (heavy rain)

avertissement *m.*   warning

avion *m.*   airplane

avoir   to have

avoir besoin (de) to need

avoir lieu to take place

avril *m.* April

baguette *f.* loaf of French bread

bateau *m.* boat

beau (belle) handsome, beautiful

beau-fils *m.* stepson, son-in-law

beau-père *m.* father-in-law

beaucoup (de) much

belle-fille *f.* daughter-in-law, stepdaughter

belle-mère *f.* mother-in-law

beurre *m.* butter

bien well

bien sûr of course

bientôt soon

bière *f.* beer

bijouterie *f.* jewelry store

billet *m.* ticket

blanc(he) white

boeuf *m.* beef

boire drink

boisson *f.* drink

boîte aux lettres *f.* mailbox

boîte de nuit *f.* nightclub

bon marché cheap

bon(ne) good

bonjour hello

bonsoir good evening

bouilli boiled

boulangerie *f.* bakery

bouteille *f.* bottle

brosse à dents *f.* toothbrush

brouillard *m.* fog

bureau de change *m.* money exchange

c'est it is

ça that

ça va okay

caisse *f.* cash register

caissier (caissière) cashier

carte *f.* menu, card

ce this, that

ceinture *f.* belt

cela that

cendrier *m.* ashtray

cent hundred

cerise *m.* cherry

ces these, those

cet this, that

cette this, that

champignon *m.* mushroom

charcuterie *f.* delicatessen

château *m.* castle

chauffer to heat

chaussettes *f. pl.* socks

chaussures *f. pl.* shoes

chemise *f.* shirt (man-tailored)

chemisier *m.* blouse

cher (chère) dear, expensive

chercher to look for

cheveux *m.* hair

chèvre *f.* goat

chez at the house (business) of

chien *m.* dog

choisir choose

chou *m.* cabbage

chou-fleur *m.* cauliflower

choucroute *f.* sauerkraut

chouette great

cinq five

cinquante fifty

clé (clef) *f.* key

combien (de + noun) how much, many

comme as

commencer (à) to begin

comment how

complet *m.* suit

comprendre to understand

comptoir *m.* counter

confiserie *f.* candy store

confiture *f.* jam, jelly

contre against

couteau *m.* knife

coûter to cost

couvert cloudy, overcast

couverture *f.* blanket

crayon *m.* pencil

crevette *f.* shrimp

croisière *f.* cruise

cuir *m.* leather

cuisses de grenouille *f. pl.* frogs' legs

cuit cooked

cuit au four baked

d'accord agreed, okay

dans in

de from, of, about, any

décollage *m.* take off

décrocher to pick up (the receiver)

défendre to defend, prohibit

déjà already

déjeuner *m.* to eat lunch

demain *m.* tomorrow

dépenser to spend (money)

depuis since

déranger to disturb

dernier(-ère) last

derrière behind

des from, of, about (the), some

deux two

deuxième (second[e]) second

devant in front of

dimanche *m.* Sunday

dinde *f.* turkey

dire to say, tell

dix ten

dix-huit eighteen

dix-neuf nineteen

dix-sept seventeen

donner to give

douane *f.* customs

douze twelve

du from, of, about (the), some

écouter to listen (to)

église *f.* church

elle she, her

elles they, them

emballer to wrap up

en some, about, from, of it, them

en arrière backward(s), behind

en bas de at the bottom of

en face (de) opposite, facing

en haut de at the top of

en même temps at the same time

en retard late (in arriving)

encore still, yet, again

enfin finally, at last

ensemble together

ensuite then, afterwards

entendre to hear

entre between

envoyer to send

escale *f.* stopover

Espagne *f.* Spain

espérer to hope

essayer (de) to try (to)

essence *f.* gasoline

est *m.* east

étage *m.* floor (story)

États-Unis *m.* United States

été *m.* summer

étiquette *f.* identification tag

étranger(-ère) foreign

être to be

être à to belong to

eux them

éviter to avoid

expliquer to explain

facile easy

faire to make, do

femme *f.* woman, wife

fenêtre *f.* window

fermer to close

février *m.* February

fille *f.* daughter, girl

fils *m.* son

finir to finish

four *m.* oven

fourchette *f.* fork

frais (fraîche) fresh

fraise *f.* strawberry

framboise *f.* raspberry

français French

frère *m.* brother

frit fried

fromage *m.* cheese

fruits de mer *m.* seafood

fumer to smoke

garçon *m.* boy, waiter

gâteau *m.* cake

gazeux(-euse) carbonated

gigot d'agneau *m.* leg of lamb

glace *f.* ice cream, mirror

gratiné browned, breaded

gris gray

guichet *m.* window

haricots verts *m. pl.* beans (green)

haut tall, big

heure *f.* hour

heureux(-euse) happy

hier yesterday

hiver *m.* winter

homard *m.* lobster

homme *m.* man

huile *f.* oil

huit eight

huître *f.* oyster

ici here

il he

il y a (+ time) there is, are; ago (+ time)

ils they

imperméable *m.* raincoat

jamais never, ever

jambon *m.* ham

janvier *m.* January

jaune yellow

je I

jeter to throw

jeton *m.* token

jeudi *m.* Thursday

jour *m.* day

journal *m.* newspaper

juillet *m.* July

juin *m.* June

jupe *f.* skirt

jus de + name of fruit *m.* juice

kiosk à journaux *m.* newsstand

la the, her, it

là there

laine *f.* wool

laisser to leave (behind)

lait *m.* milk

laitue *f.* lettuce

lapin *m.* rabbit

le the, him, it

léger(-ère) light

légume *m.* vegetable

lendemain *m.* next day

lentement slowly

les the, them

leurs their

librairie *f.* bookstore

lire read

livre *m.* book

location de voitures *f.* car rental

loin (de) far (from)

longtemps a long time

louer to rent

lui him, to him, her

lundi *m.* Monday

madame *f.* Mrs.

mademoiselle *f.* Miss

magasin *m.* store

mai *m.* May

maillot de bain *m.* bathing suit

maintenant now

maison *f.* house

malade sick

manger to eat

manquer (rater) le vol to miss the flight

manteau *m.* overcoat

marcher to walk, work

mardi *m.* Tuesday

mari *m.* husband

marron chestnut

mars *m.* March

mauvais bad

me me, to me

médecin *m.* doctor

médicament *m.* medicine

meilleur better

mercredi *m.* Wednesday

mes my

météo *f.* weather

métro *m.* subway

mettre to put (on)

midi *m.* noon

mieux better

mille *m.* thousand

milliard *m.* billion

minuit *m.* midnight

moi me, I

moins less

mois month

monsieur *m.* Mr.

monter go up

montre *f.* watch

montrer to show

musée *m.* museum

n'est-ce pas isn't that so

n'importe it doesn't matter

ne … jamais never

ne … plus no longer

ne … rien nothing, anything

neiger to snow

nettoyer to clean

neuf new, nine

neveu *m.* nephew

noir(e) black

noix *f.* walnut

nord *m.* north

nos our

notre our

nous we, us, to us

nouveau (nouvelle) new

novembre *m.* November

nuage *m.* cloud

objets trouvés *m. pl.* lost and found

octobre *m.* October

oeuf *m.* eggs

oie *f.* goose

oignon *m.* onion

on one, we, they, you

onze eleven

or *m.* gold

orage *m.* storms

où where

ouest *m.* west

ouvert open

pain *m.* bread

pamplemousse *m.* grapefruit

pantalon *m.* pants

paquet *m.* package

par by, through, per

parapluie *m.* umbrella

parc d'attractions *m.* amusement park

parfois sometimes

parler to speak

pâtisserie *f.* pastry shop

pelouse *f.* lawn

pendant during

perdre to lose

père *m.* father

petit small

peu (de) little

piment *m.* pepper

piscine *f.* swimming pool

piste *f.* slope, track

plage *f.* beach

pluie *f.* rain

plus more

pneu *m.* tire

poignée *f.* door handle

poire *f.* pear

poireaux *m. pl.* leeks

pois *m.* peas

poisson *m.* fish

poivre *m.* pepper

pomme *f.* apple

pomme de terre *f.* potato

porte *f.* door, gate

portefeuille *m.* wallet

poulet *m.* chicken

pour for, in order to

pourquoi why

pouvoir to be able to

premier (première) first

prendre to take

près (de) near

presque almost

prêter lend

printemps *m.* spring

prix *m.* price

prochain next

provisoirement temporarily

prune *f.* plum

pruneau *m.* prune

puis then

quand when

quarante forty

quart d'heure *m.* quarter of an hour

quatorze fourteen

quatre four

quatre-vingt-dix ninety

quatre-vingts eighty

que that, what

quel(le)(s) which, what

quelquefois sometimes

qui who, whom

quinze fifteen

raisin *m.* grape

raisin sec *m.* raisin

recevoir to receive

reçu *m.* receipt

réduire to reduce

regarder to look at, watch

remercier to thank

remplir to fill

remporter to bring back

rencontrer to meet

rendre to give back, return

renseignements *m.* information

rentrer to return

répéter to repeat

répondre (à) to answer

rester to stay, remain

réveiller se to wake up

rez-de-chaussée *m.* ground floor

roman *m.* novel

sa his, her

samedi *m.* Saturday

sans without

saucisse *f.* sausage

saumon *m.* salmon

savoir to know

savon *m.* soap

seize sixteen

sel *m.* salt

semaine *f.* week

sept seven

septembre *m.* September

ses his, her

seulement only

soeur *f.* sister

soie *f.* silk

soixante sixty

soixante-dix seventy

soleil *m.* sun

somnifère *m.* sleeping pill

son his, her

sortie *f.* exit

sortie de secours *f.* emergency exit

souliers *m. pl.* shoes

sous under

sous-sol *m.* basement

souvent often

stade *m.* stadium

sucre *m.* sugar

sud *m.* south

sur on

ta your (familiar)

tante *f.* aunt

tard late

tarif *m.* price, rate

tasse *f.* cup

te you, to you

tempête *f.* storm

tes your (familiar)

thé *m.* tea

thon *m.* tuna

timbre *m.* stamp

toi you

ton your (familiar)

tonnerre *m.* thunder

tôt soon, early

toujours always, still

tout quite, entirely, all, every

tout à coup suddenly

tout à fait entirely

tout à l'heure in a while

tout de suite immediately

tout droit straight ahead

tout près nearby

travailler to work

traverser to cross

treize thirteen

trente thirty

très very

trois three

trop (de) too much

trouver to find

tu you

un(e) one

valeur *f.* value

veau *m.* veal

veille *f.* eve

vendredi *m.* Friday

vent *m.* wind

verglas *m.* sleet

verre *m.* lens, glass

vers toward

vert green

vêtements *m. pl.* clothing

viande *f.* meat

vide empty

vieux (vieille) old

vin *m.* wine

vingt twenty

vite quickly

voir to see

voiture *f.* car

vol *m.* flight

volaille *f.* poultry

vos your (polite)

votre your (polite)

vouloir to want

vous you, to you

vraiment really, truly

y there

English to French

able, be able to pouvoir

about (the it, them) de (du, de la, de l'), (en)

above au-dessous de

accompany accompagner

across à travers

act agir

ad annonce publicitaire *f.*

address adresse *f.*

afraid, be afraid (of) avoir peur (de)

after après

afternoon (in the) après-midi *m.* (de l')

afterward après, ensuite

again encore

against contre

aged âgé

agency agence *f.*

ago (+ time) il y a (+ time)

agree (with) être d'accord (avec)

air conditioning climatisation *f.*

airline ligne aérienne *f.*

airplane avion *m.*

airport aéroport *m.*

all tout

all right c'est entendu

almost presque

already déjà

also aussi

always toujours

American américain

answer répondre (à)

April avril *m.*

arrive arriver

ask demander

at à

August août *m.*

aunt tante *f.*

autumn automne *m.*

bad mauvais

baggage claim area bagages *m.*, bande *f.*

bakery boulangerie *f.*

ball-point pen stylo à bille *m.*

band-aid pansement adhésif *m.*

bank banque *f.*

bathing suit maillot de bain *m.*

bathroom salle de bains *f.*, toilettes *f.*

be être

beach plage *f.*

beautiful beau (belle)

bed lit *m.*

before avant

begin commencer (à), se mettre à

behind derrière, en arrière

belong to être à

below au-dessous de

beneath au-dessous de

besides d'ailleurs

between entre

big grand, gros(se)

black noir(e)

blanket couverture *f.*

blue bleu

boat bateau *m.*

book livre *m.*

bookstore librairie *f.*

booth (telephone) cabine téléphonique *f.*

borrow emprunter

boy garçon *m.*

bread pain *m.*

break se casser, rompre

bring (person), bring (thing) amener, apporter

bring back remporter

brother frère *m.*

brown brun

bus autobus *m.*, bus *m.*

bus stop arrêt de bus *m.*

business center centre d'affaires *m.*

businessman(-woman) homme (femme) d'affaires

busy être en train de + infinitive, occupé

butcher shop boucherie *f.*

butter beurre *m.*

by par

cake gâteau *m.*

calculator (solar) calculette (solaire) *f.*

call appeler

camera appareil-photo *m.*

can boîte *f.*

candy store confiserie *f.*

cane canne *f.*

car auto *f.*, voiture *f.*

car rental location de voitures *f.*

carbonated gazeux(-euse)

card carte *f.*

care, take care of s'occuper de

carry porter

cash (check) toucher

cash register caisse *f.*

cashier caissier (caissière)

cat chat *m.*

cathedral cathédrale *f.*

celebrate célébrer, fêter

chair chaise *f.*, siège *m.*

cheap bon marché

cheese fromage *m.*

chicken poule *f.*, poulet *m.*

child enfant *m.* or *f.*

choose choisir

church église *f.*

cigar cigare *f.*

cigarette cigarette *f.*

clean propre

clock pendule *f.*

close fermer

clothing vêtements *m.*

coffee café *m.*

cold rhume *m.*

cold, to be cold (person) avoir froid

cold, to be cold (weather) faire froid

comb peigne *m.*

consulate consulat *m.*

contact lens lentille *f.* de contact, verre *m.* de contact

cookie biscuit *m.*

cooking cuisine *f.*

cool, to be cool (weather) faire frais

corner coin *m.*

cost coûter

counter comptoir *m.*

cream crème *f.*

cup tasse *f.*

customs douane *f.*

dangerous dangereux (-euse)

dark foncé

daughter fille *f.*

daughter-in-law belle-fille *f.*

day jour *m.*

day after tomorrow après-demain *m.*

day before yesterday avant-hier

dear cher (chère)

December décembre *m.*

delicatessen charcuterie *f.*

dentist dentiste *m.*

department store grand magasin *m.*

departure départ *m.*

dial composer (faire) le numéro

difficult difficile

direction, in the direction of du côté de

dirty sale

disturb déranger

do faire

doctor docteur *m.*, médecin *m.*

dog chien *m.*

door porte *f.*

downstairs en bas

downtown en ville

dozen douzaine de

dress robe *f.*

drink boire

drink boisson *f.*

dry cleaners teinturerie *f.*

during pendant

ear oreille *f.*

early de bonne heure, tôt

earn gagner

east est *m.*

easy facile

eat manger

egg oeuf *m.*

eight huit

eighteen dix-huit

eighty quatre-vingts

elevator ascenseur *m.*

eleven onze

embassy ambassade *f.*

emergency exit sortie de secours *f.*

empty vide

end terminer

enough assez de

enter entrer

entire entier(-ère)

entrance entrée *f.*

even même

every tout

excuse me pardon

exit sortie *f.*

expensive cher (chère)

explain expliquer

eye oeil *m.* (plural: yeux)

face figure *f.*, visage *m.*

false faux (fausse)

famous célèbre

far (from) loin (de)

father père *m.*

father-in-law beau-père *m.*

fax télécopie *f.*

fax machine télécopieur *m.*

February février *m.*

fifteen quinze

fifty cinquante

finally enfin

find trouver

finish achever, finir

first premier (première)

fish poisson *m.*

five cinq

flight vol *m.*

floor (story) étage *m.*

flu grippe *f.*

food aliments *m.*

foot pied *m.*

for pour

foreign étranger(-ère)

forget oublier

fork fourchette *f.*

forty quarante

four quatre

fourteen quatorze

French français

Friday vendredi *m.*

friend camarade *m.* or *f.*, ami *m.*

frighten faire peur à

from de, de la, de l', des, du, en

from (+ time) dès

front, in front of devant

fun amusant

funny comique, drôle

garden jardin *m.*

gasoline essence *f.*

generally d'habitude

gentle doux (douce)

gift shop boutique *f.*

girl fille *f.*

give donner

give back rendre

glass verre *m.*

glove gant *m.*

go aller

gold or *m.*

good bon(ne)

grandfather grand-père *m.*

grandmother grand-mère *f.*

grape raisin *m.*

grapefruit pamplemousse *m.*

gray gris

green vert

grocery store épicerie *f.*

ground floor rez-de-chaussée *m.*

hair cheveux *m. pl.*

haircut coupe de cheveux *f.*

hairdresser coiffeur (coiffeuse)

half hour demi-heure *f.*

ham jambon *m.*

hamburger hamburger *m.*

hand main *f.*

handkerchief mouchoir *m.*

hanger cintre *m.*

happy heureux(-euse)

hard dûr

hat chapeau *m.*

have avoir

have to devoir

he il

head tête *f.*

hear entendre

hearing aid audiophone *m.*

heart coeur *m.*

heavy lourd

hello bonjour

help aider

her (to) elle, la, sa, son, ses, (lui)

here ici

him (to) le (lui)

his sa, son, ses

honest honnête

hope espérer

hot, to be hot (person) avoir chaud

hour heure *f.*

house maison *f.*

how comment

how much, many combien (de + noun)

hundred cent

hungry, to be hungry avoir faim

husband mari *m.*

I je

ice cream glace *f.*

ice cubes glaçons *m. pl.*

identification tag étiquette *f.*

immediately tout de suite

in dans

information renseignements *m. pl.*

instead (of) au lieu (de)

introduce présenter

invite inviter

it le, la

it is c'est

January janvier *m.*

jar bocal *m.*

jeans jean *m.*

jelly confiture *f.*

jewelry store bijouterie *f.*

juice jus *m.*, jus de + name of fruit

July juillet *m.*

June juin *m.*

keep garder

knife couteau *m.*

know savoir

landing (plane) atterrissage *m.*

last dernier(-ère), passé(e)

late tard

late (in arriving) en retard

later, see you later à tout à l'heure

leather cuir *m.*

leave (behind) partir, quitter (laisser)

Lebanon Liban *m.*

left, to the left (of) à gauche (de)

lemon citron *m.*

lend prêter

less moins

letter lettre *f.*

like aimer

listen (to) écouter

live (in) demeurer, habiter

look at, watch regarder

look for chercher

lose perdre

lost and found objets trouvés *m.*

love aimer

luggage (carry-on) bagages *m.* (à main)

maid fille de chambre *f.*

mailbox boîte aux lettres *f.*

make faire

man homme *m.*

March mars *m.*

match allumette *f.*

matter, it doesn't matter n'importe

May mai *m.*

meat (chopped) viande *f.* (hachée)

mechanic mécanicien(ne)

medicine médicament *m.*

menu carte *f.*, menu *m.*

middle, in the middle (of) au milieu (de)

midnight minuit *m.*

milk lait *m.*

million million *m.*

mineral water eau minérale *f.*

  carbonated gazeuse

  noncarbonated plate

mint menthe *f.*

minute minute *f.*

mirror glace *f.*, miroir *m.*

Miss mademoiselle *f.*

miss manquer, rater

mistake, (make a mistake) faute *f.*, erreur *f.* (se tromper)

mitt gant *m.*

mix mélanger

model mannequin *m.*

moderate modéré

modern moderne

moisturizer crème hydratante *f.*

Monday lundi *m.*

money argent *m.*

money exchange bureau de change *m.*

money order mandat-poste *m.*

monkey singe *m.*

monkfish lotte *f.*

month mois *m.*

moon lune *f.*

more plus

moreover d'ailleurs

morning (in the) matin *m.* (du)

Morocco Maroc *m.*

mother mère *f.*

mother-in-law belle-mère *f.*

motor moteur *m.*

mountain montagne *f.*

mountain climbing alpinisme *m.*, escalade *f.*

mousse mousse coiffante *f.*

mouth bouche *f.*

mouthwash dentifrice *m.*

mow tondre

Mr. monsieur *m.*

Mrs. madame *f.*

much beaucoup (de)

mumps oreillons *m.*

museum musée *m.*

mushroom champignon *m.*

musician musicien(ne)

mussels moules *f.*

mustache moustache *f.*

mustard moutarde *f.*

mutton mouton *m.*

my mes

mystery mystère *m.*

nail ongle *m.*

nail file lime à ongles *f.*

nail polish vernis à ongles *m.*

nail polish remover dissolvant *m.*

nail clippers coupe-ongles *m. pl.*

naive naïf (naïve)

napkin serviette *f.*

near près (de)

nearby tout près

neck cou *m.*

necklace collier *m.*

need avoir besoin (de), avoir envie (de)

negligee peignoir *m.*

nephew neveu *m.*

net filet *m.*

Netherlands Pays-Bas *m. pl.*

never jamais, ne … jamais

new neuf, nouveau (nouvelle)

news informations *f.*

newspaper journal *m.*

newsstand kiosk à journaux *m.*

next prochain

next to, beside à côté (de)

nice aimable, gentil(le), sympathique

niece nièce *f.*

night, to be night nuit *f.* ,faire nuit

nightclub boîte de nuit *f.*, cabaret *m.*

nine neuf

nineteen dix-neuf

ninety quatre-vingt-dix

no non

no longer ne … plus

noncarbonated plat

noon midi *m.*

north nord *m.*

North America Amérique du Nord *f.*

Norway Norvège *f.*

nose nez *m.*

nose drops gouttes nasales *f. pl.*

note noter

notebook cahier *m.*

nothing ne … rien

notice remarquer

nourish nourrir

novel roman *m.*

November novembre *m.*

now maintenant

nurse infirmier (infirmière)

nylon nylon *m.*

obey obéir

oblige obliger

oboe hautbois *m.*

observe noter

ocean océan *m.*

October octobre *m.*

octopus poulpe *m.*

of (the) de, de la, de l', du, des, en

of course bien entendu, bien sûr

often souvent

oil huile *f.*

okay ça marche, d'accord, ça va

old âgé, ancien(ne), vieux (vieille)

olive olive *f.*

omelet omelette *f.*

on sur

one on, un, une

oneself soi

onion oignon *m.*

only seulement

onyx onyx *m.*

open ouvert

opinion, in my opinion à mon avis

opportunity, to have the opportunity avoir l'occasion (de)

opposite en face (de)

optician opticien(ne)

orange orange *f.*

orangeade orangeade *f.*

orchestra orchestre *m.*

order commander

order, in order to pour

oregano origan *m.*

organize organiser

our nos, notre

out, to go out sortir

outdoors en plein air

oven four *m.*

microwave à micro-ondes

self-cleaning auto-nettoyant

over au-dessus de

overcast couvert

overcoat manteau *m.*

own posséder

owner propriétaire *m.* or *f.*

oxtail queue de boeuf *f.*

oyster huître *f.*

P.M. de l'après-midi

pacifier sucette *f.*

package paquet *m.*

pad bloc *m.*

pain douleur *f.*

painter peintre *m.*

painting tableau *m.*

pajamas pyjama *m.*

pamphlet brochure *f.*

panther panthère *f.*

panties culotte *f.*

pants pantalon *m.*

pantyhose collant *m.*

paper papier *m.*

paper clip agrafe *f.*, pince *f.*

paper, toilet papier hygiénique *m.*

paper, wrapping papier d'emballage *m.*

parade défilé *m.*

parasailing parachutisme *m.*

parcel colis *m.*

pardon pardonner

park parc *m.*

parsley persil *m.*

participate participer

partridge perdreau *m.*, perdrix *f.*

pass passer

passport control contrôle des passeports *m.*

pastry pâtisserie *f.*

pastry chef pâtissier (pâtissière)

pastry shop pâtisserie *f.*

pâté pâté *m.*

path sentier *m.*

pay, to pay for payer

peach pêche *f.*

pear poire *f.*

pearls perles *f. pl.*

peas pois *m. pl.*

pedicure pédicurie *f.*

pen (ball-point) stylo à bille *m.*

pencil crayon *m.*

pencil sharpener taille-crayon *m.*

pepper poivre *m.*

pepper shaker poivrière *f.*

per par

perch perche *f.*

perfect parfait

perfume parfum *m.*

perfume store parfumerie *f.*

permanent permanente

pheasant faisan *m.*

phone téléphone *m.*

phone card télécarte *f.*

photocopy photocopie *f.*

photographer photographe *m.* or *f.*

piano piano *m.*

piccolo piccolo *m.*

pick up (the receiver) décrocher

picture tableau *m.*

pie tarte *f.*

pig cochon *m.*

pigeon pigeon *m.*

pike brochet *m.*

pillow oreiller *m.*

pills pilules *f. pl.*

pilot pilote *m.*

pineapple ananas *m.*

ping-pong ping-pong *m.*

pink rose

pipe pipe *f.*

place poser

place setting couvert *m.*

place, to take place avoir lieu

plaid en tartan

plate assiette *f.*

platinum platine *f.*

play jouer

play a game of faire une partie de

please faire plaisir à, plaire à

please s'il vous (te) plaît

plum prune *f.*

pneumonia pneumonie *f.*

poached poché

pocketbook sac (à main) *m.*

Poland Pologne *f.*

pole (ski) bâton *m.*

police officer agent de police *m.*

police station commissariat *m.* de police

police story film policier *m.*

polio poliomyélite *f.*

polite poli

political movie film à sujet politique *m.*

polka dotted à pois

polyester polyester *m.*

pond étang *m.*

poor pauvre

popular populaire

pork porc *m.*

pork chops côte de porc *f.*

pork sausages andouilles *f. pl.*

porter porteur *m.*

porterhouse steak chateaubriand *m.*

Portugal Portugal *m.*

possess posséder

postcard carte postale *f.*

post-its billets *m. pl.*

postage affranchissement *m.*

postal code code postal (régional) *m.*

postal meter machine à affranchir *f.*

postal worker facteur (-trice)

poster poster *m.*

postmark cachet de la poste *m.*

potato pomme de terre *f.*

poultry volaille *f.*

pound of demi-kilo *m.* de, cinq cents grammes de half pound of deux cent cinquante grammes de

powder poudre *f.*

practice pratiquer

prawns langoustines *f. pl.*

prepare préparer

prescription ordonnance *f.*

present présenter

preservative conservateur *m.*

president président *m.*

pretend faire semblant de

pretty joli

price prix *m.*, tarif *m.*

prime rib côte de boeuf *f.*

private road allée privée *f.*

problem problème *m.*

programmer programmeur(-euse)

prohibit défendre

protect protéger

proud fier(-ère)

provision provision *f.*

prune pruneau *m.*

puck palet *m.*, rondelle *f.*

pull tirer

pull out arracher

pullover pull *m.*

pumpkin citrouille *f.*

punish punir

pureed en purée

purple mauve

purpose, to do on purpose faire exprès

put (on) mettre

quickly vite

raincoat imperméable *m.*

rate tarif *m.*

read lire

really vraiment

receipt quittance *f.*, reçu *m.*

receive recevoir

red rouge

reduce réduire

regret regretter

remain rester

remove enlever, ôter, quitter

rent louer

repair réparer

repeat répéter

replace remplacer

reserve réserver

right, to be right avoir raison

right, to the right (of) à droite (de)

room chambre *f.*, pièce *f.*, salle *f.*

sad triste

salesperson vendeur(-euse)

salt sel *m.*

same (all the same) même (tout de même)

Saturday samedi *m.*

saucer soucoupe *f.*

say dire

scarf écharpe *f.*, foulard *m.*

scissors ciseaux *m. pl.*

sea mer *f.*

seat place *f.*, siège *m.*

second deuxième (second[e])

see voir

sell vendre

send envoyer

send for faire venir

September septembre *m.*

seven sept

seventeen dix-sept

seventy soixante-dix

share partager

she elle

shirt (man-tailored) chemise *f.*

shoes chaussures *f. pl.*, souliers *m. pl.*

shopping, to go shopping faire des achats (emplettes) (du shopping)

short court

show montrer

show spectacle *m.*

sick malade

sign signer

silk soie *f.*

silver argent *m.*

since depuis

single célibataire

sister soeur *f.*

six six

sixteen seize

sixty soixante

size taille *f.*

skate patiner

sleepy, to be sleepy avoir sommeil

slice tranche *f.*

slowly lentement

small petit

smell sentir

smoke fumer

soap (bar of) savon *m.* (savonnette *f.*)

socks chaussettes *f. pl.*

soda soda *m.*

soft doux (douce)

some de, de la, de l',des, du, en

sometimes parfois, quelquefois

son fils *m.*

soon bientôt, tôt

south sud *m.*

speak parler

spend (money) dépenser

spend (time) passer

spring printemps *m.*

stain tache *f.*

stairs escalier *m.*

stamp timbre *m.*

stationery papier à lettres *m.*

stay rester, séjourner

stepbrother demi-frère *m.*

stepdaughter belle-fille *f.*

stepsister demi-soeur *f.*

stepson beau-fils *m.*

still encore, toujours

stop arrêter (s' … de)

stopover escale *f.*

store magasin *m.*

storm tempête *f.*, orage *m.*

straight ahead tout droit

strawberry fraise *f.*

string ficelle *f.*

student élève *m.* or *f.*, étudiant *m.*

study étudier

subway métro *m.*

suddenly tout à coup

sugar sucre *m.*

suitcase valise *f.*

summer été *m.*

sun soleil *m.*

Sunday dimanche *m.*

supermarket supermarché *m.*

swim nager

swimming pool piscine *f.*

tailor tailleur *m.*

take prendre

take away emmener

take off (plane) décoller

take place avoir lieu

tea thé *m.*

telephone téléphone *m.*

television télévision *f.*

tell dire, raconter

temporarily provisoirement

ten dix

thank remercier

thank you merci

that ce, cet, cette. cela, que, ça

the le, la, les

their leur(s)

them (to) les, elles, eux, (leur)

then alors, ensuite, puis

there là, y

there is/are il y a (+ time)

these ces

they ils, elles, on

think (about, of) penser (à, de)

thirsty, to be avoir soif

thirteen treize

thirty trente

this ce, cet, cette

those ces

thousand mille *m.*

three trois

through à travers, par

Thursday jeudi *m.*

ticket billet *m.*

time temps *m.*, heure *f.*

time, a long time longtemps

time, at what à quelle heure

time, from time to time de temps à autre, de temps en temps

time, to have the time to avoir le temps de

time, on time à l'heure, à temps

tissue mouchoir en papier *m.*

to à

to the à la, à l', au, aux

today aujourd'hui *m.*

together ensemble

toilet paper papier hygiénique *m.*

tomorrow demain *m.*

too aussi

too much trop (de)

tooth dent *f.*

toothache rage *f.* de dents

toothbrush brosse à dents *f.*

toothpaste pâte dentifrice *f.*

top, in (at) the top of au (en) haut (de)

toward du côté de, vers

towel serviette *f.*

train train *m.*

travel voyager

trip (take a) voyage *m.* (faire un)

try (to) essayer (de)

Tuesday mardi *m.*

turn tourner

twelve douze

twenty vingt

two deux

umbrella parapluie *m.*

uncle oncle *m.*

under sous

understand comprendre

United States États-Unis *m. pl.*

until jusqu'à

upstairs en haut

us, to us nous

use employer, se servir de

usually d'habitude

value valeur *f.*

vanilla vanille *f.*

vegetable légume *m.*

very très

wait (for) attendre

waiter garçon *m.*

waitress serveuse f.

wallet portefeuille *m.*

want vouloir

warn avertir

watch garder, surveiller

watch montre *f.*

we nous, on

wear porter

weather météo *f.*

Wednesday mercredi *m.*

week semaine *f.*

well bien

west ouest *m.*

what qu'est-ce que, que, quel(le)

when quand

where où

which quel(le)(s)

which one lequel, laquelle

white blanc(he)

who qui

whom qui

why pourquoi

wife femme *f.*

wind vent *m.*

window (ticket) guichet *m.*

wine vin *m.*

winter hiver *m.*

wish souhaiter

without sans

woman femme *f.*

wool laine *f.*

work fonctionner, marcher

work travailler

worthwhile, to be worthwhile valoir la peine (de)

wrap up emballer

write écrire

wrong, to be wrong avoir tort

wrong, to have something wrong avoir quelque chose

year an *m.*, année *f.*

years, to be … years old avoir … ans

yellow jaune

yesterday hier

yet encore

you (to) on, toi, tu, te, vous

your (familiar) ta, ton, tes

your (polite) vos, votre

Index

A

B

C

D

E

F

G

H

Q

R

S

T

U-V

W

X-Y-Z